Plan Nº 1.

Wood Framing of Ground Floor

Good Money

The INDEPENDENT INSTITUTE

THE INDEPENDENT INSTITUTE is a non-profit, non-partisan, scholarly research and educational organization that sponsors comprehensive studies of the political economy of critical social and economic issues.

The politicization of decision-making in society has too often confined public debate to the narrow reconsideration of existing policies. Given the prevailing influence of partisan interests, little social innovation has occurred. In order to understand the nature of and possible solutions to major public issues, the Independent Institute adheres to the highest standards of independent inquiry, regardless of political or social biases and conventions. The resulting studies are widely distributed as books and other publications, and are publicly debated in numerous conference and media programs. Through this uncommon depth and clarity, the Independent Institute expands the frontiers of our knowledge, redefines the debate over public issues, and fosters new and effective directions for government reform.

Good Money

BIRMINGHAM

BUTTON MAKERS,

THE ROYAL MINT, AND

THE BEGINNINGS OF

MODERN COINAGE,

1775–1821

Private Enterprise and Popular Coinage

George Selgin

The INDEPENDENT INSTITUTE

THE UNIVERSITY OF MICHIGAN PRESS
ANN ARBOR

Copyright © by The Independent Institute 2008
All rights reserved
Published in the United States of America by
The University of Michigan Press
Manufactured in the United States of America
⊗ Printed on acid-free paper

2011   2010   2009   2008   4   3   2   1

A CIP catalog record for this book is available from the British Library.

Library of Congress Cataloging-in-Publication Data

Selgin, George A., 1957–
     Good money : Birmingham button makers, the Royal Mint, and the
     beginnings of modern coinage, 1775-1821 / George Selgin.
          p.   cm.
     Includes index.
     ISBN-13: 978-0-472-11631-7 (cloth : alk. paper)
     ISBN-10: 0-472-11631-2 (cloth : alk. paper)
     1. Coinage—Great Britain—History.   2. Money—Great Britain—
History.   I. Title.

     HG938.S45   2008
     332.4'043094109033—dc22   2007052543

Endpaper Illustrations: Drawings of Matthew Boulton's steam-powered
coining mill, from his 1790 patent specification. Image courtesy of the
Birmingham City Archives and Patent Office.

À Pepette,
toujours inimitable

Contents

Abbreviations

BL Add. MSS	British Library Additional Manuscripts
BPP	British Parliamentary Papers
BWP	Boulton & Watt Papers, Birmingham Central Library
CRO	Cornwall Record Office, Boulton & Watt Collection (Archive Document 1583, in 10 volumes)
GM	*The Gentleman's Magazine*
Hansard	*The Parliamentary Debates (Hansard), Official Report*
MBP	Matthew Boulton Papers, Birmingham Central Library
PRO	Public Record Office

Foreword

This book details the fascinating history of the development, production, and use by the private sector of token copper coins during the early years of the Industrial Revolution, 1787–1817. The Industrial Revolution moved workers off the land into factories and thereby greatly increased the demand for small-value transactions money, to pay the wages and to allow the workers some choice in their use of their wage receipts to buy food, drink, and other goods. For a variety of reasons, nicely described by George Selgin, neither the Royal Mint nor commercial banks were willing or able to provide such small-value currency. There was a dearth of small change available to pay wages. The shortage was so severe that it was proving a serious hindrance to the industrial development of Great Britain.

Where there is a shortage, there is also a profitable opportunity to satisfy that demand. Selgin tells the story of how the private sector, led by Anglesey copper mine owner Thomas Williams and by James Watt's partner Matthew Boulton, started to strike its own token copper coins. As part of his effort, Boulton built the world's first steam-powered mint. The enthusiastic public reception of Williams's and Boulton's prototype coins led to the opening of numerous other private mints, which eventually supplied Great Britain with hundreds of tons of copper pennies, halfpennies, and farthings.

Since these copper coins were neither full weight nor legal tender (e.g., for the payment of taxes), what made them (locally) acceptable? There were, I believe, three criteria for this. First, the suppliers of the coins promised to make them redeemable (convertible), on demand, either into gold or silver coin produced by the Royal Mint or into Bank of

England notes. Second, that promise was credible because the supplier was often a rich, established, well-known local industrialist or merchant. Third, the coins were well made by innovative and complex techniques that were difficult to counterfeit. Indeed, so successful and acceptable were some of these coins that they were at times preferred to the scarce and often badly worn (and easily counterfeited) regal copper coins that had been previously coined by the Royal Mint.

Nevertheless, despite the success of such coins in filling a vacuum, the authorities were far from happy with having part of their nation's coinage privately produced. This concern was aggravated when private producers moved on from the issue of copper tokens to the issue of silver tokens and even to the issue of gold tokens, as was done by Reading's John Berkeley Monck in 1812 (see chap. 6). Of course, any suggestion that the authorities might make such private coinage illegal would make holders tend to take up their redemption option (i.e., to run from the currency), thereby making complaints against private currencies self-validating. Anyhow, goaded by Monck's threat to create a private gold standard, the government under Spencer Perceval moved to make private coins illegal. The government was prevented from doing so immediately because of the lack of alternative (small-value) coinage, but eventually, on New Year's Day, 1818, the passing of almost all private coins became illegal. Only tokens issued by the Sheffield and Birmingham workhouses were temporarily exempted.

The story that Selgin has to tell is nowadays largely unknown and is both important and gripping. There are many interdisciplinary facets to this book. It throws light on, among other things, major chapters in the histories of coinage and numismatics, of the industrial revolution and engineering developments, and particularly of Birmingham and the manufacturers of that great city.

But Selgin and I are both monetary economists (and monetary historians). The main lesson of this book for him is that the private sector can produce and provide good money (hence the book's title) that may in some (technical) respects be better than the government's own money. I certainly agree that when the government fails to provide a satisfactory money, substitutes will be forthcoming, whether foreign money (e.g., U.S. dollars) or private tokens. But to me, the main lesson of this book is not so much about whether money should be produced by the public or private sector but the support the book gives, in my view, to the Cartalist theory of the essence of money. In effect, the balance between the metallic content and the face value of a coin represented the credible commitment of the issuer. Local confidence that an IOU could and would be honored meant that coins could generally be accepted and used in exchange. The better the credit of the issuer, the wider the circulation, and the less need for intrinsic value of the money object.

Selgin, I would guess, sees the almost universal provision of currency by the state as an unnecessary and undesirable consequence of coercion to protect a profitable monopoly (seigniorage). In contrast, I see the state's role in this respect as the almost inevitable consequence of the fact that the state is—admittedly in large part because of its coercive and tax powers—the most creditworthy institution in the country. Whichever of us may be correct, it makes no difference to the fact that this is an excellent and fascinating book.

CHARLES GOODHART

Norman Sosnow Professor of Banking and Finance
London School of Economics

Preface

Economists, everyone knows, distrust state-sanctioned monopolies and are inclined to think that private firms can do a better job supplying goods and services than governments are capable of doing. This overall stance allows for some exceptions, of course. Of these, none is more universally recognized than that concerning coinage.

That governments alone are fit to coin money has been a commonplace of economic thought since ancient times (Monroe 1923). It is, furthermore, a commonplace that even the most doctrinaire champions of laissez-faire have scarcely ever questioned. Among well-known authorities, British social philosopher Herbert Spencer (1851, 396–402) alone dared to contradict it.

Spencer's challenge drew a pointed response from his compatriot William Stanley Jevons, an economist of unassailable classical liberal credentials.

> Though I must always deeply respect the opinions of so profound a thinker as Mr. Spencer, I hold that in this instance he has pushed a general principle into an exceptional case, where it quite fails. He has overlooked the important law of Gresham . . . that better money cannot drive out worse. In matters of currency self-interest acts in the opposite direction to what it does in other affairs . . . and if coining where left free, those who sold light coins at reduced prices would drive the best trade. . . .
>
> In my opinion there is nothing less fit to be left to the action of competition than money. In constitutional law the right of coining has always been held to be one of the peculiar prerogatives of the

Crown, and it is a maxim of the civil law, that *monetandi jus principum ossibus inhaert.* To the executive government and its scientific advisors . . . the matter had better be left.   (JEVONS 1882, 64–66)

Jevons added that his view "is amply confirmed by experience," mentioning, among other instances, Great Britain's late eighteenth-century experience with private copper tokens.

The multitude of these depreciated pieces in circulation was so great, that the magistrates of Stockport held a public meeting, and resolved to take no halfpence in future but those of the Anglesey Company, which were of full weight. This shows, if proof were needed, that the separate action of self-interest was inoperative in keeping bad coin out of circulation, and it is not to be supposed that the public meeting could have had any sufficient effect.   (65)

It was this brief passage, from Jevons's *Money and the Mechanism of Exchange,* that first drew my attention to Great Britain's private token coins. Intrigued, I decided to investigate further. What I discovered amazed me, not the least because, instead of confirming Jevons's position, it did just the opposite. The Stockport resolution, for instance, was actually a resolution among traders to accept privately minted Anglesey pennies instead of official ("regal") copper coins: the resolution came too early to have been directed against other private tokens. This little berg alone was enough to stave Jevons's argument. Yet it was but a fragment from a large ice field into which the great Victorian economist had unwittingly steamed, full speed ahead, fully laden with conventional wisdom.

Thanks to their many varieties and often splendid engravings, Great Britain's commercial coins, also known as "tradesmen's tokens" and (among American collectors) "Conder tokens," have long fascinated numismatists. Economists and historians, on the other hand, have tended either to ignore them or to write them off as nothing more than a curiosity—strange little weeds allowed to sprout around a temporarily derelict Royal Mint. But they were much more than that. They were, in fact, the world's first successful money for the masses, whose tale is long overdue for a telling.

So many persons have assisted me in researching and writing *Good Money* that I cannot pretend to recall and credit all of them by name. I would like to single out five persons who were generous enough to read and comment on first drafts of each chapter. Penny Watts-Russell seems to know all there is to know about the British copper business during the time of my story and has prevented me from making several incorrect statements about it, while spotting dozens of other minor errors I managed to overlook. Besides pointing out further factual mistakes, Richard Doty, the Smithsonian's curator of numismatics, has been a constant source of guidance and encouragement. So has my brother, Peter Selgin, whose expert stylistic advice has been invaluable. My colleague David Robinson spotted and corrected numerous grammatical and typographical infelicities and errors. Finally, Bill "Copperman" McKivor provided moral support while constructively criticizing my reading of several historical episodes.

Bill McKivor was also one of several persons to assist me with images of important tokens. Two others who assisted in this way were Ken Elks and Gary Sriro, who went so far as to prepare numerous original photos just for this book. Would that I could have had space in which to publish them all! For help in getting hold of many hard-to-get publications, I owe special thanks to the Interlibrary Loan Department of the University of Georgia Main Library and to its director, Virginia Feher, as well as to Harold Welch, librarian for the Conder Token Collector's Club.

A research grant from the University of Georgia's Willson Center for Humanities and Arts relieved me of my teaching duties for a semester, allowing me to work on this project instead. Terry-Sanford research awards from the Terry College of Business in turn allowed me to devote several summers to this work, and I am grateful to Mary Virginia Terry and her late husband, C. Herman Terry, and to Charles Sanford for making those awards possible. The British Numismatic Society, the British Numismatic Trust, and the University of Georgia Research Foundation provided financial support for research in Great Britain, as did Aaron Edelheit, president of Sabre Value Management, through his establishment and continued support of the monetary studies fund of the University of Georgia Department of Economics.

I also wish to thank the Independent Institute, and its President David Theroux, for sponsoring the publication of this book. The Institute's staff has been of invaluable assistance throughout.

Finally, I benefited greatly from the moral support of my colleagues at the Terry College of Business, including my department chair, Bill Lastrapes, and my former dean, George P. Benson. The last named deserves my particular thanks for going out on a limb to support research on a topic far removed from the day-to-day fare of business schools.

Prologue

It's a late summer Saturday evening in 1787, and a workman is quaffing a pint of ale at a crowded inn in the tiny bustling port town of Amlwch, in North Wales. A couple of miles south of the inn stands the world's biggest copper mine, where he and eleven of his mates have been "working the bargain"—for a percentage, that is. It's been a decent, though hardly stellar, week: their group raised 120 tons. That makes a quid each, since the last setting put copper ore at two shillings a ton. After stopping part of the worker's pay for steels, candles, the doctor's fee, gunpowder purchased on credit at the company store, and his share of the evening's victuals, the company owes him exactly twelve shillings and sixpence.

So the pitman makes his way to the pay table to collect his earnings. After confirming his figures, the steward hands him two badly worn shillings and four rolls, or "papers," of copper pennies worth half a crown each. Upon opening one of the papers, the worker finds that the pennies aren't ordinary British coin. Instead of portraying George III or some other British sovereign, their faces show a Celtic priest surrounded by a wreath of oak leaves and acorns, and their backs bear a monogram in large, curly script, surrounded by the legend "We promise to pay the bearer one penny." The legend continues, along the coins' edges, in incuse letters: "on demand in London, Liverpool, or Anglesey."

But who is "We"? Not the Royal Mint: it hasn't struck copper coin for years. It turns out that no branch of the British government had anything to do with the coins, which come from Birmingham—a place that's a byword for counterfeit money.

Should our hardworking miner protest? The thought never crosses his mind. On the contrary: he accepts the coins, and gladly, not because they are the most beautiful and well-made coins he's ever set eyes upon—he couldn't care less about that—but because the merchants and publicans actually prefer them to regal coins. Word has it they even take them in London. They are called Parys Mine or Anglesey Druids, and they are just the first of many examples to come of privately minted "commercial" coins that will make up the bulk of Great Britain's small change throughout the next, crucial decade of its industrial development.

Had it not been for commercial coins, Great Britain's Industrial Revolution, instead of accelerating to a gallop as the nineteenth century approached, might have slowed to a saunter, if not a snail's pace, for until these coins made their appearance, manufacturers had to struggle to pay their workers, while retailers had to struggle to make change. Technical and administrative changes pioneered by private coiners also proved crucial to the reform and modernization of official coinage arrangements.

In short, if our coins today are any good—if we have enough of them and are reasonably certain that they are real rather than fake—we have Britain's private coin makers to thank for showing the way. This book tells their story.

Gresham's law, n. [gréshamz láw], fr. Sir Thomas Gresham, founder of the Royal Exchange, d. 1579. (econ.) The tendency for bad money to drive good money out of circulation.

—*The Universal Dictionary of the English Language*
(London: Routledge and Kegan Paul, 1956)

CHAPTER I

Britain's Big Problem

O Yes! O Yes! Can any say,

Where all the Money's run away?[1]

People aren't used to dealing with cash shortages these days. Of course, they grumble about being short of money. But their complaint isn't about a shortage in economists' sense of the term. They wish more wealth would come their way; but whatever they've got coming to them comes more or less the way they want it, as ready money. They're able to swap checks for notes and coins, or vice versa, as they see fit. No one has to struggle much to change a twenty-dollar bill, or even a C-note. On the contrary: to judge from the little cups of free pennies found next to most cash registers or (if I may offer a personal example) from the overflowing bowl of change on my dresser top, ours is an age not of small-change shortages but of small-change surpluses.

Nor does anyone worry much about the condition or legitimacy of their coins. Counterfeit bills remain a peril, but no one even suspects that their dollar coins, quarters, or dimes—much less their pennies—might be fakes.[2] Coin markings are for the most part clearly visible, uniform, and official looking. The occasional queer coin is merely a curiosity. It is something to give to one's nephew, not proof that things have gone awry at the mint.

---

1. From the "Old turn[pike] man's hue-and-cry after more money" (London, 1721), cited in Gaskell 2000, 162.

2. Although some fake British one-pound coins have been discovered, the Royal Mint estimates that they make up only about 1 percent of the total of such coins.

Wanting Change

Two centuries ago, the situation was entirely different. Nations routinely suffered from coin shortages, and especially from shortages of small-value coins.[3] Great Britain was no exception. Shortages of small money there can be documented at least as far back as the Middle Ages, when commoners routinely petitioned Parliament and the king for more farthings and halfpennies. Urgent appeals for more small money were heard in 1380, again in 1404, and yet again in 1444.[4] Yet those shortages were nothing compared to the one that first broke out in Ireland at the onset of the eighteenth century. "We are in great Want of Half-pence and Farthings, are almost stripped of all Sorts of Silver Coin, and have very little of the small Gold Species," wrote Thomas Prior in 1729. "'Tis our Misfortune," he added, "not only to have little Money current among us, but even that Little to consist of such Sorts, as are the most unfit for the Management of our Domestick Dealings" ([1729] 1856, 293–94).

The Irish coin shortage quickly spread to Great Britain, becoming especially serious there during the critical first stages of the Industrial Revolution. That revolution, which is supposed (by some historians at least) to have begun around 1760, generated a huge demand for coins suitable for paying wages of miners, factory workers, and journeymen. By 1771, an anonymous writer was telling anyone in Parliament who would listen, "The scarcity of Change has been severely felt by People in Trade for upwards of these Ten years past, and this Scarcity increases daily; and base designing People avail themselves of it, by getting Credit for trifling Sums, which they never intend to pay."[5]

Besides witnessing an accelerating rate of population growth, the last, "revolutionary" decades of the eighteenth century also saw an unprecedented shift in employment away from agriculture and toward manufacturing, with a corresponding increase in the number of wage earners. Back during the mid-sixteenth century, less than a quarter of Britain's population depended on money wages; by the end of the eighteenth century, the fraction was close to three-quarters. According to Barbara and John Lawrence Hammond (1911, 97–106), this shift was largely a consequence of the burst of parliamentary enclosures of common fields between 1760 and 1780. The enclosures forced many small proprietors

---

3. See Sargent and Velde 2002.

4. See Redish 2000, 111. Redish refers to Ruding (1840, 111–25, 238–75) and also Peck (1970, 1–8).

5. Anonymous 1771, 3.

and a still greater number of cottagers and squatters to give up their "scratch-as-scratch-can" existence and to seek employment as landless laborers, either on enlarged farms or, increasingly, in the growing numbers of urban workshops and factories: "Those fenceless fields the sons of wealth divide, / And e'en the bare-worn common is denied."[6]

But if enclosures pushed people out of the countryside, it is no less true that industry lured them out. The broadening of foreign markets, together with momentous mechanical innovations, served to substantially increase the productivity and real earnings of labor, especially nonagricultural labor. The benefits of industry—of Goldsmith's "ten thousand baneful arts combined"—served not merely to "pamper luxury," as Goldsmith himself would have it, but also, eventually, to increase workers' living standards.[7] Besides, most rural villages were, as George Crabbe insisted, a far cry from Sweet Auburn:

> Ye gentle souls, who dream of rural ease,
> Whom the smooth stream and smoother sonnet please;
> Go! if the peaceful cot your praises share,
> Go look within, and ask if peace be there.[8]

Nor should we overlook the liberating capacity of money earnings, so well appreciated by Samuel Johnson. Those who lived off the land, he observed, were also bound to it, having no portable wealth. Wages paid in gold, silver, or copper, in contrast, supplied "power of resistance and means for escape" from what was, essentially, a feudal system.[9]

Whether the Industrial Revolution was liberating or not, the fact remains that, thanks to it, large numbers of families that had once pastured animals on the waste while obtaining gleanings, brushwood, and turf from common fields now had to purchase their butter, flour, and

---

6. Goldsmith 1770.

7. Ibid. Although a debate raged for some years concerning whether the industrial revolution really did bring about a sustained improvement in workers' living standards, most authorities now agree that it did so, but only starting around 1820 (see, e.g., Lindert and Williams 1983). Until then, the demands of the Seven Years' War and the American and French revolutionary wars often left workers impoverished, despite immense improvements in the British economy's overall productive capacity. That Great Britain managed, despite a huge diversion of efforts toward making arms, financing foreign governments, and filling the ranks of its army and navy, to accumulate the stock of capital that would eventually provide for substantial improvements in its citizens' well-being, was itself quite a remarkable achievement.

8. Crabbe 1783.

9. Johnson to Boswell, July 22, 1777, in Johnson 1992.

fuel, and to purchase them with money. Having lost their cows, the new "waged proletariat" found themselves utterly dependent on their coppers (Rule 1992, 87–90).[10] But while landless workers multiplied, the supply of good money, and of good small money especially, dwindled.

By the 1780s, even prosperous firms were fighting an uphill battle to pay their wage bills. Although most workers earned fewer than fifteen shillings a week, some firms had huge payrolls. The cotton textile industry alone employed over 150,000 workers, half of whom were weavers. Individual textile mills often employed hundreds of workers. In Stockport in the autumn of 1786, for instance, Samuel Oldknow had three hundred weavers working for him. That translated into a monthly wage bill of over £1,000. A second mill in Anderton cost Oldknow another £500 a month in wages. Yet the reign of "King Cotton" was just beginning, the industry having only just begun to take advantage of opportunities made possible by steam power. By the spring of 1792, Oldknow's wage bill had risen to over £750 a week. A few years later, that figure, too, would be eclipsed, with Oldknow finding himself the owner of no fewer than twenty large textile mills (Unwin, Hulme, and Taylor 1924, 45, 107).

Mining companies operated on a still grander scale. The Parys Mine Company in Wales employed a thousand workers, as did Cornwall's Chacewater and Dolcoath copper mines. Cornwall's Consolidated Copper Mines was even bigger, with fifteen hundred workers to provide for. Yet all the copper mines together, with just over seven thousand workers, were puny beer compared to the coal mines, which boasted close to fifty thousand. Abraham Darby and John Wilkinson, the great ironmasters, each employed over a thousand workers, including colliers; and some of their less famous rivals were not far behind. The largest single employers of all, however, were the principal royal dockyards at Portsmouth, Plymouth, and Chatham, which—thanks to the Seven Year's War and then to the American insurrection—employed a staggering sixty-five hundred workers.

Coming up with enough coins of any kind of the denominations needed to meet such enormous payrolls was never easy, while getting hold of enough *good* coin for the purpose was well-nigh impossible. And matters seemed bound to get worse: the recent appearance of rotary

10. Arthur Young (1776) guessed that peasants' cows were worth approximately five to six shillings per week to them and their families. No commons, no cow. By 1780, unskilled adult male wage laborers earned only about seven or eight shillings a week.

steam engines had vastly increased opportunities for the profitable exploitation of factory labor, while earlier marriages and reduced mortality rates were causing England's population to grow more rapidly than ever. The decennial population growth rate, which was about 3 percent before 1751, had doubled by 1781 and would come close to doubling again before the end of the century.

No one can say exactly how British industry would have fared had the shortage of good money not been addressed somehow. But in calling the shortage a cause of "much inconvenience and social disharmony," T. S. Ashton (1955, 167) exemplifies the British penchant for understatement. In fact, John Rule (1992, 304) has observed, "Complaints both of an absolute shortage of coin, especially of small denominations, and of the deficiency in weight of those [coins] that remained in circulation were frequent, bitter and widespread." Disharmony was the least of it: the coin shortage threatened to delay, if not halt, the process of industrialization that offered displaced peasants their best hope of earning a livelihood instead of having to pick oakum in dreary workhouses. Had Britain not managed somehow to come up with a substantial quantity of decent coins, British industry, instead of rushing toward the next century, might have barely managed to limp along.

Coining Words

What was behind Great Britain's small-change shortage? One economic historian's answer—that the Royal Mint's "obsolete" equipment kept it from meeting "the heavy demands of an expanding industrial society" (Whiting 1971, 20)—won't do: it was, as we shall see, not so much the mint's equipment as its policies that prevented it from supplying enough small change. Understanding those policies means coming to grips with some monetary jargon, which isn't all beer and skittles. Fortunately, the jargon is here mainly confined to the next few pages, after which it seldom turns up.

A nation's *standard money unit* is the principal unit in which prices are posted and accounts are kept. In the United Kingdom, the unit has long been the *pound sterling*, represented by the symbol £ (derived from the Latin word *libra* referring to a Roman pound). Principal money units are usually accompanied by one or more subsidiary units. Nowadays, these tend to be based on decimal fractions (e.g., the U.S. cent is one-hundredth of a dollar), but in the United Kingdom until 1971, they were based on vulgar fractions. A *shilling* (1 s, with the abbreviation derived from the Latin word *solidus*) was one-twentieth of a pound sterling, while a *penny* (1 d, with the abbreviation derived from the Latin *denarius*), was one-twelfth of a shilling, making 240 pennies, or pence, to the pound (see table 1).[11]

In a *metallic standard*, the money unit refers to a precise quantity of some metal, usually gold or silver, or to a particular coin made from that metal. Originally, the pound sterling was just what it sounds like: a Tower

---

TABLE 1. British Money Units and Coins and Their Purchasing Power, circa 1787

Basic Monetary Unit: The pound sterling (symbol £, from the Latin *libra*), equivalent to 113 grains of fine gold.

The government did not yet supply coins denominated in pounds. Banknotes were typically denominated in pound units, the smallest permissible denomination being one pound in Scotland and five pounds elsewhere in Great Britain.

Basic Coin Units:
  Silver: The *shilling* (symbol s, from the Latin *solidus*), with 20s = £1.
  Gold: The *guinea*, with 1 guinea = 21s (or £1 1s).
  Copper: The *penny* (symbol d, from the Latin *denarius*), with 12d = 1s; thus £1 = 240d.

Relatively Common Coin Types:
  Copper: Minted at equivalent of 23d per pound avoirdupois copper.
    Halfpence = $\frac{1}{2}d$
    Farthing = $\frac{1}{4}d$

  Silver: Minted at equivalent of 62s per troy pound of standard silver.
    Threepence ("Thruppence") = $\frac{1}{4}s$ = 3d
    Sixpence = $\frac{1}{2}s$ = 6d
    Shilling = 1s = 12d
    Half Crown = 2s 6d = 30d
    Crown = 5s = 60d

  Gold: Minted at equivalent of 44½ guineas per troy pound standard gold.
    Guinea = 21s = 252d
    Half Guinea = 10½s = 126d

Purchasing Power: One British pound in 1787 was the rough equivalent of $90 in today's money, making a shilling roughly equal to $4.50. Most adult male industrial workers earned between one and two shillings per thirteen-hour day.

---

11. Scottish coin denominations were made uniform with those of England and Wales by the Treaty of Union of 1707. The Irish pound, however, remained a distinct unit until it was abolished in 1826. A proclamation of June 1701 made thirteen Irish pence equivalent to one English silver shilling.

pound, or 5,400 grains, of sterling silver, which was equivalent to 4,995 grains of fine silver.[12] By the beginning of the seventeenth century, the pound had been reduced to only 1,719 grains of fine silver, where it remained for more than a hundred years. Then, in the first decades of the eighteenth century, the term *pound sterling* ceased to refer to any quantity of silver, becoming instead a unit consisting of 113 grains of fine gold. As we shall see, this happened quite unintentionally.

Coinage is the conversion of metal ingots, or *bullion,* into disks meant to represent standard money units. Since ancient times, coinage has usually been the exclusive prerogative of monopolistic government mints. In Great Britain, it is and has long been the prerogative of the Royal Mint, which throughout the eighteenth century was housed in the Tower of London. When coinage of a metal is *free,* anyone can have any amount of the metal coined at the mint. If coinage is *gratuitous,* the mint charges nothing for this service, its costs (and profits, if these are allowed) being paid out of the public purse. Gold and silver were both coined gratuitously in England from 1663 to 1816, with the Royal Mint's coining costs and profits set forth in contracts, known as *indentures,* drawn between it and the government.

The *mint price* of bullion is the nominal or "face" value of coins given in exchange for bullion brought to the mint, while the *mint equivalent* is the nominal value of coins actually made from the bullion. When coinage is gratuitous, as it was in Great Britain, the two values are equal. Otherwise, the mint price will fall short of the mint equivalent by the charge for coinage, which may include a profit to the mint or government. That profit is known as *seigniorage,* after the lords, or seigneurs, who exercised the right of coinage in medieval France. During the seventeenth and eighteenth centuries, the mint price (and mint equivalent) of a *troy pound* (twelve ounces, each of 480 grains) of silver was sixty-two shillings. As long as Great Britain's standard money units were understood as silver units (as they were for much of this period), for the Royal Mint to have made more than sixty-two shilling coins from one troy pound of silver would have been tantamount to redefining the pound sterling, the shilling, and the penny.

Under *bimetallism,* the government allows free coinage, usually with little or no seigniorage, of two metals, assigning a mint equivalent and corresponding mint price to each. The *mint ratio* is the ratio of mint prices for the two metals, which represents the relative values assigned to them by the mint. For example, if the mint pays £44 10s (or 890 shillings) in gold coin for each troy pound of gold brought to it, while paying £3 2s (or 62 shillings) in silver coin for each troy pound of silver, the gold/silver mint ratio is 890 ÷ 62 = 14.355. A pound of gold is, in other words, officially worth 14.355 times as much as a pound of silver.

In a gold and silver bimetallic arrangement, silver is said to be *overvalued* and gold *undervalued* at the mint if the gold/silver mint ratio falls short of the ratio of the metals' market prices. Suppose, for example, that a pound of gold is worth thirteen times as much as a pound of silver in the open market. In that case, a mint ratio of 14.355 overvalues gold while undervaluing silver. Even if some mint ratio is initially consistent with market prices, changes in the metals' relative scarcity are likely eventually to cause one to become officially undervalued relative to the other.

Which brings us to Gresham's Law. That law refers to the tendency, under certain conditions, for "bad" money to drive "good" money out of circulation. The law is named, rather misleadingly, after Sir Thomas Gresham, a financial agent of the British government who advised Queen Elizabeth and founded the Royal Exchange.[13] But the tendency it describes is as old as coinage itself. In ancient and medieval times, the tendency was most often observed in connection with coin *debasements*, which were reductions in mint equivalents achieved by adding extra base metal to gold or silver coins, so that newer coins might appear just as heavy as old ones despite containing less precious metal. "Bad" (debased) coins then tended to drive "good" (finer) ones out of circulation. In a bimetallic context, Gresham's law typically refers to people's tendency to stop bringing an officially undervalued metal to the mint and (especially) to their tendency to melt officially undervalued coins, or to lighten or "short" them by clipping or filing them or by "sweating" them in nitric acid until the metal still in them is worth no more than their de-

---

13. A line in one of Gresham's letters to Elizabeth—telling her that it was her "latte ffather" who had caused all of England's fine gold to be "convayd out of this your realme" by "abasing his quoyne from vi ounces fine to iii ounces fine"—induced Henry Dunning MacLeod to assign Gresham's name to the tendency in question. In fact, the tendency had been referred to by many writers before Gresham, including Copernicus, Oresme, and Aristophanes. It was, by the way, not Elizabeth's father, Henry VIII, but his successor, Edward VI, who reduced the fine silver content of English coins all the way down to just three ounces to the troy pound.

clared values.[14] The outcome is that only "bad" (impaired) coins made from overvalued metal still circulate.

Gresham's law only takes effect where officially undervalued coins cannot command a premium, for such a premium might make up for the coins' official undervaluation, removing the usual motive for melting or lightening them. It also has to be the case that officially overvalued coins are taken at face value (or by tale), rather than at a discount (or by weight), because a discount applied to officially overvalued coins would have the same effect as a premium on legally undervalued ones. These requirements have often been satisfied historically, thanks to the inconvenience of valuing coins at other than their face values and also to *legal tender laws,* which often prohibit the passing of official coins at anything save their official ratings.[15]

A *fiduciary coin* or *token coin* (or, simply, a *token*) differs from a *full-bodied coin* in having a face value that is substantially above the value of the metal it is made of—that is, substantially above what is often referred to, again misleadingly, as the coin's "intrinsic worth."[16] The free coinage of tokens establishes a high mint price for the metal they're made of. Because simultaneous free coinage of both token and full-bodied coins would amount to an especially unstable form of bimetallism, governments usually mint token coins on their own account and in limited quantities. Doing so serves to keep the tokens from driving more valuable, full-bodied coins out of circulation.

Finally, a word or two concerning official eighteenth-century British coin types. Before 1662, all British coins were hand struck or *hammered* money. But in that year, hammered money gave way, in the case of gold and silver, to *milled* money, so called because it was stamped, using a screw press, from blanks punched from strips of metal, called *fillets,* that had been flattened to the required thickness in a horse-powered rolling mill.[17]

---

14. In "The Jockey's Tale" George Borrow writes: "I told you that my grandfather was a shorter. . . . Filing and clipping he employed in reducing all kinds of coin, whether gold or silver; but aquafortis [nitric acid] he used merely in reducing gold coin. . . . By laying a guinea in aquafortis for twelve hours, he could filch from it to the value of ninepence, and by letting it remain there for twenty-four to the value of eighteenpence, the aquafortis eating the gold away, and leaving it like a sediment in the vessel" (Borrow [1857] 1906).

15. See Selgin 1996 and 2003a.

16. The expression is misleading because all economic values are subjective rather than intrinsic to goods themselves.

17. Confusingly, the term *mill* came also to refer to the screw press itself, while the term *milled money* is sometimes used to refer not simply to coins made with the help of me-

The first British milled coins were made of gold, at forty-four and a half pieces to the troy pound, and were known as *guineas,* after the Guinea Coast, where the gold came from. Although the guinea was originally assigned an official value of 20*s,* guineas never traded at that rate. Instead, they commanded a premium that rose as high as 30*s* in 1694, when the silver coins were badly degraded, settling afterward at 21*s* 6*d*—the rate at which guineas were received by officers of the revenue following the Great Recoinage (of silver) of 1696–99. In 1717, Isaac Newton, who was then master of the mint, convinced the government to lower the official rating of the guinea to 21*s*, where it remained throughout the remainder of the century. Five guinea, two guinea, and half guinea coins were also minted during the eighteenth century. Quarter guineas were tried as well, in 1718. But they were quickly discontinued because the public found them inconveniently tiny.[18]

British silver coins included shillings (minted at sixty-two to the troy pound of silver), crowns (= 5*s*), half crowns (= 2*s* 6*d*), and sixpence.[19] Copper, finally, was coined into halfpennies and farthings (worth one-quarter of a penny), at the rate of 23*d* to the pound avoirdupois (for Great Britain) or 26*d* to the pound (for Ireland).[20] No official copper pennies were struck before 1797.

A Standard "Blundered Into"

How might the eighteenth-century British government have tried to supply its citizens with small change? Having defined its basic monetary unit in terms of one precious metal, the government faced three options. It could

---

chanical presses but specifically to those having "grained" or vertically striated edges, which were first introduced in connection with the switch to screw presses. In fact, until the very end of the eighteenth century, "milled edges" were not applied to coins directly when they were stamped but were applied to blanks in advance of coining, by means of a special edge-marking tool.

18. Quarter guineas made another brief appearance in 1762.

19. Twopenny, threepenny, and fourpenny silver coin denominations had ceased to be current after the Great Recoinage, though their production was revived starting around 1730 for inclusion in Maundy money presentation sets (Craig 1953, 247).

20. The avoirdupois pound, equal to 7,000 troy grains, was the preferred weight unit of private traders but was adopted by the Royal Mint for its copper coinage only. Mint prices and equivalents for silver and gold were reckoned in terms of the troy pound of 5,760 troy grains, which replaced the mint (or Tower) pound of 5,400 troy grains in 1526.

1. strike both large- and small-denomination coins from the standard metal, with the coins' weights corresponding to their face values;

2. resort to bimetallism, with low-denomination coins made from the less valuable metal, and large-denomination coins made from the more valuable one; or

3. issue avowedly fiduciary or token small-denomination coins, on government account.[21]

Each option had its drawbacks.[22]

Under the first option, if the standard metal was sufficiently valuable, coins of lower denominations would be too small to be practical, as happened with Great Britain's quarter guineas. A still more egregious case was that of the silver farthings the Royal Mint issued in 1464. Weighing only three troy grains each, these were "lost almost as fast as they were coined" (Snelling 1766, preface). The standard metal could, of course, be one from which convenient small-denomination coins might be made; but then large-denomination coins of the same metal would end up being too bulky.

A bimetallic system might have avoided the problem of undersized or oversized coins.[23] But it suffered from its tendency to give effect to Gresham's law, with one metal alone being taken to the mint for coining and with coins of the other metal being clipped, filed, sweated, or melted. The nation would then be exposed to shortages of decent small or large change, depending on which metal was overvalued. The situa-

---

21. Sargent and Velde (1999) and, following them, Redish (2000, 21–24), consider a fourth option: reliance on freely minted coins all made from different alloys of a common metal. However, as Redish (ibid., 21) observes, this approach was "not feasible for a variety of metallurgical reasons."

22. What follows is a much-simplified analysis of the small-change problem. For details, see Redish 2000. Edwin Cannan (1935, 33–42) provides a brief, excellent discussion. Because the elaborate formal theory developed by Sargent and Velde (2002, 15–36, 335–72) assumes a monometallic system, while abstracting from costs associated with the use of very large or very small coins, it isn't capable of shedding light on the British situation. Concerning this and other shortcomings of Sargent and Velde's theory, see Wallace 2003.

23. I say "might" because two metals alone may be inadequate to the task of providing conveniently for all needed coin denominations. In principle, though, trimetallism or some even more involved form of multimetallism can cover any conceivable denomination range. All multimetallic arrangements are, of course, subject to the working of Gresham's law, with the number of opportunities for overvaluation and undervaluation being proportional to the number of metals involved.

tion might not be much better, in other words, than if the mint stuck to a single metal.[24]

The token coinage alternative, finally, had its own peculiar drawback: the large difference between token coins' nominal, or face, value and their "intrinsic worth" would tempt counterfeiters. Unless legitimate coins could be distinguished from fake ones (by mint authorities, if not by the general public), false coiners would foil the mint's attempts to keep the supply of token coins in line with the demand for them, causing both real and fake token coins to be discounted. If the mint tried to limit the supply and prop up the value of its token coins by offering to redeem them in full-bodied (silver or gold) coin, counterfeiters might take the mint to the cleaners. If, on the other hand, it avoided losses by refusing to take back unwanted coins, counterfeiting might give rise to a glut, eventually driving the tokens' value down to a level no greater than their "intrinsic worth," and making them no more fit to serve as money than matches, nails, or . . . buttons.

Which option did the British government rely on? The answer depends on whether one speaks of the solution actually relied on or the one the government pretended to rely on. As far as British officialdom was concerned, the pound sterling, the shilling, and the penny continued throughout the eighteenth century to be *silver* monetary units, as they had been since Queen Elizabeth's day—corresponding to twenty, one, and one-twelfth shillings, respectively. As we have seen, gold guineas, which had had a free-floating value for a time, were assigned an official value of twenty-one shillings in 1717. From that point onward, Britain was officially committed to bimetallism, with both gold and silver coins commanding unlimited legal tender status for most of the remainder of the century.[25]

But there was a wrinkle to Britain's official bimetallism. The Royal Mint also struck copper coins—farthings and halfpennies—that were supposed, according to a 1672 proclamation, to contain "as much Copper in weight, as shall be of the true intrinsick value and worth of a halfpeny [*sic*] or farthing respectively." The government pretended, in other

---

24. This summary is, I admit, rather unfair to bimetallism, which still has its defenders, who argue that it has worked reasonably well in some instances (see Redish 2000, 180ff.; Flandreau 2004; Friedman 1992). Although such exceptions did exist, eighteenth-century Britain wasn't one of them.

25. In 1774, the acceptance of silver coin by tale ceased to be compulsory for payments above twenty-five pounds. This limitation lapsed in 1783 but was reinstated in 1798.

words, to provide for all of Great Britain's small-change needs without making any use of tokens—that is, without issuing any coins having a declared value substantially above their "intrinsick value." Because there was no free coinage of copper, that metal had no official mint price, so it wouldn't be quite right to characterize this policy as official trimetallism. Nevertheless, the mint adhered throughout the century to a policy of making forty-six halfpennies or ninety-two farthings from every pound avoirdupois of copper that it coined. Because it appeared to assign an official value to copper while suggesting a tight link between that value and copper's market price, Britain's official coinage policy might fairly be characterized as a sort of pseudo-trimetallism.

Great Britain's actual eighteenth-century small-change system turned out to be a far cry from what was officially proclaimed. First of all, the pound sterling had ceased, sometime during the first decades of the century, to be a silver unit, having come to refer instead to a distinct quantity of gold—namely, 20/21 of a gold guinea. The change "came about without any action, or indeed any thought of action, on the part of the legislature" (Carlile 1901, 12). It was so subtle that many people, including the great Adam Smith, failed to notice it, thinking instead that because values continued for the most part to be quoted in pounds, shillings, and pence rather than in guineas, they could only refer to quantities of silver.

The spontaneous switch to gold units took place in part because of the increasing scale of payments, which made gold coins convenient for an increasing share of transactions, but also because the full-weight silver coins so abundantly supplied during the Great Recoinage of the 1690s had taken flight or had become badly impaired (Ruding 1840, 2:87). The term *shilling* thus ceased to have a clear meaning when reckoned as a quantity of silver: while sellers liked to think of it as standing for the sort of full-weight silver coin last seen in 1699, buyers insisted on treating it as a name for the grossly underweight and decrepit silver pieces still on hand. Under the circumstances, to have gone on treating pounds, shillings, and pence as silver units would have been asking for trouble, for this was bound to revive the endless haggling and disputes that had been all too familiar during the days before the Great Recoinage. Back then, Macaulay (1856, 499) relates,

> The workman and his employer had a quarrel as regularly as the Saturday came around. On a fair day or a market day the clamour, the re-

proaches, the taunts, the curses, were incessant: and it was well if no booth was overturned and no head broken. No merchant would contract to deliver goods without making some stipulation about the quality of the coins in which he was to be paid. Even men of business were often bewildered by the confusion into which all pecuniary transactions were thrown. . . . The labourer found that the bit of metal, which, when he received it, was called a shilling, would hardly, when he wanted to purchase a pot of beer or a loaf of rye bread, go as far as sixpence.   (1856, 499)

By agreeing, implicitly, to treat the shilling and the pound as gold units while using worn silver coins as mere counters or claims to gold (to be accepted at face value only in limited quantities), merchants were able to avoid confusion and to keep things civil. Workers, however, were hardly better off than they had been just after the Glorious Revolution, for they were seldom, if ever, paid in gold and were often compelled to receive silver coins by tale. To save silver for larger purchases was to expose oneself to a loss, so this added up to real hardship.

What happened to all the good silver coins? Gresham's law happened: silver was overvalued relative to gold at the time of the Great Recoinage and remained so for a century afterward, despite Newton's decision to fix the value of the guinea at twenty-one shillings. Newton's effort to stem the outflow of silver appears halfhearted in retrospect, for although he lowered the mint ratio to just under 15¼ to 1, the new ratio was still well above the market ratio. So silver kept right on flowing east, where just thirteen pounds of it might buy a pound of gold.

So it happened that for most of the eighteenth century, the Royal Mint remained "closed to silver as effectually as if [it] had been closed by statute" (Carlile 1901, 14). Between Newton's reform and 1760, fewer than two million ounces of silver (about £500,000 worth) were sent there for coining (Ashton 1955, 171). Of this amount, £136,431 consisted of the spoils from George Anson's voyage around the world, while another £79,198 in shillings and sixpences was commissioned, at a loss, by the Bank of England to be handed out to its customers at Christmastime (Craig 1953, 246). For the remainder of the century, the mint made no silver coins at all—apart from minuscule (£60) batches of Maundy money—except on two occasions: in 1762–63, it produced £5,791 in threepennies and shillings using silver booty taken at sea; and in 1787, it once again obliged the Bank of England with £55,459 worth of Yuletide

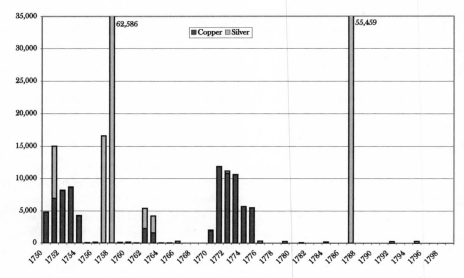

Fig. 1. Royal Mint silver and copper coin output in pounds sterling, 1750–99.
(Data from Craig 1953, 417–18.)

silver (see fig.1).[26] In contrast, during 1717 alone, the East India Company exported close to three million ounces of silver bullion, much of which came from heavier silver coins that were culled from circulation and tossed into bullion dealers' melting pots (W. Shaw 1896, 231).

That the melting and exportation of coin was illegal hardly mattered, because the law was unenforceable. Dealers merely had to swear, under oath, that they made their bullion from foreign coins or silver plate. And the payoff from flouting the law was substantial.

By law, 62 shillings are to be coined out of One pound, or 12 ounces of Standard Silver.—This is 62 pence an Ounce. Melt these 62 shillings, and in a Bar this Pound Weight *at Market,* will fetch 68 pence an ounce, or 68 Shillings. The difference therefore between coined and uncoined Silver in *Great Britain is now* 9 2/3 per Cent.

([WHATLEY] [1762] 1856, 519)

Although gratuitous coinage was supposed to help by making coins more plentiful, in Great Britain's bimetallic arrangement it did just the

---

26. According to Craig (1953, 246), "the Bank doled these treasures out without extravagance and had £22,800 still in stock in 1798."

opposite by making it profitable for dealers to melt good silver coins as soon as the relative market value of silver rose even slightly above the value implicit in the mint ratio. Also, because it assigned the costs of coining not to those who stood to gain most by having more coins at hand but to the government, gratuitous coinage gave the government reason to overlook any want of small change "until the pressure of that want [became] extreme." (Ruding 1799, 12).

Not all silver coins were melted and exported: so long as gold coins couldn't serve as small change, some silver money stayed behind. But market forces saw to it that the coins that remained had shrunk enough, either through natural wear or through deliberate shorting, to render their export unprofitable. Thus time, assisted by shears, files, aqua fortis, and even the vigorous shaking of half-filled money bags, raised the de facto mint equivalent of standard silver from sixty-two to no fewer than sixty-eight shillings to the pound. In this way, at least some British silver was prevented from being used "to grace the bodies of women in India, to provide votive offerings in the temples of China, or simply to swell hoards in these far-off places" (Ashton 1955, 169).

According to a Royal Mint study reported by Oman (1967, 357), a sample of silver coins circulating in 1786 revealed half crowns to be 12 percent below their proper weight, on average, with shillings and six-pence 23 and 36 percent below, respectively.[27] Besides being light, the silver coins that stayed behind were badly defaced, if not mere blanks. As long as such dilapidated coins could be put off, even in limited quantities, at their face value—and especially to the extent that officers of the revenue received them at that value—they were in truth not full-bodied coins at all but fiduciary ones "held up in value by gold" (Carlile 1901, 12). They were, in other words, mere tokens—unacknowledged tokens, to be sure, but tokens nonetheless.

So, just as it had, in Walter Bagehot's famous formulation, "blundered into" its Cabinet government, Great Britain blundered into a gold standard supplemented by token silver coins. But these were token coins of the very worst sort, because they were so easy to counterfeit and because the mint couldn't add to their supply, since no one would supply it

---

27. Indeed, after 1760, a rise in the relative market value of gold caused it to become undervalued at the mint, not relative to the de jure mint equivalent for silver, but relative to the de facto equivalent, as measured by the number of actual, worn silver shillings it took to make up a pound weight of standard silver. Consequently, guineas and half guineas began to be aggressively and illegally trimmed, in what came to be known as the "yellow trade," and Great Britain soon found itself deprived of good full-bodied coins of any kind.

with silver. If the stock of silver money grew at all, it did so thanks only to counterfeiting. *Good* silver money, on the other hand, was altogether unobtainable. And no wonder: the mint couldn't be expected to administer properly a token coinage whose very existence it refused to acknowledge.

"Let the Vulgar Wait"

The shortage of silver coin meant that copper halfpennies and farthings not only had to serve for all transactions below sixpence but also had to take the place of missing silver in larger retail and wage payments. On paper, as we've seen, the Royal Mint's copper coins were full-bodied coins, allowance being made for coining costs only; in reality, their nominal value was for most of the century roughly twice the market value of the copper they contained. They, too, were tokens, in other words—ones that also were all too easy to counterfeit.

While fraudulent coppers multiplied, authentic copper coins grew more and more scarce as the eighteenth century wore on, partly because many genuine copper coins, "underweight" as they were, were melted down to be turned into still lighter fakes, but also because the mint chose periodically to stop coining copper altogether, and did so even while industry pleaded for more. So there was never enough good regal copper coin around to make very small change with, let alone to fill the void left by the exportation of silver.

Some coinage historians blame the shortage of regal copper coin on officials' disdain for the metal, which mint officers condemned as "base in virtue and dishonorable" (Powell 1993, 50). British monarchs are likewise supposed to have considered it beneath their dignity to have their images stamped on such an "unworthy" material. There's something to this, for although the Royal Mint first began to make copper coins in 1672, mint officials could claim even as late as 1782 that copper coinage was not an activity "properly belonging to the Mint" (Craig 1953, 250). In truth, mint indentures never provided for any copper coins. The minting of copper was instead treated by the mint (and also by Parliament) as an extracurricular affair, undertaken on the basis of special contracts, known as "royal warrants," negotiated between the autonomous Company of Moneyers and the Crown (Craig 1953, 174–75, 250). So although the king didn't actually mind having his portrait done on copper, Parliament never included the cost of such portraits in its regular budgets.

There were also what are nowadays termed "public choice" reasons for the government's disdain for copper: copper money was, after all, money for the middling and especially the poorer classes, and the poor had no clout. The well-heeled wanted gold guineas and silver crowns—the former for large payments, especially among gentlemen; the latter for profitable exportation (if good) and for commercial transactions (if bad). An anonymous bard put it succinctly:

> 'Tis Gold buys Votes, or they'd have swarmed ere now,
> *Copper* serves only for the meaner Sort of People;
> *Copper* never goes at Court.
> And since one shilling can full Twelve Pence weigh,
> Silver is better in *Germany*.
> 'Tis true the Vulgar seek it, What of that?
> They are not Statesmen,—let the Vulgar wait.   (ANONYMOUS 1739)

The Company of Moneyers itself profited more from coining gold and silver than from coining copper. Before 1799, the master of the mint was paid a commission on output, which he shared with the moneyers. Before 1770, that commission was based on the value of money being struck, rather than the number of pieces (Ashton 1955, 167–68). Coining costs tended to be proportional to the number of pieces struck, rather than to their value: material costs aside, a farthing cost almost as much to make as a guinea. Consequently, both the master and the moneyers preferred to devote their efforts to making large-value coins. Indeed, they might never have coined copper at all had the Privy Council not asked them to start doing so in 1672.

But the mint's disdain for copper, considerable though it may have been, was just one aspect of a more complicated picture. Although mint indentures didn't provide for any copper coinage until the nineteenth century, the coining of copper was frequently made possible from 1672 onward through royal warrants procured by the Treasury in response to the public clamor for small change. While the mint produced very little copper coin between 1700 and 1728, it issued substantial, if less than adequate, quantities of farthings and halfpennies between 1729 and 1753 and again in 1762–63 and 1770–75 (see fig. 1).[28]

What has to be addressed, then, isn't simply the mint's low regard for

---

28. Official copper pennies would not be issued until 1797 and would not be produced by the Royal Mint until 1821.

copper, which alone might have kept it from coining that metal altogether, but its tendency to coin copper by fits and starts. The explanation for the pattern is twofold. First, the token nature of regal copper coins, (that is, the fact that they were valued at over twice their metallic worth), together with their indifferent—if not wretched—quality, caused them to be aggressively counterfeited. Legitimate copper coins were sometimes melted down and turned into a larger nominal stock of lightweight fakes. The mint thus found itself inadvertently boosting the output of spurious copper coins whenever it tried to add to the quantity (and improve the average quality) of genuine ones.

Second, both real and counterfeit regal coppers tended to make their way from publicans' tills to the strongboxes of London brewing companies, where they piled up. Banks wouldn't take them, and the mint never seriously entertained the idea of providing for their redemption. Also, as Sir John Craig (1953, 251) points out, "no substantial transaction could be negotiated nor Bill of Exchange bought with coppers, and they were refused for tax and excise." In consequence, by midcentury, many London breweries, as well as other London wholesalers and even a few retail firms, found themselves "burdened with £50 to £500 each of halfpence." The same thing happened in the half decade or so leading up to 1763 and during the one ending in 1775.

In response to complaints from London brewers and merchants and also in order to stop the flow of raw material to counterfeiters, the mint ceased producing copper coins from 1701 to the accession of George I in 1714, from 1755 to 1762, from 1764 through 1769, and yet again after 1775. Each of these attempts to relieve London of its surplus copper coin was, however, met by another chorus of complaints, from different sources. For in the provinces, many tradespersons and, after 1775 especially, manufacturers and mining companies found themselves shorter than ever of decent coins for making change or for paying their workers.

Indeed, even when the mint was producing copper coin, the coin might never get to some places where it was most needed, for royal warrants made no provision for the distribution of copper coins, delivering them in five- and ten-shilling packets at the Tower only. That made Tower halfpence a bad deal for anyone outside London, since the mint "sold" its coins at their full face value. Many provincial manufacturers, especially those in the far north, found the burden of the delivery cost too great to bear and therefore had either to hope that new Tower issues would trickle up to them somehow or to turn to copper counterfeiters, who at least had the virtue of delivering their products for no more than a modest markup above cost.

So, a dilemma: the mint could either try, however inadequately, to please desperate manufacturers at the cost of saddling London's brewers and merchants with more unwanted coins, or it could please the brewers and merchants at the cost of depriving manufacturers of means for paying their hands. Either option seemed to encourage counterfeiting, for the first rewarded counterfeiters with a ready supply of raw material, while the second increased the public's willingness to accept obvious forgeries for want of anything better. For a generation starting in 1775, the mint stuck to the second strategy, producing no copper coins at all. This was, remember, a time during which Gresham's law kept the mint's silver output to a mere trickle. It was also the crucial, takeoff phase of the Industrial Revolution.

One gets some idea of the severity of the resulting small-change shortage from a 1785 mint estimate that, allowing for a downward adjustment to correct for an error in the mint's production figures, put the total outstanding face value of legitimate copper coin at £306,000, or just three shillings' worth per person. That wasn't enough by a long chalk, especially considering the lack of good silver coin. Yet a large portion of this meager stock of regal copper was resting in the coffers of brewers and merchants who didn't want it, instead of being available for wage payments. "The roots of the problem," Sir John Craig (1953, 252) rightly insists, "were not in the two score halfpence a head but their maldistribution." He explains,

> Not only was there no power, had there been knowledge, to direct provision by the Mint towards or away from particular areas according to need; there was no organization whatever . . . to redistribute the burdensome loads which silted up certain cities.

As long as the British government failed to officially recognize the fiduciary status of its silver and copper coins, it couldn't be expected to take seriously the requirements for an adequate token coinage and especially the requirement that such a coinage be safeguarded from counterfeiting. As long as it denied relying on tokens, the government felt obliged to retain the appearance, if not the reality, of bimetallism (if not trimetallism). Great Britain's blundered-into gold standard was therefore forced to lead a shadowy existence, playing mistress to an economy still married, in the eyes of the law, to a silver standard, and giving birth to a bastard token coinage system that public authorities disavowed. To relieve the gold standard and its offspring of their ignoble status, the government would have to stop pretending that the pound sterling was a silver unit, while admitting the existence of official token coins. That, in turn, meant finding a way of distinguishing the Royal Mint's tokens from counterfeits. Regrettably, so far as the mint was concerned, no fool-proof means existed for doing this: its own copper coins and those made in Birmingham's back alleys were, in some instances at least, as alike as identical twins.

Making Do

How did eighteenth-century British employers cope with coin shortages? To start with, many "spent days riding from place to place" in search of small change, sometimes paying a premium for it and often having to settle for bad halfpence (Ashton 1962, 99). To pay his weavers, Samuel Oldknow was willing to look to anyone, "however distant, whose business brought a regular supply of currency and who was prepared to give credit" (Unwin, Hulme, and Taylor 1924, 176); even humble journeymen having one or two apprentices spent hours every week seeking change (Merrey 1794, 68). In importing cash from far-off places, employers had to take special steps to avoid becoming the prey of highwaymen. One of Oldknow's principal cash sources—his uncle Thomas—made a point of hiding his regular shipments of one hundred to two hundred pounds in bales of goods (Unwin, Hulme, and Taylor 1924, 177).

Because even the most intense searching couldn't make up for an overall shortage of cash, businessmen also resorted to the partial substitution of payment in kind for money payments, bucking the trend that had given rise to the waged proletariat in the first place. In fact, almost every trade offered its workers some sort of nonmonetary remuneration, often consisting of waste products, each known by precise (if peculiar) argot, as in the following tally by Peter Linebaugh:

cabbage to the tailor, blue-pigeon flying to the plumbers and glaziers, chippings to the ship-wrights, sweepings to porters, red sail docking to navy yard workers, flints and thrums to weavers, vails to servants, privileges to west country clothiers, bontages to Scottish agricultural workers, scrapings and naxeses to coopers, wastages to framework knitters.   (QUOTED IN RULE 1992, 182)[29]

Skilled workmen and apprentices were also often supplied with raw materials and tools, the costs of which were deducted from their money wages. Finally, large factories and mines ran company stores, or "Tommy shops," where workers could buy goods using company-issued "Tommy notes" paid them in place of coin of the realm. Some firms also arranged to have their Tommy notes taken by independent local retailers (Rule 1992, 180–89). Oldknow, for example, supplied houses, milk, coal, meat, and beds to many of his workers, deducting the costs of these items from their wages. During the financial crisis of 1793, when cash was especially scarce, Oldknow resorted to paying his workers' net wages almost entirely in notes that local shopkeepers agreed to accept, limiting his cash payments to "no more than two shillings in the pound" (Unwin, Hulme, and Taylor 1924, 187).

Some economic historians attribute the persistence of truck and Tommy shops to employers' attempts to get around wage regulations (see, e.g., Hilton 1960). Others attribute it to workers' fondness for "old customs" (see, e.g., John Styles 1983, 184). It's clear, however, that shortages of good money were also to blame (see, e.g., Unwin, Hulme, and Taylor 1924, 197ff). Far from making life easier for either employers or their workers, reliance on truck was both a nuisance and a potent generator of industrial ill will. "The system," the Hammonds (1917, 67) observe, "poisoned the relations of masters and men, and it vitiated the calculations of the wages paid." Journeymen complained that their employers assigned inflated values to equipment and materials they supplied, while factory and mine workers, conscious of similarly "stuffed" prices at company stores, resented pay practices that forced them and their families to obtain necessities on credit, which often meant either patronizing the factory shop or going without toiletries, fuel, or food:

You Boatsmen and colliers all,
Come listen to my ditty,
I'll sing you a song before its long,
It is both new and pretty;

---

29. The terms' meanings can generally be guessed. "Thrums," for example, are web ends left in a loom after removal of finished cloth.

It is concerning the Tommy shops,
And the high field ruffian
He pays you with a tommy note,
You must have that or nothing
    Fal de riddle ral . . .
Then to the tommy shops we go,
To fetch our week's provision,
Their oatmeal, sugar, salt and soap,
Short weight and little measure . . .
Saying if we had money instead of this,
Provisions we could have plenty,
The profit they get out of us,
Is nine shillings out of twenty . . .[30]

Wherever workers were allowed partial payment in leftovers, the line separating perquisite from purloining was often vaguely drawn. With means of payment left literally lying around, the temptation to pilfer was great. Workers "saw to it that the crumbs from their master's table were ample" (Ashton 1955, 209), and abuses sometimes amounted to what T. S. Ashton calls "barefaced robbery" (ibid.). Receivers did a brisk business with Sheffield nailors, who helped themselves to whole spools of wire, and with Birmingham brass workers, who did the same with scrap metal. Colliers thought nothing of adding an extra draught or two to their coal allowances, while shipwrights could be spotted taking home wood "chips" that looked suspiciously like deliberately divvied-up lengths of timber.

In more than a few cases, it should be admitted, embezzlement affected a kind of crude justice, as when workers in the royal dockyards allowed themselves interest, in the form of sailcloth, on wage payments that were often months in arrears (Rule 1992, 185). According to Ashton (1955, 209), "there was a close connection between 'long pay' and embezzlement," both practices being ultimately attributable, at least in part, to the shortage of small change. Official justice was, however, blind to such extenuating circumstances, and many a poor worker ended up in jail just for trying to approximate the pay he or she had been promised to begin with. Evidence from the royal dockyards, where government investigations produced an unusual wealth of information, also provides some idea of the extent to which in-kind perks might supplement cash payments.

---

30. Raven 1977, 53–54.

When, starting in 1797, new regal copper coins produced at Matthew Boulton's Soho Mint finally allowed the navy to commute daily chip allotments into cash payments, the workers asked for eight pence, which was almost a third of their daily monetary wages before the reform.[31]

Predictably, as the shortage of good small money became more severe, the purloining of materials grew worse—a fact reflected in increasing penalties as well as in increasing arrests. In 1703, a worker found guilty of the offense had "merely" to forfeit twice the value of whatever he or she stood accused of pilfering, with corporal punishment in the offing for those who could not or would not pay the requisite fine. In 1740, prosecution costs (or more lashes or stock time) were added to the old penalty. Nine years later, what was once a mere breach of contract was made a crime punishable by fourteen days' imprisonment; and in 1777 the sentence was lengthened—to three months for a first offense and six for repeat offenders (Ashton 1955, 210).

Another way in which employers dealt with coin shortages was by arranging payments so as to minimize the need for small change without otherwise altering their money wage bills. Many insisted on "group pay," which meant that several workers had to share one or more gold guineas, half guineas, or banknotes (Craig 1953, 247; Bell 1963, 9). Unless the group happened to consist of members of the same family, as was sometimes the case, group pay was a pain in the neck. A manufacturer explained:

> If the work of two men comes to near a guinea, or three men to near two guineas, we give them the gold and they must go together till they can get change by purchasing what they want. If they go to a grocer he will not give change unless the quantity of sugar, tea, &c. amounts to a certain sum, and then he stipulates for their taking a certain quantity of [bad] halfpence. . . .
>
> It very often happens that groceries are not wanted by poor men who come from villages around, who seldom care to take tea and sugar home; but they generally have a public house in the market town at which they call to refresh; And to it these two or three fellows (though not all countrymen) go, with a good excuse to get their gold changed: if they find, after drinking a pint or two, that they cannot succeed, what can they do but go to another house. . . . [B]ut whether

---

31. The workers eventually settled for three to six pence, depending on their trade (Morris 1983, 104).

they get change at the first or second attempt, they are not served
without taking several shillings in copper, and this of the worst quality
that can be forced into circulation.   (MERREY 1794, 67–68)

An equally troublesome and common practice was "long pay," by which
workers were made to wait several Saturdays instead of just one or two between reckonings. Employers also staggered wage payments, so that the
same batch of coins might do double or even triple duty. A Lancashire
cotton spinner, for instance, paid a third of his workers first thing in the
morning and then let them go to town so that he could retrieve coins
they'd spent from the shopkeepers and victuallers later that same day, to
use in paying a second group of workers. The spinner had recovered
many of the coins once more by early evening, for use in a third and final
round of payments (Ashton 1962, 99–100).

A less cumbersome way of making available coins go further involved
setting up "pay tables" at alehouses. This practice saved employers the
trouble of retrieving surplus coins from pubs only to have them taken
back the same evening. To reduce their wage bills, employers arranged
with pub owners to have their workers drink "on the strap." They then
deducted the workers' tabs from their pay, settling them collectively at
closing time using guineas or banknotes. With beer at three pennies a
quart, deductions could reduce employers' small-change needs substantially. In his *Autobiography*, Ben Franklin (2003, 45) observes that when
he was working for a London printer in 1725, his fellow workmen were
all "great Guzzlers of Beer." One "drank every day a Pint before Breakfast, a Pint at Breakfast with his Bread and Cheese; a Pint in the Afternoon about Six o'Clock, and another when he had done his Day's-
Work," thus causing "4 or 5 Shillings to pay out of his pay-table Wages
every Saturday Night."

Pay tables were seen by many as evidence of a conspiracy of employers and brewers aimed at encouraging workers to tipple, with employers
sharing in brewers' profits:

> But if to an alehouse they customers be,
> Then presently with the ale wife we agree;
> When we come to a reckoning, then we do crave
> Twopence on a shilling, and that we will have,
> By such cunning ways we our treasure do get,
> For it is all fish that doth come to our net.[32]

---

32. From *The Clothier's Delight*, reproduced in Mantoux 1927, 75–77.

Tippling was, to be sure, a serious problem, with many a poor worker returning home after midnight as bereft of money as ever and drunk to boot. Wives complained, blows were struck, arrests were frequent, and Saint Monday—an unofficial weekly "holiday" created by hungover workers—was zealously kept (George 1925, 287ff.):

And when at night he staggers home, he knows not what to say;
A fool is more a man than he upon a fuddling day
For it's drink, drink, smoke, smoke, drink, drink away
There is no pleasure in the house upon a fuddling day!

But there's no need to suppose that employers were in league with brewers or publicans or were otherwise interested in promoting domestic unrest, which reduced their own firms' productivity. More than a few resorted to pay tables because they couldn't meet their wage bills otherwise. Had there been enough good coin, they might better have served their own interests by linking wage payments to Sunday sermons.

Brummagem Ha'pence

Understandably, shortages of official small change boosted the production and circulation of all sorts of unofficial substitutes, including large quantities of counterfeit copper coin. The very nature of the counterfeiting trade rules out precise estimates of its magnitude. But there is no doubt that it was a big business, with Birmingham and London serving as its manufacturing headquarters, and that its magnitude grew as the eighteenth century wore on. Already in 1676, only four years after regal copper coins were first introduced, extensive counterfeiting triggered an Order in Council putting a temporary stop to regal copper coin production. In 1693 and again in 1701, the copper coinage was assigned to private patentees, with even more disastrous consequences. In 1717, the Royal Mint took charge again, but neither that step nor other legal reforms and private initiatives sufficed to put a stop to false coining. By midcentury, according to an informed contemporary estimate and also to the contents of a hoard of that period's copper coins unearthed many years later, close to half of all the copper coins in circulation were fake. By the end of the century, the fraction had grown larger still, with estimates placing it between five-sixths and over nine-tenths.

A popular view paints counterfeiters as solitary and shadowy figures, forging their wares "in the dark lanes of Birmingham and London"

(Raspe and Tassie 1791, p. xlii) and surreptitiously taking smallish parcels of them in person to the marketplace to fob them off on unsuspecting retailers or to sell them quietly at discount to unscrupulous factory owners. Though true in parts, this view distorts important features of the counterfeit trade in eighteenth-century England, especially in Birmingham, where techniques developed for making metal coat buttons were easily adapted to making fake copper coins. For one thing, the trade was to a surprising extent conducted in the open and on a large scale. This was especially so toward the end of the century, despite a substantial harshening of penalties in 1771. Thus in 1780, *Aris's Birmingham Gazette* noted with regret the "amazing Quantity of Counterfeit Halfpence now in Circulation" and the "great Effrontery with which they are given in Payment, in open Contempt, or Defiance of the Laws for their Suppression" (quoted in Langford 1868, 231). Another Birmingham witness, writing some decades later, observed similarly that "the trade was carried on so openly, that I often wondered at people's hardihood considering the severity of the punishment" (*The Morning Chronicle,* February 10, 1851, quoted in Powell 1993, 49). At the tail end of the century, as he was preparing to launch his own (authorized) regal coppers, Matthew Boulton also noted (in a letter to Sir George Shuckburgh-Evelyn, MP) that "Many of our Knights of the Saddle Bag, take out on their journeys, pattern cards of halfpence to get orders from us regularly as they do of Buttons" and that some counterfeit manufacturers even had "the audacity to hang up Signs in the street ALL SORTS OF COPPER COINS MADE HERE" (MBP 253/251). In London, the trade was so extensive that, according to police magistrate Patrick Colquhoun (pronounced "Calhoon"), scarcely a wagon or coach left town that wasn't laden with boxes of fraudulent coin bound for various provincial camps, seaports, and manufacturing towns (1800, 16).

Second, like legitimate commercial token makers who appeared on the scene starting in 1787 and unlike the Royal Mint, counterfeit manufacturers generally did not participate in the retail end of the business. Instead, they acted as artisans or journeymen, selling their products in bulk to large dealers for, depending on quality, anywhere from one-half to about a fifth of their face value. The dealers resold the shams for a smaller discount to manufacturers, merchants, and other clients who placed regular orders for small change, as well as to retail utterers or "smashers." In London, counterfeit smashers consisted, according to Colquhoun, of Irishmen and the "lower orders of the jews," with certain dealers holding "a kind of market every morning where from forty to fifty of those German Jew boys are regularly supplied with counterfeit halfpence" (ibid. 182).

The abundance of counterfeits toward the end of the century points to the huge scale of the counterfeit manufacturing business. Colquhoun, having examined the problem at length in preparing his influential *Treatise on the Police of the Metropolis,* found that in the course of a six-day week, two or three persons could stamp and finish counterfeits worth (in face value) two to three hundred pounds, or between 96,000 and 144,000 halfpennies. By the midnineties, there were over fifty counterfeit manufacturing operations at work, mainly in Birmingham, London, and Bristol, with several large-scale operations running several presses at once.

Although counterfeiters' scale of production was impressive, the quality of their products was often anything but. This brings us to a distinction that plays a crucial part in the discussion to follow: that between "good" counterfeits, meaning those that were convincing enough to fool even Royal Mint authorities, and "bad" ones, meaning those that at best fooled members of the general public only and probably not many of them. "Bad" counterfeits were far more common than good ones. Up to midcentury, all counterfeits were cast rather than stamped, despite the fact that the Royal Mint had not made use of cast copper blanks since the reign of William III. In the early 1750s, counterfeiters began using screw presses, with dies intentionally cut shallow to imitate old "milled" Hanoverian coppers. But even these stamped products were usually very much inferior to regal halfpennies (or at least to regal halfpennies in mint condition), being typically made to a standard of seventy-two pence per pound of copper compared to the Royal Mint's forty-six pence. By century's end, the proportion of "bad" counterfeits was especially high, with few counterfeiters even bothering to endow their coins with engravings resembling those on their official counterparts. Instead, many produced "plain halfpence," possessing no engravings at all, or so-called regal evasives, which bore legends that just barely got around the anti-counterfeiting statutes. One eyewitness recalled years after the fact: "Almost any kind of rubbish used to pass as copper money. . . . And all this made the trade of the false coiner more easy" (*Morning Chronicle,* February 10, 1851, quoted in Powell 1993, 49).

Some writers lay the blame for such obvious frauds on widespread illiteracy. But while illiteracy might conceivably account for someone being unable to tell the difference between "GEORGIUS III REX" and "GOD SAVE US ALL," it can't explain all the plain and decidedly un-

derweight halfpence. A better explanation is that the lack of legitimate
regal copper coins and (before 1787) the lack of any commercial substitutes forced people to accept obvious fakes rather than forgo payment
entirely. "Ordinary folk," Royal Mint historian Sir John Craig has observed, "if short of small change, cared nothing about intrinsic value,
high quality of copper, pattern or limits of legal tender" (Craig 1953,
253). Indeed, when provincial shopkeepers attempted, as they did on
numerous occasions, to cooperate with each other in refusing counterfeit money, their resolutions merely succeeded in curtailing sales and
sparking riots.[33]

Publick Virtue?

In light of the facts just considered, modern historians have tended to
treat eighteenth-century counterfeiters as criminals whose crime was not
only victimless but largely beneficial, like the conduct of so many Robin
Hoods. "In point of fact," Feavearyear (1963, 169) observes, "so long as
the Government was unable to find a method of providing the country
with a sound and adequate coinage [counterfeiting] was a good thing,"
as the counterfeiter "tended to fill up the void" and "could do no harm
to the standard."

There is much to be said for this view: after all, people needed small
money, and the poor needed it most of all; and even shoddy money was
better than nothing. Paradoxically, the very badness of the clumsiest
counterfeits made them particularly benign, because such miserable
coins could only gain acceptance where good coin was in short supply.
"Bad" halfpennies can for this reason be said to have made the general
public better off than it would have been otherwise. But let one speak on
its own behalf:

> In these modern times, though I am often found among the mean
> and the vulgar, I am more frequently to be met with in pompous
> courts and palaces. Without me, many think trade and commerce
> would dwindle to a shadow, and the retail trades be totally ruined. In
> short, there is scarce any situation whatever, in which I am not partic-

33. Individual retailers were powerless to do anything about counterfeits. If one attempted independently to refuse them, he merely drove his business away to rivals. Retailers could also err in the opposite direction: when one Birmingham hawker went so far as
to advertise his willingness to trade for counterfeits, his audacity landed him in court (Wager 1977, 16).

ularly serviceable; and yet such is the ingratitude of mankind in general, that my name in public is universally despised and disowned, even by those who in private endearingly caress me.[34]

"Good" (that is, convincing) counterfeits were another matter, for while they also appeared to alleviate shortages, their ability to fool even Royal Mint authorities meant that they could be placed into circulation even where legitimate coins weren't in short supply, potentially leading to a surplus. So long as official coins weren't redeemable, such a surplus could drive the entire stock of small change to a discount, seriously undermining the efficiency of exchange. If, however, official coins were made convertible into full-bodied ones on demand, the multiplication of good counterfeits would undermine their convertibility by exhausting the issuing authority's reserves of legal tender. Good counterfeits thus threw a wrench in what might otherwise have been a smoothly working small-change system. Rather than simply making up for shortages of official coin, they deserved at least part of the blame for those shortages, for as long as the Royal Mint had reason to fear that its tokens might be convincingly and profitably copied, it didn't dare offer to redeem them; and as long as the mint refused to redeem its tokens, it couldn't address local shortages without adding to surpluses elsewhere.

So good counterfeits made room for bad ones. For that reason, even though bad counterfeits were far more abundant and were more likely to be refused, the good ones ultimately did the most damage to the British monetary system, preventing it from addressing the public's small-change needs. Unless someone could come up with a way to rule such counterfeits out, British manufacturers and workers would have to muddle their way through the rest of the century without an adequate coin supply, even if that meant slowing down (if not putting off) the Industrial Revolution.

Yet the Royal Mint, far from doing whatever it could to make its copper coins hard to fake, did next to nothing. So far as the mint was concerned, making good coins was strictly a matter of putting legally authorized amounts of metal in them. When, in February 1788, Lord Hawkesbury, the president of the Board of Trade, asked the mint's officers to respond to the suggestion that they might make regal copper coins harder to fake by resorting to fine polishing and lettered edges, the officers dismissed both ideas as "a departure from the simple primitive

34. Anonymous 1772.

Institution of Material Money,—that of carrying full weight for value,—which is its only natural and best Security" (BL Add. MSS 38421, 221, February 8, 1788). This opinion was, mind you, offered less than two months after the same authorities reported that at least half of Great Britain's copper coins were fake (PRO PC1/37/114, December 1787).

Paper Money

Today, excepting traveler's checks, "private money" is practically synonymous with bank deposits that can be transferred using checks or plastic cards. During the eighteenth century, however, checks were rarely used. Instead, private banks issued their own circulating paper notes. Although paper notes wore out too rapidly to take the place of copper coin, they might at least have filled in for silver, thereby going a long way toward addressing Great Britain's overall coin shortage. As it happened, though, oppressive regulations prevented them from doing even that much.

The first British bank to gain widespread acceptance for its notes was the Bank of England, founded in 1694—not, as some suppose, to shore up the British monetary system, but to fund Great Britain's ongoing war with France. Besides coming up with the million pounds the government needed as fast as you can say "monopoly," the "Old Lady of Threadneedle Street," as the Bank came to be known, proved to be exceedingly profitable. But for reasons difficult to square with the profit motive, the Bank refused to set foot outside of the City until the government forced it to set up branch offices in 1826. The Bank thus earned its second (since forgotten) moniker, the "Bank of London." Moreover, the Bank refused to issue notes for less than the princely sum of twenty pounds before 1759 or for less than ten pounds before 1793, when it began to issue five-pound notes. Bank of England notes were seldom seen in the provinces and were of no use at all to most workers, let alone paupers, even in London.

It was up to other banks, especially banks in the countryside, to supply paper currency that could serve in retail trade and in the payment of wages. Unfortunately, an act of 1708 had given the Bank of England a monopoly of joint-stock banking in return for its agreeing to purchase some exchequer bills that the government badly wished to sell, causing so-called country banks to remain undercapitalized and to fail disconcertingly often. As Lawrence White has observed (1984, 39), "It became popular in England to attribute the instability of these banks to their issues of small notes rather than their undercapitalization." Parliament responded by banning all banknotes for less than one pound in 1775. In 1787, the minimum legal denomination was made five pounds, and the ban, which originally had to be renewed every few years, was made indefinite.

North of the Tweed, banking was free from many of the constraints and privileges that hindered it in England and Wales. By midcentury, several "public" or joint-stock banks had been established there, and both they and smaller "private" banks issued notes for less than one pound beginning in the 1750s. Some private banks made small notes their specialty, issuing paper worth as little as one shilling. As such notes became more abundant, complaints arose, mainly (according to one Victorian-era source) from "country gentlemen, led on by some who visited Edinburgh occasionally," and given to "exaggerated assertions, fallacious inferences, and ridiculous fears."[35] Whether warranted or not, the claim that Scotland was in the grips of a "small note mania," which representatives of Scotland's chartered banks were all too happy to affirm under oath, eventually caused Westminster to intervene, by prohibiting, in 1765, the issuance in Scotland of notes under one pound. After 1777, the one-pound notes of Scottish banks, which had already been circulating in northern England, gained greater currency there and could even be found further south. But by that time even Scottish banks were powerless to counter shortages of smaller change.[36] In short, as Jonathan Rule (1992, 203) points out, "however impressive historians may find the range of accepted paper in use in the eighteenth-century economy, for the bulk of the population money still meant coin, and that was short in quantity and poor in quality."

Commercial Coins

Deprived of small banknotes, ignored by the Royal Mint, sick of having to deal with bad shillings and doubtful halfpennies, and unable to make

---

35. Boase 1867, 2, cited in L. White 1984, 29–30. Compare Macleod 1892–93, 436ff.

36. The Bank of England had been issuing redeemable notes since its establishment in 1694, and Scottish banks had been doing the same for many decades before 1776. Sargent and Velde (2002, 263) thus err in writing that Adam Smith "proposed that banks be allowed to issue paper notes if they would promise to convert them into specie on demand" and that he got the idea by observing the successful private issuance of copper tokens. Smith could not propose what was already established practice. Nor did he propose any further liberalization of Scottish banking law. On the contrary, he endorsed the 1765 ban on small notes.

do with such except by aggravating, if not further injuring, their workers, manufacturers and other businessmen desperately sought some other source of relief. Finally, in 1787, one of them decided that if the mint wouldn't supply his firm with decent small change, he'd do it himself, by issuing private tokens bearing his firm's own markings. Others followed his example, and before long, Great Britain found itself equipped with a brand-new "commercial" small-change system.

This wasn't the first time unauthorized tokens served as Britain's principal small change. A similar arrangement flourished following the failure of Lord Harrington's copper farthings. Those farthings, issued under royal patent starting in 1613, had been especially light and shoddy and were therefore aggressively counterfeited. Not surprisingly, Harrington refused to honor his commitment to redeem them in silver, turning the farthings, which were not legal tender even in small payments, into so much junk copper. Harrington's copper farthing patent was extended to others until 1644, when Charles I finally put a stop to further issues.

The unauthorized private tokens (mostly farthings and halfpennies, with some pennies) that came in the wake of Harrington's failed effort were, unlike Harrington's coins, redeemed in silver, though only locally. Their issuers were mainly reputable town authorities or councils and some private tradesmen and shopkeepers. Precisely how these private issuers protected themselves from counterfeiters isn't clear: although their tokens were certainly better than Lord Harrington's, they were still on the whole of mediocre design and execution. In any event, they never circulated very widely, and there weren't all that many of them.[37]

For a while, the government tolerated the unauthorized tokens, but then it made up its mind to reaffirm its coinage prerogative by ordering milled copper coins from the Royal Mint and declaring the private tokens illegal. Despite the availability of regal substitutes, the private tokens proved so popular that the 1672 proclamation declaring it "His Majesty's pleasure that no person or persons should for the future make, coin, exchange, or use any farthing or tokens, except such as should be coined at His Majesty's mint" had to be followed by others on October 17, 1673, and December 12, 1674. The last proclamation prolonged tokens' legality until February 5, 1675, after which magistrates were under strict orders to prosecute offenders (Snelling 1766, 36).

That the law proscribing private tokens was still on the books made

---

37. See Berry 1988.

renewed resort to such tokens during the late eighteenth century risky. Despite this, the new tokens were issued on a far vaster scale than their seventeenth-century predecessors had been—a scale exceeding, in the space of a decade, the combined regal copper issues of the previous half century. The new tokens proved to be some of the best and most beautifully designed coins ever made anywhere. They were also the first token coins to be sufficiently counterfeit-proof to carry redemption pledges credible enough to make them current not only where they were issued but, in some cases, many miles away.

Great Britain's commercial coins were, in short, the best small change the world had ever seen. And their appearance couldn't have been more timely, for it was partly thanks to them and the people who made and issued them, that Great Britain managed to become the world's first industrial nation.

The story of Great Britain's commercial coinage is, above all else, as John Roger Scott Whiting (1971, 11) puts it, "a story of the initiative of local authorities, companies and individuals in the face of state ineptitude." But it is also the story of intense and often cutthroat competition among the commercial token makers themselves, competition that was the ultimate force driving them to produce coins of such exceptional quality, but that had little in common with economists' textbook notion of "perfect competition." In particular, the commercial coinage story is the story of a superficially cordial but often rancorous battle of wits between two of Great Britain's industrial giants: Matthew Boulton, the visionary and fatherly "Prince of Soho," and Thomas Williams, Anglesey's hardboiled "Copper King."

CHAPTER II

Druids, Willeys, and Beehives

Take care of the pence,

And the pounds will take care of themselves.[1]

The Great Discovery

The late eighteenth-century commercial coin regime might never have come about had it not been for an ill-chosen tune and a much-coveted bottle of booze.

Back in the 1690s, young Alexander Fraser (or Frazier), master of Lovat, was minding his own business at a wedding in Beauly, Scotland, when some bagpipe player, who was either impudent or stupid or both, started blowing "the biotag Mac Thomas." It happens that "the biotag Mac Thomas" was a tune highly offensive to the house of Lovat. Consequently, Fraser, in a fit of rage, stabbed the bagpiper dead. This sort of thing was not allowed then, even in the Highlands, so Fraser got himself quickly on a ship, fleeing Scotland and the gallows. Where Fraser was headed is anyone's guess. But he ended up on the rocky shore of the Welsh island of Anglesey, his ship having been lost in the Menai Straits, where it was either swallowed by the Swillies or smashed into bits on Platters Rocks. And in Anglesey Fraser remained until his death in 1776 at the ripe old age of 109—fugitive from justice, rightful heir to his father's estate, and codiscoverer of the world's biggest copper mine.

Such, at least, was the tale told by "Lord Lovat" himself, who, by the

---

1. Attributed to William Lowndes, Great Britain's secretary to the Treasury under William III and George I.

time of what came to be known as the "Great Discovery," was a grizzled and gray hermit living in a shack on the eastern side of Anglesey's Parys Mountain, close to where the copper was found. The locals, for their part, were more than happy to believe him, as were his four sons, who continued to press their claims upon the Beauly estate after their father's death. The senior Fraser looked ancient enough, after all, to have brandished a knife back in the 1690s. And as for reports that the real Alexander Fraser was killed at the Battle of Claverhouse and buried at Kirkall back in November 1692 . . . well, what better tale for getting the law off a fugitive Scotsman's back?[2]

Concerning the great copper find there is less room for doubt. In 1761, Fraser had been doing some prospecting for Sir Nicholas Bayly, owner of the Cerrig y Bleddia sheep farm, which covered the eastern half of Parys Mountain. He discovered some lumps of melted copper and traces of charcoal—remnants, it seemed, of an ancient Roman copper mine. That summer, Bayly had Fraser accompany a mine agent to the site. The two came back with a favorable report, and crews started mining the following year. Three shafts in all were sunk on Bayly's land, deeper and deeper, until, at last, every one of them struck . . . water; lots of water.

Come 1764, Bayly was just about fed up with mining when Charles Roe & Company, which had been working Bayly's mines for him for the past year, offered to lease them from him for twenty-one years in exchange for an 8 percent share of any ore produced. Three years later, the Cerrig y Bleddia mines remained sodden money pits so that, in late February 1768, a chagrined Charles Roe asked Jonathan Roose, foreman of one of his lead mines on the mainland, to explore other sites on Cerrig y Bleddia, in what seemed a futile attempt to recover his substantial investment. Roose sent out several search parties, but all came back empty-handed. Then he offered a bottle of brandy[3] (and a rent-free cottage, in case that helped) to the first man to find ore. That did it: on March 2, St. Chad's Day, just as the search was about to be given up, a cry rang out. Just three yards below the surface, Parys Mountain's mother

---

2. To add to the confusion, there was another Alexander Fraser—son of the infamous Simon Fraser, eleventh Lord of Lovat, who was tried in absentia, sentenced to death, and eventually outlawed for various acts of violence. When the Crown later remitted his death sentence, Simon showed his gratitude by supporting the rising of 1745, whereupon the "bonny Traytor" was captured, impeached by the House of Lords, and, on April 9, 1747, executed on Tower Hill. His son, who was born on July 1, 1729, is supposed to have died without issue, on August 7, 1762. For further details, see Mackenzie 1896.

3. Some sources say whiskey.

lode—what turned out to be the world's biggest vein of copper ore—had been found, and residents of the tiny fishing hamlet of Amlwch watched a lucky miner on horseback being escorted down the mountain in triumph, waving an empty bottle.

The Copper King

Sometime during 1769, Roe & Company, having riddled Cerrig y Bleddia with a streak of shafts later to be known as the Mona Mine (after the Roman name for the island), started picking at the northwestern tip of the streak, which marked the boundary of their leasehold. This was asking for trouble, for although Sir Nicholas held a lease on the entire western half of Parys Mountain and owned half of it, his share consisted not of a particular parcel but of an undivided moiety. The rest belonged to a man named Lewis, who had recently died. Lewis's heirs, including his niece Mary and her clergyman husband, Edward Hughes, objected to the encroachment, claiming, understandably (what can one do, after all, with a half share of a crater?), that Bayly's lease didn't include mineral rights. Bayly sought relief in a court of equity, whereupon the Hugheses turned to their family solicitor, Thomas Williams, for advice. By the time litigation ended in 1778, Williams, in stereotypically lawyerlike fashion, had advised himself into full control of the Lewis holdings.

Williams then joined forces with Edward Hughes and a London banker named John Dawes to form the Parys Mine Company, doing so just in time to help satisfy the rapidly growing demand for copper for ships' sheathing. To manufacture the sheets, Williams erected extensive works in Holywell, including two complete rolling mills and a steam-driven drop hammer capable of delivering eighty blows a minute. He also formed a partnership with a Birmingham manufacturer named John Westwood, whose patented methods of cold rolling allowed Williams to manufacture copper bolts capable of holding the sheathing in place without corroding.[4] Finally, in 1785, Williams gained control of the Mona Mine and hence of the whole of Parys Mountain:

---

4. The combination of copper sheathing and iron bolts had proven most unfortunate, thanks to galvanic action: in August 1782, it caused the hull of HMS *Royal George* to split open, killing all nine hundred people on board. The failure of iron fastenings is also suspected of causing the French prizes *Ville de Paris, Glorieux,* and *Centaur* to sink during a storm off the Grand Banks a few weeks later, with thirty-five hundred men lost.

Now his hard hands on Mona's rifted crest,
Bosom'd in rock, her azure ores arrest.[5]

The country lawyer from Llanidon thus became principal owner of the world's largest copper mine.

And "largest" meant gigantic: ascending to the top of the western side of Parys Mountain, one found oneself standing on the verge of a vast chasm, over fifty yards deep and twice as wide, its sides of deep yellow and dusty slate streaked here and there with bluish green veins. Not so much as a blade of vegetation was to be seen for half a mile in any direction, thanks to sulfur fumes rising from numerous kilns where the ore was roasted. To the northeast, the Parys Mine's open cast gave way to Mona's streak of shafts—145 of them in all—with a blotch of collapsed shafts marking the transition from one mine to the other.

Several crude timber stages perched along the tops of the chasm's vertical walls. Miners and buckets were lowered from them by means of a rope attached to a whimsey. The miners found a foothold on the walls and commenced their picking and blasting, creating little pockets and eventually little caves, and eventually big caves, some of which would eventually collapse. But never mind: day miners earned about fourteen pence a day, which was good pay in those parts, even for dangerous work; and miners who "worked the bargain," meaning those who got paid by the ton, could earn many times more, depending on the price of ore as established by the last setting or "sheeting" of the bargains. Considering that there were over a thousand miners at work, producing over forty thousand tons of ore a year, not to mention another thousand workers in the smelting plants and elsewhere, this added up to quite a payroll.

Quite a payroll. And no good money with which to pay it, just worn-out shillings and lots of Brummagem halfpence and gold guineas or five-pound notes—if the pitmen would consent to share the last. Imagine what Williams must have thought, without a single decent copper coin to his name, and all that inexpensive copper ore laying about. If only the government . . . But why wait for the government to act, when he might take the initiative? Good old Westwood, clever fellow, knows something about coinage: he produced those lovely medals for Garrick's Shakespeare festival. Why not let Westwood find an engraver to make a model, and start making blanks (unmarked metal disks) in Holywell? Why not

---

5. Darwin 1791, *Economy of Vegetation,* canto 1.

indeed! If the government drags its feet, P.M. Co. can at least pay its own workers. And should the government decide to act, well, who better to supply the copper, if not the new regal coins themselves, than Wales' own Anglesey mines?

At first, Williams tried to interest the government in his plan. In a March 1785 audience with Lord Effingham, then master of the mint, he proposed to strike regal copper coins bearing lettered edges applied using a new procedure that was probably another of Westwood's inventions. The edges would make the coins much harder to fake than the Royal Mint's copper. In a follow-up letter, Williams offered to instruct the Royal Mint in his new edge-marking technique, so as to guard "against the Treachery of Workmen who, on any difference with us, might communicate ye same exact mode of stamping the Letters to those who ought by all means to be kept ignorant of it" (PRO Mint 8/1, Williams to Lord Effingham, April 5, 1785). As if this weren't generous enough, Williams offered his coining services gratis, on the understanding that the copper for the new coins was to come from his own mines, rather than from Cornwall.

In retrospect, it seems that the government had been given a unique opportunity to repair its copper coinage. Yet for the better part of two years it took no action. It was then that Williams decided to take matters into his own hands. If the government wouldn't undertake a new copper coinage, he would do it himself, not by striking regal coins without permission—for that would be counterfeiting—but by striking his own money, the nonpareil Parys Mine Druids.

The Druids

Precisely how the first Druid coins were made is one of many enduring mysteries of the commercial coinage episode. All sources agree that Westwood supervised the coinage and that the very first Druid dies were engraved by John Milton, the Tower Mint's assistant engraver, who presumably had little else to do. It is also pretty certain that the first Druid blanks were prepared at Williams's battery works at Holywell, where Parys Mine copper was rolled into ships' sheathing and bolts and where Williams once made blanks for some Dutch East India Company coins. Some sources claim, however, that the Druid blanks were cut out at the nearby Greenfield Copper and Brass Company, a Mona Mine subsidiary.

Things start getting murky when it comes to the actual coining. According to Milton himself, as related by collector Thomas Welch via token cataloger Charles Pye, only a few proof pieces were struck using his dies. These were quickly superseded by ones made from dies sunk by John Gregory Hancock, one of Birmingham's best metal engravers. But no one knows just how many of this second series were struck, what sort of equipment was used, or even where the coins were made.

According to Matthew Boulton, as of late March 1787, or about a month after the Druids' initial appearance, the "Copper King" (as Boulton styled Williams) had four blank cutting presses at his disposal but only one coining press. Boulton also supposed that the coining press belonged to the Royal Mint. Perhaps the edge-marked blanks were delivered from Holywell to London to be struck either at the Royal Mint itself or at Milton's shop on Fetter Lane, but a more popular theory has them struck at the Parys Mine Company's works in Holywell. Still another view, endorsed by Pye (among others), asserts that they were coined in Birmingham, at the Parys Mine Company's warehouse at 9 Great Charles Street; but that view is contradicted by evidence suggesting that the warehouse, which would eventually produce most of the Druids, was not equipped for coinage until mid-June. Most experts think the Holywell story correct, but because Williams's papers disappeared long ago, only Clio herself knows the truth.

What is certain is that the first striking of Druids for circulation took place no later than late February 1787, when Samuel Garbett, a major Birmingham manufacturer and a close friend of Matthew Boulton's, got hold of one of the coins. In a letter to Boulton, Garbett managed to give Hancock's work short shrift, declaring the Druid head to be "tolerably well executed" (MBP 309, quoted in Hawker 1996, 6). The general verdict concerning the coins' design and execution proved far more enthusiastic, with collectors to this day regarding them as some of the most exquisite coins ever struck.

Whether or not they appreciated the Druid's aesthetic merits, Parys Mine Company employees welcomed them with open palms. What's more, the coins quickly found their way to the mainland, thanks in part to Williams's astute decision to provide for their redemption in Liverpool and London as well as in Anglesey itself. By March 23, word about them reached London, causing the following, rather inaccurate report to appear in the *Daily Universal Register*, forerunner of the *Times*.

> There is a new coinage, by contract with the Government, now going on in the Isle of Anglesey at the great copper mine there. This coinage consists of one penny pieces, not one halfpenny as hereto-

fore. The die is, a Druid on one side, and the King's head on the
other; and the size is about half-a-crown. One hundred tons are said
to be the quantity agreed for; and forty shillings per ton to be allowed
for coining: the contractors finding their own copper. They are to be
in London in about a month.

Evidently the *Register* had not actually seen the new coins, the reverse
of which displayed not the king's head but the Parys Mine Company's
monogram. Also, there was no government contract, much as Williams
might have wished there had been. That would come later—much later
and it would go not to Williams (who by that time had long given up
coining) but to Matthew Boulton of Soho, outside of Birmingham. As for
the claim that Williams coined for forty shillings a ton, that can only have
been a misprint for "forty pounds," if not "forty guineas," per ton. A few
days later, the *Register* tried again:

> The new money, which, by permission of the Government, The An-
> glesea Company has issued, is a species of promissory coin for one
> penny, struck upon copper, intended only for the convenience of pay-
> ing their men. The die is most beautifully conceived and executed,
> and the intrinsic value of the copper is nearly a penny. A Druid, en-
> circled by a wreath of oak, occupies one side. The reverse has a
> cypher, P.M. Co, i.e., 'Parry's Mine Company,' over which are the let-
> ters (D) Denarius, encircled with the following words; "We promise to
> pay the bearer one penny"—on the outside of the rim, are the words,
> "On demand, in London, Liverpool, or Anglesea." There are several
> of these pieces in town, but they are picked up with great avidity.

Much better. Only Williams never obtained official permission to issue his coins. Others made inquiries at the Royal Mint concerning the
Druids' legality, and the mint responded with a shrug: since the Druids
were made of copper, rather than silver or gold, they were not proper
money and so did not infringe on the mint's prerogative. In truth, Royal
Mint officials were more than happy to let private industry supply its own
small change if it could, so that they could be left to enjoy their sinecures
in peace. That stand turned out to be penny-wise and pound-foolish, so
to speak, though it would take several years for the mint to appreciate
just how badly it had miscalculated.

As for the Druid's "intrinsic value," although Richard Doty (1986),
the Smithsonian's curator of numismatics, accurately describes them as

"massive, heavy pieces," he and the *Register* and a host of other writers err in saying that they contained close to their intrinsic value in copper. In truth, although the first Druids were manufactured at a rate of sixteen pennies per pound of copper and although the Royal Mint never exceeded this standard either before or since, manufactured copper cost only a bit above nine pence per pound during the late 1780s. Williams, of course, had to cover his coinage costs somehow; in fact, he could make copper sheets more cheaply than anyone and was thus able to earn perhaps a farthing's profit on each of his Druids, to the extent that they weren't quickly redeemed. It is just as well that he did so, for had his coins actually been worth no more than their "intrinsic" (i.e., metallic) value, they would have fallen victim to Gresham's law as soon as the market value of their raw material increased even slightly. Indeed, the value of copper did rise, sharply, during the 1790s, driving into melting pots most of those early Druids that hadn't yet taken refuge in collectors' cabinets.

Having made their debut in London, Druids eventually toured the rest of the country, where they were for the most part eagerly received. In April 1789, when the Parys Mine Company had switched from pennies to halfpennies, a correspondent from Hope, near Manchester, informed Lord Hawkesbury that a "Gentleman" from a neighboring town, inspired by "*Compassion* to the Poor grievously injured by the *bad* halfpence," had placed seventy-five thousand Druid halfpence into local circulation and that merchants of the same town intended to receive the "Welsh" money until a new coinage of regal halfpence appeared (BL Add. MSS 38422, 12, April 8, 1789).[6] In June 1790, the well-traveled and penny-pinching John Byng (later fifth Viscount Torrington)[7] was surprised to receive both Anglesey and later Macclesfield halfpennies as change from a turnpike gate near the spa town of Buxton, a good 150 miles from Parys Mountain. The surprise was a pleasant one, for the coins struck Byng as being "of more beauty than that of the mint, and not so likely to be counterfeited." They were certainly a damn sight better than the bad copper turnpikes customarily fobbed off on innocent travelers as change for banknotes, guineas, or shillings, as if the implic-

---

6. The correspondent, it should be said, disapproved of private tokens, opining that they represented "an improper interference with the Executive Government, and his Majesty's royal Prerogative."

7. Not to be confused with Admiral John Byng (1704–57), son of the first Viscount Torrington, who, having retreated to Gibraltar when he ought to have been relieving Minorca from the French, was court-martialed and shot "pour encourager les autres."

itly unfavorable exchange "was part of the profit" (Andrews 1970, 167, 232). If even turnpikes were handing out Druids, it could only mean that they had plenty to spare. Indeed, Druids became common enough to allow communities of merchants, in Stockport and elsewhere, to resolve to "[t]ake no other halfpence in future than those of the Anglesea Company" (BL Add. MSS 38422, 13).

The first Druids were so popular, in fact, that Williams quickly found himself once again short of means for paying his own workers. The tendency for Druids to circulate far beyond Anglesey meant that relatively few of them found their way back to the company through its redemption agents in Anglesey and in Liverpool and London; and Williams's original coining facilities were far from being capable of supplying an entire payroll's worth of fresh coins every payday. So, in mid- or late March 1787, Williams made up his mind to erect a larger-scale mint at the Parys Mine Company's Birmingham warehouse, at 9 Great Charles Street, and to transfer all his coining operations there as soon as the refurbishing was complete. But ill fortune intervened, when the sudden and unexpected death of William Welch, the warehouse's manager, caused the move to be delayed until a new man could be found. In the meantime, Williams once again engaged John Gregory Hancock to make dies, this time for a far more extensive Druid coinage that would include halfpennies as well as pennies. He then began to inquire after additional coining presses, while contracting with John Westwood to have sheet copper delivered to the Great Charles Street mint from Westwood's rolling mill in Whitton (west of Birmingham). In case Westwood came up short, Williams also made arrangements with Thomas Dobbs, another metal roller (who himself eventually went into token making).

Finally, on June 13, Williams hired Charles Wyatt, a former Boulton employee, to manage the Great Charles Street mint.[8] By then, Williams was in desperate need of more coin—so desperate that he asked Boulton his price for coining two tons of Druid pennies to tide him over while his new mint was being completed. As it happened, Boulton was still working on his own mint and so could not help Williams for many months. But Wyatt came through with flying colors: besides proving to be a competent manager, he was, like his father, an accomplished mechanic, who was able to supply Parys Mine Company with at least three additional coining presses, all of his own making.

Although John Westwood would one day dismiss Wyatt's presses as

---

8. Concerning Charles Wyatt and his relationship with Boulton, see Selgin 2005.

"the worst he ever saw" (MBP 150/29, Matthew Boulton to Thomas Williams, May 24, 1789) they cannot have been all that bad, for if the numbers handed down to us are to be believed, they sufficed to accomplish one of the most impressive feats in the history of coining. What those numbers say is this: from the time when the Parys Mine Company first began coining at its Great Charles Street facility, during late June or early July 1787, to Wyatt's receipt of Williams's order transferring responsibility for Druid coinage to Boulton two years later, the mint at 9 Great Charles Street managed to strike 250 tons of Druid pennies and another fifty tons of Druid halfpennies—nearly thirteen million coins in all. Moreover, the mint produced the vast majority of these coins during late 1787 and 1788, when it was also minting coins for John Wilkinson. More impressive still, both the penny Druid and Wilkinson's coins (which were originally issued as pence but later called in and reissued as halfpence) were struck in restraining collars—broad, washer-shaped devices that were placed over a coining press's lower die—so as to limit the outward expansion of blanks upon striking and thereby guarantee a more perfectly circular finished product.

Even when not striking coins "in collar," a skilled press crew back then would have had to hustle to sustain an output of thirty coins per minute for an entire eleven-hour shift. Striking in collar normally slowed things down a lot, because struck coins tended to get stuck in the restraining collars, instead of dropping from the press automatically. Even a rate of ten collar-struck coins per minute could prove challenging. At that rate, working regular shifts, a single ordinary screw press would have taken over four years to produce all nine-million-odd Druid pennies and another half year at least to produce the Druid halfpennies (which were struck without collars). To put these values in perspective, the Royal Mint's record copper coin output, achieved during 1771, consisted of just fifty-five tons of halfpennies (about 5.7 million coins) and a trivial amount of farthings, all of which were struck without collars at a mint with at least half a dozen coining presses at its disposal.

Of course, the Parys Mine mint also employed several coining presses. Although it may have had access to only one press (besides its four cutting-out presses) before its move to Birmingham, we have seen that Charles Wyatt furnished it with several more—correspondence suggests at least three. It may have acquired others besides, though just how many it ended up with isn't known. We do know that when Boulton eventually agreed to coin for Thomas Williams, he also agreed to buy Williams's presses, which were then assigned a value of five hundred guineas, or £525. According to a contemporary pamphlet on coining, a decent manual screw press could be had for as little as twenty guineas. Even allowing that the price assigned to Williams's presses was grossly inflated (as Boulton insisted), it's hardly likely to have been more than triple the market price. It follows that, if we allow £52.5 per press and assume that half of the presses in question were for blank cutting, Parys Mine Company had not one but five coining presses at its disposal, or enough to handily coin all those Druid pennies and halfpennies in under one year without working overtime.

All of this assumes, of course, that the Parys Mine mint really did coin three hundred tons of Druids at Birmingham. But did it? The number originates with Charles Pye (1801, 3), who claimed to have gotten his information from the Birmingham coiners themselves, and who therefore didn't hesitate "unequivocally to assert that my statement of the tokens struck in Birmingham is correct." There are nonetheless at least two reasons for doubting Pye's figure. First, he made no allowance for Druids struck before the move to Great Charles Street, apart from the small number of proof pieces struck using Milton's dies. His numbers therefore appear to lump together Druids coined at Great Charles Street with those coined at Greenfield (or wherever else Druids were coined before June 1787). Allowing for this means that Williams actually had several more months' time in which to manage three hundred tons; however, the difference hardly matters assuming (as Boulton claimed) that Williams managed to produce only about a ton of Druid pennies a month during those early days, when he really did have only one coining press at his disposal (Hawker 1996, 10).

Second, as Colin Hawker (ibid., 50–54) explains in his painstaking study of the Druid tokens, Pye's figures may include at least twelve tons of Druids manufactured at Great Charles Street during the summer of 1789 not by the Parys Mine Company itself but by Matthew Boulton. Williams had agreed by then to get out of the coining business and to let Boulton coin for him. Boulton, however, had only one steam press up and running at his Soho Mint, and that press was already committed to making coins for Charles Roe & Company. Consequently, Boulton had to rely on the old Parys Mine mint, which he took over for the purpose, to strike the first part of what would eventually be a thirty-ton order of Druid halfpennies. It follows that any reckoning that adds Boulton's Druid commissions to the Parys Mine Company's own output may involve some double counting. But here again, the error is relatively small: a matter of twelve or thirteen tons out of three hundred. Juggle the figures all you like, there's no denying the Parys Mine Company mint its laurels.

The Salamander

Druids weren't the only tokens being churned out at the Parys Mining Company's Great Charles Street mint. Joining them were tokens made for Williams's close friend John Wilkinson. Besides being (according to some sources at least) a junior shareholder in the Mona Mining Company, Wilkinson was also, in his own accurate (if immodest) assessment, the founder of the South Staffordshire iron trade.

Wilkinson is often mistakenly credited with having been the first man to smelt iron using mineral coal instead of charcoal, thereby freeing Britain's iron industry from its dependence on the nation's rapidly dwindling forests. But credit for that innovation belongs not to Wilkinson but to Abraham Darby I, who pioneered the use of coal at his Coalbrookdale furnace in 1709, almost two decades before Wilkinson's birth (Trinder 1973, 20–22). The key to Darby's success was his prior conversion of coal into coke, which (after much experimentation) proved capable of making iron that was sufficiently free of sulphur to be suitable for forging. But not all coal lent itself readily to coking, which meant that, despite Darby's innovation, wrought iron could not be produced economically in places—including South Staffordshire—where iron ore and high-sulphur coal were both abundant but trees were lacking. John Wilkinson's contribution—or, rather, one of his many contributions—consisted of his developing means for making malleable pig iron using powerful blast furnaces fueled not by coke but by coal itself (Davies 1999, 9–11).

John's father, Isaac, had been smelting iron using the blast from a water-powered bellows in Bersham, Wales, for several years when, in 1757, John and several other partners took over an old furnace about half a mile south of Broseley, near the Severn in Shropshire, establishing the New Willey Company. Not long afterward, Isaac went bankrupt, and John and his brother William took over his former business, forming the New Bersham Company. Unlike their father, they proceeded to turn a tidy profit. Then, in 1766, John went to Staffordshire, where, in Bilston Parish, he set up his Bradley ironworks. Here Wilkinson eventually perfected the smelting process that was to further blacken South Staffordshire's "Black Country."

Besides having figured out how to make high-quality iron much less expensively than ever before, Wilkinson was, according to Alfred Neo-

bard Palmer (1898, 28–29), "convinced of the applicability of iron to almost every purpose for which stone, brick, or wood had hitherto been
used." He made good on his convictions at every possible opportunity.
He built a cast-iron chapel for the Wesleyans at Bradley and equipped its
Sunday school with perpetual cast-iron copybooks, consisting of square
boxes filled with casting sand, to be written on with an iron skewer. In
1780, in partnership with Abraham Darby III and several junior investors, he built the famous iron bridge across the Severn, so that materials might be conveyed between the Broseley and Coalbrookdale iron-
making districts even in the wintertime, when the river froze over.[9]
Finally, on July 6, 1787, while his copper tokens were being coined some
miles away in Birmingham, Wilkinson launched the *Trial,* the world's
first commercially significant iron boat, which was supposed to be able to
convey materials along the Severn even in midsummer, when conventional wooden boats drew too much water to be useful under heavy
loads. The hundreds of spectators who lined the Willey Wharf and surrounding roads to witness Wilkinson's latest conceit expected the *Trial* to
do rather worse—by sinking right to the bottom. To their immense surprise, it drew only nine inches, eliciting a round of applause that could
be heard even above the din of a prearranged thirty-two-cannon salute.

Concerning cannons, although highly innovative uses of iron may
have secured Wilkinson's fame, more pedestrian ones secured his fortune. One of these was the making of armaments. Being free of the
Quaker scruples of the Darbys, his main rivals, Wilkinson supplied many
of the guns, grenades, and shells used by British forces during the Seven
Years' and American wars and by both sides during the war between Russia and Turkey. Then, when revolutionary France went to war with Great
Britain, Wilkinson once again supplied plenty of heavy arms, to the
British forces naturally, but also, it has been alleged, to the enemy.

Wilkinson's cannons were especially sought after because, starting in
1774, he employed a special machine that allowed him to bore them
from solid castings, making them especially true and, consequently, far
less liable to blow up. The same boring machine was also responsible for

---

9. Here again, Darby deserves pride of place, for he was the senior subscriber (albeit
by only a slim margin), and the iron for the bridge was cast at his works. The iron bridge,
it should be admitted, went over budget: it was supposed to cost £2,700 but ended up costing £2,737. Friedrich Engels ([1844] 1968, 20) managed to credit neither Darby nor
Wilkinson but Thomas Paine with having built the first important iron bridge. In truth, although Paine drew some plans for an iron bridge, his bridge was never built. Evidently, the
Manchester Guardian had not pointed this out.

Wilkinson's initial involvement with Boulton & Watt's steam-engine business—an involvement that grew into a rather complicated relationship, with Wilkinson becoming not only the chief supplier of parts to Boulton & Watt but also one of that firm's most important clients and, finally, one of its major (though illicit) rivals.

To make his engine as efficient as possible, Watt needed a cylinder that didn't leak. The problem was that the tin cylinder installed on Watt's experimental prototype, which he had brought with him to Soho in 1774, wasn't up to the job. In fact, it was shitty, and literally so, having been sealed, in some trials at least, with horse manure.[10] Boulton, who had first met Wilkinson at his Bersham works in 1766, had been buying cast iron from him ever since and was well aware of the superior quality of his iron castings and of his recently patented device for boring perfectly straight cannons. Asked to help Watt with his engine, Wilkinson jumped at the challenge, boring the first, eighteen-inch engine cylinder at the New Willey works and shipping it to Soho in April 1775, to be installed in Boulton & Watt's very first "Parliament" engine. The cylinder proved more than satisfactory, varying less than the width of an old shilling (about one thousandth of an inch per inch) from Watt's specifications (Soldon 1998, 114).

Wilkinson went on to supply cylinders, together with many other parts, for the vast majority of Boulton & Watt steam engines. But the original boring machine at New Willey couldn't handle the substantially wider cylinders needed for more powerful engines. Wilkinson therefore proceeded to build a new, large-capacity lathe at New Bersham. Boring the wider cylinders perfectly round proved especially daunting (the massive cylinders tended to sag while resting horizontally) and kept Wilkinson's engineers busy for the rest of the decade in perfecting a suitable shape-preserving cradle. By the early 1780s, the bugs had been worked out, just in time for Boulton & Watt's new rotative engines. Nothing now stood in the way of employing steam engines in place of waterwheels and horse gins, even for the most power-intensive applications.

Having helped to make Watt's engine far more efficient than its nearest rival, Wilkinson proceeded to become one of Boulton & Watt's most enthusiastic and daring customers. Besides employing several of their reciprocating engines for the conventional purpose of raising water from mine shafts, he also used one for the very first time for a different

---

10. Other attempted sealants included tallow, papier-mâché, felt, and pasteboard. They weren't any better.

purpose: to blast air directly into his New Willey furnace. That innovation was what allowed Wilkinson to generate the powerful blast needed to smelt iron using coal, and to do it even in places, such as South Staffordshire, where water mills capable of working bellows were lacking. The iron industry was thus freed once and for all from its traditional dependence on proximity to wood and water.

Not surprisingly, when Boulton & Watt began making rotative engines, Wilkinson was eager to adopt their new product. Indeed, the very first Boulton & Watt rotative was installed during March 1783 at Wilkinson's Bradley works, where it proved capable of delivering a staggering 240 blows per minute from a forge hammer of seven hundredweight—more than the forge operator could handle, in fact, because such rapid blows made holding and controlling the metal impossible.[11] All told, between 1776 and 1784, Wilkinson purchased ten Boulton & Watt engines, seven of which were employed in making iron (Soldon 1998, 250).[12] During the subsequent decade, Wilkinson installed eleven more Watt-type engines at his various works. But these last engines differed from the rest in one important respect: Boulton & Watt knew nothing of them. They were "pirate" engines, made secretly and in violation of Watt's patent. Besides making eleven pirates for himself, Wilkinson made and sold another dozen, including one for his friend Thomas Williams, who needed an engine to power a hammer at his Ravenshead smelting facility and couldn't get a licensed engine cheaply and quickly enough to suit his plans.[13]

Boulton and Watt had begun to suspect Wilkinson of making unlicensed engines several years before getting the goods on him in 1795. However, their lack of proof, combined with their desire to preserve what had become a crucial business relationship (Wilkinson was still their only reliable source of engine parts), kept them from taking any action. Boulton's son, Matthew Robinson, who (together with James Watt Jr.) had recently been made a partner in what was now Boulton, Watt & Sons, also suspected John Wilkinson and, unlike his father, felt no com-

---

11. The rate was adjusted to a "mere" one hundred blows per minute. Wilkinson had tried once before, at New Willey in 1778, to power a forge hammer using a steam engine. But at that time, only reciprocating engines were available, and the experiment failed: instead of delivering sixty blows per minute, as it was supposed to do, the engine ended up knocking itself into little cast-iron bits (Soldon 1998, 63).

12. Of the remaining three engines, one was for a lead mine in which Wilkinson was part owner, and the remaining two were exported to France.

13. This was in 1785, when Williams, Boulton & Watt, and Wilkinson were all partners in the Cornish Metal Company. It was a small world.

punction about taking action. He also lacked proof, however, until it was handed to him by his future father-in-law, who happened to be none other than John's brother and former partner, William.

Although William was co-owner of the Bersham works, he left them in John's hands when he went to France in 1777, only to return, a decade later, convinced that John was cheating him out of his fair share of the company's profits. That John refused to show William the books didn't help matters. For eight years, while he was kept in the dark, Williams's anger smoldered. Finally, in March 1795, it broke out in a fury. According to James Stockwell, a relative (William had married his paternal aunt), William

> collected . . . a great number of men in the town of Wrexham in Wales, and marched them to the large iron works at Bersham, and there, with sledge hammers and other instruments, began to break up the expensive machinery. On intelligence of this reaching John Wilkinson, he collected a still greater number of men, and followed exactly his brother's example, so that in a very short time the famous Bersham Iron Works became a great wreck. . . . Perhaps these two brothers thought this was the most politic way of dissolving partnership.
>
> (STOCKDALE, *Annales Caermoelenses,* QUOTED IN SOLDON 1998, 215–16)

Mind you, Stockdale was only two years old at the time, and although he claims to have heard the story straight from the Wilkinson brothers themselves some years later, the whole thing does seem incredible. But the rift between William and John was real enough: their partnership was dissolved, and an arbitration committee declared the silenced Bersham works (or what was left of them) John Wilkinson's sole property that May.

As for William, although he got a cash settlement for his share of Bersham, he remained bitter. That autumn, while John was away, William took his revenge by revealing John's engine piracy to young Matt through evidence William had uncovered from John's business ledgers. William then followed up by giving twenty-five-year-old "Jammy" Watt, who had only recently fled France to join his father's firm, a look at several pirated engines at John's recently established Brymbo works. Finally, William provided Boulton, Watt & Sons with a complete reckoning of John's pirated engines (Soldon 1998, 231). Eventually, "the Salamander," as Matthew Boulton had come to refer to John, agreed to pay back royalties amounting to over seven thousand pounds to young Jammy, who collected them on behalf of his and his father's firm. It was, after all, a pittance to a man who by then was worth at least one hundred thousand pounds.

Willeys

Until their falling-out in 1795, Wilkinson had had dealings not only with Boulton & Watt but also with Matthew Boulton's Soho Mint, which had been supplying tokens to Wilkinson since late 1789, when Thomas Williams withdrew from the coining business.[14] During the 1780s and 1790s, Wilkinson was one of Great Britain's largest employers, with as many as five thousand workers to provide for at his various works. Like many industrialists, he resorted to group pay, monthly "reckonings," and Tommy shops (like the one at his Bradley works). He also provided many of his workers with housing at low rates or even gratis, as well as with coal and, occasionally, ale (Soldon 1998, 165). But as we've seen, such practices were clumsy substitutes for good coin. When Williams decided to make his own coins, Wilkinson did not hesitate to ask him to mint on his behalf as well.

Williams's Parys Mine mint manufactured only a few tons of "Willeys," so named not in flippant reference to their issuer but because their edge markings declared them payable at the New Willey plantation as well as at Wilkinson's other works. Boulton would supply several more tons, and so would Westwood and Hancock after leaving Williams's employment and setting up their own mint. Although these coins were originally meant to address Wilkinson's own payment needs only, they, like the Druids, quickly earned the status of coin of the realm. Unlike the Druids, however, they were never meant to impress government officials. Consequently, Wilkinson saw no need to make them surpass the regal standard of twenty-three pence (or forty-six halfpence) to the pound of copper. Instead, he originally assigned his coins, which bore no express denomination, a value of one penny despite the fact that they weighed only half as much as Druid pennies. Boulton, on first getting his hands on one in

---

14. Boulton had first made preparations to coin for Wilkinson back in 1788, when he asked Jean-Pierre Droz to work on models he hoped to present to Wilkinson as a New Year's present. As usual, Droz failed to come through, so Boulton didn't produce his first Willeys until the winter of 1789. These were made using Hancock's original dies and edge-marked blanks left over from the Parys Mine coinage. Consequently, they are dated 1788 and are, to the dismay of collectors, indistinguishable from earlier Parys Mine mint issues (Vice 1990, 3).

August 1787, complained to John Motteux, his London banker, that Wilkinson was earning "a rare profit" and that unless the government made him stop, "every manufacturer in Birmingham will coin his own copper money" (Vice 1990, 2).

In fact, it proved unnecessary for the government to interfere. Wilkinson's workers and tradesmen where his works were located refused to accept the great ironmaster's tokens at the rate he assigned to them, forcing him to cry them down, as it were, to half their originally intended value. Considered as halfpennies, the Willeys were as good as their Druid counterparts, and only at this rating did they first gain widespread acceptance. Wilkinson had inadvertently discovered an important difference between commercial and regal coins: that while the Royal Mint could take advantage of its copper coins' limited legal tender status to make them as light as it wished, commercial coins could be lightened only subject to the public's approval, without which they could not circulate.[15]

Although Wilkinson's first tokens ended up being just as heavy as Williams's Druids, their appearance set them apart. For while Williams's coins paid homage to an anonymous Celtic priest, Wilkinson's celebrated the great ironmaster himself by means of a bust-right portrait obverse. The portrait, rendered by Hancock, bore a more than passing resemblance to that of His Majesty, as stamped on the Tower Mint's products. Trademark infringement was the least of it: Wilkinson understood fully well the implicit claim of sovereignty his gesture signified, and so, apparently, did the public. In December 1787, when numbers of Willeys had found their way to the capital, a versifying correspondent to the *London Magazine,* like anyone who examines the tokens today, couldn't help noticing their most conspicuous feature: Wilkinson's cheek.

> In Greece and Rome your men of parts,
> Renown'd in arms, or form'd in arts,
> On splendid coins and medals shone
> To make their deeds and persons known.
> So Wilkinson, from this example
> Gives of himself a matchless sample!
> And bids the *Iron Monarch* pass

---

15. Following the initial Parys Mine mint issue, Wilkinson, responding in part to complaints that both his original coins and the Druids were too bulky, decided to lighten his coins somewhat, making his standard thirty-six halfpennies to the pound. Later, he would reproach Boulton for reverting, without permission, to the earlier, heavier standard.

Like his own metal wrapt in Brass!
Which shows his *modesty* and sense,
And *how,* and where, he made his pence.
As *Iron* when 'tis brought in taction,
Collects the *coppers* by attraction,
So, thus, in him 'twas very proper,
To stamp his brazen face—*on copper.*

But the very fact that Willeys had become notorious in the capital meant that, brazen or not, Wilkinson's face was making the rounds well beyond the confines of his plantations in North Wales and Staffordshire. Officially, as the Royal Mint was quick to point out, Willeys, being copper, weren't money at all. Economically, they were nothing less.

True to its name, *The Gentleman's Magazine,* in its issue for the same month, refrained from lampooning Wilkinson, settling instead for an illustration accompanied by a general description of the tokens—their obverses bearing, besides the "proprietor's head," the inscription "John Wilkinson, Iron Master"; their reverses showing a "large striker [hammer], and a forge, with an artificer at work"; and their edges marked "Willey Snedshill Bersham and Bradley." Concerning Wilkinson himself, the article, though still perfectly polite, was far from accurate, describing him as being "of Worcestershire"; stating that his daughter had married Dr. Priestley; and claiming that he was worth eighty thousand pounds, "all acquired by his own industry." Actually, Wilkinson then lived not in Worcestershire but in Shropshire; and Priestley married not Wilkinson's daughter but his sister. Finally, Wilkinson built his fortune not only with his own labor but also by having married, in 1755 and again in 1763, ladies who were themselves quite wealthy.[16]

Wilkinson's copper tokens had not been his first attempt to issue his own circulating money, nor would they be his last. Back in 1773 and 1774, he paid some of his workers in his own three-shilling, five-shilling, and seven-shilling promissory notes. It was partly in reaction to these particular notes that Sir George Savile's ban was imposed. In the fall of 1788, or about a year and a half after introducing his copper coins,

---

16. Here Wilkinson resembled Boulton, who married two coheiresses in turn, each of whom brought his firm a fortune of fourteen thousand pounds (Hopkins 1989, 87). But Boulton managed to procure a son from his second wife, whereas Wilkinson found it necessary to have a mistress produce his three sons, the last of whom was born when Wilkinson was seventy-eight.

Wilkinson was planning to issue silver pieces rated at 3s 6d each, but he desisted after striking only one hundred pieces, having learned that the Royal Mint was not about to put up with his plan.[17] Several years later, in 1792 and 1793, Wilkinson tried paper again. This time, instead of issuing his own, tiny promissory notes, he got hold of some French assignats, which, once countersigned by his chief clerk, were also assigned a value of 3s 6d each. The assignats were used to pay Wilkinson's men at Bersham and were soon circulating around there freely. One made its way to Worthenbury, where Peter Whitehall Davies stuffed it in an envelope bearing the following message to Lord Kenyon:

> Broughton, December 19, 1792
>   My Lord,—I take the liberty to trouble your lordship with another letter, in which I have enclosed an assignat, made payable at Bersham Furnace, endorsed by Gilpert Gilpin: I am informed he is the first clerk of Mr. Wilkinson, whose sister married Dr. Priestley. With what view Mr. Wilkinson circulates assignats is best known to himself. It appears to me that good consequences cannot arise from their being made current, and that very pernicious effects may. Mr. Wilkinson, in his foundry at Bersham (where I am informed he has now a very large number of cannon), and in his coal and lead mines, employs a considerable number of men. They are regularly paid every Saturday with assignats. The Presbyterian tradesmen receive them in payment for goods, by which intercourse they have frequent opportunities to corrupt the principles of that description of men by infusing into their minds the pernicious tenets of Paine's "Rights of Man," upon whose book I am told public lectures are delivered . . . by a Methodist. The bad effects of them are too evident in that parish.
>
>   (QUOTED IN RANDALL 1879, 39–40)

Though the notion of burly ironworkers being corrupted by Methodist preachers might seem laughable, Davies's letter gave rise to an act of Parliament (33 Geo. III *c* 1), putting paid to Wilkinson's assignat scheme, which Edmund Burke, one of the measure's supporters, termed "a treasonable fraud" (Thompson 1981, 201). The act did not, however, put a

---

17. The one hundred specimens were privately distributed as "medals." A die resembling the reverse "ship" die used for their production was subsequently used to strike a small and now eagerly sought-after run of copper halfpennies.

stop to rumors that "Wicked Will" was in league with the French, the most pernicious of which alleged that iron water pipes he had been shipping to Paris were really cannon in disguise.[18]

If French sympathies did in fact play some role in Wilkinson's monetary experiments, Wilkinson's sympathy for his workers—a trait he shared with Boulton (whose Soho works were a model workplace)—played a far more important one. Whatever minor aid Wilkinson's assignat scheme may have given to the Jacobins, it and his other "wage token" arrangements undoubtedly contributed toward his and other workers' welfare, by making it easier for them to enjoy the fruits of their labor and by tiding them through rough times during which workers elsewhere went begging. No less than the ale he dispensed, which he also made himself, Wilkinson's tokens endeared his workers to him, to the point of making him into a kind of folk hero, whom they saluted in song.

> Ye workmen of Bersham and Brymbo draw near,
> Sit down, take your pipes, and my song you shall hear;
> I sing not of war or the state of the nation,
> Such subjects as these produce nought but vexation.
>   Derry Down, Down, Derry Down.
> But before I proceed any more with my lingo,
> You shall all drink my toast in a bumper of stingo;
> Fill up, and without further parade,
> JOHN WILKINSON, boys, that supporter of trade.
>   Derry Down . . .
> May all his endeavors be crown'd with success,
> And his works ever growing posterity bless;
> May his comforts increase with the length of his days,
> And his fame shine as bright as his furnace's blaze.
>   Derry Down . . .
> That the wood of old England would fail did appear,
> And tough iron was scarce because charcoal was dear;
> By puddling and stamping he cured that evil,

---

18. They were, in fact, water pipes, made for the Paris waterworks in a project aimed at preventing fires, like the terrible one that had destroyed the city hall in 1773. William Wilkinson had gone to France in 1777 to build a cannon foundry. But France and England were not at war at the time, and the foundry was almost finished when they went to war on July 10, 1778. The project was, moreover, entirely Williams's affair, John Wilkinson having played no part in it. That being said, there is little doubt that John Wilkinson, like many freethinkers, sympathized with the French revolutionaries at least until the onset of the Terror.

So the Swedes and the Russians can go to the devil.
    Derry Down . . .
Our thundering cannon too frequently burst,
A mischief so great he prevented the first;
And now it is well known they never miscarry,
But drive all our foes with a blast to Old Harry.
    Derry Down . . .
Then let each jolly fellow take hold of his glass,
And drink to the health of his friend and his lass;
May we always have plenty of stingo and pence,
And Wilkinson's fame blaze a thousand years hence.
    Derry Down, Down, Derry Down.   (QUOTED IN SOLDON 1998, 159)

Such sentiments couldn't have been further removed from ones expressed by some of Wilkinson's fellow industrialists, many of whom hated the fellow most earnestly. "Wilkinson," Professor Trinder (1973, 202) observes, "drove harder bargains than his contemporaries, his prices were higher and his credit terms shorter." That his metal was, up to the mideighties at least, also the best around had something to do with his being able to make tough terms; but that detail didn't keep his clients, let alone his rivals, from loathing him.

Boulton and Watt, as we've seen, had reason to keep things civil, despite suspecting the worst, at least until the Soho foundry was finished in 1796. Boulton, moreover, could not help admiring Wilkinson "for his decisive, clear and distinct character, . . . a first-rate one of its kind" (quoted in Dodd 1971, 140). Others were neither generous nor restrained. Even Wilkinson's most trusted clerk, the very same Gilbert Gilpin whose signature appeared on Wilkinson's assignats (and who, incidentally, would issue tokens himself in 1811), referred to Wilkinson as "Old Shylock." Lord Dundonald (Archibald Cochrane), a talented inventor (he had a knack for discovering valuable by-products of coal) who was, unfortunately, as financially inept as Wilkinson was clever, went further, calling him one of Britain's most "malevolent Old Scoundrels" and likening his heart to pig iron.[19] One wonders whether Wilkinson got wind of the last remark and, if he did, whether he might perhaps have considered it a compliment. Wilkinson's detractors may also have borne a grudge against him for his alleged French sympathies: Lord Dundonald, for one, was a former navy man whose eldest son was exchanging

---

19. Dundonald died in poverty in Paris on July 1, 1831.

cannonballs with regicides while Wilkinson was busy handing out their paper money.[20]

Wilkinson died, appropriately enough, on Bastille Day, 1808.[21] But he had not quite finished being eccentric. In his will, he expressed his desire to be buried either within a chapel he had built for the purpose at Brymbo or in the garden at his Castle Head estate in Lancashire, depending on which was closer to the place of his death. "Iron-mad" to the end, Wilkinson arranged to be interred in a coffin cast from his favorite metal, having left two such coffins (the second reserved for his daughter), complete with screws and a spanner, in his Bradley hothouse. He tried to make things easy for his executors by dying at his house at Hadley, which was closer to Castle Head and hence to the coffins. But Castle Head was an island at high tide and was surrounded by soft sand at low. As the hearse bearing Wilkinson's body approached it, its wheels sank into the sand up to their axles, notwithstanding the combined effort of four horses. Eventually, another wagon had to be brought to rescue Wilkinson's body from the surf. When the body, which had been encased in a conventional wood and lead coffin, finally reached Castle Head, the iron coffin proved too small to accommodate the wooden one, and a new coffin had to be ordered. Then, when Wilkinson was secure in the new coffin, it turned out that it couldn't be buried until some rock was blasted away to make room for it. It seems that John Wilkinson, outsized in life, proved no less so in death.

Indeed, Wilkinson's stature in the eyes of his workmen was such that many couldn't bring themselves to believe that he was gone for good. Instead, they became convinced somehow that he would reappear at Bradley on the seventh anniversary of his death—astride a gray mare no less. When the appointed day came, thousands of his former employees were waiting to greet him. Alas, neither he nor the horse showed up; but the keen disappointment felt by so many, so long after Wilkinson's departure, speaks volumes of their fondness for and dedication to the man who had relieved them of their surplus labor.

Posterity did not bless Wilkinson's works, after all. Instead his estate, reputed to have been worth over £130,000, was frittered away during

---

20. Young Cochrane would eventually come to be known as "the Sea Wolf," having distinguished himself as one of Nelson's finest frigate captains.

21. This date, July 14, should please numerologists: Wilkinson first arrived in Staffordshire on July 14, 1756; he attended a grand banquet given in Paris in his honor on July 14, 1786; and he launched the *Trial* on July 14, 1787.

years of legal wrangling between his natural children, whom Wilkinson had named as beneficiaries, and his nephew, who challenged their claims. By 1828, the Bersham works were derelict, while the rest of Wilkinson's former holdings were in the process of being sold, bit by bit, to pay outstanding legal fees. A few old buildings at New Willey, remnants of old furnaces here and there, and Wilkinson's former homes at Broseley and Castle Head are all that's left of his once vast empire.

The Princely Boulton

Although plenty of people were grateful when Druids and Willeys began to circulate, Matthew Boulton wasn't one of them. Had Boulton had his way, the Parys Mine mint would never have struck a single commercial coin (let alone several hundred tons' worth), and neither would Boulton himself have struck any. Yet he ended up being one of England's largest commercial coin makers.

To understand Boulton's dim view of commercial coins, and of Williams's coins especially, we must delve into Boulton's reasons for becoming involved in coinage in the first place; and to do that, we must know something about Boulton's general business background. To the extent that Boulton's name rings a bell today, it is likely to do so only because he joined forces with James Watt in 1775 for the purpose of developing and manufacturing Watt's steam engine. But before he ever shook hands with Watt, Boulton was already one of Birmingham's leading figures, who, besides running what was by then the Midland's most impressive manufactury, also played a prominent role in Birmingham's civic and cultural life. Well before going into business with Watt, he helped found the famous Lunar Society, so named because its monthly meetings were held on the day of the full moon, to facilitate participants' late-night return journeys. The prestigious society's dozen members included, among others, Joseph Banks, Erasmus Darwin, and Joseph Priestley. In 1773, Boulton led Birmingham's successful campaign to have its own assay office and hallmark. Finally, had it not been for Boulton, Watt himself might never have become a household name. A statue in today's Birmingham commemorating the invention of the steam engine quite properly joins Boulton with Watt and Soho employee William Murdock (who played a crucial part in perfecting Watt's engine), for had it not been for Boulton's keen lobbying skills, Watt would never have obtained the twenty-five-year extension of his separate condenser patent that ultimately clinched his fame, to the point of causing him to be mistakenly identified, outside Birmingham at least, as the "inventor" of the steam engine.

Boulton's beginnings, though comfortable enough, were hardly spectacular. Born in Birmingham in 1728, he entered his father's small toy business seventeen years later, became a formal partner in 1749, and took charge of the firm upon his father's death in 1759. Some years before the last date, young Boulton, having already set his sights far beyond what his father's small factory could satisfy, talked his father into buying Sarehole Mill—an old corn mill that's now a museum—so that the firm could use it to make its own sheet metal (Doty 1998, 4; Pelham 1963, 81–82). Once on his own, in 1761, Boulton made a second move, purchasing a site on the Hockley Brook, just across the Staffordshire border, for one thousand pounds. This proved to be the very last water mill to be developed within a five-mile radius of Birmingham (Pelham 1963, 79). It also ended up being the most famous mill of all, for it was here that Boulton built Soho, the world's first modern factory, where he was to make a vast array of products, including buttons, buckles, candlesticks, salvers, sword hilts, bread baskets, and, at length, copper coins.

Just when did Boulton first become interested in coining? The standard view, which originates in an 1810 statement by Watt (Doty 1998, 24), has him expressing an interest in the possibility of coining, by steam power no less, back in 1774. But this claim is more than a little suspect, because Watt had a habit of getting his dates wrong,[22] because there is no other evidence to support it, and especially because it is hardly likely that Boulton could have conceived of a steam-powered coining press years before the invention of rotary-motion steam engines.

A more plausible view has Boulton taking an interest in *the coinage question* during the seventies, when he played a minor part (as a receiver of old coins and disburser of new) in Savile's gold recoinage. This view traces Boulton's interest in *coining* no further than 1782, when Boulton's friend Samuel Garbett and Garbett's son Francis were preparing their report concerning the operations of the Royal Mint. Parliament had commissioned the report in reaction to the gold recoinage, which took three years and cost £750,000, much of which ended up lining politicians' and

---

22. For instance, he gives the date of the eighteenth-century gold recoinage as "178_," when it in fact took place during the 1770s.

mint officers' pockets: the master of the mint, Lord Cardogan, alone earned eighty thousand pounds—most of it sheer profit. Edmund Burke condemned the recoinage as "a great expense to the nation, chiefly for the sake of members of parliament." A mint, Burke insisted,

> is a *manufacture,* and it is nothing else; and it ought to be undertaken upon the principles of a manufacture; that is, for the best and cheapest execution, by a contract upon proper securities, and under proper regulations.   (DYER AND GASPAR 1992, 441)

Burke followed up his speech by proposing, as part of his famous Economic Reform Bill, that the Royal Mint be abolished and that its responsibilities be assumed by the Bank of England. Although the proposal got nowhere, it at least led to the commissioning of Garbett's investigation into "the state and charge of the management of the mint." Garbett sought Boulton's advice and opinions concerning coinage, as was only natural given (1) Boulton's earlier role in establishing the Birmingham Assay Office (an important aspect of the report dealt with the Royal Mint's procedures for assaying gold and silver); (2) his involvement in the gold recoinage; and (3) his ownership of the world's largest, best-equipped, and most quality-conscious hardware factory. At the time, Boulton & Watt was also developing its rotative engine; and it is in Boulton's correspondence with Garbett that we first find him advocating "other modes of Manufacturing" coin as a possible way to reduce costs and deter counterfeiters (Doty 1998, 25). Although "other modes" has generally been taken to refer to the possible use of steam-powered presses, this assumption is based solely on hindsight and may therefore be mistaken.

Although there's no firm proof that Boulton was looking to coin for the government (much less to make coins using steam) before Garbett submitted his report in March 1783, he was certainly contemplating these possibilities not long afterward. Soho's Cornish mining agent and sometime mechanic William Murdock later recalled having had several conversations with Boulton during 1784 or 1785 concerning "different modes of working Eight Coining-Presses by means of a sliding-rod connected with the [steam] Engine by a Crank" (quoted in ibid). The successful debut of Boulton & Watt's rotative engine, the likelihood of a new copper coinage being undertaken, the Royal Mint's lack of interest in copper, and Boulton's close relationship with Garbett (as well as his other connections in William Pitt's government) convinced him that he was better placed to renew the nation's copper money supply—and more capable of doing it competently—than the Royal Mint itself.

As of early 1786, however, Boulton faced two important hurdles: he had to figure out exactly how to make coins using steam (his original proposal to Murdock having come to naught), and he needed a commitment from Pitt's government. He did his best to overcome these hurdles by arranging to coin money for the East India Company—thereby gaining crucial practical experience while demonstrating his ability to coin on a large scale—and by having Garbett lobby energetically on his behalf in London. He also managed to meet, in Paris, an ingenious engraver and inventor named Jean-Pierre Droz, whose innovative screw press and segmented "collar" seemed ideally suited for adaptation to steam. Boulton convinced himself that if he could only lure Droz to Soho, the business of regal copper coinage would soon be his.

Then, in late February 1787, Boulton learned of Williams's coinage coup, which put him in high dudgeon. "I wish he would mind his own business of making copper," he fumed in a letter to John Vivian, the deputy governor of the Cornish Metal Company, "and not trouble himself about . . . money making, but leave it to those who understand it better than himself" (quoted in Harris 1964, 73–74). That the Druids were getting favorable press was bad enough. More disturbing still was the news that Williams was making inroads with the government: Westwood had managed to finagle an audience with the king, for the purpose of showing off Williams's coins (Dykes 1999, 182), and he and Hancock were in the process of distributing impressive pattern cards for copper and silver coins to every member of the House of Commons (Harris 1964, 74). The two coiners even had the effrontery to "speak publicly of their going to reside in the Tower very soon to manage the . . . coinage," a much-alarmed Boulton informed Garbett. "Hence it appears," he concluded, "that Williams seems sure of the contract" (Dykes 1999, 182).

Two months later, Williams still had no contract. Boulton, however, didn't even have a specimen to show the king (or anyone else for that matter), Droz having so far produced nothing but a series of demands for more money. To Droz, Boulton now wrote pleadingly that Williams had "hired the 2 best Die Engravers in England in order to prevent other persons from benefit by their service" (Hawker 1996, 10; cf. Dykes 1999, 182). Garbett responded by instructing his son Francis to do his best in London to foil Williams's plans, "presumably," Richard Doty (1998, 29) writes, "with the idea that no copper coinage at all was preferable to one produced by the wrong man." Williams, for his part, did what he could to spike Boulton's guns, in part by trying to hire Droz away from him, so as to deprive Boulton of what seemed his last hope for securing the services of a top-notch engraver. In the end, Boulton succeeded in keeping Droz, though he lived to regret it.

By the end of 1787, Boulton had regained his confidence. Williams still hadn't received any commitment from Pitt's government, while Boulton's East India coinage project had been completed successfully, if not very profitably. Droz, having visited Soho that fall, was back in Paris, where he claimed to be working at long last on Boulton's halfpenny pattern pieces. Most promisingly, the Privy Council Committee on Coin, having finally heard the petitions of Boulton, Garbett, and their friends, summoned Boulton to London to be interviewed. Boulton postponed the meeting twice, because of pain from a kidney stone and also because Droz had yet to supply the much-awaited patterns (Doty 1998, 32). Come January, he could delay no longer and so went to face the lords without so much as a halfpenny to show them. No matter: the Garbetts had done their homework, and Boulton emerged from the meeting all but assured that the regal copper coinage would be his.[23]

Boulton's faith in the government was now so great that he did not wait for the actual order to come from London before starting, in April, the construction, on what had been his farmyard, of his Hôtel de Monnaie—better known as the Soho Mint. By late November 1788, the building was ready, and serious work on the mint's coining machinery, including the first of eight specially designed coining presses, had begun. All appeared to be in or falling into place, save Pitt's eagerly awaited blessing.

"A Very Good Kind of Man"

Why was Boulton so determined to land a regal coining contract? The traditional answer, which has come down to us from Boulton himself directly or by way of James Watt and Samuel Smiles, emphasizes Boulton's altruistic motives. Boulton claims merely to have wanted "to gratify Mr. Pitt in his wish to put an end to the counterfeiting of money" so as to protect innocent workers from unscrupulous employers and retailers and also so that convicted counterfeiters might no longer be seen "dangling from gibbets on Handsworth Heath" (Boulton to Woodman, November

---

23. Boulton finally got his proof pieces on March 6, 1788.

13, 1789, quoted in Smiles 1866, 387–88). In his superb history of the Soho Mint, Richard Doty (1998, 26) admits that Boulton was interested in private profit as well as in the "public weal," but he insists that the last consideration had to have been more important, in light of the modest profit (about fifteen pounds per ton of copper coined, by Doty's reckoning) that the Soho Mint would eventually clear. On the whole, Doty concludes, Boulton "seems to have been inspired by laudable motives" (27; cf. Mantoux 1927, 389–90).

Nevertheless, Boulton's pecuniary interest in an improved copper coinage was far greater than what previous authorities have acknowledged, for even if a regal coinage contract could only be expected to yield a modest return to the Soho Mint, Boulton originally saw such a contract as perhaps the only means for keeping his other undertakings afloat. To understand why, we must take a bird's-eye view of Boulton's various business ventures as of the mid-1780s. These were the Plate Company at Soho, Boulton & Scale (Soho's button-manufacturing division), Boulton & Watt (steam engines), Boulton & Watt's Cornish copper mine holdings, and Boulton & Watt's ill-fated Albion Mill in London (Cule 1935, 203). The last-named enterprise—a steam-powered corn mill Boulton first dreamed up in 1783—wasn't set working until May 1786. It then proceeded to become "a constant drain on the steam engine firm" until March 1791, when some prototype Luddites decided to do Boulton a favor by sneaking into his mill, spiking the cistern cock, waiting till low tide, and setting the place ablaze (Lord 1965, 164–66).

Concerning the Plate Company's affairs before 1793 very little is known, except that, to judge from his correspondence, Boulton took little interest in it (Cule 1935, 216). Boulton & Scale got going in mid-1783, following the death of Boulton's original Soho partner, John Fothergill. Boulton's share of its nine-thousand-pound capital was six thousand pounds. The rest came from John Scale, who also served as the company's manager, with profits and losses being divided accordingly. Although the company got off to a good start, it ran into serious trouble at the onset of 1785, when Denmark and Prussia restricted the import of various British goods, including buttons. A sanguine bard of the time wrote:

At LONDON, LEEDS, and MANCHESTER,
Fear not but trade will briskly stir;
And BIRMINGHAM shall have her share,
As long as mankind BUTTONS wear.

Never let it be said,
In the land that TRADE is dead;
'Twill sometimes droop, I'll not deny,
But TRADE in ENGLAND ne'er shall die . . .

Imperial JOSEPH'S mandate ne'er,
A British heart shall strike with fear![24]

But Boulton & Scale had plenty to fear, for the company was heavily dependent on foreign sales. That April, Scale wrote to Boulton:

I almost tremble to look at our orders, not because we have too many
but because we have scarce any. At this season we used to have three
or four months work before hand, but alas tis now but about so many
days.

(MBP, SCALE TO BOULTON, APRIL 9, 1785, QUOTED IN CULE 1935, 208)

As if this weren't bad enough, the French government, later the same
year, imposed its own *arrêt* on English manufactured goods. Then some
Russian customers turned out to be deadbeats. By autumn, Boulton and
Scale, desperate for business, realized that they would have to drum it up
in Britain somehow. That, Boulton perceived, would be no easy matter.
"It will not do to send out a rider once in two years," he wrote to Scale
that October, adding, "the thing must be well planned and steadily executed if begun, whether foreign orders do or do not come in."[25]

And the engine company? Because Boulton & Watt's first rotative engine was set working at Wilkinson's works only in March of 1783, and because the first rotatives proved to be considerably less profitable than
pumping engines had been as of 1785 or so, almost all of the firm's earnings consisted of annual premiums generated by its reciprocating engines. Those annual premiums were set equal to one-third of the savings
in coal that could be attributed to the use of Watt's engine instead of a

---

24. John Freeth, "Trade in England Ne'er Shall Die," in Freeth 1790.

25. Although no records for the company can be traced for 1786, there is no reason
to think that its fortunes improved much that year. In 1787, it managed to earn a decent
profit. But the company's finances would later become precarious again: from John Scale's
death in 1792 to 1796, when the company was finally wound up, its books show an accumulated loss of £701 (Cule 1935, 213). According to Eric Hopkins (1989, 87), Boulton's
original hardware partnership, Boulton & Fothergill, had fared no better: "in spite of the
glittering facade provided by Boulton's activities, the firm . . . was often near to bankruptcy."

"common" (Newcomen, or atmospheric) engine.[26] More than half of the premiums—almost nine thousand pounds—came from twenty-one engines being used to pump water from the deep shafts of Cornwall's copper mines. The mines were located far away from the nearest practical source of coal, in South Wales, and therefore had every reason to take advantage of Watt's invention.

Thanks to the Cornish mines, Boulton & Watt was firmly in the black, and Boulton was able to cover losses suffered in his other ventures. Indeed, Boulton and Watt's stake in the mines' success was so large that they took shares in them, so as to have a voice in their management and to safeguard their premiums. "If I can keep the present Cornish Battery of 21 great guns going," Boulton confided in his London agent, "I have no doubt but I shall soon vanquish all my difficulties" (MBP, Boulton to William Matthews, January 11, 1782, quoted in Lord 1965, 160n1).

Starting in the early 1780s, however, the Cornish mines found themselves not merely in water as usual but in hot water. The government had limited British copper exports, closing off foreign markets. At the same time, Williams's Anglesey mines were so fecund that they allowed him to sell copper cake profitably for as little as fifty pounds a ton, while Cornwall needed eighty pounds a ton just to break even (Harris 1964, 42). Throughout 1784 and 1785, the market for Anglesey copper widened, while that for Cornish ore shrank. Even Soho itself couldn't resist buying from Williams. "Upon examining my Christmas account," Boulton wrote to his Cornish agent John Wilson in January 1784, "I was astonished to find that I have bought between £5 and 6,000 worth of copper the last year from the Parys Mine Company, which is certainly a reproach either to me or the smelters of Cornish ores" (CRO, Wilson MSS, quoted in Harris 1964, 54). The culprit was the manager of the Plate Company, who, upon being asked why he would buy copper from Anglesey while knowing of his master's interest in the Cornish mines, observed that Anglesey copper was not only cheaper but better, so that even if Cornish copper had been offered at two shillings a pound less, he and Boulton "should be losers by the bargain" (ibid.).

Boulton, it seems, was bound to be a loser one way or another. As Anglesey's yields increased, the market price of copper continued to de-

---

26. At first, Boulton & Watt charged the same premium for rotative engines as it had for its pumping engines, failing to allow for rotatives' considerably greater production and operating cost. It was not until 1786 that Watt succeeded in coming up with a standard measure of "horsepower," allowing the firm to assess a modified premium of five pounds per horsepower.

cline. If it fell any further, many of the Cornish mines would have no choice but to shut down, leaving their employees to fish for pilchards. As J. E. Cule (1935, 249) succinctly puts it, "If the beams ceased to rock in Cornwell, the bailiffs entered Soho." Only two things could possibly keep the beams rocking. These were a mining cartel, in which Williams would also have to be involved, or a substantial new source of demand for copper, akin to the demand that had arisen following the Royal Navy's adoption of copper sheathing.

Much has been written concerning Boulton's role in engineering the truce between Anglesey and Cornwall that would lead, in September 1785, to the formation of the Cornish Metal Company (see Harris 1964, 54–68). John Wilkinson, the company's major shareholder, had also been instrumental in getting it off the ground. Although, as J. R. Harris (1964, 69) observes, "a brief calm settled upon the copper trade" in consequence of this arrangement, the terms of the cartel did not take effect until May 1786. Even then, the cartel was a victory more for Anglesey than for Cornwall. Although the new scheme guaranteed a price of eighty-six pounds for cake copper, which was sufficient to cover Cornwall's costs, the metal company had to do its own marketing, and when it came to finding customers, the Cornish Metal Company proved a singular failure.

By June 1786, copper had been piling up for some time in the metal company's Birmingham warehouse, causing Watt to become "seriously alarmed." "No sales yet," he wrote to Wilson, "nor likelihood of any, no measures taken that I know of to promote sales abroad, and considerable remnants of copper in the hands of the Old [smelting] Companies" (CRO, Wilson MSS, Watt to Wilson, June 8, 1786, quoted in Harris 1964, 70). Watt darkly hinted that Williams was cheating the cartel by selling copper at less than the agreed price, but the evidence suggests that Williams was simply a more competent salesman (ibid.). Whatever the reason, Cornish copper sales remained in a slump. By August, a reckoning could be delayed no longer: it had become necessary to close some of the larger mines.

The miners' and Boulton & Watt's best hopes now lay in finding some further outlets for copper (ibid., 71). According to Harris (1964, 74–78), "[i]nstead of making real efforts to improve their sales organization, Cornishmen began to turn hither and thither in search of some grand project which would sell vast quantities of copper and end their difficulties at a blow." A new regal copper coinage, which would be good for copper sales of several hundred tons a year for several years, became

Boulton's own preferred grand project for saving the Cornish mines and hence for saving Soho. "The situation of the Cornish Metal Comp^y gives me great uneasiness," he wrote Wilson from Soho on May 6, 1787, continuing:

> & I am so sensible of the importance it is of, to obtain a *speedy consumption of a large quantity* of their Copper that I have anxiously promoted it in many shapes. . . . I & my friends moved the Towns in this Neighbourhood to petition parliament for a Coinage, & I took measures to secure for Cornwall not only their proportionate share of it, but laid the foundation for its proving a Mode for Cornwall to recover the start Mr Williams has got them in Sales.   (CRO 2/47)

Boulton added that in putting himself to considerable trouble and expense to "perfect the Art of Coining," he had "always heartily had in view to promote the most speedy consumption & greatest quantity of Cornish Copper possible" (ibid.).

By mid-1787, Boulton and Watt had more reason than ever to be banking on a new copper coinage. The Anglesey mines, Watt wrote Wilson in despair, were "in a better state than ever." Unless Williams (an asthmatic) cooperated by dropping dead, nothing else could possibly revive Cornish copper sales. "And there is," Watt lamented, "no immediate prospect of William's [*sic*] death." As long as the government renewed the coinage, Boulton was certain that, Williams's Druids notwithstanding, Cornwall would "have a fair share of the copper contract." "[O]therwise," he said, "there is no faith in prime ministers" (ibid., 74). Still, it would be far better for Boulton to undertake the coinage himself, both so as to have more say concerning where the copper came from and so that he might give alternative employment to the button company's languishing equipment and personnel. In a 1788 letter to Pitt, Boulton expressly offered the Cornwall situation—which he summarized by listing mine closings and the number of workers they affected—as grounds for letting him undertake a new copper coinage (Cule 1935, 250–51).

In short, far from having been a secondary consideration, the pecuniary gains Boulton hoped to derive from a government coining contract were immense. They are to be reckoned not merely in terms of direct profit to be earned on every ton of coins the Soho Mint churned out but in terms of those gains plus equally large or larger indirect gains to

Boulton & Watt, not to mention the saving of their direct investment in the Cornish mines. Smiles and Doty and others, to the extent that they overlook these indirect pecuniary gains, give us an exaggerated sense of Boulton's selflessness.[27] The man may have been public-spirited. But he was also very much concerned with saving his own skin.[28]

Subtle (and Not-So-Subtle) Monopolizers

Boulton had prosaic reasons aplenty for wanting to land a regal coinage contract. By early 1788, he seemed well on his way toward getting it. But so long as he did not have a contract in hand, Williams posed a threat, and Boulton was anxious "to Clip his wings and disarm him" (CRO 3/13, Boulton to Wilson, March 10, 1788).[29] Fortunately, doing so proved to be relatively simple, for in late 1788, Williams volunteered to withdraw from the tussle: he was prepared not only to abandon the idea of coining for the government but also to allow Boulton to coin his Druids.

Williams first sought Boulton's help in coining Druids over breakfast at Soho, where Boulton claims to have answered "that for a Broth[r] Miner I would do them at his own price" (Hawker 1996, 10–11). That was back in mid-1787, when Williams was still struggling to get his Great Charles Street mint in order. Boulton was far from being prepared at the time to coin for Williams, both because he had no mint and because he had no one capable of preparing suitable dies, so nothing came of this first offer. By mid-1788, the Parys Mine mint, having gotten off to a slow start, had reached its stride. Nevertheless, that autumn, Williams agreed in principle to get out of the coinage business, leaving the field open to Boul-

---

27. Although he admits that "other circumstances, doubtless, concurred in keeping [Boulton's] attention directed to the subject" of coinage, Smiles (1866, 388) refers only to Boulton's substantial inventory of copper purchased from the "Copper Mining Company [*sic*] . . . at a time when they could not dispose of it elsewhere." Smiles grasps the elephant's tail but fails to notice the elephant.

28. I am being literal: besides facing bankruptcy, Boulton also faced the wrath of thousands of unemployed Cornish miners, who tended to blame their lot on their employers. When he visited Cornwall in October 1787, Boulton was surrounded by an angry mob of four hundred pitmen. The men had heard a rumor to the effect that Boulton, upon being told that closing the mines might mean starvation for them and their families, suggested that such an outcome could be avoided by handing out liberal doses of arsenic. The miners only let Boulton go after he handed out twenty guineas (Cule 1935, 249–50). On this occasion, one supposes, halfpenny tokens would not have sufficed.

29. Although the Cornwall Record Office has "corrected" the dating of this item, changing "1788" to "1789," the context suggests that the former date was in fact accurate.

ton, who had then begun to build his own mint, and allowing him to take over Druid production, with Hancock thrown into the bargain.

Why had Williams, who had promised only a year before to coin "25 Ton per week" for Mr. Pitt (at two pence per pound or for nothing if two pence proved insufficiently tempting) and who was closer than ever to being capable of living up to that promise, decided to give up coining entirely and to yield to a hostile opponent who still didn't have a single working coining press? Recall that Williams chose to make his own coins and to offer to coin for the government so as to take full advantage of the low cost of Anglesey copper. As long as the government contracted to pay him no less for his copper than it might have paid for Cornish ore, Williams could even offer to coin free of charge, and expect to profit by doing so, because his profits from the copper sales would then have more than compensated him for the costs of coining. That was back in 1786, when the Cornish Metal Company had fixed the price of copper cake at eighty-six pounds a ton and when Anglesey copper ore cost only fifty pounds a ton. Under the cartel agreement, both the Anglesey and the Cornish mines were independently responsible for marketing their copper at the agreed-on price. Williams therefore had every incentive to drum up business, especially big business, for his mines.

All that began to change in November 1787, when the Cornish miners, led by Wilkinson (who now had a large stake in Cornish ore sales), made Williams "the despotic sovereign of the copper trade" (the expression is Watt's) by agreeing to let him sell all of their copper for the next five years for a 2 percent commission (Harris 1964, 86), on the condition that he limit Anglesey's sales for the first year to one-third of total sales. Once this agreement was struck, Williams was certain to profit from a new regal copper coinage whether or not he did the coining himself. Moreover, by early 1788, doubts had begun to grow concerning whether the government would act at all: the king was suffering one of his bouts of mental illness, and no coinage could proceed except by his authority. Finally, Anglesey's yields were starting to shrink, and Williams was beginning to doubt whether he could meet his other copper commitments while still having enough left over for a new regal coinage.

Matthew Boulton, however, was determined to go ahead with his own coining plans and so began building his own mint that April. Having gotten wind of Williams's change of heart, he jumped at the chance to remove his sole rival from the field. Toward the end of the year, he had drafted an agreement in which he offered to purchase Williams's presses and other coining equipment for five hundred guineas (£525), in exchange for Williams's agreeing that "he would neither by himself or his Agent direct or indirectly make any opposition to him in the business of Coining for Government or other persons" (quoted in Hawker 1996, 17). If the government offered Boulton a contract to coin one thousand tons or more, Boulton was to pay for Williams's equipment in cash; otherwise, Boulton would deduct seven pounds out of every thirty-one pounds he charged Williams for coining Druids, until the presses were paid for. That Boulton was still not absolutely certain that he, not Williams, would gain the government's support is revealed by his inclusion of a clause absolving him from any obligation to purchase Williams's presses "if Gov^t should give their order to T.W. or his agents" (ibid.). Williams finally signed the agreement on March 3rd, 1789. It was a fine victory for Boulton. It was also rather bad news for John Westwood.

"An Ingenious, Shabby Fellow"

Although Boulton once dismissed him as a "mere striker of blanks" (MBP 378/51), John Westwood Sr. had a hand in making all the pre-Soho Druids as well as in making the first Willeys. Alone at Holywell and together with Charles Wyatt at 9 Great Charles Street, Westwood supervised Parys Mine Company's coining operations. Later on, at his own facility just down the street from the Parys Mine Company warehouse, he would manufacture another sixty-five tons or so of tokens for various clients, making him far and away the most productive mint master of his day. The two mints Westwood supervised were, moreover, Soho's only rivals before 1791, for it was only in that year that other private mints began appearing on the scene.

Westwood also made some of the most sought-after commercial coins. Collectors prize his products not only because they bear John Gregory Hancock's superior engravings but also because they include coins made for several of the Industrial Revolution's leading figures. This distinction was largely a by-product of Westwood's pioneer status, for in the first years of the commercial coinage episode, only industrial giants were capable of commanding both the credit needed to get workman to accept their tokens and the confidence required to challenge the Royal Mint's coinage monopoly. Their successful examples were, however, to pave the way for large numbers of smaller-scale token issuers.

Westwood turns out to have been a rather tragic figure, in part because he usually gets no credit for most of the tokens he produced. Much of the blame for numismatists' neglect of Westwood's achievement must, however, be laid squarely on his own shoulders, for Westwood's "shabby" reputation (as usual, the adjective is Boulton's) caused him to maintain the low profile that led to his subsequent neglect.[30] Rumors of shady undertakings—including Westwood's involvement in counterfeiting—allowed Boulton to brand him "unfit to run a mint" (ibid.), and can only have encouraged Williams, while he was still contemplating coining for the government, to make light of Westwood's role in Druid making.[31] Westwood himself appears to have been fully aware of his damaged reputation, which caused him to allow his talented die sinker to front for what was really Westwood's own coin-making firm. By the time Charles Pye got around to gathering his "firsthand" information about who produced what, poor Westwood had been dead for several years, while Hancock was still alive and kicking and, apparently, more than happy to go on taking full credit for what had really been Westwood's token commissions—commissions that Hancock had merely (though often brilliantly) designed (Dykes 1999).

Westwood began his career as an engraver (a pretty good one, it seems) of copper plates for book illustrations—just the sort of background required, one can't help thinking, for forging banknotes. Whatever his illicit undertakings may have been, Westwood's first aboveboard venture into numismatics took place in the late 1760s, when he branched into medal making, producing, among other things, medals for the Shakespeare Jubilee celebrations at Stratford. Several years later, Westwood went into business with his brother, Obadiah, whose specialty had been stamping brass "furniture" (mountings, handles, and ornaments) for coffins, using equipment of his own invention. During the late seventies, the brothers relocated from Newhall Street to 20–22 Great Charles Street, just a few doors down from the Parys Mine Company warehouse, which William Welch was then still managing. John Westwood and Welch got together to form a copper and brass casting and rolling business, and in the early 1780s, Westwood developed his new method for hardening copper by cold rolling. It was presumably Welch who first put Westwood in touch with Thomas Williams, who then proceeded to employ Westwood's process of cold rolling at Holywell to

---

30. I would have neglected him myself had it not been for D. W. Dykes's (1999) welcome clearing of the record.

31. Westwood's nephew, John Westwood Jr., a chip off the old block, also gained a reputation for counterfeiting—producing, among other fakes, imitations of some of his uncle's more famous tokens.

manufacture the copper bolts he and Westwood and another inventor, named William Collins, patented in 1784.

Although those copper bolts would eventually be said, in 1799 testimony before a parliamentary committee, to have given the British navy an "incalculable advantage" in its clashes with Napoleon's fleet (Prosser 1881, 127), Westwood did not live to enjoy this buffing of his tarnished reputation or the large Admiralty royalties that might have gone with it. Instead, he died, quite bankrupt, in March 1792, before the navy completed its necessarily lengthy trials of his bolts and while the "Little Corporal" was still an inconspicuous junior officer in the Corsican Volunteers.

Westwood's financial troubles appear to have begun sometime in the early fall of 1789, when Williams was in the process of transferring responsibility for Druid production to Boulton. Williams appears to have kept Westwood in the dark concerning his agreement with Boulton, allowing Westwood to hope, on first learning that Williams was shutting down the Parys Mine mint, that he might continue to coin Druids for Williams at his own mint. Consequently, Westwood, now in partnership with Hancock, decided to set up his own coining operation during May and June of that year. Having borrowed heavily from John Hurd, Matthew Boulton's copper business partner, Westwood went shopping for coining presses and for new coin commissions to go with them.

Boulton, having by then agreed to purchase Williams's presses, tried to get Westwood to buy them instead. He did this, he says, for Westwood's own good, "as I knew it would be injurious to Westwood to get new Presses made" (Dykes 1999, 183), but also, one assumes, to save himself five hundred guineas. Westwood, however, demurred—it was on this occasion that he called Williams's presses the worst presses he'd ever seen. Eventually Westwood would order several "fast thread" presses, which, according to Hancock, could coin for half as much as Boulton's prototype steam-powered press. In the meantime, though, he and Hancock had landed their first independent commercial coin commission. This was a contract awarded them in March 1789 to coin two distinct series of tokens, forty-two tons in all, at £36 10s a ton, for Charles Roe & Company's manufacturing subsidiaries at Macclesfield in Cheshire and its copper mines at Cronebane in County Wicklow, Ireland. Charles Roe (who started out, sure enough, making buttons), founded the Macclesfield silk industry during the 1750s and then went on to build the Macclesfield Copper Company, which leased and worked Cerrig y Bleddia until Uxbridge and Williams decided to work it themselves in 1785, a few years after Roe's death. In 1787, the Macclesfield partners, including Roe's son William, decided to purchase the Cronebane copper mines, thus forming the subsidiary they named the Associated Irish Mines Company. They then proceeded to invest forty thousand pounds in the mines over the course of the next decade and were rewarded with an annual output of about one thousand tons of ore, which yielded regular net returns of 3 to 4 percent.

Because Westwood had no coining presses when he first arranged to coin for Roe & Company, Boulton, despite having only one of his own new presses in running order, was able to persuade him to hire the Roe & Company commission off to Soho: Boulton would act as his "journeyman," striking Roe's tokens using edge-marked blanks supplied by Westwood and splitting Roe's fee, with just over half (£18 10s) going to Westwood; Roe & Company would supply the necessary copper cake to Westwood. Because Westwood owed money to Hurd, it was arranged that Boulton would collect the full amount, keeping his part and remitting the rest to Hurd on behalf of Westwood. After some vacillation (and the failure of original Roe "beehive" dies), the Cronebanes were given priority, thus securing the honor of being the very first coins to be struck in substantial quantities at the Soho Mint.

Boulton had struck over twenty tons of Cronebane halfpennies (1,674,185 pieces) when Zacchaeus Walker Sr., his brother-in-law and business associate, informed him in early September that "all is not right with John Westwood" (MBP 358/181). Upon discovering soon after that Westwood was on his beam-ends, Boulton stopped the presses, fearing that Roe & Company, which had yet to pay him a shilling, might be among Westwood's creditors and so might withhold all or part of its payment pending favorable settlement of Westwood's account. That December, *Aris's Birmingham Gazette* published a notice to the effect that "John Westwood, Castor of Medals," had gone to the dogs. Sure enough, Roe & Company now flatly refused to tender Westwood's share to Boulton, agreeing to pay Boulton's striking expenses only and forcing him to get in line with the rest of Westwood's creditors to collect whatever they could of Westwood's part.[32]

Although Westwood found himself in financial straights not long after Williams awarded Boulton his first, thirty-ton Druid commission in

---

32. According to David Vice (1991 and 1996, 51), Hurd suffered most from Westwood's bankruptcy: when Westwood's estate was finally settled, almost a year after his death in March 1792, his creditors, including Boulton (who had agreed to serve as Hurd's agent), had to settle for fifteen pence on the pound.

July 1789 (when he'd taken delivery of the new coining presses he and Hancock had ordered), his biggest difficulties seem to have stemmed not from losses on his coining account but from ones connected to copper rolling. The *Gazette* notice specifically refers to Westwood's metal business affairs. "Hancock's" token manufactory remained a going concern despite Westwood's bankruptcy.

Whatever its cause, Westwood's bankruptcy dealt his coining business a blow, in part because Boulton took advantage of it to steal some of Westwood's business. Having apparently ceased to be deeply concerned about Westwood's well-being, he appropriated a commission Westwood had secured in June to coin for Walter Taylor & Company, the Southampton naval contractors, convincing them to cancel their original order after Westwood had already completed a small run. Later, he made off with two more clients with whom Westwood had made tentative agreements. Still, Westwood's coining business survived and eventually prospered, becoming the first private mint of the era to operate without so much as an inkling of any possibility of coining for the government.

By the time of his death, Westwood had arranged to coin for eleven clients in all, all but two of whom placed orders for either five or ten tons of halfpennies. They included John Wilkinson, who, after the closing of the Parys Mine mint, first took his business to Boulton and then (to Boulton's great annoyance) decided to let Westwood have some of it as well. Somewhat more surprisingly, Roe & Company also returned to Westwood: rumor has it that when Boulton abruptly ceased coining for it, the company first took its business to an unknown coiner in London, who, using dies Hancock had been working on when Boulton suspended Roe's coinage, struck for them another ton of "beehives," so named because the Roe & Company cypher on their obverse is surmounted by a neat hive surrounded by tiny bees. (The coins' reverse shows Genius seated and holding a drill-cum-scepter in one hand and a cogged wheel in the other.) In March 1790, however, the company turned to Westwood again, ordering twenty-five tons of Macclesfield halfpennies (which were originally to have been part of the Westwood-Boulton commission). Numismatists claim that only ten tons were struck: what became of the rest is anyone's guess. Whatever their amount, the coins— which bear the same reverse as the beehives but with Charles Roe's bust portrait on their obverse—are considered to be some of Westwood and Hancock's most beautiful products and hence some of the best coins of any kind ever made.

When John Westwood Sr. died, his part of the coining business was taken over by his brother, Obadiah, and Obadiah's son, John Westwood Jr., who (still in partnership with Hancock) kept making commercial coins until 1795. But their story belongs to a later chapter.

Matthew Boulton was, in the meantime, expanding his own list of commercial clients, which by 1792 included (besides Williams; Wilkinson; and Taylor & Company) the Cornish Metal Company, Glasgow's Gilbert Shearer & Company, and France's Monneron Frères. But while John Westwood Sr. could take unalloyed pleasure in every one of his new commercial coin commissions, Boulton could not help viewing his own growing involvement in commercial coinage with considerable dismay, for Pitt's government had not followed through, after all, with its promise to let him coin for the entire nation. That left Boulton little choice but to seek other uses for the world's most modern—and most expensive—mint.

CHAPTER III

Soho!

. . . Where GENIUS and the Arts Preside,

EUROPA'S wonder and BRITANNIA'S pride;

thy matchless works have raised Old England's fame,

And future ages will record thy name.[1]

World's Biggest Factory

It's hard for a writer with a weakness for clichés to resist saying that Matthew Boulton was not a man for half measures. Yet the cliché hardly does Boulton justice, for while he certainly didn't settle for half measures, he was often no less dissatisfied with full ones. For Boulton, in other words, "enough" frequently meant "too much." "To understand the character of Mr Boulton's mind," wrote fellow Lunar Society member James Keir, "it is necessary to understand that whatever he did or attempted, his success and failures were all on a grand scale" (MBP 290/112, Keir's Memorandum 1809, 9).

Consider the Soho works, Boulton's factory (or "manufactory," to use the contemporary term) in Staffordshire's Handsworth Parish, just northwest of old Birmingham.[2] When Boulton's father died in 1759, his toy business consisted of a cluster of workshops surrounding the Boulton residence at 7 Snow Hill. The shops employed a handful of workers only

---

1. James Bisset, in Bisset 1800, 12.
2. Handsworth Parish was incorporated into the city of Birmingham in 1911.

and specialized in a small range of items, including fancy buckles and buttons. But young Matthew, their new proprietor, had something far more ambitious in mind, and the Handsworth property, which he'd had his eyes on for some years, was just what he needed to carry out his bold plan. Equipped with his inheritance, he at once began negotiations with the leaseholders. Two years later, the thirteen-acre heath, including all of Soho Hill and the steep slope running down from it to the Hockley Brook, was his.

The tract's previous owners had already made a half-mile "cut" in the brook, damming it to form a mill pond that fueled a rather feeble mill. They'd also knocked down an old warrener's cottage at the hill's bleak summit to make way for a more substantial residence they called Soho House.[3] Having purchased their lease for little more than what these improvements cost, Boulton enclosed part of the heath's remaining commons, dismantling "a few miserable huts with idle people" (Uglow 2002, 66), adding a drop or two to Great Britain's growing pool of unskilled wage laborers and thereby exacerbating ever so slightly the small-change shortage he would eventually help eliminate. Boulton finished Soho House, installing his mother and sister there. He also replaced the original rolling mill with a better one, which was to be the nucleus of nothing less than "the largest Hardware Manufactory in the World" (MBP 135/68, Boulton to J. H. Ebbington, March 2, 1768).

Finishing Boulton's grand project would cost a great deal more than his modest inheritance. But here Old Exile came to the rescue, for just months after his father's death, Boulton's first wife, Mary, suddenly passed away. Having inherited three thousand pounds upon her own father's death in 1750, Mary was supposed to split another twenty-eight thousand pounds with her sister, Anne Robinson, upon their mother's death, with brother Luke picking up the residual. Now Anne stood to inherit both her own and Mary's share. Whether spurred on by his own cupidity (as many suspected) or by Cupid's arrow (as he himself insisted), Boulton at once began courting his deceased wife's sister. In June 1760, despite considerable public brow knitting, ecclesiastical sanctions, and Luke's smoldering misgivings, they married, thereby placing all twenty-eight thousand pounds of Robinson-family wealth within Boulton's grasp. So much for half measures.

Flush with new resources, Boulton joined forces in 1762 with John Fothergill, who, having matched Boulton's capital contribution of

---

3. The name is supposed to derive from the hunter's cry "So-ho!"

£6,207 with £5,400 of his own money, was awarded the keys to Soho House. Two years later, Luke Robinson stuck his own spoon in the wall, leaving his share of the Robinson estate to Anne and, hence, unwittingly, to that gold-digging husband of hers, who proceeded to pour several more thousand pounds into Soho. By 1765, the manufactory had grown large enough to allow Boulton to shut down his Snow Hill workshops and to commandeer Soho House, which he set about enlarging and embellishing, with lovely terraced gardens, decorative pools, and stately evergreens. Below the house, halfway between it and the works, Boulton built a block of stables. Due west of it, he erected a strip of outbuildings, including a menagerie he called his "Fairy Farm," a tea room in which to entertain guests, a fossil room, and a laboratory. In 1789, Samuel Wyatt, of the famous Wyatt family of architects, was commissioned to further improve the house, adding a water closet and central heat, among other things. In 1796, his brother James would improve it still more.

> Behold yon MANSION flank'd by crouding trees,
> Grace the green slope, and court the southern breeze.
> Genius and Worth with BOULTON there reside,
> BOULTON, of the arts the patron and the pride!
> Commerce with rev'rence at thy name shall bow,
> Thou fam'd creator of the fam'd SOHO!

The Wyatts were also responsible for the stately red brick buildings that made up "the fam'd SOHO" factory itself.

That factory set a new standard in industrial architecture, at once turning it into the Midland's biggest tourist attraction. Soho's "Principal Building," finished in 1767, was designed by William Wyatt, whose uncle John, the ill-starred Birmingham inventor, and cousins Charles and John Jr. were then working for Boulton. The building was in the shape of an elongated E, its nineteen-bay front looking uphill toward Soho House and its five-story rear facing the brook. It was supposed to bring to mind a duke's palace but has been likened by at least one authority to an oversized stable block. The central part of the building, which was adorned with a Palladian entry surmounted by an octagonal clock cupola, contained Soho's silver-plate works, countinghouse, warehouses, and display rooms. The gabled side wings supplied further workspace on their lower floors and dwelling space for Soho's middle managers and foremen upstairs.

The rear of the Principal Building faced the so-called Great Yard, below and beneath which were three more yards or courts surrounded by buildings devoted to metal rolling, slitting, grinding, casting, forging, drilling, and turning, as well as to making some of Soho's nonmetallic products. After Boulton drew the yoke together with Watt, the eastern-most of these lower yards became Soho's "engine works," where parts for Boulton & Watt engines were designed, made, and assembled.[4] As the engine business grew, a second and larger engine yard was built just below the original, extending the manufactory across the Hockley Brook. About twenty yards to the east of the Principal Building, between it and the Fairy Farm, Boulton erected another long and narrow three-story building to house Soho's latchet works. All told, by the late 1770s, Soho's various structures took up almost five thousand square yards of space and were capable of providing workspace for up to one thousand workers.

No less impressive than Soho's vastness was the scope of its undertakings. According to the late Sir Eric Roll, whose *An Early Experiment In Industrial Organization* (1930) remains the most insightful treatment of Soho from an economists' perspective, Boulton, "a man of great vitality and diversified taste, which found a suitable outlet in the manufacturing of a great number of different articles," was "not . . . a man of specialization" (10). That's putting things mildly. Here is Boulton's own 1774 reckoning of Soho's products, as delivered to some London silversmiths:

> All sorts of buttons, gilt, plated, platina, steel, inlaid, both of yellow metal, and superfine buttons of various colours, and with foil. Women's and men's chains of steel, and inlaid with gold, or with gilt metals, or quite common ones. Men's and women's gilt chains from the most common to the most fine ones, and with cameos and different colours. All manner of silver and silver plated articles such as tea kitchens, bread baskets, candlesticks, waiters; all sorts of vases, mounted in strong gilt or ormulu, geographical and astronomical clocks, also clocks upon a construction quite new, having but one

---

4. In truth, the only engines actually manufactured at Soho, apart from those installed there, were prototypes. Otherwise, Boulton & Watt engines were erected on site, in accordance with drawings supplied by Boulton & Watt but using parts made by other firms. Although Boulton and Watt, in their capacity as "consulting engineers," insisted that customers obtain engine cylinders from Wilkinson and recommended Wilkinson for other castings as well, they themselves supplied only a few particularly demanding engine parts before the completion of the Soho Foundry in late 1795.

wheel in them. Gilt glass and filigree trinkets and steel sword-hilts, all sorts of sleeve buttons, viz., platina, steel, inlaid, tortoiseshell, plain and inlaid boxes, instrument cases, toothpick cases, sundry articles in silver filigree, in shagreen, chapes of all qualities and sorts, and sundry more articles. (DELIEB 1971, 57)

Boulton left out saltcellars, candlesnuffers, patented cheese toasters and coffee machines, and the firm's entire painting and japanning division, among other things. His list also fails to convey the scale of many of Soho's individual divisions: Soho strove to outdo France in ormulu, London in sterling silver, and Sheffield in Sheffield plate. Finally, Boulton's list predates his partnership with Watt, which would add not only steam engines but also copying machines (another of Watt's inventions), Argand lamps (introduced in 1784), and, starting in 1789, coins and coining equipment.

Nor would Soho be bested when it came to quality. Its products were, according to Boulton's friend and fellow Lunar Society member Erasmus Darwin, "wrought up to the highest elegance of taste and perfection of execution." Apart from his other ambitions, Boulton aspired almost single-handedly to blot out "the bad reputation from which Brummagen goods were suffering" (Roll 1930, 9).

Yet Boulton also insisted on underselling other quality-conscious manufacturers. He believed he could do so and still "make the neddy,"[5] by selling "great quantities [for] small profits" using newfangled machines (MBP 137/87, Boulton to V. Green, 6 August 1775, quoted in Quickenden 1980, 284). "It was always in Mr Boulton's mind," wrote James Keir, "to convert such trades as were usually carried on by individuals into great manufactures by the help of machines, which might enable the articles to be made with greater precision and cheaper than those commonly sold" (MBP 290/112). By 1768, according to Darwin, Soho's mechanical contrivances included special lathes, drills, and lapping and sorting machines, often designed by Soho's own staff and "superior in multitude, variety and simplicity to those of any manufactory in the known world" (Roll 1930, 8). In a letter to designer and architect Robert Adam, Boulton himself boasted of having equipped his workshops with "almost every machine that is applicable to these arts" (Roll 1930, 11; cf. Smiles 1866, 144).

---

5. I.e., get rich (Brummie).

For all this equipment, Boulton needed plenty of power. His quest for such power drew him to the Hockley Brook, the area's other waterpower sources having already been spoken for (Pelham 1963).[6] Water from the brook was diverted to Soho's mill pool, from which it passed beneath the eastern wing of the Principal Building and toward the rolling mill.[7] There it engaged Soho's large waterwheel, which powered the rolling mill as well as "a prodigious number of different tools" (Roll 1930, 8). From the wheel's tailrace, the water took a sharp turn to the east, running beneath the lower yards and into the Soho Pool, where, having descended twenty-four feet in all, it was finally reunited with the brook.

But the Hockley Brook alone couldn't meet Boulton's ever-expanding needs, especially during spring and summertime droughts, when the mill pool often got so low that work had to be either suspended or cut back to just a few hours a day. Paradoxically, this very shortcoming of the original Soho plant would eventually make Boulton a rich man, for it got him thinking, toward the late 1760s, about steam. Rotary-motion steam engines were still more than a dozen years away, so Boulton could scarcely have dreamed of employing steam to directly power his machines. He was instead thinking of using a Savery pumping engine to recirculate water from his waterwheel's tailrace to the mill pond, when John Roebuck, Sam Garbett's partner and one of Birmingham's most famous inventors, mentioned to him a young Scotsman in his employ named Watt, who was toying with a better sort of engine. Boulton invited Watt to Soho during the summer of 1768 and was so taken by the young engineer that he resolved to lure him there permanently.

The catch was that Roebuck held a two-thirds stake in Watt's engine and wasn't willing to part with his young inventor, despite the latter's bouts of depression and snaillike progress. Then, in 1772, the spectacular failure of the Ayr Bank ruined Roebuck, among many others, forcing him into bankruptcy within the space of a year. Roebuck's unsettled debts included a twelve-hundred-pound charge from Boulton & Fothergill. Boulton offered to cancel the debt in return for Watt's em-

---

6. In 1755, Boulton persuaded his father to acquire Sarehole Mill, in Hall Green. The Boulton firm rolled metal here until 1761, when Boulton acquired the Soho Mill. Although Sarehole Mill thus missed its chance to become the location of one of the world's great manufacturing marvels, it became famous nonetheless as the inspiration for J. R. R. Tolkein's Middle Earth and is now a museum open to the public.

7. The mill pool was also fed by a small stream that cascaded downhill from Soho House's decorative Shell Pool, where Anne Boulton's dead body was discovered floating, face down, on July 11, 1783. Whether Anne committed suicide or died accidentally is uncertain.

ploy and for Roebuck's share of Watt's engine (Uglow 2002, 245–46).[8] Some months later, Watt's dismantled prototype made its way from Kinneil to Soho, where Soho mechanic Joseph Harrison reassembled it in one of the lower yards. Once up and running, the engine—known first as "Beelzebub" and eventually (and more fondly) as "Old Bess"—was set to work replenishing the mill pool (ibid., 248).[9] Watt himself turned up at Soho in May 1774. The rest, as they say, is history.

In short, Boulton was unique among his manufacturing peers. In a district known for shoddy products, he insisted on making goods of the highest quality; while most other toy makers specialized in a handful of products, he produced a vast array; and at a time when most producers worked on a small scale, he favored a gigantic one. Also, while most Birmingham entrepreneurs operated as factors only, subletting the manufacturing and marketing sides of their business to small masters and independent merchants, Boulton and his partners both made and marketed all of Soho's products, drawing the necessary workmen together in a single huge facility over which they exercised full technical and economical control (Roll 1930, 5–6). Finally, Boulton sought to automate his manufacturing processes as far as technological know-how would permit, while other producers relied almost entirely on simple, manually operated machines.

So Boulton pushed things far indeed. But why suggest that he pushed too far? Because, fantastic showpiece though it was, Soho was also an impressive money loser. As Jenny Uglow (2002, 68) remarks, "the wonderful manufactory, which looked so fine, nearly ruined both partners." Boulton spent lavishly, selling or mortgaging much of his original property, tying up Fothergill's capital, and drawing promiscuously on the Robinson estate. The Principal Building alone was supposed to cost two thousand pounds—a stunning sum at the time—and ended up costing nine thousand.

The firm's early returns didn't even come close to justifying such huge investments, and Boulton and Fothergill were soon being pressed by their creditors. Come mid-June 1778, Fothergill was ready to toss in the towel. "Better stop payment at once," he wrote Boulton, "call our creditors together, and face the worst, than go on in this neck and neck

8. Poor Fothergill, having had his fill of Boulton's grand, but often financially unsound, schemes, decided for once to play it safe. Refusing the one-third share of Watt's engine Boulton offered him, he instead took the six hundred pounds he had coming to him.

9. Until Old Bess's arrival in 1774, Boulton relied on a horse gin, installed in 1767, to turn Soho's waterwheel during dry spells.

race with ruin" (Uglow 2002, 287). Boulton instead managed to keep Soho's bankers at bay, but the firm went on hemorrhaging money. By 1780, its bill (overdraft) account had risen to twenty-five thousand pounds, with accumulated losses of eleven thousand pounds on a capital of twenty thousand. The painting and japanning division, having alone suffered an average annual loss of five hundred pounds, was shut down that year (Roll 1930, 99), as was the ormulu business. The sterling silver branch, yet another money loser, was aggressively downsized (Quickenden 1980, 277, 288).

As we saw in chapter 2, Boulton & Scale, the partnership Boulton formed after the long-suffering Fothergill passed away in June 1782,[10] fared no better than Boulton & Fothergill had done. The hopes of Boulton & Watt, the steam-engine division, rested precariously on the fate of the Cornish mines up until "the devil of rotations" came to the rescue. Until then, Boulton & Watt's uncertain cash flow made the Hockley Brook seem like a raging torrent in comparison. In late December 1781, for instance, the engine company couldn't come up with its workers' regular wages, let alone their Christmas bonuses, and had to draw for the purpose on Boulton & Fothergill's already flattened cushion of liquid assets (Uglow 2002, 64).

The roots of Soho's dismal economic performance lay, according to Sir Eric Roll (1930, 98–99: see also Quickenden 1980; Cule 1935), in the very scale and scope that made it such a marvel. Boulton had expanded his firm's productive capacity "far beyond the limits justified by the fluctuating nature of the demand for its products." At length, the engine business would save Soho, ensuring its lasting fame and amply justifying the standard view of Boulton as a man who combined "shrewd business practices, extraordinary luck, and real vision" (Doty 1987). Still, the fact remains that the general industrial philosophy, with all its emphasis on gigantism and high-tech, that was to make Boulton & Watt such a spectacular success also turned most of Boulton's other undertakings up to the mid-1780s into equally spectacular flops. And that very same philosophy was about to be applied, uncompromisingly, to coining: Boulton

---

10. Though some of Boulton's biographers fail to mention it, the Boulton & Fothergill partnership came to an end while Fothergill was still alive and kicking. Boulton gave Fothergill the sack in November 1781, after accusing him of cheating the firm. Fothergill died, bankrupt and broken, the following year. He was thus spared the final indignity of having to watch Boulton grow rich thanks to the only one of his many grand ventures that Fothergill had refused to take part in.

would settle for nothing less than the world's largest, most quality-conscious, and most technologically advanced mint.

"The Soho"

Anyone relying on any save the most recent works on the Soho Mint will come across the following "facts": first, that a prototype steam-powered mint had its trial run in striking coins for the East India Company in 1786; second, that although the mint was perfected by 1788, Royal Mint opposition kept it from producing regal coins until 1797; third, that the entire coining process, from metal rolling to striking, took place within the confines of the original Soho factory; fourth, that the mint operated on an assembly-line basis, with materials being conveyed automatically from stage to stage of the coining process by way of conveyer belts and chutes; fifth, that its machinery was entirely steam-powered (Boulton having first determined to apply steam power to coinage in 1774); and, sixth, that its steam-powered presses could coin ten times faster than manual ones.

Thus Samuel Smiles (1866, 389) writes that Boulton first conceived of coining using steam power in 1774 and that "he successfully applied the engine for the first time in executing his contract with the East India Company for above a hundred tons of copper coin" in 1786.[11] Boulton's prototype mint, says Smiles, was "violent and noisy," as well as too tiny to fulfill the regal copper coinage contract Boulton anticipated. He therefore remodeled and expanded it. By late 1788, the perfected mint was ready to start coining, with six coining presses on line and another two in the works. Officials at the Royal Mint were able, however, "by mere passive resistance, to delay the adoption of the new copper coinage for more than ten years" (Smiles 1866, 392), forcing Boulton to take up commercial coining to keep his mint going. At last, in 1797, the mint began striking regal copper coins, eventually striking forty-two hundred tons' worth (ibid., 398).

Concerning the arrangement of Soho's coining facilities, a much-cited account from 1800 (Anonymous 1801: cf. Morfitt in Pratt 1805, 362; Roll 1930, 133) first identifies the mint then operating at Soho with

---

11. Quite a few more recent—as well as more scholarly—works include statements to the same effect. See, for example, Dyer and Gaspar 1992, 445. Mitchiner (1998, 1962) gives the date for the first steam-struck coins as 1775, perhaps confusing Boulton & Watt's first sale of a steam engine with Boulton's earliest use of a steam-powered coinage press.

the one built, according to it, in 1788. The source then goes on to observe how "[i]n adjoining apartments all the preparatory processes are carried on with equal facility," including "the rolling of copper into sheets, cutting them into blanks, and shaking them into bags clean and ready for the die." The separate steps are, moreover, supposed to have been linked in assembly-line fashion so as to achieve what, according to Sir Eric Roll (1930, 134), "can only be described as a very early anticipation of the modern organization of manufacturing processes."

> Without any personal communication between the different classes of workman . . . the blanks are conveyed to the room where they have been shaken, and from thence to the coining-room in boxes moving with immense velocity on an inclined plane, and accompanied by a ticket of their weight."   (ANONYMOUS 1801)

According to Erasmus Darwin, among others (e.g., Morfitt in Pratt 1805, 362), the whole process was powered "by an improved [Watt] steam-engine, which rolls the copper for half-pence finer than copper has ever before been rolled for the purpose of making money; it works the coupoirs or screw presses for cutting out the circular pieces of copper; and coins both the faces and edges of the money at the same time" (Darwin 1791, 29n). Finally, Lord Liverpool (Jenkinson 1805, 229) tells us that besides saving labor, the combination of steam power and Boulton's ingenious coining apparatus allowed Soho "to coin at least ten times as many pieces, in a given time, as [could] be coined at the [Royal] Mint" using ordinary screw presses.

Such is the standard view. But the Soho archives tell a different story. To start with, there was no such thing as *the* Soho Mint. Instead, as Richard Doty (1998, 23–24) explains, there were no fewer than three Soho mints, not counting the East India affair (treated further anon) or later mints established by James Watt Jr. and Ralph Heaton. The original Soho Mint, known by its creators simply as "the Soho," began striking coins in 1789 and lasted less than a decade—that is, just long enough to complete Boulton's first five-hundred-ton regal coin commission. That job, with its oversized tuppence "cartwheels," nearly shook Boulton's coining machine to pieces. Consequently, in 1798, Boulton tore down his original mint and built another from scratch, using a coining press assembly altogether unlike the one he'd patented eight years before. This second Soho Mint handled the bulk of Boulton's regal copper commissions, as well as some later, smaller jobs, before being mothballed for a decade starting in 1813. Finally, in 1824, Matthew Robinson Boulton, after first having briefly revived the old mint, began constructing a third and last Soho Mint, only half the size of its predecessors. That mint shipped its last batch of tokens in January 1850 to Melbourne's Annand Smith & Company and was afterward unceremoniously auctioned off (Doty 1998, 337). Evidently, the mint that dazzled so many Soho visitors during the first years of the nineteenth century was not the pioneer steam-powered mint Boulton built in the 1780s. Because they mix these two mints up, early sources give readers an entirely false impression of the success of Boulton's original design, understating by a decade the time it took him to come up with a truly reliable means for steam striking heavy coins.

Hard facts also give the lie to the oft-repeated claim that the first steam-struck coins were the ones Boulton made for the East India Company's Bencoolen settlement in Sumatra. In truth, although sheet copper and round blanks (also known as "planchets" or "dubbs") for the Bencoolen coinage were prepared at Soho, using copper cake paid for by John Company, the coins were struck not at Soho but at a makeshift mint set up in a warehouse at the French Ordinary Court in London (Gould 1969; Doty 1998, 299).[12] That mint was equipped with manual screw presses, the Privy Council (which authorized the East India coinage) having allowed two hundred pounds for the purchase of up to three such machines. This was but a tiny fraction of what Soho's steam-powered coining equipment would cost.

Nor did Soho make the manual presses that were used in London, for no one there had any idea how to make a decent screw press. Instead, Boulton and John Scale (who managed the East India coinage) commissioned Anthony Robinson, an independent Snow Hill machinist, to make two of them. Joseph Harrison, the well-liked, though intemperate, "father" of the Soho workman (his drinking problem, a common malady among Soho employees, caused him to let at least one steam engine run wild and break down), was also assigned to the project. Harrison reported the presses' arrival in London at the end of September and then invented an automatic blank "layer-in" to go with them (Vice 1996, 50–51). In the following summer, Robinson was asked to make a third

---

12. The blanks themselves had to have been made without the help of steam power, as the last box of them was sent from Soho to London on January 19, 1788 (Gould 1969, 274; MBP 140/201, Greenhow to Boulton, January 20, 1788). The famous "Lap" engine that would eventually be used to power Soho's blank-cutting presses was not installed until June of that same year.

press, but he couldn't start on it until October, because he first had to build a press for . . . John Westwood (Gould 1969, 274; MBP 235/199, Thomas Greenhow to Boulton, October 12, 1787).

Thanks in part to some clever digging done in the 1990s by industrial archaeologist George Demidowicz,[13] we also know that Soho's coining processes were never entirely steam-driven. Neither were they all performed in "adjoining apartments." In fact, only the final stages, including the actual striking of coins, took place in the mint building itself, which stood not within the main Soho manufactory but tucked behind the Fairy Farm, one hundred yards away. The original Soho Mint consisted of a broad shed containing a "coining room," measuring approximately forty-two by twenty-eight feet. The room was eventually equipped with eight coining presses, each of which was attended by a twelve- or thirteen-year-old boy, whose only job was to stop his press (each machine had its own clutch) when necessary and then set it going again. The presses were arranged in a circle and activated by means of a large rotating wheel housed in the loft above. An additional structure was added in 1791 to provide space for an office, a warehouse, a smith's shop, a carpenter's shop, and rooms for scaling blanks and for annealing, or "pickling," them. The mint had its own rotative steam engine, which was housed between the mint building and Boulton's tea room. The engine powered both the coining presses and the shaking machines that delivered finished blanks to them.

Earlier stages of the coining process were carried out not at the mint but within the original Soho manufactory. Copper cake was flattened into sheets by the firm's water-powered rolling mill, located in the westernmost lower yard. The mill had been redesigned in anticipation of the East India coinage and further improved two years later and so could handle both the hot rolling of copper cake into ingots and rough sheets and the fine rolling of the latter cold into polished sheets of uniform coin thickness. Although Old Bess was called on, as she would be for another fourscore years, to replenish the mill pond, Soho's rolling mill was never converted to steam power. Once the copper had been rolled, pickled, and polished, it was cut into short strips or fillets, which were then fed into Soho's battery of six blank-cutting presses. Those presses were located in a tiny (eighteen by thirteen feet) "cutting out" room on the first floor of Soho's lapping mill, which adjoined the rolling mill but was

---

13. See, if you are able, the fascinating *Time Team* documentary on Soho, originally broadcast by Channel 4 Television (UK) on January 19, 1997.

powered, starting in June 1788, not by water but by Soho's renowned rotary-motion Lap Engine.[14]

So, contrary to what early sources say, Soho made coins using not one
but two steam engines. Yet the image those same sources convey of a
coining operation that was thoroughly steam-powered and thoroughly
automated is exaggerated, for as we've seen some of Soho's machinery
was water powered; and while some stages of Soho's coining processes
anticipated standard coining practices of the mid-nineteenth century,
others differed little from their counterparts at the old Tower Mint.[15]

Turning to Liverpool's claim that Soho's presses could coin ten times
faster than those used at the old Tower Mint, the truth never even came
close. According to Soho's Cornish agent Thomas Wilson, Tower
officials considered two and one-half hundredweight of regal halfpennies (or, using the standard of forty-six halfpennies per pound avoirdupois and assuming a ten-hour working day, just shy of twenty-one and
one-half coins per minute) "a good Days work" for one of their manual
press teams (MBP 303/57). In contrast, in June 1789 (when the Soho
had not yet begun striking coins "in collar"), James Lawson reported that
despite "many little hindrances," its one functioning press was able to
strike twenty-four hundredweight of coins in a week. The press might, in
other words, accomplish in six days what the Royal Mint's presses could
do in ten. That was a considerable improvement, to be sure; but it fell
well short of tenfold.

Moreover, Soho's maximum coining speed could only be achieved
with the aid of shallow dies, Lawson having determined that "[t]he smallest difference in the height of the dies makes 2 or 3 strokes difference pr
minute" (MBP 322/10, Lawson to Matthew Boulton, June 27, 1789).
Eventual improvements allowed Soho's presses to strike between 50 and
120 low-relief coins per minute (depending on the size of the coins they
were making), even when restraining collars were used to keep the coins

---

14. The double-acting Lap Engine was the first rotary motion engine to incorporate a
governor. It was originally used to drive as many as forty lapping and polishing machines
for metal toys. Like Old Bess, it remained in use until 1848, when Soho was abandoned. After that, the engine, or at least much of it, made its way from museum to museum until it
finally ended up at London's South Kensington Science Museum, where both it and Old
Bess can be seen today.

15. According to Jenny Uglow (2002, 212), what I have said concerning the first Soho
Mint was also true of manufacturing processes at Soho generally: "Although Boulton . . .
had all the different processes in one place, each workshop still operated independently,
under a separate foreman: the only rough move towards a production line was in trying
(not always successfully) to orchestrate the making so that it proceeded stage by stage."

perfectly round. Such rapid striking of coins "in collar" was perhaps Boulton's most impressive coining achievement. Yet even it represented an improvement by no greater a factor than six over what the Parys Mine mint accomplished using the worst screw presses John Westwood ever saw.

To insist that the Soho was not quite the wonder some sources make it out to have been isn't to deny that incredible effort and ingenuity went into it. By any measure, Boulton's mint was a tremendous and extraordinarily difficult achievement. "God only knows," Lawson recalled in a letter to Matthew Robinson Boulton, "the anxiety & unremitted perseverance of your Father to accomplish the end. . . . [O]ften He attended & persevered in the experiments 'till we were all tired" (quoted in Doty 1998, 24).

Although William Murdock says that Boulton first suggested to him the idea of a contrivance for driving eight coining presses by steam power "around 1784 or 1785" (quoted in Doty 1998, 25), work on the Soho didn't begin until April 1787, when Boulton was still attending to the East India coinage. The new project started with the erection of the gable-roofed mint engine house, equipped with its ten-horsepower rotary engine. The mint building itself was readied by November. Then came the hard part: equipping the mint. Boulton and his crew had to come up with a way to deliver power from the engine to the mint's coining presses. That meant devising a gadget that would convert the motion of a rotating shaft into the rapid lifting and plunging of a sequence of vertical screws.

The solution they settled on, which was to serve both in the mint itself and, on a smaller scale, in the cutting-out room, consisted of a huge merry-go-round-like device, with the presses arranged in a circle, like so many wooden horses, within a hefty wooden frame and below a huge, horizontally mounted cast-iron wheel. In place of their usual "flys," the presses were equipped with special arms, or "plates." Complementing the plates was a set of five S-shaped press-driving arms attached to the upper surface of the great wheel.[16] Power from a rotating shaft inserted between two of the presses made its way to the wheel by means of a vertical

---

16. Because he neglects to consider that the great wheel supports not one but five press driving arms, the usually meticulous Dickinson (1936, 142–43) miscalculates the coining rate for the entire eight-press assembly as $12 \times 8 = 96$ coins per minute (which would imply a rate per press of only 12 coins per minute) instead of $12 \times 8 \times 5 = 480$ coins per minute, implying 60 coins per minute per press—a rate consistent with the range claimed by Boulton.

axle and a set of beveled gears. Numismatist Jim Reeves tells how the thing worked (or how it was supposed to work) better than I could ever hope to.

> As the wheel rotated, it actuated the presses individually [as] an arm from the wheel engaged with an arm on the screw coining press which it turned over part of the revolution. This movement of the press arm was resisted through chain connections to two pistons, housed in airtight cylinders, for each press. . . . Later in the rotation cycle the press arm was released from its connection with the driving arm and the vacuum on the pistons drove the press arm back to strike the coin, thus the main shock of the striking was not transferred back to the driving wheel. (REEVES 2001, 18)

As 1788 drew to a close, drawings for Boulton's coining carousel were prepared and various parts were ordered, including the huge iron wheel, which was cast at Wilkinson's Bradley works. The carousel was installed in the mint the following spring, and in June, a solitary coining press was up and running. Although Boulton didn't bother to patent his apparatus at first, he changed his mind when the thought that a certain Swiss associate (whom we shall get to know shortly) might copy it gave him a bad case of the cobbywobbles. The patent documents for Boulton's "coining mill" were prepared during the summer of 1790 and received the royal signature and seal that October.[17]

Two more agonizing years would pass, however, before Boulton would see all eight coining presses called for in his original plan up and running. Why did it take so long? The basic problem, which Boulton had already experienced in setting up the East India mint, was that there just weren't that many people around who knew how to make a decent run-of-the-mill coining press, let alone the special presses Boulton wanted for his mill. Besides having to be equipped with custom-made arms instead of ordinary flys, these presses had to be fitted with special blank feeding, or "laying-in," devices that could keep up with their rapid striking speeds.

Boulton knew all along that he'd have to make special arrangements to get his presses made; but he thought he'd found an ideal solution—

---

17. What Boulton patented was not, as some have claimed, the idea of making coins using steam power but a particular means for operating screw presses using power transmitted from a rotating shaft. The shaft might just as well have been connected to a water mill or horse gin. Steam power per se was of course not patentable.

not only to this problem, but to several other challenges he faced in preparing his mint—in the shape of a talented and cocky Swiss engraver and mechanic named John-Pierre Droz. Poor Boulton had no idea what he was getting himself into.

Drozing Off

The Droz saga starts in December 1786. While Scale, who would rather have been making buttons, agonized over the East India coinage, Boulton and Watt and Boulton's son Matthew Robinson were inspecting the waterworks at Marley, France, where water was pumped from the Seine all the way to Versailles. During a side trip to Paris, while young Matt tried on the latest French fashions, Boulton and Watt took advantage of authority given them by the British Treasury to pay an official visit to the Paris Mint. There they were shown a pattern *écu de Calonne* (so-named in honor of France's controller general of finance) that Droz, one of the mint's engravers, had executed. The ecu made an immediate impression on Boulton. Besides sporting a superbly engraved portrait obverse, its edge bore an intaglio inscription that was said to have been added to the coin by the same blow that struck its faces, using a six-segmented collar Droz had invented. The pieces of the collar separated automatically after each blank was struck, allowing finished coins to be easily dislodged from it.

Before long, Droz himself showed up to demonstrate his collar to Boulton and Watt and also to Thomas Jefferson, who happened to be present gathering ideas for his own country's coinage (Doty 1998, 26).[18] Droz then took Boulton and Watt to see the press he used, which he'd also designed, letting Boulton try his own hand at striking an edge-lettered crown. (Boulton kept his handiwork as a souvenir, which he'd later enjoy showing off to William Pitt.) Later that evening, Droz came to Boulton and Watt's rooms to give them a closer look at his segmented "plateau" and to regale them with his other coin-making feats. He alluded, among other things, to a new way he'd come up with for multiplying coining dies, so that a single set of original hand-engraved matrices might yield hundreds of identical working copies.

18. According to Pollard (1968, 243), several months after Boulton and Watt's visit, on February 18, 1788, Droz "reported to Boulton from Paris . . . that representatives of the American Government had visited him, but that he had shown nothing to any of them but Jefferson." Jefferson eventually tried, unsuccessfully, to get Droz to come to the United States.

Here, Boulton afterward remarked to Watt, was just the man to help out with the new regal copper coinage he and Garbett were lobbying for. Droz knew how to engrave a head and could presumably manage a likeness of George III, and his new technique for multiplying dies would allow precise copies of his engraving to appear not just on a few tons of coins but on five hundred or even a thousand tons. Finally, Droz's segmented collar and special press could make perfectly round edge-marked coins faster than they'd ever been made before. Imagine hooking several of those presses to a rotative engine. . . .

Once back in England, Boulton was still waiting for a green light from Pitt when, in February, Williams's Druids made their debut, goading Boulton (who feared being a step behind his rival) into action that was to prove premature. On March 7, he wrote to Droz, apologizing for not having written sooner. "Your own experience will have taught you," Boulton explained, "that what ever depends on the determination of Ministers advances slowly" (Pollard 1968, 254). Boulton asked Droz to prepare a die bearing King George's head and to strike twenty or thirty silver shilling pieces with it using his special press. After he'd begun constructing his mint in April, Boulton wrote to Droz again, this time asking for permission to reproduce Droz's press. He offered Droz one hundred pounds for the requisite drawings plus another one hundred for each press built according to them. After Droz upped the price of the drawings to two hundred pounds, a deal was struck.

Although Droz finished the shilling patterns in early May, Boulton was still anxiously waiting a month later for the press blueprints he needed to complete his mint. Then, in early June, Williams had his son, Thomas Jr., visit Droz in Paris to find out, in Richard Doty's words, "whether he and Boulton were in treaty and, if so, whether he would break that treaty and come to work for the Anglesey group" (Doty 1998, 28). Although Droz refused to betray him, Boulton, upon learning what Williams had been up to, resolved to bring Droz to England, where he could "keep him to his cakes and milk"[19] and where the two of them, working together, could make more rapid progress on the presses and proof pieces.

After many entreaties from Boulton, Droz finally agreed to come to England in September. But he would come only for a month and without the desperately needed press drawings. Despite his disappointment, Boulton asked Droz to prepare copper halfpenny patterns, to allow him

---

19. I.e., keep a close watch on him (Brummie).

to supply Pitt with indisputable proof of his ability to cap Williams's Druids. He also got Droz to agree informally to come back to Soho as a salaried employee. Apart from that, the visit produced little save some magniloquent talk contrasting orthodox, outmoded coining methods with Boulton and Droz's cutting-edge alternatives.

After Droz returned to Paris, Boulton, expecting to be called on to supply regal halfpennies at any moment, decided he could wait no longer for Droz's drawings and so went ahead and placed an order with Hodgells, Harrison & Greenbaugh (HH&G) for one cutting-out and two coining presses.[20] Otherwise, he was still banking on his Swiss secret weapon. When the Privy Council followed through that December with some questions regarding Boulton's coining plans, Boulton's replies left no doubt concerning the crucial part Droz was to play, albeit without referring to him by name. Asked how he intended to invest his coins with "the most inimitable" workmanship, Boulton responded with the following recipe:

1st . . . . The copper should be rolled of a fine Polish, which hath never yet been done for half-pence.

2nd . . . . The Dies should be engraved by the best Engraver in Europe.

3rd . . . . An Inscription should be struck round the edge of the Piece at the same time and with the same blow that strikes the Two Faces, and should not be milled upon the Edge as those are, which are called the Anglesey Druid Pence; or as the Milling or our Guineas are, but the Letters should be in relief, for Reasons I can give, like the new Six Livre Piece which was intended for France.

4th . . . . These Operations should be performed by Machinery on such new principles, as will produce Effects evidently different from those of any Presses now known or used in England.

---

20. The Harrison of HH&G was the very same Joseph Harrison we've met with twice before, who had evidently come to realize that making coining presses was good business. Confusingly, Jenny Uglow (2002, 245, 255) refers to the Harrison who set up Watt's Kinneil engine at Soho as "John," while Doty (1998, 297) refers to the Harrison who handled the East India coinage as "William." Uglow seems to confound Joseph Harrison with the inventor of the naval chronometer and hero of Dana Sobel's *Longitude* (1995)—to whom Uglow refers elsewhere in her book (ibid., 206), who died in 1776, while Doty has apparently confused him with his son, who also worked at Soho as an engine erector and, starting in 1800, as foreman in the small engine shop of the Soho Foundry but who had nothing to do with the East India coinage project.

5th . . . . The machinery should be capable of working with more Expedition, and with fewer Workmen than the Machines now in Use, in order to save Expence and make dispatch.

Ingredient 2 refers, of course, to none other than Droz, while ingredients 3 and 4 refer to Droz's inventions. (The other ingredients point to Soho's improved rolling mill and to the steam-powered coining facility then in the works.)

Throughout the remaining winter months, as HH&G worked on Boulton's presses, Droz dallied in Paris. Boulton showered him with increasingly urgent letters begging him to get his drawings, his pattern halfpennies, and himself to Soho as fast as possible. At last, in January 1788, Droz wrote back, not to gratify Boulton, but to say that though the HH&G press design was rubbish, Boulton might as well go ahead with it while Droz prepared three of his own presses together with a plaster model. Three more excruciating months would pass before Droz's presses finally made it to Soho, together with the elusive drawings. Even at that late date, two of the presses still needed some work, while the third was a mere skeleton.

While Boulton waited for his presses, Droz got around at last to finishing some pattern halfpennies. The first of them reached Soho on February 18 but consisted of a lead piece without edge markings of any kind, which was hardly likely to impress the Privy Council. In early March, Droz followed up with six gilt and eight bronze pieces, to which he added, two months later (following the replacement of a fractured reverse die), fifty-four gilt specimens. Although these coins sported milled edges, they were of a guilloche pattern only and were otherwise a big step down from Droz's pattern ecus. Boulton wrote diffidently that June that perhaps Droz could be so kind as to send some better ones "struck up perfectly on your great Press" (Doty 1998, 34). For the time being, though, Boulton had to settle for the guilloched specimens: with luck, the Privy Council Committee on Coin would forget his previous insistence on the need for raised letters.

Around this time, Boulton, after much cajoling, finally persuaded Droz to come back to Soho for two years, in return for an annual fee of five hundred pounds and rent-free accommodation in a house Boulton had already built for him. That was on top of the money already paid or promised to Droz for his presses. But when it came to fulfilling his part of the bargain, Droz pithered yet again, arriving at long last, with several assistants in tow, during the first week of October 1788.[21] By then, Boulton was beginning to have doubts about his regal coinage contract. But, having already paid Droz several hundred pounds, including an advance on his salary, he was determined to get his money's worth one way or another.

Just what did Droz offer to do during his two-year stint? He agreed, first, to assist Boulton in perfecting his coining presses, especially by getting his segmented collar to work as he had promised it could. Second, he agreed to engrave original dies and puncheons to be used in the actual regal coinage, bearing an improved portrait of the king (for which Boulton hoped the king would sit). Finally, he agreed to teach the Soho staff the improved methods of die multiplication of which he'd boasted.

And what did Droz end up doing? Next to nothing. He complained incessantly and about practically everything. He concocted elaborate excuses for his poor performance. He meddled and made trouble and otherwise got on the nerves of the regular Soho mechanics—James Lawson, John Southern, and Peter Ewart—who (despite occasional help from Watt) had to work overtime to ready Boulton's mint while the far more generously remunerated Swiss goofed off. Droz also refused to divulge to anyone his secrets of die making and die multiplication, while taking his sweet time in making dies and punches on his own. He even had the brass gall to take a two-week holiday just after he'd promised to finish some badly needed dies as swiftly as possible (Doty 1998, 36, 42).

All this was more than enough to make a parson, let alone a hard-bitten manufacturer, swear. Yet because he looked on Droz both as a friend and as a gentleman, Boulton insisted on giving him the benefit of the doubt. It took Zach Walker Sr., among others, to convince him that Droz was dead to honor.

> From your description I can not conceive Mr Droz either honest in Principal [sic], or good in disposition—Honesty in Principal will not warrant one man in taking another's Money without performing what he promises and rendering the agreed value of the money—and a good disposition could not suffer a friend to be injured by such neglect—Indolence, idleness, or any such excuse is too barefaced.
>
> (WALKER QUOTED IN DOTY 1998, 39)

---

21. Upon Droz's arrival, the cases containing his plateau and dies were seized by custom agents at Dover, causing him to go into hysterics and terrifying Boulton, who feared that Royal Mint officials would discover Droz's secrets. They needn't have worried: if mint officials did see Droz's tools, they weren't impressed enough to bother keeping them.

Eventually, Boulton realized that he had to do something. But just what could he do? No written contract had been drawn between him and his Swiss engraver: Boulton had incautiously relied on a gentleman's agreement. That at least would have to change. At last, in mid-November, Boulton and Droz drafted a formal contract spelling out more or less the same terms they had informally settled on almost a year and a half before. But despite the contract, the old Soho hands continued to complain about Droz's general uselessness. Come January, Watt, having had enough, advised Boulton not to pay Droz another halfpenny "unless compelled by law," as doing so would only allow him "to feed his lawyers" (Doty 1998, 341). For his part, Droz, who was as fed up with Soho as Soho was with him, seemed pleased to have been given a legal excuse for breaking his promises.

The standoff went on until March 1790, when Boulton, who had by then come to view Droz as "the most Vain, humoursom [*sic*], troublesome, tedious, & trifling" man he'd ever had any concern with (MBP 309/92, Boulton to S. Garbett, March 29, 1790), proposed to settle matters with him by arbitration. During the ensuing months, a panel of arbitrators was chosen, and documents were submitted for their consideration. One of those documents, James Watt's written testimony, which he sent to Boulton on July 7, was to prove especially damaging to Droz's case. In it, Watt gave his erstwhile friend credit for "his exceeding neatness and good workmanship in graving his dies" as well as for "having his tools made more accurately than was usual at Birmingham." But he also observed that had Droz only "chosen to make some progress" with his engravings, his dispute with Boulton might never have arisen (quoted in Pollard 1968, 251).

More damning still, considering its source, was Watt's appraisal of Droz's mechanical contributions, which made the Swiss out to be a right spoofer. Concerning Droz's "improved" presses, Watt wrote:

> In my opinion and as far as I can remember the only new thing & in which consists the merit of Mr D's press are first the coining the edges at the same blow with the piece and it remains to be proved whether that will answer in practice. . . . Second the improvement in the layer-in which you had before you saw him.
>
> Third an easier method of fixing and adjusting the dies, not so perfect however as he told us at Paris. Fourth the substituting the carriage in place of the bolt formerly used. . . .
>
> The other parts of the machinery have been contrived as far as I

know by yourself by Mr Southern and me, though my share has been little.   (IBID.)

As a matter of fact, Droz's celebrated, segmented collar, to which the first part of Watt's comment refers, turned out to be a pig in a poke: the hand-engraved segments wore out quickly and were hard to replicate, because their junctions had to match perfectly (ibid., 257). Consequently, the collar, though fine for making a handful of impressive proof pieces, was too costly for regular coining. As for Droz's "improved layer-in," Boulton noted, against the February 18, 1788, entry of his "Extracts . . . Correspondance" (MBP 306/27), that it was virtually the same as the layer-in "w*ch* I used at y*e* East India Mint except making his move in a straight line instead of a circle but both worked by the motion of the great Screw" (Gould 1969, 275). Indeed, at one point in the rush to finish Boulton's mint, Lawson asked Ewart to dig up one of the old East India mint devices in London so that it might be refurbished for use at Soho (ibid.).

Finally, Droz's superior device for die multiplication ended up being a white elephant. Droz had hopped-up an ordinary die multiplication "engine" (essentially a beefier version of an ordinary manual coining press) with a rudimentary hydraulic contrivance. Only the hydraulic contrivance didn't really help: according to Watt, it was "very lame & a thing which the laws of nature would not permit unless she had pleased to alter the times of the vibrations of pendulums." Consequently, "a common press would have answered . . . as well, perhaps better."[22] In short, to judge by Watt's appraisal, if the Soho Mint ever did finally manage to get up and running, it would be no thanks at all to Droz, since scarcely a trace of any of his vaunted innovations was likely to end up in it.

The proposed settlement of July 1790 was, not surprisingly, largely favorable to Boulton. He was to pay Droz a final amount of £819 17s 8d on top of the £1,087 5s 4d he'd already paid him, while Droz was supposed

---

22. Boulton's assessment of Droz's success in improving Soho's die multiplication practices was equally negative: "Not done, and he uses only the means used by everyone else in Birmingham" (Pollard 1968, 250). Reading too much into the word *engine,* Pollard incorrectly supposes that Droz's special die-multiplying apparatus was steam powered rather than hydraulic. Sargent and Velde (2002, 61) go even further, crediting Droz with having "invented" die hubbing around 1780, by which time the practice was well established in Birmingham (see chap. 8). They also err in crediting Droz with the invention of a modified portrait lathe, or *tour à portrait,* for multiplying dies. Credit for that innovation belongs to Jean Dupeyrat, who sold such a lathe to Boulton in the autumn of 1790 (Pollard 1971).

to hand over all the dies and puncheons he'd been working on at Soho (some of which Boulton still hoped to employ for his regal coinage) and fulfill his promise to teach Boulton's staff how to multiply dies using his special equipment, for whatever that was worth. After that, Droz was to promptly quit Soho bag and baggage and go back to France. He might just as well go to Coventry, for all Boulton cared, so long as he wasn't able to steal any of Boulton's coining trade secrets.

But Droz wasn't through annoying Boulton. He first refused to hand over the dies and then got a court to set aside the arbitration agreement, provoking Boulton to get Sir Joseph Banks to intercede on his behalf, which Banks did that November. At last, in February 1791, thanks to Sir Joseph, Boulton took delivery of the materials Droz owed, along with Droz's own list (reproduced in Pollard 1968, 253) of every item he'd prepared during his stay. Besides the seventeen objects (twelve puncheons, four matrices, and a die) specifically mentioned in the settlement, the list named sixteen matrices, ten puncheons, two pairs of dies, some wax models, and two "plates or machines which strike the tranche complete"—that is, two of Droz's useless "plateaus." It was, by any measure, a paltry tally, especially considering that it cost Boulton seven hundred pounds more than what he'd paid for his two-thirds share of Watt's engine.

Still, Boulton was happy to be rid of the troublesome Swiss who had given him and his staff so much grief. But having unburdened himself of one hindrance, he faced another, bigger one: Droz, it emerges, was not the only person who let him down.

Pitt Stop

Perhaps British testimony has been unfair to Droz. That testimony was, after all, mostly one-sided, coming either from Boulton himself or from Boulton's close friends and associates. Nor can the judgment rendered by the arbitration committee be taken at face value, for that committee also ended up being one-sided: although it first had three members, Droz's own choice, Justin Vuilliamy, withdrew before the judgment was rendered (Doty 1998, 42).[23]

Also, as Pollard (1968, 242) observes, Droz's disastrous interval at Soho was "only a brief episode in a generally distinguished career." Droz

23. The other committee members were John Motteux, chair of the East India Company (Boulton's choice), and Sir Joseph Banks (by mutual consent).

made a good name for himself in France before coming to Soho, and he was no less well regarded there when he returned. In 1799, he went back to work at the Paris Mint, serving as keeper of coins and medals and, from 1804, as keeper of the Mint Museum, where his coins, presses, and other contributions to French coinage history are now proudly displayed. Droz retired in 1814 and died, wreathed with honors, in 1823.[24]

Finally, if Droz broke his promises, Boulton broke his as well. In particular, Boulton got Droz to come to Soho by telling him that he was about to be called on to reform Great Britain's copper coin. Droz thus looked forward not just to the pecuniary gains Boulton offered but to basking in the glory that such a reform was bound to convey to its instruments. But although there were times when the government seemed ready to summon Boulton to its aid, all turned out to be false alarms. By the end of Droz's two-year stint, the promised regal contract was nowhere in sight. If Droz was guilty of not getting anything done, Boulton was no less guilty of not having at hand any project worthy of "the best Engraver in Europe."

What had become of Boulton's regal coinage contract? Smiles's (1866, 392) claim that the Royal Mint managed single-handedly to hold it up for a whole decade by mere "passive resistance" is a long way from the truth. In fact, the Royal Mint only played a bit part in a rather involved political drama.

Let us recall the setting. The government seemed bound to do something about the coinage ever since the Garbetts submitted their polite but damning report in 1782. By the summer of 1786, rumors of an imminent recoinage were flying, and by that autumn—about a year before the formation of the Privy Council Committee on Coin—Samuel Garbett and Boulton were lobbying for permission to coin the king's copper.

The men to whom Garbett and Boulton made overtures were William Pitt, the prime minister, and Charles Jenkinson, president of the Board of Trade—the Privy Council committee to which difficult economic matters were referred. Pitt was a green, though fiercely eloquent, Reform MP when, during December 1783, he found himself, paradoxically

---

24. Droz did not lack French detractors. Augustin Dupré, engraver general of French coins from 1791 to 1803, wrote: "As sire Droz announced the discovery he claimed as his own, he was confronted by contradictions, and not just the one denying him the honor of his invention. He was also shown that his method would only make coining more difficult while addng to its expense the costs of using and maintaining his machine" (author's translation of French original in Darnis 1988, 178). For a less critical French perspective on Droz, see Gallet 1902.

enough, appointed first lord of the Treasury, chancellor of the exchequer, and prime minister, by the very king whose power he so fervently wished to curtail. In accepting these appointments, Pitt saved the Crown from the still greater threat posed by Charles Fox's political coalition, which would have gone so far as to deny the king his prerogative of choosing his own ministers. The king, in turn, supported Pitt even when that meant going along with reforms he didn't like (Duffy 2000, 33).

The stiff and pompous Jenkinson was, in contrast, a died-in-the-wool representative of the "old politics of the Court," who, as leader of the king's friends in the House of Commons, had far better access to His Majesty than any member of Pitt's cabinet. He therefore posed a real danger to Pitt. Yet Pitt himself assigned "Jenky" to the Committee of Trade in 1784 and put him in charge of that same body two years later (when it had become the Board of Trade), while rewarding him a peerage as Lord Hawkesbury. Pitt chose Jenkinson to handle the nation's economic affairs—despite his politics—because of his exceptional knowledge of trade and finance and also because of his role in orchestrating the gold recoinage of the early 1770s.[25] In short, as Pitt explained to his mother, although politically the selection might "sound a bit strange," Jenkinson had "really fairly earned it" (Gash 1984, 8). Indeed, when it came to the coinage, Jenkinson was to be a far more unswerving and tireless advocate of reform than Pitt himself. Still, Pitt remained wary of his appointee and kept him out of his cabinet until 1791, by which time events had drawn the views of the two men much closer together.

Although the coinage question was first referred to the Board of Trade, a special committee of the Privy Council, headed by Lord Camden (the lord president), was established during the autumn of 1787 to deal exclusively with it. Toward the end of the year, the Committee on Coin, as it came to be known, wrote to Boulton to ask for further details concerning his plan, to request specimens of his proposed coins, and to invite him to London for an interview. After stalling for time, Boulton responded to the committee's demands during the first months of 1788.

After that came the first indications that the government might be less anxious than Boulton was to get going on a new copper coinage. Several months passed while Boulton heard nothing—nothing from Pitt, nothing from Hawkesbury, nothing even from the Privy Council. The si-

---

25. The 1911 *Britannica* notwithstanding, Charles Jenkinson was never master of the Royal Mint and never had any other official connection with that institution (Craig 1953, 242). Rather, Charles's son Robert, the second Lord Hawkesbury (and later prime minister), held that position, albeit only for twenty months.

lence appears to have been due to the committee's decision to attend to the gold coinage before renewing its deliberations on copper, not (as Smiles suggests) to resistance—passive or otherwise—from the Royal Mint. On October 16, a frustrated Boulton wrote Hawkesbury to try and get things moving again. "I have held myself in readiness all this Summer," he stated, "to Obey any summons I might be honored with from your Lordship or the Privy Council" (BL Add. MSS 38421, 271). He added that the Soho Mint would be ready as of New Year's Day to coin one thousand tons per year—more if necessary.

But Boulton had readied himself in vain, for during the evening of the very next day, before his letter even reached Hawkesbury, the king suddenly doubled over with a violent stomachache and then started foaming at the mouth and babbling incoherently. At first, the royal physician thought that his gout had somehow gone to his head; but soon it became clear to all concerned that George III was, at least temporarily, insane. With the king far gone, Boulton's prospects for coining regal copper seemed far gone as well: as Boulton explained to Wilkinson in a letter of November 28, 1788, the Privy Council would take no action on the coinage until the king regained his "health" (Doty 1987, 681).

The problem wasn't just that the king had to personally sign off on Boulton's contract. Pitt's political survival was at stake, for unless the king recovered, a regency would have to be declared, and the Prince of Wales would waste no time in dismissing Pitt and his cabinet in favor of his opposition friends. Pitt managed to cling to power in the immediate aftermath of the crisis, thanks mainly to Prinny's unseemly reputation—which made the idea of handing the regal reigns to him extremely unpopular—and to the fact that Fox was traipsing around Italy with his mistress when he might best have forced the issue of a regency. But Fox eventually returned, and even the half-mad Prinny, womanizing sot though he was, was better than an outright lunatic.

Come January, Boulton, fearing the worst, wrote Hawkesbury again. His letter (BL Add. MSS 38422, 1) seems worth quoting in full, if only because it is such a fine example of the self-righteous spin Boulton liked to put on his interest in coining copper.

My Lord

I have been silent for some time past upon the Subject of the Copper Coinage because it was evident, that your Lordships Mind hath been occupied by Subjects of a higher and more important Nature, and, though I must unfeignedly [sic] lament the derangement of our beloved Sovereign's health and the probable fall of the prosperity which this Country so recently and eminently enjoyed, yet amidst these Calamities, I cannot help turning my thoughts to the loss I am likely to sustain by the probability of the Copper Coinage falling to the ground: My primary Motive for taking that Matter up arose from a full persuasion, that I could put a final stop to the counterfeiting of Money, and to the retrieving the honor of that branch of the Mechanick Arts, but after I had put myself to a considerable expense (which was necessary even to make the Specimens which the right honorable the Lords of the Privy Council ordered me to do): It was natural that I should then calculate not only upon the repayment of that expense, but likewise upon the gaining a [sic] small profit, and for this purpose I have remounted my Rolling Mill and made it the best in England, I have built a Building in my Garden detached from all other buildings or Manufactories for the purpose of carrying on the Coinage, I have erected two Fire Engines for that purpose and have contrived and executed such new machinery as is sufficient to Coin Gold, Silver & Copper for half Europe, similar to the specimen for a French Crown, which I had the honor to present to your Lordship: I have made an engagement with Mr Droz the Engraver upon terms that will fall very heavy upon me, but without which I could not have attained that degree of perfection I have aimed at: I have neglected my other Persuits [sic] in a great degree, and have already expended several thousand Pounds in making preparations to execute the Coinage upon such terms and in such a manner as to put an end to the evils and inconveniences resulting from counterfeiting, and such as there is little probability of being accomplished by any Other Person.

Hence I am impelled by my Duty to my Family &c. to most humbly crave your Lordships advice and assistance at this important Crisis.

If it were possible for the Lords of the Privy Council to make any Order or any Contract with me respecting the Coinage, before any great change takes place in the Government, it would relieve my Mind from a great degree of Anxiety, or if your Lordship should think it necessary that I should come to Town directly, I will instantly conform to your Advice.

A Meeting of the Inhabitants of Birmingham is called by publick advertisement for Friday next to sign an address of thanks to Mr Pitt &c. which is not likely to meet with any Opposition for although there may be sometimes maneuvering by Agents at these Meetings Yet it is

evident that there is but one Sentiment pervades the Minds of all the
People of this Nation who are not fettered by Party or biased by Interest. Wishing your Lordship and all that are Dear to you Health and
many many happy Years I remain with the highest respect My Lord

> Your Lordships
> Most faithful
> & Most Obliged Obed^t: hble. Servt.
> Matt^w: Boulton

Hawkesbury's reply to Boulton (ibid., 31) seems no less worth quoting,
for the sake of the ever-so-subtle hint of scorn that lurks between its lines:
the king lay gravely ill, with Pitt's government hanging by a thread, and
here was this *manufacturer* lamenting the loss of a coining contract he
hadn't been granted in the first place.

Dear Sir

I have received the favor of your Letter of the 12th and I am much
concerned to think that among the many Evils that will necessarily
arise from the Derangement of Our beloved Sovereign's Health it is
likely that you will be exposed to your share of Loss & Inconvenience
in consequence of your Zeal for the Publick Service. You know very
well how zealously I was disposed to prosecute the Business of the
Copper Coinage, and that it was my Wish also to remedy many defects
in the Gold and Silver Coin and to place them both on a better Foot-
ing than that at which they stand at present, and I was happy in thinking that Government would have the advantage of being adjusted by
your Abilities & by the Discoveries you have made, in accomplishing a
Work of this Importance. In the Midst of these Pursuits a terrible
Calamity has fallen upon Us which has put a stop to all our Proceedings for it would be idle to prosecute a Measure which We shall not be
suffered to bring to a Conclusion. . . . I had talked to M^r. Pitt on this
Subject before I received your Letter & He agrees with Me in thinking
that you had better on this account come to Town if it will not subject
you to great Inconvenience. I am happy to hear that the Gentlemen
of Birmingham think so favourably of the present Administration &
particularly of the Measures they are now pursuing.

> I am Y^e (etc.)
> Hawkesbury

At the end of the month, Boulton did in fact call on Hawkesbury in London to see whether he'd raised his case with Pitt again. But Hawkesbury had gotten nowhere: Pitt, who didn't tend to answer letters anyway, was far too preoccupied with his own survival to bother answering one concerning the misfortunes of a Staffordshire factory owner.

Disappointed by Hawkesbury in London, Boulton, upon returning to Soho, tried directly petitioning the Committee on Coin. He began by reminding them that he had made extensive preparations for coining up to fifteen hundred tons of copper, at a cost of "upwards of Four Thousand Pounds and the Loss of one Year's attention to my other Business." "Therefore," he resolved,

> As it is probable the present derangement of his Majesty's Health may interrupt the carrying into execution the aforementioned plan, and thereby subject me to a Loss too heavy for me to bear.
>
> I must humbly pray that your Lordships would take my Case into Consideration, and grant me such relief as may in your Candor and Justice seem meet.   (BL ADD. MSS 38422, 5, FEBRUARY 6, 1789)

Before the committee could respond to Boulton's petition, the king began to recover—thanks, some say, to the ministrations of a parson named Willis, who cured him through frequent bleedings, forced vomiting, cold baths, and, mainly, therapeutic sessions involving "a straightjacket, iron clamps, a chair and a length of rope" (K. Shaw 1999, 42), which appear to have worked by scaring him back *into* his wits.[26] By March, the lord chancellor was able to report his full recovery, reviving the prospects for action on the coinage and thereby rendering Boulton's request for relief moot.

In June, Boulton was back in London, where he spoke to the king and delivered specimens of his halfpence to him and his ministers. The king's perfectly sound mind—Boulton noted how he recollected details of a conversation they'd had seven years previously—so convinced

---

26. Although it is widely believed that King George suffered from porphyria, research on porphyria undertaken since the 1960s has failed to establish any connection between the disease and temporary mental illness. According to Karl Shaw (1999, 50), had George actually suffered from porphyria, "there should have been a far greater concentration of porphyriacs in the British Royal family, and a much greater distribution throughout the royal families of Europe." Historians have thus begun to revive the view—from before the 1960s—that George III suffered from a psychiatric disorder (ibid., 51).

Boulton that his coining prospects were near at hand that he now worried not so much about getting his contract as about getting copper with which to fulfill it (CRO 3/85, Boulton to Wilson, June 29, 1789). For the first—but hardly the last—time, Boulton complained to Wilson that the Copper King was purposefully withholding supplies from him, though he asked Wilson to keep the complaint to himself, for otherwise it would "soon come round again to Mr. Williams for he has more pimps than one at Truro" (ibid.)

While Willis's therapy may have helped the king to recover, thereby saving Pitt's government, it also left him in such a state of exhaustion that he decided he would henceforth "expect others to fulfill the duties of their employments, and only keep that superintending eye which can be effected without labour or fatigue" (Barnes 1939, 202). The king intended, in other words, to pile more work on the cabinet (ibid., 203).

Deprived of the king's active support, Pitt had his hands full promoting parliamentary reform, revision of the Test and Corporation Acts, and abolition of the slave trade. There being not a moment to spare for the coinage, it was shoved to the back burner. Hawkesbury informed Boulton of the situation, while passing the buck to Lord Camden, in a letter dated April 13: "[S]ince His Majesty's Recovery the Pressure of Public Business has been so great, that it has been impossible to resume that of the Copper Coin, & tho' I may have some share in this Transaction, yet it properly belongs to the Lord President, who is at the Head of the Committee appointed for that Purpose" (BL Add. MSS 38442, 35). So it appeared that the lovely medal Boulton commissioned that same month to commemorate the ending of the crisis (and to remind the king of the unfinished coinage business)—the one significant numismatic product of his partnership with Droz—would be struck and distributed in vain.

Unaware of the brush-off then on its way from Hawkesbury, Boulton sent him a memorandum on April 14 in which he added the distress of the Cornish copper miners and the growing trade in private tokens to his list of reasons for expeditiously reforming the copper coinage. Concerning Cornwall, Boulton wrote:

> There are now more than half the Copper mines [there] stoped [sic]
> & the Miners are in great Distress & that Daily increasing. A sale of
> 1500 Tons or 2000 Tons of Copper to Gover*mt.* would relieve Cornwell of a tax of near ten thousand pounds a Year . . . which must
> shortly terminate in the annihilation of the Cornish Miners & in giving a Monopoly to the Anglesey Co. . . . [E]very ensuing Year will de-

crease the power of Cornwell & increase those of Anglesey, whose Controller General aims at Power, & is now Canvasing [*sic*] at Great Marlow in Buckinghamshire for a Seat in Parliament.　(IBID., 13)

As for the private tokens then in circulation, including Williams's Druids, Boulton warned that "these examples will be followed by others, unless the growing mischief is put a Stop to by the hand of Power" (ibid.). Precisely what "mischief" he had in mind Boulton didn't say, though he may well have had in mind the mischief tokens might do to him if their number grew large enough to make a new regal copper coinage seem unnecessary: Boulton was already facing the prospect of having "to Discharge some valuable Workman & put an end to my Expenses relative to the Coinage both of which I shall do with great reluctance, after all the pains I have taken" (ibid.). Boulton's memo ends on a decidedly despondent note.

Indeed my Lord it hath been my misfortune to expend a large portion of my Life & fortune in improvements of various kinds; which have been of more use to our Manufacturers, & to the publick, than to my self, & I fear the present case will prove another instance of Serious loss to my Family, unless your Lordship stands my Friend: which I do not ask upon any other ground, than that of my doing the business better & cheaper, and more effectually put an end to the evil complaind [*sic*] of, than if done by his Majesties [*sic*] Mint, or any other persons in the Kingdome but I fear the plan will die away unless it is revived & cherished by your Lordship.

I beg once more to implore your Lordships favour and protection & remain with the highest regard [etc.].

Hawkesbury could only repeat with renewed emphasis what he'd said in his letter of April 13: that Boulton ought to address himself not to the Board of Trade but to the Committee on Coin. "It is not proper," Hawkesbury explained, "for me to take the Lead in the Business, tho' I shall be ready to lend any Assistance which it is in my power to give." He ended by reminding Boulton of the storm the government had just weathered: "You cannot be surprised at the Delay which has hitherto occurred in Consequence of the Calamity to which We were lately subject & which is now happily at an End" (ibid., 15).

The calamity may have ended, but Pitt's troubles had not. Compounding them was his ongoing conflict with the lord chancellor, Lord

Thurlow, who was "in open warfare" with him from 1788 onward (Duffy 2000, 57). Thurlow had been rankled by Pitt's appointment in 1788 of Secretary of the Treasury George Rose to the House of Lords post of clerk of the parliaments—a post Rose had hoped to add to his already impressive collection of sinecures (ibid., 58). Another flap occurred in 1789, when Pitt sacked Thurlow's friend Francis Hargraves from the Counsel of the Treasury. During the regency crisis, Thurlow all but openly endorsed the Prince of Wales. Yet the recovered king kept him at his post, which was tantamount to blocking Pitt's reforms. Because Thurlow and Hawkesbury were friends and because Hawkesbury himself was sincerely dedicated to reforming the coinage, Thurlow didn't directly seek to scuttle a recoinage. Nevertheless, by running interference with Pitt's other reforms, Thurlow forced him to devote all his energy to them, leaving him no time to devote to Britain's small-change problem.

Despite Pitt's preoccupation with other matters, the Committee on Coin renewed its activity during the autumn of 1789. It called on Boulton to meet with it again and thereby restored his hopes for prompt action. On December 11, 1789, while on the road home from one of his many trips to London, Boulton wrote to Hawkesbury to express his hope that the Privy Council might get around to the "business of the Coinage" before the holidays, indicating his readiness "to obey their Lordships orders at a moments notice" (BL Add. MSS 38422, 37).

The same flurry of activity that revived Boulton's hopes also aroused the usually slumbering Royal Mint, which now revealed its growing fear of a privatized copper coinage by aiming a defensive salvo straight at Boulton's plan. In its "Memorandum against the Proposed Alteration of the Copper Coinage" (MBP 249/234), the mint opposed the whole idea of a new copper coinage, declaring:

1. There will be no necessity for it.
2. It will produce no Advantage to the Public.
3. It will cost a great deal of Money to the public.
4. It will be productive of many Crimes & Offences.

The mint also claimed, in essence, that the only people who were adversely affected by counterfeit money were those who "wilfully [sic] and knowingly" trafficked in the stuff.

Boulton's status as a major manufacturer allowed him handily to refute the mint's self-serving and false assertions (MBP 249/235). Garbett did his part as well, spoiling Hawkesbury's holidays with a barrage of information bearing on the mint memorandum, including a copy of the mint charter. In his understandably delayed response, Hawkesbury explained that he'd been "extremely occupied with the Coin Business, & with a Marriage that is just going to take Place in my Family." He then reported that the charter proved to his full satisfaction that mint officials enjoyed "no Powers or Rights that can stand in the Way of a Reform" (BL Add. MSS 38422, 92). That the Royal Mint could have a coinage reform forced down its throat if need be was certainly welcome news. But the news didn't prevent Boulton's own holiday from being ruined by "a most unwelcome holiday present": word from William Matthews, on Christmas day, that the government decided to put off further coinage hearings "until at least the following February" (Doty 1998, 41).

In fact, the tidings were to be worse still, for although Boulton didn't know it, Samuel Garbett, who had heretofore been so supportive of his coining ambitions, was now distancing himself from him. The reason had to do with the price of copper cake, which had been as low as sixty-eight pounds a ton back in 1787 but had since risen to as much as eighty-six pounds. Although the high price of copper was good news for the Cornish miners, it was killing Birmingham's toy and button manufacturers, and Garbett, as president of the Birmingham Commercial Committee, felt duty-bound to oppose any project that was likely to raise it much further.

Although Garbett first began to reveal his misgivings concerning any large-scale minting of copper at the beginning of 1790,[27] he completely unburdened himself in a letter of April 12 to Hawkesbury.[28]

----

27. See, for example, his January 11 reply to a request from William Fawkener, clerk to the Privy Council, for his opinion concerning a proposal for making the nominal value of new copper coins equal to their cost of production.

28. Unlike me, Richard Doty (personal communication, May 21, 2003) does not believe that Garbett's reversal could have played any crucial role. "Garbett," he observes, "was something of a crank . . . and he [Boulton] knew it." But what mattered was not Boulton's opinion of Garbett but that of those persons in the government who would decide whether or not to proceed with Boulton's coinage proposal. Hawkesbury, for one, took Garbett quite seriously and encouraged the king to do so as well: Garbett, he explained to His Majesty in a letter of October 6, 1794 (BL Add. MSS 38422, 236), is "a principal manufacturer at Birmingham and a Person of most influence in that Town, he is an honest man, and very ingenious, but very active, punctilious, and a little apt to be troublesome; Lord H. would recommend therefore, that some general attention should be paid to him." Bear in mind also that Hawkesbury, who was certainly no crank when it came to coinage, continued to heed Garbett's opinions on the subject after having given Boulton the cold shoulder. On January 25, 1790, for instance, Hawkesbury, after agreeing to postpone the coinage business in favor of other matters until he could meet with Garbett, wrote to him, "You & I differ in Opinion with respect to the general Principles of Coin, on no Point but that which relates to Seignorage, and which I shall be ready again to discuss with you when you come to Town" (ibid, 48).

The Truth is, that I realy [*sic*] dread an opinion prevailing that from my intimacy with Mr Boulton I promoted a heavy Coinage of Copper, as I am sure whenever it is begun the public confusion will be intolerable, & I expect dangerous, *as no Remedy can . . .* be applied for the Miseries it will produce, & therefore on every occasion I have always (as Self-Defense) reprobated the Design. As I dare not interfere farther, I will shew Mr Boulton a Copy of this Letter, & give him permission to say to your Lordship that I did so.   (BL ADD. MSS 38422, 120)

Boulton, oblivious to Garbett's change of heart, continued to turn to his old friend for sympathy and aid. On March 29, he wrote to commiserate:

I find myself in a very unpleasant situation. On the one hand, I am teired [*sic*] to death by Mr Droz, who is tired of doing nothing, and who only wants to get all the money he can from me & then return to France. (His late conduct hath convinced me that I was mistaken in his Moral Character) and on the other I am kept in a ruinous Suspence; for I am obliged to continue all my Expensive workmen. If I was to discharge them I could not recruit them again suddenly if calld upon by Goverment to execute the proposed Coin.

Moreover these artists & Workman would be eagerly taken by our Birmingham Coiners, under the idea of possessing themselves of my inventions, & rivaling me in the favour of Goverment.

I wish his Majesties [*sic*] Ministers would allow me to make a small beginning if it was for no other use than to prove by a regular course of work wither all my apparatus is perfect as well as to enable me to judge whether I shall stand in any need of Mr Droz further assistance. . . .

Let me beg of you to tell me whither you have any Idea when the Lords of the Council propose to resume the Subject, or whether you think it will be set about this Spring or Summer. I have heard nothing of it for some time past.   (IBID., 119–20)

Garbett, feeling torn, enclosed a copy of Boulton's letter with his own letter of April 7 to Hawkesbury that spoke, among other things, of the increasingly bellicose state of Birmingham's manufacturers. Hawkesbury's immediate reply read, in part, as follows:

I am concerned to hear that Mr Boulton is under the Distress you mention. I have really a personal regard for him, but I always told him

that the Business of Coin did not belong particularly to my Department and tho' I would give every Assistance in conducting it yet that I
would not undertake it by myself without the concurrent Aid and
Opinion of the Rest of the King's Servants. . . . I should however before now have reminded Mr Pitt of it if the many other Branches of
Business with which I have been occupied for the last three Months
had not taken up the whole of my Time, and they are indeed so various and many of them so difficult that I hardly find either my Understanding or my Health equal to the Management of them. I am sorry
to hear of the Disturbances prevailing in Birmingham concerning the
Supply and Price of Copper.   (BL ADD. MSS 38422, 50–51)

In short, although Boulton never ceased to entertain the hope of receiving his "final orders . . . to begin upon the Copper Coinage" (MBP
150 (Letter Book Q), Matthew Boulton to Perregaux, April 29, 1790), by
the spring of 1790, a combination of adverse circumstances made fulfillment of that hope less likely than ever. Those circumstances were to remain essentially unchanged for another two years. On October 29, 1791,
Matt Robinson Boulton wrote to Wilson lamenting his father's situation:

[A] new range of shops has been built, he has brought Artists at a considerable expense from Paris, erected several new presses & entered
into engagem^{ts} for the delivery of large quantities of Coin, these are
all now upon the point of standing still. . . . The stoppage of his Works
will be a very considerable loss to him, but in the eyes of a Man of Honour the loss of Character is a much greater consideration & therefore you cannot be surprised that my father should feel himself chagrined at the disappointment.   (CRO 4/104)

In late May 1792, the impediment to action posed by Lord Thurlow's
interference was finally removed, Pitt having decided to force matters by
telling the king that either he or Thurlow would have to go. Cornered,
the king dismissed Thurlow. Thus Pitt secured full control of his cabinet
at long last (Duffy 2000, 60). But he quickly found himself preoccupied
with France's increasingly aggressive foreign policy, including its attempts to encourage rebellion in Holland and the threat that such a rebellion would pose to Britain's trade and naval power. Thurlow's post, in
the meantime, remained vacant, with the great seal put in commission,
until January 1793. Less than a month later, on February 1, France declared war on Great Britain.

The war made a new copper coinage less likely than ever before, for it meant, first of all, that the government would have no funds to spare to cover the expense of a recoinage and, second, that the price of copper, which was heavily influenced by the demand for ships' sheathing, would reach unprecedented heights even without a new copper coinage. Besides unleashing turmoil in Birmingham, the unstable price of copper made a recoinage especially risky, for if the price rose high enough, newly made copper coins might quickly end up in melting pots, and the whole effort would be a gigantic waste. On the other hand, were the price of copper to fall again in the near future (owing, say, to a quick end to hostilities), any recoinage undertaken beforehand would also prove wasteful, for the government would in effect have bought copper high in order to sell it low.

Paradoxically enough, although the French war would be responsible for delaying Boulton's coinage for several more years, an episode connected to that same conflict would ultimately cause the government to decide to produce a new copper coinage after all. But that would not happen until 1797—Pitt's annus horribilis—a full decade after Boulton first began to build his mint.

A Coining Millstone

In the meantime, Boulton had to find some way to recoup at least part of the seven thousand pounds he'd invested in his mint. Although he tried to do so on more than one occasion by offering to sell his mint lock, stock, and barrel, the best he could do in the end was to offer to coin money for clients other than the British government. Just as Boulton & Fothergill had once looked abroad for new button customers, Boulton now looked on foreign governments as potential purchasers of his coins.

At one point, the newly formed U.S. government looked like a likely prospect. In September 1789, a well-connected American acquaintance of Boulton's named John Hinckley Mitchell met with President Washington in New York to discuss his plan for supplying the new nation with two hundred thousand pounds in gold, silver, and copper coin. Mitchell intended to let Boulton do the actual coining at Soho, in return for a commission. Washington's response was encouraging, so Mitchell advised Boulton to prepare a bid specifying his charges (Mitchell 1931, 13). Boulton did so on November 25, giving his price for copper coin as £46 13s 4d per ton (or fourteen pence per pound, inclusive of packing and freight to the port of Bristol) and encouraging Mitchell to bring the business "to a conclusion as soon as possible that I may arrange my own time & business properly, for besides the British Copper Coinage, I am now in treaty with some other European States for the conduct of the whole of their Coinage" (ibid., 17–19).

On April 7, 1790, Mitchell's proposal was laid before the U.S. House, which referred it to Thomas Jefferson in his capacity as secretary of state. Jefferson reported back on it a week later. He was, of course, acquainted with the unnamed "Undertaker" referred to in the proposal and also with the "first Artist . . . in Europe" who was to engrave the dies for the proposed coinage. He did not doubt that these two men were "truly in a condition to furnish Coin in a state of higher perfection, than has ever yet been issued by any Nation." Yet Jefferson's conclusion was unfavorable. Like some modern opponents of dollarization, he believed that to allow foreign production of a nation's money was "to submit [that exercise] to another Sovereign" (Mitchell 1931, 26). He feared, among other things, that Mitchell's plan would expose the U.S. coinage system to enemy interference in time of war, and therefore recommended that the United States establish its own mint with help from Mitchell's "Undertaker" (ibid., 27). Congress did eventually resolve to establish a U.S. mint. But that was not until the spring of 1792, when Jefferson had decided to take personal charge of the project, leaving Boulton entirely out of the picture.[29]

While his American prospect was still alive, Boulton took the considerably more daring step of offering to coin money for France. In a letter of April 26, 1790, to John Perregaux, his London banker, he worried that word would get out concerning his offer. "[F]or god's sake," he told Perregaux, "dont say a word . . . , for if it should appear that I had any inclination to serve a Foreign Country, it may be of material injury to me" (MBP 150 (Letter Book Q)). Boulton especially feared that word might reach his old friend Samuel Garbett. Boulton knew full well that Garbett loathed the revolution, and Boulton was depending on him and his son Francis (who was then being considered for the position of comptroller of the Royal Mint) to keep his hopes for a regal coining contract alive. Still, Boulton persisted, forming a liaison with a German chemist named

---

29. Boulton responded belatedly to Jefferson's adverse report and plans then in place for an initial U.S. coinage, in a letter of November 5, 1792. "I agree," Boulton wrote, "with Mr. Jefferson that the coinage of money is one of the attributes of sovereignty and ought to be done in every great State, but I have considered America as a newborn child that needed doddering strings before it could walk and my offer was to furnish them" (Mitchell 1931, 37).

Swediaur, who had connections in high French places, and authorizing him, in a letter of February 7, 1791, to secure a French coinage contract on behalf of the Soho Mint or, alternatively, to sell the mint itself—that is, the coining mill "with all its appurtenances"—to the French government (Doty 1998, 45).

Swediaur didn't sell the French government on either proposal. He did, however, put Boulton in touch with Monneron Frères, the Parisian *negocians,* who awarded Soho a large private token commission. Completing that commission proved more difficult than Boulton had imagined: copper, which not long before was so abundant as to threaten the very survival of the Cornish mines, was now so scarce that Boulton had to struggle to come up with it (Doty 1998, 46). Writing to the French brothers, Boulton claimed that the shortage of copper was just another attempt by Williams to foil him: "We are annoyed and attacked by the great monopolist in conjunction with his spies, pimps and cats" (MBP 151 (Letter Book R), Boulton to Monneron Frères, October 27, 1791). In truth, a month before, Boulton had pleaded with his supposed nemesis to supply him copper at below its market price, on the grounds that he would otherwise lose money on the Monneron Frères deal. An unmoved Williams responded by telling Boulton that such deals "injure the copper trade as well as your own interests" and that it would be worth Boulton's while "to give me a very handsome commission to make those contracts for you" (MBP 368/66, Williams to Boulton, September 30, 1791).

No less troubling than the scarcity of copper was the fact—for which Williams could hardly be blamed—that Boulton's mint wasn't up to the job: the French tokens, which were thicker and heavier than any of Britain's commercial coins, wore out both dies and presses. To limit breakdowns, the presses were slowed to just forty-five strokes a minute. Still, things fell apart: in mid-February of 1792, a chagrined Boulton explained to the French brothers that the great force used "to strike the 5 sous pieces has broke, bent, & deranged, most of the parts about the press's [*sic*]." The force even snapped off part of one press's balance bar, which landed on and smashed the arm of one of Boulton's best workers (Doty 1998, 47).[30] In a follow-up letter, Boulton tried to lay rose-tinted varnish on what was in fact a dismal picture.

> You must not conclude that my plan of Coining is any worse than I have always represented & always thought it. . . . I assure you upon my

---

30. What, one wonders, had happened to those twelve-year-old boys who were supposed to be operating Boulton's coining presses?

honour, it is not, but the Strengths & proportions of all the particular
parts can only be ascertained by Experience & I am more confident
than ever that all the imperfections will be overcome very soon

(IBID.).

However, far from being "overcome very soon," the problems continued:
one press after another broke, so that, more often than not, only a single
press could be kept running. So matters remained until the spring of
1792, when Soho's coining mill was yanked back from the brink of anni-
hilation by the sudden bankruptcy of Monneron Frères in March and
then, following the firm's reorganization in April, by a law of May 3 forbidding further production of French private tokens.[31] One wonders how
the mint would have fared had the government come through with its
thousand-ton contract back in 1788. The outcome might well have been
disastrous—especially if the government had insisted on ordering heavy
coins. But one needn't leave too much to the imagination, for something
like a larger-scale repeat of the trials encountered in making the Monneron Frères tokens is exactly what Soho was to experience in 1797.

Three other foreign coining contracts—all for British colonies—
came Soho's way during the early nineties. One was a second order from
the East India Company, which was approved in late February 1791
(Doty 1998, 305). This time, the order was for the company's Bombay
settlement, and the amount of coins ordered—one hundred tons'
worth—far outstripped Boulton's other early coinage undertakings. The
largest coins required for this commission were, fortunately, only slightly
bigger than unimpaired copper halfpennies, so Boulton was able to keep
his presses and dies together, finishing the entire order in just nine
months (Doty 1998, 305–6).[32] Boulton's next colonial commission came
from the Sierra Leone Company, which needed silver dollars and copper
pennies for use in its West African colony. The order involved fewer than
a million coins in all, which were struck during December 1792 and May
1793; that was, for the time being at least, all that the tiny colony needed

31. In September, further legislation suppressed private tokens altogether, including
ones that had been placed into circulation before May 3. These measures, which anticipated similar ones introduced sometime later in Great Britain, were taken despite the fact
that private tokens were France's best small change at the time, as may be readily
confirmed by touring the historical coin displays at the Paris Mint Museum.

32. Boulton had reason, however, to resist making coins that were very small, for his
contracts generally specified a certain payment per ton of coined metal. Consequently, because the labor cost involved in making small coins was not necessarily lower than that for
making large ones, Boulton might find himself losing money on smallish coins, as happened during the last stages of his first East India Company commission (Doty 1998, 305).

(ibid., 308–9). The third colonial order, for Bermuda, was smaller still—a mere 90,042 coins, including one hundred proof pieces. Like the Sierra Leone commission, this order was also placed at the end of 1792 and completed in May 1793 (ibid., 309).

Foreign coin commissions alone, however, could not keep the Soho Mint's staff fully employed, let alone defray the mint's huge capital cost. Consequently, Boulton found himself reluctantly expanding his involvement in Great Britain's commercial token business. As we saw in chapter 2, Boulton's initial forays into this field were aimed not so much at establishing a permanent commercial clientele for the Soho as at discouraging Williams and Westwood, his rivals for a regal coinage contract. Having failed to convince the government to force those rivals out of business, Boulton tried absorbing them instead, lest they should divert attention from his own plan. He thus offered to coin Druids for Williams and Cronebanes in partnership with Westwood. Williams eventually agreed to quit coining his own money; and although Westwood's mint survived Boulton's poaching of its clients, its importance dwindled after John Westwood's death.

So it happened that, by the early 1790s, Boulton was close to having the entire British token market to himself. And he needed it, for by that time he had lost all hope of coining copper for the British government and—setting aside his earlier, expressed opposition to commercial coins—began actively to seek orders from private clients. Boulton took his big first step in this direction with the Southampton brewer Walter Taylor, of Taylor, Moody & Company. Back in 1789, Boulton had talked Taylor out of placing an order for coins with Westwood, by assuring him that Soho would soon be preparing new regal coins. By the spring of 1791, Taylor had given up waiting for the government to act and was shopping for tokens again. This time, Boulton, instead of trying to talk him out of it, took Taylor's order himself, depriving John Westwood of yet another client.[33]

Another of Boulton's early commercial clients was the Cornish Metal Company, which, as noted in chapter 2, was formed back in 1785 to save the Cornish copper mines. Although John Vivian first approached Boulton back in August 1789, when he anticipated ordering one hundred tons of halfpennies, Boulton did not get around to making an initial

---

33. As it happens, Taylor may have wished he'd stuck to Westwood, for when the first batch of his tokens arrived, they were so "tarnished, nicked, and scratched" that he threatened to cancel the remainder of his order (Doty 1998, 306). Boulton eventually placated Taylor by cleaning the offending tokens and by striking him a complimentary set of polished pieces.

batch of coins for him until mid-1791. Although the coins, the obverses of which resembled Williams's Druids, had been beautifully executed by Droz's replacement, Rambart Dumarest, Vivian had by then begun to reconsider the scale of his original proposal, which was eventually revised downward to just over one ton of tokens only (Doty 1998, 307). Dumarest was also responsible for the lovely and immensely popular "Glasgow halfpennies" Boulton delivered to Gilbert, Shearer & Company during October 1791 and February 1792 (ibid). After the last batch of Glasgow halfpennies was delivered, there came a lull in Soho's coin-making activities that lasted until the early months of 1793.

How, one might ask, was Boulton's mint succeeding so far in its capacity as an entirely commercial venture? The answer, alas, is that it was not succeeding at all. Like so many of Boulton's other purely private ventures (apart from the steam-engine business), the Soho Mint was a money loser. On September 13, 1792, William Brown, Soho's clerk, prepared a report on mint profits and losses, giving Soho's total net loss on its coining operations as £6,475 for the period ending in 1791. Adding amounts spent on Williams's useless presses and on a new mint building added in 1791 brings the loss to £7,780 (Doty 1998, 49–50). During 1792, Soho made another £5,285 in coining revenues; but even assuming (generously) that only a third of this gross amount represented production costs, it cannot have reduced the accumulated loss to below half its value the year before. "In truth," Richard Doty (ibid., 50) concludes, "the Soho Mint was *not* a going concern and would not become one until its master secured its first regal coining contract in 1797."[34]

Until then, Boulton had no choice but to try and sign as many commercial coinage contracts as he could lay his hands on. But while many such contracts would come his way, making a profit from them would be far from easy. Although it looked for a time as if Boulton might command monopoly rates for his tokens, that was no longer the case by 1793: the government's failure to act, either by producing more coins of its own or by suppressing commercial alternatives, had given rise to a whole new crop of commercial coin makers; and Matthew Boulton, who had wanted a peaceful copper coin monopoly, suddenly found himself fighting it out in a cutthroat coinage industry.

---

34. In treating the entire £5,285 sum as if it represented net revenues or profits, Doty actually understates Soho's losses.

CHAPTER IV

The People's Money

But when should people strive their bonds to break,

If not when kings are negligent or weak?[1]

No Problem?

In the autumn of 1790, John Wilkinson found himself in a hobble. Boulton had offered to coin for him after shutting down the Parys Mine mint. But he took forever to get started, and by late spring, he'd turned out only five hundredweight of Willeys—a mere trickle. Wilkinson, desperate for change, turned to John Westwood Sr., who promised to deliver him fifteen hundredweight of coins per week.

Once he tumbled to Wilkinson's plan, Boulton, feeling betrayed, withdrew his services in a huff. Then Westwood proved unable to deliver his quota, let alone make up for Boulton's withdrawal. So, come October, the desperate ironmaster had no choice but to get Boulton—who then had several presses working—to change his mind. Boulton agreed to do so, but not before allowing himself to "discharge a little bile."

> Allow me to remark that I expended more than ten guineas in dies to coin for you . . . and that when I found you had pitted Westwood against me I stopped short, as it would have been cowardly to have run against such a competitor. Splitting of halfpence is the next thing to splitting of farthings. I do not love things in the ½ and ½ way, yet

---

1. Dryden 1681.

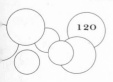

nevertheless if you choose to order any quantity of ½ pence worth engraving new dies for . . . I will contract to make you as many per week
as you please.   (MBP 367/34; SEE ALSO VICE 1990, 3–4)

In accepting Boulton's terms, Wilkinson let loose a little bile of his own.

It has been from inaction or indecision on your part that I have been
obliged to get any [tokens] elsewhere. Independent of my inclination
the execution of your coin would commend my preference. But . . . a
beefsteak to a man that is hungry will be preferred, to venison, when
waiting for it is a condition.   (VICE 1990, 4)

Poor Wilkinson would have to go hungry a little longer, for the ever-
pithering Droz, having made heavy weather of Soho's first Willey dies,
would hold up the new ones as well. Eventually, Dumarest came to the
rescue, allowing Boulton to deliver specimens in December. Wilkinson
found these eyeable enough—they were, after all, faithful copies of Hancock's perfectly good originals.[2] But a rub remained, for so far as Wilkinson was concerned, the coins were too faithful to the originals, being
made to the old Parys Mine Company standard of thirty-two to the
pound. Wilkinson thought this too heavy. "Whatever Politicians and
Statesmen may judge to be a proper standard," he told Boulton, "I shall
incline (until some regulation shall prevent it) to oblige my Customers
particularly where it is so much to my own interest" (MBP 367/41,
quoted in Vice 1990, 4). Wilkinson wanted his coins made to the regal
standard of thirty-six halfpennies per pound, and he wanted them fast: "I
trust . . . that 5 ton of a proper size or rather weight will soon follow—if
you know my distress in the want of Copper I think you would have supplied me sooner" (ibid.).

The significance of this little affair consists of the glimpse it gives us
of the coin situation in England as 1791 approached: the affair reveals
that despite the first onslaught of tokens, including all the Druids, the

2. Dumarest had engraved new matrices based on Hancock's original Willeys. The
master dies for Boulton's first Willey strikings were, in contrast, made by mechanically
copying, or "hubbing," Hancock's own matrices—a procedure that caused Hancock considerable dismay once he learned of it. On April 12, the Birmingham engraver wrote his
former master, regretting "so great a falling off from the generous man," who "by endeav-
oring to get a Hubb from my Die [deprived] me of any further benefits arising from my
Labour." Hancock indicated that he would have charged Boulton all of five pounds to prepare new dies for him, which was a fraction of what Droz asked for in addition to his (all
too generous) salary (MBP 236/103).

change shortage was still going strong. Yet the same affair's denouement a scant two years later paints an utterly different picture. Having by then taken delivery of just over six tons of Soho Willeys, Wilkinson found himself encumbered by a surplus. "There are so many private coinages on foot," Wilkinson informed Boulton in November 1792, "that I cannot vend in my own works one-fourth of what would have passed without trouble a year ago. I must decline giving any orders till we meet" (BWP 20/6, quoted in Vice 1990, 5). Wilkinson expected his supplies to last another "two or three months" (ibid.). In fact, they were to last more than a year.

Wilkinson would eventually place two more orders, each for a mere seven casks. But that would be all: by March 1795 (when the last seven casks were delivered), Great Britain had all the Willeys—and, for the most part, all the small change—it needed. "The formerly coin-starved parts of the country," David Dykes (2000, 90) writes, "were, on the whole, well served by tokens." Even Matthew Boulton couldn't help paying tokens an unintentional compliment, by complaining repeatedly that their widespread acceptance was prejudicing his chances of ever receiving a regal coinage contract (Vice 1990, 3).

In a word, private-sector coiners had solved Britain's big small-change problem.

Every Man His Own Mint Master

Or so it seemed, at least for a time. Besides meeting the coinage needs of manufacturing districts, the first "industrial" tokens, especially Druids, earned the status of "money of the realm," circulating as widely as regal copper (as stray finds attest) and being everywhere preferred to it (W. Davis 1904, xiv; Byng 1970, 167, 172).[3] "Such is the amazing estimation the money of Anglesey is held in here," a Liverpool correspondent told *The Gentleman's Magazine* (February 25, 1789), "that you will really seldom meet with a Tower halfpenny, and even these are refused if a pretext for so doing can possibly be suggested." The Black Country was, as

---

3. A register of coin finds kept by the National Museum in Cardiff, for instance, shows that, besides being well-served by Druids, both North and South Wales witnessed the circulation of (often considerable) quantities of tokens issued in various English counties and, more surprisingly, by the Irish mining companies. Scottish finds similarly attest to the circulation of various English tokens there. Based on such finds, Ken Elks affirms (personal correspondence, February 25, 2006) that many commercial coins circulated "well outside the immediate area where they were issued."

we've seen, replete with Willeys and other tokens,[4] while Wales itself was, of course, well stocked with both Druids and Macclesfield halfpennies. "All the copper coin in Wales," John Ferrar (1796) wrote while traveling there in August 1795," "is heavy and good." In Ireland, the "Cronebane" halfpennies of the Associated Irish & Hibernian Mine Company—Roe & Company's sister operation—together with "Camacs" issued by its bitter rival, the Hibernian Mining Company, almost entirely replaced regal coin and would continue doing so well into the nineteenth century (M. Smith 2002). Tradesman's tokens even found their way to North America, whose cash-starved merchants welcomed them just as warmly as their British counterparts.

The early "industrial" tokens were just the beginning, for their success brought forth a flood of new entrants into the business. The commissioning and issuing of commercial coins, which had been the preserve of a few industrial and mining firms, was taken up by all sorts of small businessmen—grocers, drapers, silversmiths, malsters, and pretty much anyone whose dealings generated a need for small coin. Well, not just anyone: even small-scale token issuers were almost always persons of good standing in their communities, whose token issues were generally modest in comparison with their capital and command of credit.

The expansion of new token issuers reached its peak in 1794, when sixty-four new tradesmen became coin issuers (Elks 2005, 23). Regal copper, in the meantime, was being resorted to less and less: in a reversal of Gresham's law, good money was driving out bad. "Provincial halfpence are," wrote Dundee coin collector James Wright Jr. in 1795, "the most common current coins of the present day," having "in some districts . . . almost totally supplanted the very base and barbarous national copper currency" (Wright 1797, 1). When, somewhat later, Joseph Moser—a London magistrate fervently opposed to private coinage—offered a Chester merchant three genuine Tower halfpence for some snuff, the merchant coolly informed him that the price was either *six* Tower halfpence or three provincial ones. Moser soon discovered, to his great dismay, that what was true in Chester was true just about everywhere: provincial tokens were "preferred to the true Government halfpence," while official copper was "frequently, and certainly illegally, refused" unless it was "parted with at less than its real value" (Moser 1798, 306).

---

4. Willeys did not disappear entirely from the Black Country for many decades. David Dykes (2004, 174n75) recalls receiving "the odd token" as small change in Swansea back in the 1950s, while Nicolas Mayhew (1999, 104) claims that the odd Willey still turned up in Birmingham's small change a decade later.

By the end of the century, approximately six hundred tons of copper had been consumed in making some forty million commercial pennies, halfpennies, and farthings, collectively worth more than one hundred thousand guineas, which entered the stream of British payments from no fewer than two hundred independent sources (Elks 2005, 36).[5] That was more copper coin, in value terms, than the Royal Mint had issued since 1750, and that's leaving aside anonymous tokens and specious ones aimed at collectors, the nominal value of which was perhaps double that of genuine commercial coins (Wright 1798). A given quantity of commercial tokens also went further than a like quantity of regal copper, because tokens, being redeemable, returned to their sources to be reissued again, whereas regal copper tended to make a one-way trip into retailers' tills or wholesalers' strongboxes, where it piled up uselessly. In economists' jargon, commercial coins had a higher "velocity of circulation" than regal ones.

The government's decision to tolerate commercial coins and to put off indefinitely the reform of its own coinage brought new mints as well as new tokens into being, dashing Boulton's hopes of monopolizing commercial coining by driving Westwood out of business. The first new entrants, Peter Kempson and William Lutwyche, appeared on the scene in 1791 and would eventually rival the Soho mint in the extent of their commissions, catering to more (though typically smaller) clients and manufacturing dozens of tons of tokens. Whereas Westwood and Boulton had waited for coin-starved industrialists to come to them, Kempson and Lutwyche, taking their cue from the button trade, had riders (traveling salesmen) roam the country to drum up trade. Of the new token issues of 1794, for example, seventeen were from Kent, where Lutwyche (or some agent of his) had gone door-to-door (Dykes 2000, 91; Elks 2005, 22–23). Kempson made similar forays into Suffolk, Norfolk, and Essex. Thanks to such marketing efforts, England's less industrial counties secured their own supplies of commercial tokens instead of having to wait for tokens to trickle down from the industrial north. R. C. Bell's (1963, 15) helpful "distribution map" of token issuers (fig. 2) shows clearly how issuers came to be located not just wherever factories and mines were to be found but in populous communities generally.

While they shared similar marketing strategies and scales of operation,

---

5. These figures refer to legitimate commercial tokens only. According to William Davis (1904, xiv), the grand total of eighteenth-century commercial copper issues (including private and political tokens and anonymous tokens for general circulation but excluding regal counterfeits) consumed "many thousand tons of copper."

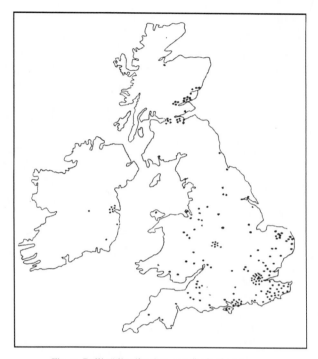

Fig. 2. Bell's "distribution map" of token issuers

Lutwyche and Kempson had little else in common. Although both produced good commercial coins,[6] Kempson is remembered chiefly for his
outstanding series of medallets depicting important buildings in London,
Coventry, and (of course) Birmingham. Lutwyche instead became notorious for his spurious coins, including both regal and commercial counterfeits. Their different bailiwicks accord roughly with the two men's social po-
sitions. Kempson (1755–1824), besides having been a well-established
button maker before and after the token episode, was a respected community figure whose civic contributions included a long stint as a Guardian of
the Poor. He died a "gentleman" at Moseley in 1824, having left his still-

6. Lutwyche's higher-end products included his own private farthings, which are of
special interest because they illustrate some eighteenth-century coinage equipment. One
series shows an old-fashioned coining press with a weighted rod on its reverse, and the goddess Moneta on its obverse; the other shows a screw press with a circular wheel, or "fly," on
its reverse, with Justice seated, holding her balance and pouring coins out of a cornucopia,
on its obverse. The significance of this design will become clear in chapter 8.

flourishing button business in the hands of his son and former partner a year earlier. Lutwyche (christened in 1754) is an obscure figure who listed himself simply as a "Copper Token-maker" in the Birmingham trade directories before dropping out of them altogether after 1801, by which time he'd given up coining. His death seems to have gone unrecorded.

Eventually a score of mints took part in making eighteenth-century commercial coins. Many of them were even more obscure than Lutwyche's.[7] We do know, however, that most of their proprietors started out as button makers and that almost all set up shop in Birmingham (see table 2).

TABLE 2. Manufacturers of Commercial Coins between 1787 and 1797

Mint proprietor/ manufacturer	Mint location	Principal occupation	Known clients	Output (tons)
Matthew Boulton	Soho	Various	17	76.61
Thomas Dobbs	Livery St.	Metal roller	2	1.50
James Good(e)	Lench St.	Button maker	9	1.10
Bonham Hammond	100 Snow Hill	Button maker	1	0.50
John Hands	Sheffield*	Die sinker	3	n.a.
Charles James	Birmingham/London[†]	Die sinker	2	n.a.
John Stubbs Jorden	Birmingham	Die sinker	1	1.00
Peter Kempson	Little Charles St.	Button maker	58	51.95
Joseph Kendrick	36 Great Charles St.	Button maker	3	1.00
William Lutwyche	Temple Row	Die sinker/Toyman	71	66.90
William Mainwaring	Birmingham	Buckle maker	4	2.25
Joseph Merry	Cherry St.	Buckle maker	1	0.07
Thomas Mynd	Whittall St.	Toy maker	5	n.a.
Parys Mine Co.	9 Great Charles St.**	Copper mine	2	300.00
James Pitt	Lancaster St.	Button maker	1	1.15
Peter Skidmore	London	Stove grates	2	0.50
Sam Waring	Bradford St.	Button maker	3	4.25
John Westwood Sr.[††]	20 Great Charles St.	Metal roller	12	82.40
O. & J. Westwood	22 Great Charles St.	Button makers	2	0.15
William Williams	London	Button maker	1	n.a.
Unknown				5.50
Total			200	596.83

Source: Selgin 2003b, 480, with revisions based partly on Dykes 2004, 170.

Note: Street addresses are all in Birmingham. Where Bell lists tokens simply as "scarce" or "common," I have, in the absence of information from other sources, assigned them quantities of zero and ten hundredweight, respectively.

*Possibly Islington, Birmingham.

[†]Moved to London ca. 1790.

**Also Holywell, Flintshire.

[††]In partnership with John Gregory Hancock.

---

7. Two of the small-scale token makers had familial connections to Soho: Thomas Mynd was married to Boulton's sister Catherine, while Thomas Dobbs's daughter married John Southern. Concerning Mynd, see Dykes 2000.

The World's Workshop

Birmingham, Brummagem, Bromwicham, Brymingham, Berminge-
ham—spell it or say it however you please, there is something queer
about the place. Even before the canal boom it managed to become England's preeminent industrial city and was well on its way to becoming
the "workshop of the world." Yet it was located far from sources of the
principal raw materials—especially copper and zinc—upon which most
of its manufacturers relied, and transport was a problem, since it was also
a good distance from any port or navigable river. Birmingham didn't
even have its fair share of streams capable of being reliable sources of
power for its hammers and rolling mills.

How, under the circumstances, did Birmingham manage to attract
and to breed such a disproportionate share of Great Britain's outstanding entrepreneurs, inventors, and skilled artisans? Why, in particular, did
it—and not London or Bristol or Sheffield—manage to become, in Edmund Burke's oft-repeated phrase, the "great toyshop of Europe"?

Although the origins of metalworking in Birmingham remain obscure, they certainly go back beyond the fifteenth century, when the
small village of Birmingham (or whatever the preferred spelling was
then) was already a source of cutting tools, nails, and swords. Until the
end of the seventeenth century, very little growth took place, but during
the eighteenth century, Birmingham acted like a magnet, attracting all
kinds of skilled artisans from every manner of trade, especially experts in
the metal trades. But why Birmingham rather than Sheffield, which was
surrounded by coalfields and good sources of waterpower, or Bristol,
which was more accessible? The explanation given in Drake's 1825 city
guide is as good as any to be had. What set Birmingham apart was, in a
word, freedom. According to Drake Birmingham enjoyed "perfect freedom . . . from all corporate and chartered dignities, honours, immuni-
ties, privileges, and annoyances." He explained further:

> No absurd forms of wearisome servitude are necessary to give the ac-
> tive tradesman a right to practice his art here. . . . The atmosphere of
> this place is free to anyone, and the consequence has been, that it has
> reaped the benefit of active talent and industry, flowing in from all
> quarters.   (DRAKE 1825, 12)

Because it wasn't incorporated, Birmingham (unlike Bristol) became
a haven for Nonconformists after the 1661 Corporation Act excluded
them from membership in town corporations. The Five Mile Act of 1665

enhanced its relative attractiveness by driving Nonconformist ministers out of incorporated towns and cities and their immediate environs. The Test Act of 1673 did its part by excluding intelligent and ambitious Dissenters from civic and municipal offices, thereby inadvertently encouraging them to try their luck in business. Although the Five Mile Act was effectively repealed and the Test Act was much weakened by the Toleration Act of 1689, Birmingham's status as a haven for Nonconformists was by then firmly established. So also was its status as the center of the buckle trade, which religious persecution drove here from its former headquarters in nearby Walsall (Court 1953, 53–60). By the 1780s, buckles had given way to buttons, but in other respects little had changed: Birmingham was still the world's chief source of metal fasteners and toys, and Dissenters continued to infuse the place with entrepreneurial energy (Uglow 2002, 19).

But the contribution of Nonconformists to Birmingham's economy, great as it was, mustn't be exaggerated. After all, most of Birmingham's growth occurred well after 1689, when Birmingham no longer offered Dissenters all that many privileges they couldn't have elsewhere. Nonconformity was, furthermore, hardly a prerequisite for being a successful manufacturer. Thus Kempson was, according to fellow button maker Julius Hardy (himself a Methodist), "a very rigid Establishment man" (Hardy 1973, 61), while Boulton, though he consorted with mavericks (including the controversial Joseph Priestley) and inclined toward deism, regularly attended services at Birmingham's St. Paul's Chapel before being entombed in Handsworth's thoroughly Anglican St. Mary's Church.

If religious freedom alone were all that mattered, Boulton and his fellow coiners might have fared just as well in Sheffield, which was Birmingham's nearest rival in the button trade and was also unincorporated. But Sheffield was held back by the authority of the Cutlers' Company and (after 1750 especially) by the general spread of craft unionism, with its attendant strikes and "rattenings."[8] Despite efforts, starting in 1800, to outlaw them, craft unions would eventually transform Sheffield into the "world's biggest closed shop" (Tweedale 1993, 32). So it was by default that Birmingham became "emphatically the town of 'free trade,' where practically no restrictions, commercial or municipal, were known"

8. Rattening was the practice of confiscating and hiding artisans' tools and wheel bands as punishment for their failure to pay union dues or to abide by union rules.

(Timmins 1866, 211) and where the notion of free trade was even to be extended, however briefly, to the nation's coinage.[9]

From Buttons to Blunt

While the forces that lured the toy trades, including button making, to Birmingham were obscure, the link between button making and coin making was plain as day, for the materials and techniques involved in each were quite similar.[10] In both cases, production began with strips of metal (copper or, for buttons, a blend of brass and tin known as "white metal") cut from rolled sheets. Round planchets, or "blanks," were punched from the strips using small hand-cranked screw presses. The blanks might then be passed through edging machines, either to mark them (as was often done with commercial coins) or simply to round them off. Finally, designs would be struck onto the edged blanks using more powerful presses, the screws on which were tipped with an engraved steel die and engaged by means of a heavily weighted dumbbell-like bar or circular flywheel.

A typical press crew consisted of between three and five men. One tended to the insertion of blanks and the removal of finished buttons; the others gave the flywheel or bar a smart hike, causing the die to spin its way through several revolutions toward a fresh blank resting on the press's lower bedplate or, in the case of coins, on a second die attached to the bedplate. The violent collision of screw and blank yielded a finished button or coin, which, still baking from the force of the blow, would be removed manually or (in the case of more advanced presses) automatically ejected into a hopper upon the rebound of the fly. A new blank would then be inserted, allowing the men to set the press agate once more. An experienced crew might bang along this way for fifteen minutes or so between short breaks.

Of course, buttons, unlike coins, bore designs on their faces only, their "reverses" being reserved for a metal shank. But those designs could be elaborate—so elaborate that a gross of gilt livery buttons might

---

9. Readers wishing to know more about what Birmingham was like not long after the private coinage episode may wish to consult an earlier, lengthier version of this section, which takes a "ramble" through that town as it was in 1829. This version is available on the author's Web site, at http://www.terry.uga.edu/~selgin/documents/Ramble.pdf.

10. On the similar manufacturing processes involved in copper coining and metal button making, see, for example, the essays "Buttons" and "Coining" in Rees 1786.

fetch 140 guineas, or more than one pound sterling per button (Hutton cited in Anonymous 1852, 346). That may seem like an outrageous price to pay just to add a little glitter to a footman's coattails. But one need only look at some of these buttons at the Birmingham Museum, or at the Victoria & Albert, to see that they could be genuine works of art, far surpassing in sheer ornateness the best of their numismatic cousins.[11]

Button making was typically a cottage industry, with most masters taking on one or two journeymen only. A few large-scale firms did exist—the most famous, John Taylor's, was so large that its metal sweepings alone were worth one thousand pounds annually—but these were exceptional. Here, too, commercial coining resembled button making, with a relatively large number of small operations competing with several large ones. Because intense competition afforded no opportunities for complacency, technical innovations were pursued by both small and large button makers, who accounted for a substantial share of the many patents granted to Birmingham entrepreneurs: during the last decades of the eighteenth century, scarcely a year passed when a patent wasn't granted to at least one of them (Prosser 1881, 55).[12] Among other sorts of patents were ones related to improved screw presses and stamping equipment, six of which were issued between 1761 and 1800.[13] Of course, for every patented innovation, there were (then as now) numerous others for which no patents were sought (Berg 1994, 269). It seems safe to assume, therefore, that even small-scale button makers furnished themselves with efficient machines, many of which also came from Birmingham, including "fast thread" presses that could close dies with a quarter turn only (instead of two complete turns) and presses equipped with automatic blank feeders.[14]

---

11. Gilding added little to the cost of buttons, as it took only five grains of gold to gild a gross of them (D. P. White 1977, 70). At least one commercial coin, Lutwyche's West Cowes halfpenny, is said to have been made using a livery button die to which a legend had been added (Samuel [1881–83] 1994, August 31, 1881).

12. Birmingham button makers secured seventy patents between 1770 and 1852. Of these, fourteen were issued between 1785 and 1800.

13. Before 1785, 111 patents had been granted to various Birmingham businesses for improvements in stamping and pressing techniques. In 1804, John Gregory Hancock secured a patent for a cam-driven "fly press" that allowed for repeated strikes through continuous rotation of the fly in one direction (Prosser 1881, 136). Hancock also secured various patents unrelated to stamping or coining. Of the other coin makers, John Westwood Sr., his brother Obadiah, James Stubbs Jorden, and (of course) Matthew Boulton each has at least one patent to his name.

14. According to Spilman (1982), by the early 1780s, even American counterfeiters were employing sophisticated screw presses.

Yet, important as novel machinery was to the button trade, the real key to that trade's efficiency was its heavy reliance on division of labor. Adam Smith's famous illustration of division of labor came from a Birmingham pin factory, where ten persons could make "upwards of forty-thousand pins in a day" (Smith [1776] 1925, 7). Smith might have made his point still more forcefully by referring to button making. "[Y]ou will perhaps think it incredible," a 1755 visitor to Taylor's button factory wrote a friend in London, "when I tell you they [the buttons] go thro' 70 different Operations of 70 different Work-Folk" (Hopkins 1989, 6–7).[15] Such thorough exploitation of gains from division of labor was perhaps the most important technical innovation of the last half of the eighteenth century, albeit one that has, despite Adam Smith's efforts, been overshadowed by various nifty but arguably less consequential mechanical inventions (ibid., p. 39).

Among their other talents, Birmingham manufacturers enjoyed a reputation for being able to leap from trade to trade or to pursue several trades at once, according to the market's dictates (Everseley 1964, 89). An old Birmingham song touts this versatility:

> I'm a roving Jack of all trades,
> Of every trade and all trades,
> And if you want to know my name,
> They call me Jack of all trades . . .
>
> In Swallow Street made bellows-pipes,
> In Wharf Street was a blacksmith;
> In Beak Street there I did sell tripe,
> In Freeman Street a locksmith.
> In Cherry Street I was a quack,
> In Summer Lane sold pancakes;
> And then at last I got a knack
> To manufacture worm cakes.[16]

---

15. Lord Shelburne, who visited Taylor's in 1766, was likewise impressed by its reliance on division of labor, which he described as involving only fifty steps (perhaps less-fancy buttons were involved) and which, he said, made producing buttons "so simple that, five times in six, children of six or eight years old do it as well as men, and earn from ten pence to eight shillings a week" (Court 1953, 40). Adam Smith himself refers to button making both in *The Wealth of Nations* ([1776] 1925, 10) and in his *Lectures on Justice, Police, Revenue, and Arms* ([1763] 1896, 255). In the latter work, he has the labor involved divided among eighty persons.

16. "Birmingham Jack of all Trades," in Raven 1977, 178–80.

So any Birmingham button maker could easily turn mint master. Indeed, only button makers were permitted to have screw presses, ownership of which had been generally banned back in February 1662. Although Royal Mint authorities were supposed to destroy any screw press discovered beyond the confines of the Tower (Craig 1953, 159), they could think of better ways of enjoying their sinecures. The government, in turn, realized that strict observance of its directive, had it been possible at all, would destroy the button industry. So officials turned a blind eye Birmingham's way, allowing it to become a capital not just of button making but also of private coining, both licit and illicit. In pointing to Birmingham as the source of most British counterfeit coins, Patrick Colquhoun (1800, 172) observed how "ingenious improvements" in button-making technique were "easily applied to the coining and colouring of false money." Not for nothing were fake British copper coins known as "Birmingham buttons," or just plain "buttons."

Enduring Impressions

Although Birmingham's Johnny-come-lately token makers catered mainly to small clients and made their tokens in correspondingly small batches, their tokens were similar in all essential respects to those that came before. The vast majority were halfpennies, with some pennies and farthings, all cut to standards not far from (and sometimes surpassing) the regal standard. Virtually all of them were made of copper.

The almost exclusive emphasis on copper tokens seems paradoxical in light of the inconvenience of copper as a medium for wage payments. At the Tower standard of forty-six halfpennies to one pound of copper, ten shillings—a typical week's earnings by the 1790s—translated into over five pounds of tokens, not counting the weight of the paper *rouleaux* in which they were bundled. In practice, of course, wages were seldom paid entirely in copper. Still, even the most considerate employers were hard pressed to keep the copper component at less than half their total wage payments, let alone keeping it at or below the legal limit of six pence per pay packet.

Why, then, didn't the private sector turn out more convenient, silver tokens? Although Peter Mathias (2004) treats the focus on copper as evidence both of the growing importance of retail sales and of the fact that regal silver wasn't so scarce as is often supposed, the truth is that silver was even scarcer than copper. Silver tokens weren't made not because silver wasn't really all that scarce but because few dared to circulate private silver pieces, for which there was no historic (let alone legal) precedent. Wilkinson flirted with the idea back in 1788; and Colonel John Fullarton was about to give it a try ten years later—with tokens bearing the portrait bust of the Prince of Wales—when Sir Joseph Banks talked him out of it (Dykes 2002). Fullarton's attempt would not be the last, for at length, silver tokens—and plenty of them—were issued. But that story comes later.

The other thing most eighteenth-century tokens had in common, which set them apart both from regal coins and from earlier tokens, was their extraordinary appearance. According to Francis Klingender, whose *Art and the Industrial Revolution* (1947) remains the outstanding work on its subject, the tokens displayed a unique "combination of intellectual vigor, social consciousness and imaginative design" (Klingender 1953, 46). Nor did Klingender, a hard-line Marxist, object to private coins' celebration of British capitalists. "It is only fitting," he says, "to find portraits of men like Roe or Wilkinson in the place that had hitherto been reserved for the likenesses of sovereign princes." Equally fitting, in Klingender's view, are the "robust" allegorical figures of Industry, Commerce, and Fame found on many tokens, for these lack "that self-conscious mawkishness which distinguishes the same symbols in Victorian designs" (ibid., 41). The Victorian coins of which Klingender speaks were, of course, not commercial but official productions.

Many of Klingender's favorite tokens were designed by John Gregory Hancock. Like many other great Birmingham die sinkers, Hancock apprenticed at Soho, his father having bound him to Boulton in 1763, when he was just thirteen (MBP 236/102). He undertook his first token commissions, including the original Parys Mine Druids, as John Westwood Sr.'s business partner and front man. Hancock's Druids, displaying (in Klingender's words) a pleasing "combination of severely classical forms with Ossianic romanticism" (Klingender 1953, 43), got things off on a high note. But when Hancock turned to his next project—Wilkinson's Willeys—he traded classical symbolism for a blend of gritty realism and industrial publicity that would form the pattern for many tokens to come. Although most issuers didn't go so far as to put their own portraits on their coins, many followed Wilkinson's lead in depicting their factories and storefronts or "the latest achievements of industrial technique," through engravings "masterly in their clear and harmonious presentation" (ibid., 41–43). In some instances, the detail is stunning: factory interiors are depicted brick by brick; ships are rigged down to the last ratline; and engravings of machines seem fit for a patent specification.

Have a look, for example, at the Plymouth halfpennies of Shepheard

Dove, Hammett & Company—a hemp and flax manufactory founded, according to Bell (1963, 30), "as a philanthropic venture to give employment to the poor, and to provide for the education and clothing of indigent children." The coins, which were struck by Lutwyche, celebrate Plymouth's sailcloth industry: a woman spins yarn on their reverse, while a man weaves the yarn into canvas on their obverse. Or consider the Westwoods' Thames & Severn Canal tokens, another Hancock design, with a Severn trow under sail and flying the Union Jack on the obverse and a meticulous rendering of the Sapperton Tunnel on the reverse. Then there are the Coalbrook-dale Iron Company tokens, engraved by Thomas Wyon and manufactured by Kempson, with Ironbridge on their obverse and Ketley's inclined plane engine, with its immense flywheel, on their reverse. Behold, above all, the splendid Carmarthen halfpennies issued by John Morgan—yet another ironmaster. Their faces, once again John Gregory Hancock's work, show painstaking interior scenes of men raking coals and working a tilt hammer. It is, of course, not possible to engrave heat. But someone forgot to tell Hancock.[17]

Two other token engravers, the brothers Peter and Thomas Wyon, deserve special mention for the indirect part they played in the improvement of Great Britain's official coins. Like Hancock, the Wyons had a Soho connection: their father, George Wyon III, worked at Soho's Silver, Plated, and Ormulu Goods department until 1783 or 1784, when he set up his own die-engraving business (Quickenden 1995, 356). During the 1790s, Peter and Thomas, having learned the trade from their father, sank dies for many copper tokens and also for Kempson's medallets, with Peter specializing in the former and Thomas in the latter.

After their father's death in 1797, the brothers turned the family business over to their younger sibling, George Wyon IV, and went their

---

17. After Westwood's death in 1792, Hancock went on making dies for Obadiah Westwood, including those for some American pattern cents. He had the help of his apprentice John Stubbs Jorden until 1795. Then Hancock struck out on his own, becoming the town's most sought-after token engraver. But Hancock's health, which was never robust, declined after the turn of the century, and he passed away at fifty-five on November 11, 1805. His death was, according to *Aris's Birmingham Gazette* (November 11, 1805) "sincerely lamented by all the friends and patrons of genius." Although Hancock Sr. is generally considered to have been Birmingham's best token designer, his son John Gregory Jr. appeared likely to eclipse him at one point, having engraved the dies for several private tokens at the turn of the century, when he was not even ten years old. But while John Gregory Jr. is listed among Birmingham's "artists" in Bisset's *Magnificent Directory* (1808), for which he supplied several engravings, attempts to discover what became of him after that, including the attempt of token collector and cataloger Thomas Sharp (who looked into the matter in 1834), have come to naught.

separate ways. Peter stayed in Birmingham, where he and his son William (whom he'd apprenticed in 1810) made dies for many nineteenth-century commercial coins. Thomas moved to London, where he managed, thanks to the recommendation of the Privy Council Committee on Coin, to land the post of chief engraver of seals at the refurbished Royal Mint on Little Tower Hill. His son and apprentice, Thomas Jr., followed him there in 1811 and proved so talented that the mint made him its youngest chief engraver ever, at the extraordinary age of twenty-three. Shortly afterward, William Wyon, having completed his apprenticeship, was made second engraver. Tragically, Thomas Jr. died in September 1817, at only twenty-five, leaving the chief engraver's post temporarily vacant. Eventually, William would fill it, securing the dynasty that would dominate British coin engraving for the rest of the nineteenth century.[18]

Designs like those engraved by Hancock and the Wyons had the unintended effect of turning commercial coins into valuable historical documents. "Issued by the people, they tell of the people, and become imperishable records of that most important estate of the realm. . . . They indicate to us their occupations and their skills, their customs and modes of life," says Llewellyn Jewitt, the famous nineteenth-century Derby antiquarian, as quoted by economic historian Peter Mathias (1979, 191). Mathias himself goes even further: for him, the tokens make up nothing less than an "illustrated history of the Industrial Revolution" (ibid.). Supporting this view is Mathias's own fine, 1962 volume combining color photographs of various tokens with his own expert commentary.[19]

To suggest that all or most tokens depicted scenes of industry or commerce would, however, be quite misleading, for in truth their designs run a cultural gamut.

> The devices shewn upon them were legion. . . . Effigies of kings, queens, bishops, peers, statesmen, warriors, men of mark in science, art and literature, . . . commemorations of national or local events; presentments of natural objects . . . and of man's ingenuity in cathedral, college, fort, harbour, ship, mine, factory and canal; graven structures of antiquity . . . ; pieces of theological, political, or social satire; quaint advertisements of exhibitions, businesses, or wares; men

---

18. Forrer's *Biographical Dictionary of Medallists* (1970, vol. 6) devotes over one hundred pages to Wyons. For further details, see Carlisle 1837; Sainthill 1844; Sainthill 1853.

19. See also Whiting 1971, which, though lacking color plates, includes descriptions (with black-and-white photographs) of seventeenth- and nineteenth-century tokens as well as eighteenth-century ones.

depicted at work at various trades, or angling, shooting, orating and
boxing; birds, beasts, fishes, insects, plants and flowers; arms, crests,
flags and emblems; musical instruments and musical notation.

(W. DAVIS 1904, XIV)

Nor was every commercial coin a work of art: some are rather desultory
affairs, displaying nothing apart from some city's arms and a cipher. Still,
taken as a whole, commercial coin designs far surpassed those found on
the vast majority of coins from government mints. Wright (1798) made
this point by posing a rhetorical question.

If even one-third only of the number of these tokens be allowed to be
estimable from variety of design, interesting objects represented, or
good execution, can the same be justly said of a like number of any series, in any metal, of any of the national coinages of kings in modern
Europe from the days of Cunobeline?[20]

Wright had no doubt concerning the answer to be expected from "every
reader intelligent on the subject and unfettered by prejudice."[21]

Why did the private sector turn out such nice coins? It did so, first of
all, because nice coins were good publicity. At a time when there was no
national press and when advertisements still consisted of mere notices,
tokens "were one of the few media where persuasive—even aggressive—

---

20. Cunobelin, or Cunobelinus, was a Celtic king of Britain (and the inspiration for
Shakespeare's Cymbeline), whose gold staters are much admired by numismatists.

21. In his "fictional biography" of Wright's feminist daughter Fanny, Edmund White
(2003) describes James Wright as "the worst sort of freethinker . . . who would have been
arrested for belonging to the infamous Friends of the People, a communistical phalanstary
in Edinburgh, had he not ridden, all alone, one misty night, out into the murky Tay, where
he drowned his devilish papers." White adds:

Mr Wright belonged to several numismatics clubs and possessed very valuable
coins; typical of his Jacobin views, he wondered why the public mints employed "the
silly morsels of heraldry" in designing coins rather than "emblems of industry and
commerce." Doubtless he wanted our shillings not to present the royal profiles but
to show milkmaids plying swollen teats, and our crowns to enshrine dustmen wad-
ing through ordure.

White's accusation is unfair. There are, first of all, no teats whatsoever on Wright's Dundee
halfpennies, which featured buildings and other mundane subjects. (The reverses of
Wright's rarer penny pieces did, however, depict Eve handing Adam an apple.) More generally, Wright, while disapproving of heraldic devices, favored (apart from "emblems of industry and commerce") depictions of outstanding buildings, great modern works, and il-
lustrious characters (Wright 1797, 1–4). For a more objective assessment of Wright as a
numismatist, see Dykes 1996.

advertising could flourish" (Mathias 1962, 36). Although every token was good for some sort of publicity, the treatment of tokens as advertising platforms is most obvious in some tokens issued by retailers. The reverses of the tokens issued by rags-to-riches London book dealer James Lackington, for instance, proclaimed him "Cheapest Bookseller in the World," in a legend surrounding the figure of Fame caught taking a breather from blowing her (i.e., Lackington's) horn. Engaging and attractive commercial coins (no less than engaging and attractive print ads today) reflected well on the enterprises they represented, while shoddy coins did just the opposite. For this reason, most coin issuers didn't hesitate to spend a few extra guineas on top-notch dies. Commercial mints had to in turn vie with one another for the services of Birmingham's best die sinkers.

But private coin issuers had a second, still more practical reason for commissioning coins of the highest possible quality. Such coins were harder to counterfeit, or to counterfeit convincingly. Their issuers were therefore better able to spot fakes and thus avoid redeeming them.

Of course, coin issuers profited most of all when even authentic coins never came back to them, for then their profit was equal to the full difference between their outlay on the coins and the coins' face value. Token collecting therefore gave coin issuers a third reason for making attractive and interesting coins. At first, this reason didn't matter much, because collectors tended to ignore commercial coins. But they could hardly go on ignoring them once they became Great Britain's principal change, especially in light of their outstanding engravings. So look they did; and no sooner had they done so than they found themselves hopelessly smitten.

Token Mania

Richard Doty (1986, 5–6) has likened the eighteenth-century commercial coinage story to a play in three acts. Act I, which lasted until 1791, involved the striking of tokens by and for leading industrialists, including Williams, Wilkinson, and Boulton. Act II, which lasted for the next three or four years, saw the entry of new mints and the spread of token issuing to small businesses all around the country.

Act III opened with a craze in token collecting that took off in 1794. According to Wright (1798), who took part in token collecting both as a collector and as a token designer, the collecting craze was a natural response to commercial coins' singular features.

Such extreme attachment cannot possibly be excited, but where there exists a high degree of esteem for its object; nor shall we wonder that this esteem should be great, if we coolly appreciate the real dignity and usefulness of COINS and MEDALS, which aspire to some *striking* and *superlative* characteristics.

Collectors went to great lengths to acquire specimens of every sort of commercial coin, paying a premium for rare and artistic pieces and eagerly looking forward to new issues (W. Davis 1904, xiv).

What the collectors did not anticipate (and would certainly not have welcomed) was the profound influence their innocent pastime would have on the future course of commercial coining. "Token mania" was to give rise to a plethora of new tokens, most of which were never meant to serve as money. Once they realized that tokens were being acquired to be put in curio cabinets, coin makers and issuers went to more pains than ever to endow them with attractive or otherwise desirable engravings. But that was the least of it, for once they realized that collectors couldn't resist a rare token, the private mints started making runs of tokens aimed exclusively at them. Before long, the market was being flooded with "instant rarities" (the phrase is Richard Doty's), including deliberate mutations of genuine trade tokens. Some of these bore altered legends or edge markings and issuer's names that were either misspelled, entirely fictitious, or randomly "plucked from some [trade] directory" (Elks 2005, 29). The redemption pledges carried by such "specious" tokens— if they bore such—were of course bogus. Most specious tokens were so-called mules, which were made by combining the obverse die from one genuine trade token with the reverse die from another. The advantage of mules was that they allowed private mints to use dies already on hand to cater to gullible collectors, while nonetheless evading the charge of having actually counterfeited any client's coins.

Besides specious tokens, including mules, commercial mints also made some legitimate products that were never meant to circulate. These included personal or "private" tokens commissioned by collectors for trade among themselves and series of "medallets" resembling tokens, though sold directly by the mints to the public. The most famous of the latter were the "buildings" series of Kempson and Peter Skidmore (see Bell 1978).[22] Finally, there were so-called political tokens, which (as their name suggests) served the same purpose as campaign buttons.

---

22. Skidmore specialized in such medallets—issuing only one circulating token out of some two hundred products.

Unlike genuine trade tokens, tokens made especially for collectors were sold directly to dealers in collectable coins—especially to unscrupulous ones—who sold the tokens to collectors at a premium. Tokens with crisp engravings and of good weight commanded the highest premiums, other things equal; so many specious tokens were, unlike counterfeits, actually of good quality. Most were also made in small (if not minute) quantities, because to have flooded the market with them would have defeated their purpose (Elks 2005, 29): if a token was rare enough, collectors might pay as much as one or two guineas for it, or several hundred times its face value, provided they didn't suspect it of being fraudulent. Private tokens, being both exceptionally rare and exceptionally well made, commanded the highest premiums, with some private farthings fetching as much as five pounds (ibid.).

Although some commercial mints were especially active in the collectors' market (Lutwyche, for instance, was a notorious mule maker), every mint took part in the collecting craze in one way or another. That the Soho Mint was no exception is evident from a number of its commissions, including the halfpennies it struck for Lancaster coin collector Daniel Eccleston in 1794. Besides being "exceptionally massive and fine" (Bell 1963, 82), Eccleston's tokens, which showed his bust on their obverse and a ship moored behind a plow and flying shuttle on their reverse, had unusually broad, legend-bearing raised rims that were to be incorporated into Boulton's first regal coins.[23] Fancier still than Eccleston's coins were the ones Soho made for Captain George Chapman's Penryn Volunteers, the last specimens of which were delivered just before Soho turned its attention to striking decidedly less ornate regal coins.

Token mania didn't last long: it reached its peak after only a year or

---

23. Peculiar as this device was, it wasn't nearly as odd as Eccleston himself, a lapsed Quaker. Having squandered his fortune on his coin collection, he never paid Boulton—although (to give the man his due) he did eventually send the great man's son a half dozen coconuts, which were hard to come by back then (Doty 1998, 311). The *Lancaster Gazette* published Eccleston's obituary in 1816, only to receive a note, supposedly from heaven, correcting some biographical details and signed:

Daniel Belteshazzar
  Fitz-William
    Caracticus
      Cadwallador
        Llewellyn
          Ap-Tudor
            Plantagenet
              ECCLESTON.

so (Doty 1986). Then a lull set in, prompted no doubt by the exploding variety of tokens—especially fake tokens, which tried collectors' patience while exposing them to ridicule. Even commercial coin dealers themselves couldn't resist having a laugh at the expense of naive collectors, as London's Matthew Denton did by issuing a specious token showing two men facing each other, surrounded by the legend "WE THREE BLOCK-HEADS BE." Small wonder, then, that collectors lost heart. Although token collecting never quite stopped, a century was to pass before a genuine revival began, which is still going strong today.

Confusion Worse Confounded?

Some numismatists claim that thanks mainly to the collecting craze, the overall quality of Great Britain's commercial coinage deteriorated over time. A few even go so far as to declare that commercial coins ended up being no better than the regal copper they were intended to supersede. According to this view, Gresham's law, having briefly and mysteriously taken leave, came back with a vengeance.

Thus Samuel Hamer ([1904] 2000, 20) says that although commercial coins at first displayed "a decided advantage" over their regal counterparts, eventually they "became a nuisance." This happened, Ken Elks (2005, 25) tells us, because the "free-for-all" triggered by the collecting craze caused better tokens to be shoved aside by "large amount of almost worthless money." By 1797, he adds, things were "so far out of hand . . . that finally the government was forced to take action," by giving Boulton the coining contract for which he'd been clamoring and by outlawing private tokens (ibid.). Bell (1963, 10, 59) and Doty (1986) likewise claim that tokens were outlawed in 1797, in part owing to the deterioration of their quality.

But the government didn't outlaw tokens in 1797 and would not outlaw them for another two decades. Furthermore (as will be seen in the next chapter), the state of Great Britain's commercial coinage had very little to do with the governments' decision to award Boulton a coinage contract. Finally, the underlying claim that Britain's commercial coinage was going to wrack and ruin is itself, at best, a half-truth.

The claim appears to involve three more specific assertions: first, that tokens were widely counterfeited; second, that the quality of authentic tokens deteriorated over time; and third, that numerous token sources and types led to utter chaos—much like that caused by the clans described in Milton's *Paradise Lost.*

Of each his faction, in their several clans,
Light-armed or heavy, sharp, smooth, swift, or slow,
Swarm populous, unnumbered as the sands
Of Barca or Cyrene's torrid soil.[24]

Let's examine each assertion in turn.

Concerning counterfeits, we've seen how they infiltrated and infected the regal copper coinage. The counterfeiting of redeemable commercial tokens should have been even more destructive, because it would have deprived legitimate token issuers of any means for limiting their liabilities, making them no better off than so many issuers of signed blank checks. Yet far from having been ruined, legitimate token issuers don't even appear to have been phased by counterfeiting. Some issues were kept going for years, while new issuers kept appearing. So far as available records indicate, no token issuer was ever driven to bankruptcy or otherwise embarrassed on account of fake tokens.

Tokens were counterfeited—no mistake. Here, Lutwyche was once again a major culprit, having made a large number of counterfeits, including some of the best. "The true extent of Lutwyche's token counterfeiting," Elks (2005, 17) writes, "has been, perhaps, largely unappreciated, since some of [his fakes] were so well-made that they have been accepted as genuine." These high-quality fakes included Willeys and Camacs as well as tokens issued by the Birmingham Mining & Copper Company.

But counterfeiting didn't do much harm to genuine token issuers, because convincing counterfeits, such as Lutwyche's, were exceptional: the vast majority of counterfeit tokens were *obviously* fake. Many announced themselves through the crudity of their engravings. But the most obvious giveaway was their weight. According to Elks (2005, 38), whose conclusions are based on a painstaking study of nearly eight thousand extant tokens, token counterfeits are almost always a quarter to a third lighter than the genuine tokens they imitate. Such "scandalously light" tokens were, according to a contemporary observer, "easily distinguished from the genuine ones" (*GM*, January 1795, 34): because counterfeits were cut to the same diameter as genuine tokens, spotting them was just a matter of observing their thinness. Obvious token counterfeits were probably accepted on the same basis as shoddy (including fake) Tower copper—that is, as a stopgap in places lacking adequate supplies of real commercial coins.

---

24. Milton, *Paradise Lost*, book 2.

Also, the quantity of counterfeit tokens was, to quote our contemporary source again, "trifling in comparison with the Birmingham halfpence [i.e., fake Tower halfpence] formerly in circulation" (ibid., 33–34). Most tokens were never counterfeited at all. The exceptions were almost all tokens issued on a large scale, including all the industrial issues of the first "act" of the commercial coinage episode (Elks 2005, 165–67). According to David Dykes (2004, 168), the "very ubiquity" of these tokens "attracted the attention of the counterfeiting fraternity on a considerable scale." Because they involved numerous authentic die variants, large-scale issues made it harder to keep track of frauds by comparing coins.

Yet even the most prominent of all private tokens were never counterfeited on a scale approaching that which undermined the regal copper coinage. Thus, among a thousand-odd tokens supposedly issued by the Parys Mine Company, Elks discovered only forty-two counterfeits— or just four times the rate of counterfeits among British one-pound coins today.[25] The low figure is no doubt due in part to collectors' diligence, but that diligence reflects the relative ease with which Druid fakes could be identified. The far greater incidence of counterfeit regal copper coin reflects, first, the fact that regal coins were made on a still larger scale than Druids and, second, the fact that the Royal Mint's relative lack of die-making expertise gave rise to especially large numbers of legitimate regal coin variants. Moreover, as we've seen, the deteriorated state of most outstanding regal coins made copying them convincingly mere child's play.

The prevalence of "industrial token" counterfeits may also have reflected a decline in the production of counterfeits over time. That decline occurred in part because the multiplication of legitimate small-scale token issues eroded the scope for counterfeiting, both by reducing the market for fake tokens and by reducing the share of tokens that lent themselves to faking. As David Dykes (2004, 172) explains, small-scale issues enjoyed a local circulation only, which depended on their being routinely redeemed. For the most part, they moved quickly from their source to local inns and alehouses and then back again, allowing frauds to be discovered in short order. Counterfeiters therefore left them alone, and it was precisely for that reason that local issues came to be preferred to nonlocal ones, even when the latter were (purportedly) from firms of great standing. "When the principal tradesman of Norwich and

---

25. Ken Elks, personal correspondence, February 25, 2006.

Coining at the Tower Mint.
(Courtesy of Science Museum/Science & Society Picture Library.)

George II halfpennies: *left,* fine; *middle,* worn; *right,* counterfeit.
(Reproduced from originals held by the Department of Special Collections of the University Libraries of Notre Dame.)

John Westwood's medallion for the Shakespeare Jubilee.
(Courtesy of Birmingham Assay Office.)

Thomas Williams.
(Portrait by Sir Thomas Lawrence. Courtesy of Amgueddfa Genedlaethol Cymru, National Museum of Wales.)

Westwood's pattern Druid.
(Courtesy of Dr. Gary Sriro.)

Early collar-struck Parys Mine Druid penny, as issued for circulation. The dies were engraved by John Gregory Hancock. *(Courtesy of Dr. Gary Sriro.)*

Rare 1788 silver Willey.
(Courtesy of Ken Elks.)

John Wilkinson.
(Portrait after Lemuel Francis Abbott. Courtesy of National Portrait Gallery, London.)

The Soho Manufactory.
(Courtesy of Science Museum/Science & Society Picture Library.)

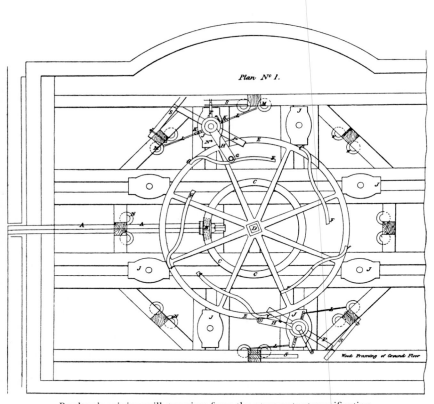

Boulton's coining mill, top view, from the 1790 patent specification.
(From the U.K. Patent Office Library. Reproduced by kind permission of the Science Library, Birmingham Central Library.)

John-Pierre Droz.
(After a portrait medallion by Eugène Dubois. ©
Bibliothèque Publique et Universitaire, Neuchâtel.)

Matthew Boulton.
(Portrait by William Sharp, after Sir William Beechey.
Courtesy of National Portrait Gallery, London.)

William Pitt.
(Portrait by J. Hoppner. Courtesy of James Smith Noel Collection,
Louisiana State University in Shreveport.)

Charles Jenkinson, Baron Hawkesbury.
(Cropped version of portrait by Charles Warren,
after Charles Benazech. Courtesy of National
Portrait Gallery, London.)

The first steam-struck coins: *top,* Macclesfield halfpenny; *bottom,* Cronebane halfpenny.
(Courtesy of Dr. Gary Sriro.)

Droz's pattern halfpenny, a later restrike of the coin presented to George III in March 1788.
(Courtesy of Bill McKivor.)

Halfpennies: *top*, Coalbrookdale; *middle*, Carmarthen; *bottom*, Deal.
(Courtesy of Dr. Gary Sriro.)

Peter Kempson's Soho Manufactory token, from his "Views of Birmingham" series.
(Courtesy of Birmingham Museum & Art Gallery.)

Caveat emptor: "1784" Parys Mine Druid, made to snare gullible collectors.
(Courtesy of Bill McKivor.)

Reverses poking fun at collectors, from the private tokens of London coin dealer Matthew Denton.
(Courtesy of Dr. Gary Sriro.)

Post-Fishguard official coins: *top*, countermarked Spanish dollar; *middle*, 1797 "cartwheel" penny; *bottom*, 1799 halfpenny. *(Courtesy of Birmingham Museum & Art Gallery* [top] *and Bill McKivor* [middle and bottom].*)*

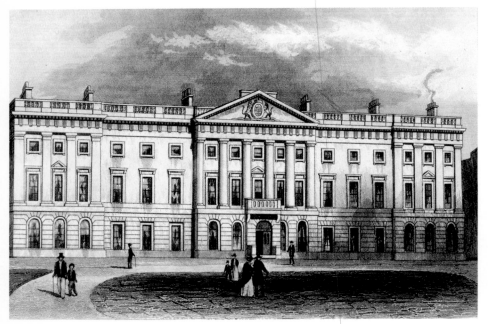

The new Royal Mint at Little Tower Hill.
(Courtesy of Royal Mint Museum.)

Soho's 1804 Bank dollar, which
gave impetus to the Royal Mint
reform. *(Courtesy of Ken Elks.)*

The coining room at the new Royal Mint.
(Courtesy of Royal Mint Museum.)

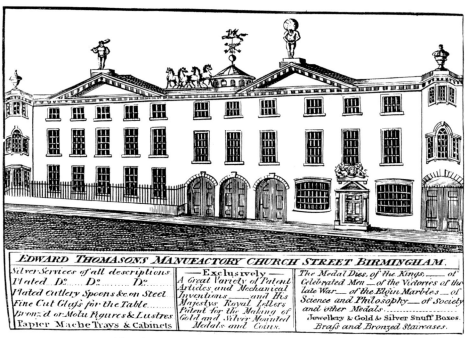

EDWARD THOMASON'S MANUFACTORY CHURCH STREET BIRMINGHAM.

Silver Services of all descriptions	—Exclusively—	The Medal Dies, of the Kings,____of
Plated D.º D.º D.º	A Great Variety of Patent	Celebrated Men ___ of the Victories of the
Plated Cutlery Spoons &c on Steel	Articles and Mechanical	late War ___ of the Elgin Marbles ___ of
Fine Cut Glass for the Table	Inventions____and His	Science and Philosophy ___ of Society
Bronz'd or Molu Figures & Lustres	Majestys Royal Letters	and other Medals
Papier Mache Trays & Cabinets	Patent for the Making of	Jewellery & Gold & Silver Snuff Boxes
	Gold and Silver Mounted	Brass and Bronzed Staircases.
	Medals and Coins.	

Advertisement for Edward Thomason's manufactory.
(From West 1830.)

Sir Edward Thomason.
*(Portrait by William Brockedon. Courtesy of
National Portrait Gallery, London.)*

Thomason's token for Bilston ironmaster
Samuel Fereday. *(Courtesy of Ken Elks.)*

Bilston silver sixpence token.
(Courtesy of Birmingham Assay Office.)

Crown Copper Company penny.
(Courtesy of Ken Elks.)

Birmingham workhouse copper sixpence token.
(Courtesy of Birmingham Assay Office.)

Troublesome token: "Henry Morgan" shilling "Issu'd by Royal Licence."
(Courtesy of Royal Maritime Museum.)

Troublesome token: John Berkeley Monck's forty-shilling gold token.
(Courtesy of American Numismatic Society.)

Spencer Perceval.
(Portrait by George Francis Joseph. Courtesy of National Portrait Gallery, London.)

Pascoe Grenfell.
(Portrait by Sir Martin Archer Shee. Courtesy of City and County of Swansea: Swansea Museum.)

James Maitland, eighth Earl of Lauderdale.
(Portrait after Thomas Gainsborough. Courtesy of National Portrait Gallery, London.)

Obverse of token maker William Lutwyche's private token, showing a manual screw press. *(Courtesy of Dr. Gary Sriro.)*

George IV crown, designed by William Wyon.
(Courtesy of Tony Bergantino Collection.)

1882 Heaton & Sons penny.
(Courtesy of Tony Bergantino Collection.)

THE SOHO MINT, NEAR BIRMINGHAM.

A CATALOGUE

OF

THE VALUABLE MACHINERY AND PLANT

OF

THE SOHO MINT,

long celebrated and in high repute with the Government of Great Britain, as also with Foreign powers in Europe, Asia and America, the East India Company, and with mercantile and other firms of eminence in all parts of the world.

THE MACHINERY

may be pronounced as the most perfect of its kind in existence, having been constructed entirely under the personal superintendence of the late proprietor, whose genius and great mechanical skill are too well-known to render further allusion necessary; it includes

FOUR COINING PRESSES,

highly finished and worked by Pneumatic Apparatus. Each Press is constructed in a massive iron frame, with 5½-inch screw, working in a heavy metal nut; the dies are placed in a steel collar, which rises as the blank is struck, thereby preserving a square edge to the Coin. It is fed by a self-acting layer on, so formed as to reject an imperfect or improper Blank, and requiring merely the attention of a child in order to the efficient operation of the Machine. The speed varies from 60 to 80 blows per minute, according to the size of the Coin.

SIX CUTTING OUT PRESSES,

worked by the Steam Engine with pneumatic balance pumps; they are highly finished and erected in a circular iron frame, with fly-wheel and gearing, and capable of cutting 300,000 Blanks per day.

THREE MILLING MACHINES;

2 Shaking Machines, with Drying Stoves; Washing and Pickling Cisterns; Annealing Furnaces and Muffles;

A POWERFUL MEDAL OR MULTIPLYING PRESS,

to work by hand, with 5½-inch screw, and metal nut, in massive iron frame; several smaller Punching Presses;

A 10 HORSE POWER CONDENSING STEAM ENGINE;

2 Steam Boilers; 2 Timber Beam Condensing Steam Engines, one of which will be considered highly interesting from the fact of its being the first erected by James Watt; 2 powerful Vacuum Pumps; 700 feet Iron Shafting; 100 pair Plummer Blocks and Brasses; self-acting Screw-Cutting Lathe; 1 self-acting Turning Lathe; 8 Engine and Foot-turning Lathes; Drilling Machines; an assortment of Taps and Dies, Stocks and Steel Tools; 50 dozen Files;

EIGHT PLATE AND BAR ROLLING MILLS,

the Rolls by "Wilkes;" Driving Pinions and Apparatus; the iron frame work for a Water Wheel; 100 Spur, Rigger and Pinion Wheels; Cutting Shears; Tilt or Stamping Hammer; Smiths' Forges, Bellows and Tools; Box, Beam and other Scales; 2 tons Weights; Crab Crane; Machine Crane and Jib; Grindstones and Frames;

AN ASSORTMENT OF EXPENSIVE PATTERNS,

including those of the Royal Mint and the East India Company's Mints at Bombay and Calcutta, also of the various Machines at the Soho Mint;

12 TONS OF THE FINEST DIE STEEL,

made expressly for the late Mr. Boulton, under his personal directions, and acknowledged to be the best Die Steel in the Kingdom; 2 tons Shear and Scrap Steel; 7 tons of best Die Iron; 6 cwt. forged Dies and Collars;

5 TONS OF COPPER AND LEAD,

in sheets and Scrap, Cisterns, Pipes, &c.; Swedish Copper for Alloy; 50 Brass Cocks;

THE EXTREMELY VALUABLE COLLECTION OF DIES

for the Coins and Medals, well-known as the Soho Collection, most beautifully executed, principally by the celebrated Kuchler, and by Droz and Philp, also the Dies for many rare Coins, hitherto considered as almost unique, including a Dollar George III., 1798, a Britanniarum Penny, many specimens of proposed Coins, of various dates, and of the French Republic, 1790 to 1792, a pattern Half-penny George III. by Droz, and Provincial Tokens; also

A CABINET OF COINS AND MEDALS,

embracing 4 sets of the Soho Collection, and many others extremely rare.

THE OFFICE FITTINGS AND FURNITURE,

including 2 Iron Strong-room Doors, an Iron Safe, Wainscot Presses, Desks, Copying Machines, Office Stove, and a large variety of miscellaneous property.

Which will be Sold by Auction, by Messrs.

FULLER AND HORSEY,

On MONDAY, APRIL 29, 1850, and following days, at 11 o'Clock,
AT THE WORKS, NEAR BIRMINGHAM. IN LOTS. BY DIRECTION OF THE EXECUTORS OF THE LATE M. R. BOULTON, ESQ.

The Machinery may be seen in motion, and the other effects Viewed, on Thursday, Friday, and Saturday prior to the Sale. Catalogues, without which no person can be admitted, may be obtained at One Shilling each, of Messrs. FULLER & HORSEY, Billiter Street, London.

Title page of Fuller & Horsey's Soho Mint auction catalog.

(From Birmingham Central Library designated archives collection MS 3147/10/74. Reproduced by kind permission of Birmingham Central Library.)

later Ipswich decided . . . to take only those tokens issued by fellow towns-
man," Dykes writes, "they were adopting a measure of self protection
against anything that was not a known quantity in their own vicinity"
(ibid.). The same tendency was, by the way, observed with respect to
banknotes, with the public preferring provincial notes to those issued by
the Bank of England—in part, perhaps, because of local loyalties, but
also because provincial notes were less susceptible to forgery.

> In some respects the small size of country bankers' issues enabled
> them to indulge in producing high quality notes by methods which
> could not be used to produce notes in quantities needed by the Bank
> [of England]. Also their notes often circulated in localized areas and
> so would be identified as forgeries sooner.
>
> (HEWITT AND KEYWORTH 1987, 46)

As local token issues became more prevalent, token counterfeiting became less worthwhile. Indeed, it became more or less pointless, because
anyone set on issuing light and irredeemable tokens found it easier to do
so in an aboveboard way, by issuing anonymous tokens for general circulation. The emergence of a collectors' market, in the meantime, offered
a far more lucrative outlet for the efforts of determined false coiners: the
making of mules and other "instant rarities."

It may be thought that this last change made little difference, for a collectable fake is still a fake, whether or not one chooses to label it a "counterfeit." But from an economic perspective, fakes aimed at collectors were
quite unlike ordinary counterfeits, for they went straight from manufacturers to crooked coin dealers, chiefly in London, who retailed them at
prices "well above their face value" (Dykes 1997, 117; Bell 1963, 9). Because specious tokens aimed at collectors never circulated, any confusion
or loss suffered on account of them was borne not by the general public
but by collectors, especially by gullible collectors. It isn't the case, therefore, as Peter Mathias (1979, 203) claims, that specious tokens aimed at
collectors "increased the difficulties of using tokens as money." Laborers,
in particular, had no reason to fear them. On the contrary, they would
have been lucky to find a mule or two in their pay packets.

Token experts have, unfortunately, adopted the practice of calling
specious tokens of all kinds "counterfeits," and so have mislead others
into thinking that the public at large was imposed on by the proliferation
of "counterfeit" tokens after 1794. A closer look reveals that this proliferation was almost entirely aimed at collectors. Thus, when, in a 1796 let-

ter to *The Gentleman's Magazine,* Charles Pye laments the fact that tokens
are being "counterfeited for the worst of purposes, to impose upon the
publick," the "counterfeits" he has in mind are actually mules ("the obverses and reverses mixed on purpose to make variety, and the inscription on the edges varied for the same purpose"), and "the publick" refers
not to ordinary persons but to Pye's fellow token collectors.

> The manufacturing of this rubbish, or, as it may properly be called,
> wasting of copper, has been systematically brought forward; and col-
> lectors have purchased without considering that they were manufac-
> tured for no other purpose than to impose on them.
>
> (*GM,* DECEMBER 1796, 991–92)

That anyone at all should have been bamboozled by fake tokens is a pity.
But to the extent that false coining hurt collectors only, it called not for a
coinage reform but for more caution on collectors' part. *Caveat emptor.*

In short, counterfeiters played considerably less havoc with the commercial coin regime than they played with the regal coinage. That fact is
remarkable enough. But it becomes still more remarkable when one
considers that the counterfeiting of commercial coins, far from being a
hanging matter, was legal—or practically so, for no statute prohibited it.
It was perhaps an instance of fraud, or "passing off," under common law,
but if so, public authorities never troubled themselves to apprehend persons guilty of it. That genuine tokens were themselves of doubtful legal
standing—the seventeenth-century ban was still on the books—didn't
help either. Had the state bothered to track down and punish makers of
false tokens as aggressively as it did makers of false regal coin, the token
regime would presumably have proven still more counterfeit-resistant.

Next let's take up the alleged decline in the overall quality of genuine
tokens over time. Sharp, for instance, writes (1834, i–ii) that early tokens, including the Parys Mine Druids, contained "nearly their nominal
value in copper" but that this ceased to be true when coining was taken
up by less scrupulous "publishers" who sought to enhance their profits
by skimping on copper. More recently, Mathias (1979, 202) has spoken
of "a deterioration in [commercial coin] standards as widespread in its
own way as the original failings of the regal copper coinage." Elks (2005,
37), finally, holds that standards started slipping in 1792, with new issuers turning out "very light tokens . . . as a means of making a little extra profit." He adds, significantly, "There is no reason to believe that
there was any rise in the price of copper at this time."

Besides begging the question of why early token "publishers" failed to exploit profit opportunities later ones couldn't resist, such claims are factually incorrect. The earliest tokens, Parys Mine Druids included, weren't worth anything close to "their nominal value in copper," which was just as well, since they would otherwise have been melted in short order. Though later tokens were indeed lighter, their "intrinsic value" was generally about the same as that of the Druids and was higher than that of Tower halfpence, for the price of copper did rise during the 1790s. As table 3 shows, that rise tended to offset the decline in tokens' average weight, leaving their intrinsic value unchanged.

We come finally to the charge that the commercial coinage episode was chaotic. That the episode produced a bewildering assortment of tokens cannot be denied: one expert claims to have identified some six thousand distinct token variants, including all die variants but excluding known forgeries (Hill cited in Mathias 2004, 70). The question, though, is, to *whom* was the assortment bewildering?

That token collectors were bewildered is evident enough, for had that not been the case, the authoring of catalogs wouldn't have become a cottage industry. Nor would collectors (and professional numismatists as

TABLE 3. Manufactured Copper Prices and Halfpenny Token Weights, 1787–1800

Year	Price of copper (d/lb) (Grenfell)	(Tooke)	Average weight (ounces)	Average "intrinsic value" (pence) (Tooke)	(Grenfell)
1787	11	9.480	0.499	0.296	0.343
1788	11	9.600	0.499	0.299	0.343
1789	11	9.600	0.452	0.271	0.311
1790	11	10.080	0.448	0.282	0.308
1791	11	10.400	0.450	0.293	0.309
1792	12	11.460	0.419	0.300	0.314
1793	13	13.230	0.372	0.307	0.302
1794	13	13.152	0.346	0.285	0.281
1795	13	13.152	0.339	0.279	0.275
1796	13	13.776	0.334	0.287	0.271
1797	14	14.400	0.351	0.316	0.307
1798	14	14.400	0.370	0.333	0.324
1799	15	15.600	0.361	0.352	0.338
1800	17	18.000	0.275	0.309	0.292
Average	12.786	12.595	0.394	0.301	0.309

Correlation coefficients: –0.879 (Grenfell)
                         –0.928 (Tooke)

Sources: Token weights: Elks 2005. Copper prices: Thomas Tooke 1838, 400 (average of reported quarterly prices); Grenfell 1814.

well) have devoted so much effort and time to distinguishing specious tokens and mules from authentic issues and to documenting variants of authentic issues. But it does not follow from this that the many varieties of tokens proved a "nuisance" to members of the general public; and the general public's perspective must be taken in reaching an economic verdict concerning commercial coinage.

One must recognize, first of all, that only several hundred of the six thousand-odd token types experts have identified are versions of genuine commercial coins, as opposed to anonymous tokens, political and private coins, and tokens made to fool collectors.[26] That's still a large number, to be sure. But just how much chaos did it cause? Considered from the public's perspective, the presence of a variety of authentic token designs was not necessarily a bad thing: as we've seen, it actually served to make counterfeiting more difficult, by limiting (and in many instances avoiding altogether) die variations for any particular coin type. Nor is there any compelling aesthetic or political reason for having all coins of any denomination look the same: Benjamin Franklin, for one, ridiculed the official British practice of "repeating continually upon every halfpenny the dull story that everybody knew," observing that "it would have been no loss to mankind if nobody had ever known, that George III was 'King of Gt. Britain, France, and Ireland'" (Samuel [1881–83] 1994, 18, July 5, 1882).[27]

The large number of independent token issuers was another matter. It meant that to keep themselves informed of every legitimate token issue (so as to be able to tell real tokens from counterfeits anywhere and everywhere), consumers and retailers would have had to shoulder an all but impossible burden. "Here," Richard Samuel ([1881–83] 1994, January 19, 1881) writes, concerning Great Britain's small change during the mid-1790s,

> we have a small proportion of regal, and probably often much worn, coins, mixed with an overwhelming quantity of bad imitations, a large

---

26. While Dalton and Hammer (1910–17) list over three thousand token types for England alone, Bell (1963, 11–12) observes that "more than three quarters" of these are private advertising tokens, unfinished proofs, special issues for collectors, or coins struck from defective dies that were soon replaced. Bell lists only 254 distinct token types for all of Great Britain, but as his criteria are (by his own admission) extremely strict, the correct number may be somewhat larger.

27. The United States did not take Franklin's numismatic device to heart until 1999, when it began issuing a series of quarters (with completion scheduled for 2008) bearing fifty distinct reverse designs, each honoring a different state.

number of honest tokens, and a host of inferior ones, all circulating at the same time; and one can well imagine that poor and ignorant people, to say nothing of others, must have had the greatest difficulty in knowing of what their change really consisted.

In practice, however, the burden was much smaller than Samuel suggests, because most tokens did not circulate all that widely. The very lack of information concerning tokens—apart from the big "industrial" issues—that managed to stray far from their place of issue constituted a sort of gradient, like the sides of a saucer, that kept most tokens close to home. Consequently, most retailers had to deal only with one or two local token types, perhaps accompanied by an equally small number of major industrial tokens from elsewhere, while their customers had only to keep abreast of what the retailers considered current. That "it needed a bold workman to present tokens to his master and demand their face value for them in coin of the realm" (Mathias 1979, 200) was perhaps true but generally beside the point, for workers could spend tokens they earned locally, leaving their redemption to shopkeepers and publicans. Only unfamiliar tokens from far-off districts tended to be refused. According to Joseph Moser (1798, 307), who wrote near the end of the century (when fear of suppression made people especially leery of non-local tokens), "you cannot now pass at Barnet, nor even at Doncaster, a Provincial halfpenny which you took at York; but still it is certainly current in the district."

Moser actually saw in this limited currency a further reason for condemning tokens: imagine, he said, the fate of a discharged Chester Canal worker who takes his severance pay with him to Shrewsbury or Manchester "or indeed to any town at twenty or thirty miles distance." That worker would "find more than half the coin which he took at the former city of little use to him on the road, and of none when he gets to the end of his journey" (ibid.). But here Moser seems to forget his own testimony to the effect that provincial tokens were by then worth more locally than genuine Tower copper, meaning that Moser's poor worker was actually better off converting his provincial tokens into Tower copper while still at Chester than he would have been had he been paid with Tower money in the first place.

The need to exchange coins so as to avoid exchange losses when going from one district to another was also less of a burden to consumers than one might suppose, for despite its ongoing commercial revolution, Great Britain remained, to a substantial degree, a "collection of regional economies" (Brewer 1982, 207). Most Britons, and workers especially, seldom ventured far from home and so had little reason to regret being paid in local coin or receiving it as change. When people did travel, they might first equip themselves with "industrial" tokens or regal copper and whatever silver they could get hold of, which might be accepted anywhere. But at home, local copper was frequently the most reliable—and least confusing—small money to be had.

In short, to reckon the "chaos" stemming from commercial coining as if all commercial coins were equally likely to be encountered anywhere is to confuse eighteenth-century spending patterns with modern ones. A proper reckoning of the confusion commercial coins created for the average British wage earner also requires that mules and other specious tokens aimed at collectors be subtracted from the total variety of tokens most people could expect to come across. In hearing token enthusiasts, both early and modern, lament the chaos into which their favorite regime is supposed to have descended, one cannot help thinking that they've conflated the chaos they and their peers have had to contend with in amassing their collections with that faced by persons who actually received tokens in exchange.

What if . . . ?

To say that Great Britain's commercial coinage was better than some writings suggest isn't to deny that it was far from ideal. Small change of a truly national character would have been preferable, assuming it worked well in other respects. Nationally accepted coins would have spared shopkeepers the burden of having to inspect and sort coins that came their way, and people would have been able to go from district to district without ever feeling obliged to change their money. Of course, no one in his right mind would imagine local coins to be anything but a nuisance in a modern, fully integrated economy.

But what matters isn't how Britain's commercial coins compare to some ideal or to modern coins but how they compared to what came before them. In that contest, commercial coins carried the day in most respects, especially in the one respect that matters most: the judgment of the people. Whatever token experts might argue, retailers and (therefore) their customers favored commercial over Tower products. In other words, if commercial coins were a nuisance, they were a welcome nuisance.

What made the favorable reception of commercial coins all the more remarkable was the fact that the Royal Mint had had centuries in which to perfect its policies and procedures, while Great Britain's commercial mints and coin issuers had scarcely a decade. Also, the Royal Mint's products were protected by strict—if not Draconian—anticounterfeiting laws, while commercial coins enjoyed no legal protection at all. Finally, the Royal Mint never had to worry about its products being suppressed, whereas commercial coin makers and issuers operated under a legal cloud from the start, having had every reason to expect the government to eventually clamp down on them.

Fears of government suppression turned out to be well-grounded. But suppose they hadn't been. Suppose that instead of suppressing commercial coins, the British government had sanctioned them? What might have happened then?

The very possibility must seem far-fetched, for no power that governments exercise is more taken for granted than their monopolization of every sort of currency. Herbert Spencer, the only prominent thinker ever to question it, observed:

> So constantly have the ideas of currency and government been associated—so universal has been the control exercised by lawgivers over monetary systems—and so completely have men come to regard this control as a matter of course, that scarcely any one seems to inquire what would result were it abolished. Perhaps in no case is the necessity of state-supervision so generally assumed, and in no case will the denial of that necessity cause so much surprise.   (SPENCER 1851, 396)

Yet deny it Spencer did. Gresham's law, he claimed, applies only when governments force their citizens to accept debased or otherwise inferior coins. The opposite tendency—a tendency for good money to drive out bad—would prevail if coinage were left to private enterprise. Strangely enough, although he made these observations in 1851, Spencer never mentioned Great Britain's commercial coinage episode. Still, it's clear that, had the decision been left to him, Spencer would have allowed commercial coining to continue, forever breaking the Royal Mint's monopoly.

Spencer was, as everyone knows, an uncompromising champion of laissez-faire and minimal government. Yet his stance oughtn't to be dismissed out of hand, for while commercial coining was still going on, many saw in it the basis for a permanent solution to Great Britain's small-change problem. "Most of these coins," numismatic historian Stephen Leake observed (1793, app., p. 7), are neatly executed, and make no small addition to the collector's cabinet; they are much heavier than our national currency, and we hope it [commercial coinage] will be the means of government attending to an improvement in that part of the coinage.

The stance taken by Patrick Colquhoun is especially worth noting, for when it came to coining outside the Tower, Colquhoun was anything but indulgent. While serving as a police magistrate, he personally tracked down dozens of counterfeiters; and if it had been up to him, he'd have gladly sent the whole lot on a one-way botanical excursion:

> Come come my jolly lads, for we must away
> Bound down in irons to Botany Bay,
> Tis no use to weep nor to complain,
> For perhaps we may see Old England again.[28]

Specifically, Colquhoun wanted to make it a felony, punishable by seven years' transportation,

1st. For any person to make or manufacture any piece of Copper or other metal, with or without any device whatsoever, with the intent that it shall pass as the *Copper Monies of the Kingdoms of Great Britain or Ireland.*

2nd. For any smith, engraver, founder, &c. or any person, except those employed in the Mint, or authorized by the Treasury, to make or mend, buy or sell, conceal or have in their possession, without a lawful excuse, any punches, stamp, die, mould, & c. on which shall be impressed, or with intent that there shall be impressed on the same, and resemblance whatever, in part or on the whole, of such *Copper Monies.*

3d. For any person to buy or sell, or offer to buy or sell, or to utter or tender in payment, or to give or offer to give in exchange, *thirty or more pieces of Copper* in any one day; such pieces resembling or being intended to resemble, or passing or being intended to pass as the current Copper Money of said kingdom.   (COLQUHOUN 1800, 197)[29]

---

28. "The Jolly Lad's Trip to Botany Bay," in Holloway and Black 1979, 145–46.

29. While Colquhoun favored stiffer penalties for copper counterfeiters, he also thought the penalties for counterfeiting of gold and silver coin—which counted as high treason—were too severe: "When we are taught . . . that it is considered by the Law a

Yet for all his urging of a veritable "war on slugs," Colquhoun was prepared to tolerate commercial coining. "It might perhaps be useful," he wrote in his *Treatise on the Police of the Metropolis,* "to legalize commercial coins on three conditions":

1. That the Copper of which they are made shall be pure.
2. That this Coin shall be at least 10 per cent. heavier than Mr. Boulton's new Coinage.
3. That the parties circulating such Coin shall be responsible to the holders, for the value in Gold or Silver, when demanded: and shall stamp their names and an obligation to that purpose on the Coins, Tokens, or Medals so issued by them.   (IBID., 198–99)

Commercial coiners generally violated only the second provision, and it is just as well that they did so, for the price of copper was unstable and rising, so that tokens made according to it would quickly have been melted down. Indeed, much of "Mr. Boulton's new Coinage" itself ended up in melting pots within a few years of being issued. Colquhoun, though a deft beak, was no political economist.

Colquhoun was, to be sure, far from being convinced that legalizing commercial coins would prove wiser than outlawing them along with other unauthorized copper. Nevertheless, the fact that he even entertained the possibility of an officially sanctioned private copper coinage suggests that even he could appreciate the utility of such a coinage. It also gives us a good reason for wondering what such a coinage would have been like and how well it might have worked.

Counterfactual history is always risky business. But with respect to private coinage, one is able to lean heavily on evidence from two related enterprises: button making and banking. Making tokens was, as we've seen, not so different from making buttons, while issuing tokens wasn't so different from issuing (small-value) banknotes.

When commercial coining got under way in 1787, British provincial banking itself was just getting off the ground. Indeed, token issuers were protobankers of a kind, whose tokens were the equivalent of very small

---

greater crime to coin a sixpence than to kill our father or mother, nature and reason revolt against the proposition" (Colquhoun 1800, 34). The prescribed penalties—offenders were supposed to be drawn on the ground or pavement to the gallows and hanged by the neck— was so severe that they proved counterproductive: judges refrained from sentencing known offenders, thus undermining the law's deterrent effect.

banknotes, except that they were made of copper rather than paper. As actual country banks multiplied, their notes came to be widely used in payments outside of London, where Bank of England notes held sway. But because regulations placed lower bounds on the size of notes and because very small notes were impractical, such notes could never take the place of coin in smaller payments. It would, under the circumstances, have made perfect sense for bankers to take over the issuing of tokens, instead of leaving the business to every sort of mercantile or industrial firm. It also would have made sense for them to issue silver as well as, or perhaps instead of, copper tokens, as silver would have been more convenient for many transactions. As we shall see, bankers did become important token issuers, and they did have recourse to silver tokens, in the early nineteenth century.

It would also have made sense for token issuers—whether nominally banks or not—to establish branch networks so as to encourage more widespread, if not nationwide, circulation of their coins. Such a move would have ended the strictly "local" status shared by most tokens. But unlike the move to silver tokens, it was never to occur, in part because the six-partner rule made it difficult for English country banks to set up branches and in part because Scottish banks, which could and did establish branch networks, were kept from branching into England.

The survival of some strictly "local" coins might eventually have given rise to specialist coin changers or brokers, analogous to the banknote brokers who plied their trade in the antebellum United States, where legal restrictions also limited the growth of branch banking. The note brokers, who had their headquarters in various large cities, offered to purchase notes at discounts that reflected any perceived risk in addition to the actual cost of returning notes to their source for redemption. They also made their price lists available, along with "counterfeit detectors" aimed at alerting merchants to fraudulent notes. Token brokers might have offered similar services to British retailers, thereby making it easier for them to accept tokens from faraway districts.[30]

Of course, private mints themselves were to blame for the existence of fake commercial coins. But it is hardly going far out on a limb to imagine that, given enough time, certain mints' bad reputations would have

---

30. Indeed, in London during the seventeenth-century token episode, one Richard Rich performed these very services, having set himself up as a "changer of farthings" on Drury Lane (Berry 1988, 5). Rich may not have been alone in this, and it would hardly be surprising to discover that the late eighteenth century also had its share of "changers of halfpence." However, no evidence of such has come down to us.

caught up with them: it was, after all, in token issuers' interest to try to avoid doing business with mints that might "mule" or otherwise misuse their coin dies. Reputable mints would likewise have had reason to take steps against their less reputable rivals, to prevent them from doing irreparable harm to the entire coining industry. Here the Birmingham button trade offers an instructive parallel, for better button makers also faced the challenge of protecting their trade against damage done to it by counterfeiters, especially by makers of phony ("washed") gilt buttons that blackened rapidly. To combat the practice, industry leaders, led by none other than Matthew Boulton, formed the Button Association in 1795. The association then proceeded to obtain legislation making the production of washed buttons a crime punishable by a sixteen-pound fine, with a ten-guinea reward for information leading to a conviction. Within two months, the association saw to the conviction of three offenders, which was enough to put paid to the gilt counterfeit trade (Langford 1868, 91):

> For a Birmingham lad knows gold from brass,
> If he don't Jemmy Johnson squeeze me.[31]

Needless to say, conjectures like the foregoing must be taken with a grain, if not a scoop, of salt, for the commercial coinage regime never had a chance to mature. Instead, the British government took steps that would snuff it out, first temporarily, and then for good.

---

31. "Birmingham Boy in London," in Holloway and Black 1979, 59–60.

CHAPTER V

The Boulton Copper

The silver coin is mostly base,

(Each Knave the public fleeces)

Of Copper little good we trace,

Save BOULTON'S penny pieces.[1]

Fright at Fishguard

February 22, 1797. We are back in Wales again, with Thomas Williams. But we are not in Anglesey. We are at Pembrokeshire, on the north coast. And we are not with Thomas Williams the Copper King but with a different Thomas Williams: Thomas Williams Esq., of Trelethin, a retired sailor. It's four bells—ten o'clock to landlubbers—and Williams has just interrupted his morning walk to peer through his telescope at a squadron of naval ships: two large frigates, a corvette, and a lugger. They are heading toward Fishguard from just off North Bishop Rock. Williams doesn't know it, but he is witnessing the long-delayed arrival of Matthew Boulton's regal coinage contract.

What Williams does know is that there's something funny about those ships. They're flying the British colors, sure enough. But if they're British and inbound, why are their decks crammed with troops, and why are the troops wearing dark—almost black—uniforms? Because, Williams gath-

---

1. Poet (John) Freeth, "More Guineas, and Less Paper Credit," in Horden 1993, 96–97.

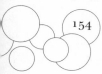 154

ers, the ships aren't British. They are French. And they are invading Great Britain.

As invasions go, the one at Fishguard was a pretty desultory affair. The landing force consisted of no more than fourteen hundred ragtag troops, many of them released jailbirds, led by a superannuated Irish-American adventurer named William Tate and armed with only one hundred rounds of ammunition each. While they disembarked during the early morning hours of February 23, two Welsh regiments and batches of locals armed with guns, swords, and pitchforks were mobilizing to meet them. As the British defenses gathered strength, the French reinforced themselves with foraged food and pilfered port, then went on a general looting spree. Throughout the day, members of the Legion Noire (so called because of their dark brown outfits)—many of whom were too top-heavy to shoot straight—were picked off in ones and twos by locals. Then, in the early evening, the Pembrokeshire militia arrived. At 8:00 p.m. Tate, believing himself outnumbered (when in fact he still had a two-to-one advantage), decided to seek terms. On the morning of February 24, the Legion Noire laid down its arms to a scratch force of Welsh volunteers.

Needless to say, Tate's invasion, considered as an attempt to conquer Great Britain, was bound to be a fiasco. But conquest wasn't the point. The real aim of the landing—or one of its aims at least (another having been that of getting Tate out from the Directory's hair)—was to deal a blow to Great Britain's economy by undermining its monetary system. With respect to this objective at least, the invasion was nothing less than a spectacular success.

As soon as he recognized the French squadron for what it was, Williams sent a messenger to St. David's. From there, other messengers were dispatched to alert the countryside. Soon, rumors of the invasion were being spread far and wide, with the usual exaggerations. The corvettes became frigates, while the frigates become ships of the line. The size of the landing party grew correspondingly, from hundreds to thousands and eventually to ten thousand soldiers. Before long, reports were being heard of a tricolor waving over Pembroke Castle and of other French landings—at St. David's itself, along Cardigan Bay, and even at Bristol. It was only a matter of days—perhaps hours—before the rumors spread beyond Wales to England, where they'd be embellished still further.

In London, in the meantime, the Bank of England teetered on the brink of failure. Since the start of the war in 1793, the Bank was repeatedly called on to make advances to the government. Its stock of bullion had deteriorated accordingly, from between £6 and £7 million in 1794 to just £2.5 million in February 1796. The Bantry Bay invasion of December 1796, though also a military failure, further worsened matters by giving the public a chronic case of invasion jitters, which provoked further hoarding of guineas. The guineas had to be handed over to the public by country bankers, who in turn cashed in their London accounts, causing the London banks to draw on their deposits at the Bank of England.

After Bantry Bay, the Bank directors lived "in constant fear that some new alarm would precipitate another crisis" (Feavearyear 1932, 167–68). On the very eve of the Fishguard landing, things had gotten so bad that a deputation of Bank directors begged Pitt to consider offering some relief, preferably by arranging to have the government repay at least part of the £11.7 million the Bank had lent it. But before the government could act on this appeal, the Bank's worst fears were realized: reports of the invasion—wildly inaccurate reports—caused the Bank to suffer its greatest cash drain yet, sending its stock price plummeting.

With their Bank now facing imminent default, which it managed to forestall only by paying its notes in shillings and sixpences, two of the Bank's directors again turned for help to Pitt, who paced back and forth in his drawing room all night before deciding what to do. On Sunday, February 26, he and the rest of the Privy Council assembled at Whitehall, where, in consultation with the king, they prepared an Order in Council reading, in part, as follows:

> [I]n consequence of the ill founded or exaggerated alarms in different parts of the country, it appears that, unless some measure is immediately taken, there may be reason to apprehend a want of a sufficient supply of cash to answer the exigencies of the public service; it is the unanimous opinion of the Board, that it is indispensably necessary for the public service, that the Directors of the Bank of England should forbear issuing any cash in payment until the sense of Parliament can be taken on that subject   (*Hansard* 1797, c. 1518).

The "sense of Parliament" was expressed in the so-called Bank Restriction Act (37 Geo. III *c* 45), which, after lengthy and often heated debates, received the Royal Assent on May 3. The measure legalized the stoppage of payments that the Privy Council had already (illegally) authorized, forbidding the Bank to pay out gold except in certain special cases, including the payment of its dividends. The act also indemnified the Bank against any legal consequences arising from its prior stoppage.

Ironically, the first reports of Tate's surrender reached London just as the Order of Council was being prepared. But before the news could elicit any official response, the Rubicon had been crossed, not to be crossed again for another twenty-one years: the government, in trying to save the Bank, inadvertently discovered a way to turn Bank paper into gold, so that the Bank might lend to it without limit. Moreover, the Bank restriction, though unprecedented, had appeased a considerable segment of the public, including most bankers and businessmen, to whom it brought considerable relief. The reaction of Matthew Boulton's London banker and confidant Charlotte Matthews was perhaps typical: "People have been struck mad with fright," she wrote Boulton on the 28th, "& had not the severe remedy taken place respecting the Specie a general Bankruptcy must have been the consequence. . . . the People here receive the Measure with great Cheerfulness & I wish the Country People may do the same" (MBP 326/7). So Whitehall was in no hurry to end the restriction. In the meantime, Great Britain would have to make do not with its official silver pound or even with the former de facto gold pound but with a paper pound, relative to which the values of both gold and silver might freely fluctuate.

If the paper pound came as a relief to most businessmen, it was to be an outright boon to Boulton himself, for it was thanks to it that he finally secured a regal coinage contract. Just how did the paper pound help Boulton? When the restriction took effect, the main source of gold coins—the only coins that were not already in markedly short supply—was cut off, while those guineas and half guineas already in circulation were stowed away or exported (Cannan 1925, xiii). So it happened that silver and copper coins, long relied on for all payments under half a guinea, now had to fill in for half guineas and guineas also, which they could not possibly do except with great inconvenience and by further aggravating coin shortages at the lower end of the denomination spectrum. Under the circumstances, for the government to continue neglecting the state of the currency was no longer simply a question of "letting the vulgar wait." Gentlemen as well as tradesmen and common folk were now feeling the brunt, and gentlemen couldn't be kept waiting.

So the first week of March witnessed a flurry of activity aimed at eliminating the money shortage, including measures aimed at relieving former restrictions on small-denomination banknotes. On March 3, a law (37 Geo. III c 28) was passed allowing the Bank of England to issue notes under five pounds. On March 10, another law (37 Geo. III *c* 32) extended the same privilege to country banks in England and Wales as well as to private persons. Eventually, a third measure lifted the separate ban on Scottish banknotes worth less than twenty shillings.[2]

While the legalization of small banknotes helped reduce the need for coin (both directly and by encouraging the spread of banking facilities),[3] it alone could hardly make up for the lack of decent coins. Banknotes were far too flimsy to be a practical circulating medium for very small payments, and although notes for as low as a half crown (2*s* 6*d*) were sometimes issued, and ones for ten shillings or a half-guinea weren't uncommon, most banks didn't bother issuing notes for less than twenty shillings or a guinea.

One Scottish banker recalled how his customers "were deprived of the means of purchasing with ready money the necessaries of life."

> [T]here were no notes of less value than twenty shillings and it was with the utmost difficulty they could get change anywhere else; for the instant it was known that payments in specie were suspended, not a person would part with a single shilling that they could keep, and the consequence was that both gold and silver specie was hoarded up and instantly disappeared. . . . Saturday was the day on which we had the severest outcry to encounter . . . as many master-tradesmen requested in the most earnest manner to have a little silver for enabling them to pay their workpeople. All we could do when sensible that their demands proceeded from *real* necessity, was privately to change a note or two by taking them into a separate room, for we durst not do it openly in the counting-house for fear of raising a riot.
>
> (FORBES 1860, 84)

Yet Scotland was better off than England and Wales, for at least some Scottish banknotes, like the better tradesman's tokens, circulated widely, while notes of English and Welsh country banks enjoyed a local circula-

---

2. Although it was originally supposed to be a very short-term emergency measure only, the legalization of small-note issues was repeatedly renewed. In 1808, notes for less than one pound were again banned, along with small checks. The minimum permissible note denomination was restored to five pounds in 1829.

3. Pressnell (1956, 140) claims that "there can be little doubt" that the lifting of the ban on small notes "helped to multiply the country banks." But he adds that "their rapid growth *before* it was granted suggests that its importance can be exaggerated." Even if the industry might have grown almost as rapidly despite the ban, the scale of banknote issues would certainly have been considerably smaller (ibid., 142).

tion only.[4] The Bank of England (which also never issued notes for less than one pound) was no exception: its notes were payable in London only and, for this reason, tended to be used only within thirty miles or so of the City. Finally, banknotes were even more subject to fraudulent imitation than were token coins, and therefore had to be treated with caution. Bank of England notes, being among the flimsiest, were especially suspect.[5]

In short, paper money could not be expected to fill the void left by the disappearance of gold coin; and if paper wouldn't do, some kind of metal would have to. The government had no choice but to supply new subsidiary coins to the public, and supply them as quickly as possible.

A Reale Blunder

Having rejected the idea of issuing notes below one pound, the Bank of England was as anxious as any firm to get hold of small change. And yet the Bank had a huge stash of silver coins—worth over £241,000—piled up in its vaults. The rub was that the coins were Spanish, or Spanish American: they were "pillar" dollars, worth eight Spanish reales (hence called "pieces of eight"), that came from Hamburg, Portugal, and the West Indies as English trade dividends and also from prize ships captured on the high seas. Because they were dollars rather than shillings, the Bank had looked on them as so much raw silver. As the market value of an ounce of standard silver had long been above 5s 4d, melting and recoining the dollars at the official Royal Mint rate of 5s 2d per ounce was out of the question. But the urgent need for change following the restriction gave rise to a scheme—hatched by the Bank and the Treasury and announced on March 3 by a warrant—to convert the dollars into English money valued at 4s 6d. Given the coins' weight and the standard of Spanish silver, that rating was expected to make them worth something more than their bullion value.

The conversion was to be achieved by having the Royal Mint stamp each coin's obverse, just below the Spanish monarch's ear, with the same tiny portrait bust of George III used to mark silver plate at Goldsmith's Hall. As some irreverent wag put it, "The Bank to make their Spanish

---

4. A few country banks arranged to have their larger notes only redeemed in London.

5. See Clapham 1945, 2:3; Coppieters 1955, 64–65. That both the Bank of England and the Royal Mint did a poor job when it came to making imitation-proof products was no coincidence: monopoly privileges tended to insulate the officers of both institutions from adverse consequences that would otherwise have befallen them as a result of such neglect.

dollars pass, / Stamped the head of a Fool on the head of an ass." For once, the mint worked quickly, and the first "Bank dollars" were about to be issued on March 6 when a last-minute jump in the market price of silver gave the Bank and the Treasury a case of cold feet. Three days later, the Bank began issuing the coins at last, but only after their official value had been raised to 4s 9d to keep them from becoming the latest victims of Gresham's law. Although the adjustment may seem small, it proved controversial, because it signified a decisive move away from the old Royal Mint price of silver, which had been in effect since 1601, and toward an avowedly token silver coinage.

At first, the new tokens looked to be a smashing success. For days, the Bank of England's Pay Hall was chock-full of people seeking the new coins; some stood in line for several hours before finally making it to a teller's window. By early August, more than 1.5 million Bank dollars, officially worth £345,000, had been claimed and had begun making their rounds from pay tables to retail stores and back again by way of the nation's banks.

There was no lack of demand for Bank dollars. Unfortunately, the Bank wasn't the only firm that stood ready to meet that demand, for although the government had finally agreed to go along with a token silver coinage, it still clung to the notion that successful coinage was simply a matter of controlling coins' metallic content. It therefore failed to appreciate the necessity of making coins—especially token ones—hard to imitate, for whenever a coin, official or not, is rated much above its metallic worth, people will be tempted to copy it.

And copying Bank dollars was a cinch. If one happened to have a hammer, some Spanish dollars (which were easy to come by), and a punch bearing a phony hallmark (which even a third-rate engraver could manage), a modest but tidy profit was just an arm's swing away. That Bank dollars weren't sanctioned by any royal proclamation made faking them all the more tempting, because people who forged them were subject to prosecution only under common law, instead of facing the much harsher penalties inflicted on persons caught counterfeiting "the king's money."

It should come as no surprise that the Bank of England's tellers, who were best able to spot fakes, started spotting them within days of the original tokens' debut. At first, the Bank chose to ignore the problem, but during the summer, as the price of standard silver fell to just 4s 10d per ounce, counterfeiting activity exploded. More sophisticated forgers, seeking greater profits, also began making lightweight Spanish dollars, to which phony stamps were afterward applied; and before long the Bank of England discovered, to its dismay, that it had been receiving and reissuing some of these fakes. From that time onward, the Bank felt obliged to scrutinize every dollar handed to it and to refuse doubtful ones even if they might in fact be genuine. That, of course, was asking for trouble, and the Bank knew it. So on September 28, the Bank announced that it was taking back its tokens, which it would pay for in hastily minted seven-shilling gold pieces; the public would have until the end of October to turn them in. Come November, any genuine tokens that remained outstanding would no longer be current: they would, in other words, be treated once again like so much junk silver.

The public, having gone into a frenzy when Bank dollars were first issued, now went into another. The Bank was only taking back dollars it considered genuine, and then only in lots of twenty or more. Most people possessed fewer than twenty Bank dollars, and even those who thought they might have the requisite number couldn't be certain, because they weren't able to tell real ones from frauds. Silver dealers profited from the distress by getting people to part with genuine dollars for little more than their metallic worth. At last, on October 10, the Bank, fearing a public relations disaster, offered to receive any good (that is, full-weight) Spanish dollars, whether bearing genuine stamps or fake ones, at the official rate of 4s 9d, for a ten-day interval only, after which it would revert to its original plan.

As one might expect, the Bank's generous offer got forgers' hammers swinging faster than ever. Anticipating trouble, Magistrate Colquhoun, who was equal parts zealot and xenophobe when it came to hunting down counterfeiters and who was especially inclined to point a finger at London's Jewish minority, proposed placing a sign in the Pay Hall reading: "All Dollars brought by Jews, to be exchanged here." The idea was to subject Jews to special scrutiny, so that they would think twice about dealing in phony silver.

Whether the Bank demeaned itself by going through with Colquhoun's scheme isn't known, but in making its first tentative moves toward an avowedly fiduciary silver coinage, both it and the government took a very public pratfall. Not until 1804 would the Bank once again attempt to issue silver tokens. In the meantime, if the small-change shortage was to be addressed at all, it would have to be addressed, not with silver, but with copper.

Doing Cartwheels

The government began planning a new copper coinage even before the first countermarked Spanish dollars appeared. On March 1, the House of Commons asked the king to authorize measures "for procuring an immediate supply of such Copper Coinage as may be best adapted to the payment of the Laborious poor in the present Exigency" (Dyer and Gaspar 1992, 446). The king complied on March 3 by assigning the new charge to the long-dormant Privy Council Committee on Coin. On that same day, Charles Jenkinson, formerly Baron Hawkesbury but now raised to the earldom of Liverpool, sent Boulton the good news.

Dear Sir

In consequence of the Difficulties which have occured [sic] in the present State of Affairs, to find a Circulating Medium for all Ranks of People and particularly those who are in less affluent Circumstances, it has been suggested, that it may be proper in such a Moment, to have a new Copper Coinage; There is no Man who can better judge of the propriety of this Measure, and of the plan that ought to be adopted, in issuing a Coinage of this Nature, than yourself; and no one will execute it with more Accuracy, and more Expedition. The Idea that has occured has been, to issue a Copper Coin of the Value of 2d or 3d so as to represent the 6th or the 3 [sic] part of a Shilling: The Value of the Copper in such Coin, should certainly be less than the Value of the Metal in Bars, that is, the Charge of coining it; should be taken out of it; perhaps something more might be taken; but We should avoid, if possible, taking so much more as may encourage others to counterfeit it. This Coin certainly will be very bulky and heavy, but I doubt much, whether this would be any Objection, to that Description of People, for whose use the Coin is principally intended. I wish you would lose no Time in turning this Subject in your Thoughts [as if it had ever stopped turning there!], and in framing a Plan conformably to the Ideas which I have suggested, or to any others which may occur to you, and, which may be more likely in your Judgement to Answer the purpose intended.

I am sensible that your Presence in Birmingham may in the present State of Things be necessary, as your Influence there is great. In such a Case you may send your opinion on this Subject, to me in Writing. But if your Presence in Birmingham could properly be dispensed with, it would be better that you should come to Town, in order to have some Conversations with M*r* Pitt and Me, upon it, as We should thereby easily settle this Business to our mutual Satisfaction.

I am

(&c.)

Liverpool

(BL ADD. MSS 38422, 171)

For Boulton, the news came just in the nick of time: the war was killing the toy trade, and Soho was struggling to pay its bills. Just days before the Fishguard landing, Boulton confided to Mrs. Matthews that "the town of Birmingham is so poor and distressed from want of trade and foreign remittances that we cannot collect our debts but are dunned for every debt we owe" (MBP 326/5).[6]

Of course, Liverpool couldn't just hand Boulton a contract. New hearings would have to be held, and alternative proposals would have to be considered. Still, there could be little doubt that Boulton would ultimately get the job, for his was the only mint capable of coining on the scale the government was contemplating, and Liverpool was now thoroughly committed to his cause. Because he was by far the most active member of the Committee on Coin, as well as the only member present at all of its meetings (and often one of only two members present), Liverpool could move quickly. Over the course of a dozen meetings held over a couple of weeks, Boulton and others (including Thomas Williams) were interviewed, information of various kinds was solicited, and rival offers (from the Westwoods and the Parys Mine mint manager, Charles Wyatt) were duly noted in the minutes. Then, on March 28, having gone through the requisite motions, the committee presented its report at Whitehall. To no one's surprise, the report awarded high marks to specimens Boulton had supplied to the committee, while proposing Boulton himself as the best person to produce millions of pieces like them. Although the Treasury, which had the last word, made a few revisions to the committee's proposal, it assented to the general plan. On June 9, the king did likewise: the Soho Mint finally had its contract.

According to that contract, Soho was to strike 480 tons of pennies and another 20 tons of twopenny pieces. These were to be the first official British copper coins to bear these denominations and the first of any denomination to be struck by steam. Boulton thought it desirable to have them embody common units of both weight and measurement, so

---

6. For the war's effect on Birmingham's economy, see Hopkins 1998.

(with the government's approval) he made the pennies weigh precisely one ounce and measure just over 1.4 inches (or 17 coins = 2 feet), while making the tuppence pieces weigh two ounces and measure 1.6 inches (or 5 coins = 8 inches).[7] At John Southern's urging, he even went to the trouble of securing a certified copy of the Royal Society's standard foot so as to get the new coins' diameters just right.

Boulton was to receive £149 6s 8d for each ton of coins he produced, of which £108 was to pay for the copper, £37 6s 8d was to cover Boulton's manufacturing costs, and £4 was to cover the expense of distributing the coins throughout Great Britain. In its report, the Committee on Coin observed that Boulton's coinage fee was considerably lower than the Royal Mint's average cost for coining copper before 1775, which Garbett had placed at no less than fifty-nine pounds per ton; it was also lower than the rate of forty-two pounds per ton at which the mint had offered to coin copper back in January 1788. Such comparisons were specious, because the Royal Mint figures refer to halfpennies and farthings and because the expense of coinage depends more on the number of coins to be minted than on their total weight. On the other hand the mint's forty-two-pound offer includes only those coinage expenses above and beyond the mint's fixed expenses, including capital depreciation and officers' salaries.

Soho's coins were also supposed to be decidedly superior to what the Royal Mint was capable of making. Their final design was the work of Conrad Heinrich Küchler, a German whom Boulton hired in 1793 as the last of three replacements (the others were Rambert Dumarest and Noel Alexandre Ponthon) for Droz. Though sullen and ill-tempered, Küchler was a skilled engraver whose special knack for portraiture had caused him to become Soho's chief medallist. His previous commissions included Boulton's Cornwallis and Lord Howe medals; and he would eventually cement his reputation by engraving the Trafalgar medal and Boulton's own memorial medal. But medals, like commercial tokens, were a stopgap undertaking at the Soho mint, to be set aside as soon as a regal coinage project was in prospect. So Küchler abandoned his other projects to come up with a good likeness of George III, which he completed to the king's complete satisfaction.[8]

On the whole, the new coins (both denominations were alike apart

---

7. Boulton first planned to have eight of his two-pence pieces measure one foot, but he changed his mind for some reason.

8. A glance at the results suggests that George III, unlike his son, preferred accuracy to flattery.

from minor details) bore conventional devices. Küchler's right-facing bust portrait of the king appeared on their obverse, surrounded by the legend "GEORGIUS III · D · G · REX." The portrait broke with tradition only in substituting a draped bust for the usual cuirassed one and in employing the initials "D · G" instead of spelling out "Dei Gratia." The reverse bore the legend "BRITANNIA" above and the date (1797) below, with that "goddess of the land" seated on a rock amid the ocean, waving an olive branch in her right hand and clasping a trident in her left. Before her sailed a triple-masted warship, and by her side rested an oval shield bearing the combined crosses of St. Andrew and St. George. On the face of the rock, just below the shield, the word "SOHO" announced, to anyone who cared to know, that these coins came not from the Tower but from a far-removed private factory. As far as the Company of Moneyers was concerned, Küchler might as well have included a tiny Tower of London in the background, so as to allow Britannia to stick her tongue out at it.

The moneyers might well have chafed at the new coins, but they could hardly claim them inferior to their own copper work. Yet, as Richard Doty (1998, 314) has observed, the coins were far less artistic than the proof pieces Boulton showed off almost a decade before.[9] Especially noteworthy was the new coins' complete lack of edge markings, a traditional means for discouraging the production of cast counterfeits—and a means on which Boulton had placed much emphasis in his original coinage proposals. Boulton's painful encounter with Droz, which got started largely owing to his desire to employ Droz's *virole brisé* to mark the edges of coins while striking them in collars, now appeared to have been in vain.

Boulton's regal coins did have one novel feature—namely, their broad, raised rims, which (together with their large size) led to their being called "cartwheels." It was along these broad rims that the coins' legends appeared, in incuse lettering. The rims were meant to prevent the shallowly engraved Britannia and the equally shallow monarch from

---

9. They were, in fact, far less artistic than had been many commercial tokens, including previous Soho products. Dyer and Gaspar's (1992, 446) assertion that "there were solid grounds for Boulton's confident assertion that his copper coins were the most perfectly executed that Great Britain had ever seen" can be accepted if one allows that commercial tokens weren't really "coins." In attempting to justify the cartwheel's less than spectacular designs as having at least represented "an attempt at artistry for what was, after all, a subsidiary coin of limited value," Doty (1998, 314) fails to consider that precisely such subsidiary coins are most in need of the protection against counterfeiting that outstanding engravings supply.

wearing down rapidly; but they also created a shallow canyon in which grime might accumulate. Although such broad rims had not appeared before on any official British coins, they had been common enough on medals (where the grime problem doesn't arise), and Boulton had tested them on his Eccleston halfpennies.

Despite their plain edges and the eight years of steam-coining experience that informed their design, the cartwheels were a poor match for Soho's equipment. What's more Boulton knew it, thanks to the Monneron Frères episode: the French five-sol tokens, which were thirty millimeters (1.53 inches) wide and weighed about nine-tenths of an ounce each, almost tore Soho's presses to pieces (Doty 1998, 47). It followed that if the somewhat smaller but heavier penny cartwheels did not rip the same presses to shreds, the twopenny coins would surely do so.

Realizing this, Boulton decided, even before the regal coinage contract was officially his, to rebuild his mint from scratch (Doty 1998, 54). But to do so would take months, and Boulton had offered to begin coining cartwheels at once. So he put John Southern to work shoring up the old mint (ibid., 51). Striking commenced on June 19; one imagines Southern and Busche and the rest of the senior mint staff standing by with their fingers firmly crossed. They certainly needed all the luck they could get, for, as Doty (ibid., 54) explains, notwithstanding Southern's efforts, the new coinage "was virtually beyond [the Soho's] capacity."

> Presses broke, dies shattered, bottlenecks were created, and harried workmen were deafened by the noise. . . . The rumbling of the overhead wheel, making a dozen revolutions per minute, added to the cacophony as iron curves and rollers banged against each other, air pumps hissed and sputtered, and dies smashed images of Britannia and the King into pieces of metal.

Despite every sort of disruption, the mint staff managed to complete Soho's original regal order by late April 1798.[10] In fewer than eleven months, they had struck over 17.5 million coins, besting the Parys Mine Company's record by a considerable margin. It was, by any measure, a spectacular accomplishment, though one that Soho itself would shortly eclipse.

---

10. Striking of the twopenny cartwheels did not begin until January 1798: for obvious reasons, Boulton chose to leave these heavier and potentially more destructive pieces for last.

Regal Paperweights

Yet from an economic perspective, the cartwheels were something of a flop. Notwithstanding all the fanfare surrounding them and all the ingenuity that went into making them, they didn't relieve Great Britain of its shortage of small change, and they didn't lift the curse of counterfeit copper. Nor could they possibly have done either.

Why not? Part of the problem was the coins themselves, starting with their denominations. The public had long been pining for good farthings and, especially, halfpennies. Yet the government chose to give them pennies and twopenny pieces. The Committee on Coin defended the move by stating, first, that, taking counterfeits into account, the available stock of halfpence and farthings "was fully sufficient for the use of such parts of the Retail Trade . . . as are carried on with Coins of this low denomination" and, second, that "an Issue, however gradual, of Copper Coins of the same denominations as those now in use, but of a superior value, might discredit the whole of the Halfpence and Farthings now in Circulation, and might thereby bring Distress upon the laborious poor."[11]

These arguments were hardly persuasive.[12] Of course, there were plenty of halfpence and farthings around, if one included all the flimsy and fake ones. But these defective halfpennies and farthings were proof of the desperate need for new official versions, not grounds for denying such a need. The concern that the appearance of new halfpence and farthings might aggravate shortages by discrediting old ones was equally at odds with the evident tendency for old and unauthorized coins to fill any gap stemming from a shortage of new, authorized ones. As long as good coins remained in short supply, it was not the mere appearance of new ones but a belief that this appearance heralded the legal suppression of old ones (as had happened after 1672) that risked discrediting the latter.

---

11. While the Committee on Coin worried that the introduction of new halfpence and farthings might not be "gradual" enough to avoid discrediting the old copper, Boulton contradicted it by expressing the opposite fear. In a March 1797 letter to Sir George Shuckburgh-Evelyn, he estimated that it would take twice as long to strike five hundred tons of halfpennies as it would take to make the same tonnage of pennies and that any more limited introduction of new halfpennies "would create confusion in that medium rather than accommodation" (Wager 1977, 45; see also MBP 152/257, Boulton to Shuckburgh-Evelyn, March 1797).

12. The same may be said of Peck's (1970, 217) claim that the larger coin denominations may have been a response to "the diminished purchasing power of the halfpenny toward the end of the eighteenth century." According to available price statistics, the British price level rose only about 25 percent between 1787 and 1797.

Consequently, if the government was anxious to keep old halfpennies and farthings around, it had only to say so publicly; that is, it had only to make clear that in proclaiming the new coins current, it did not intend to revoke the currency of old ones. Ideally, the government would allow old coins to remain current until it had all the new ones it needed to replace them.[13]

Unfortunately, Pitt's government did nothing to assure the public that it wasn't planning to decry the old copper money soon after it started issuing cartwheels. The government therefore ended up doing precisely what it sought to avoid doing—that is, aggravating the small-change shortage—despite not having issued a single new halfpenny or farthing. The cartwheels' appearance had an especially chilling effect on the commercial coinage industry, as issuers, fearing exposure to mass redemptions, stopped placing further orders. It was fear of impending suppression—not a general preference for the new regal copper, which in any event could not take the tokens' place until new regal halfpennies appeared in 1799—that caused commercial token production to fall off to a mere trickle after 1797. The same fear also hampered the circulation of existing tokens, regardless of their quality. "I should be glad to send you some Macclesfield and Anglesey halfpence if they pass with you," Burslem merchant John Sherwin wrote Sheffield file maker Peter Stubs in September 1797, "because they are stopped with us" (Ashton 1939, 121).

Finally, even if the Committee on Coin's reasons for deferring production of new halfpennies and farthings had been valid, the inference it drew from them—that pence and tuppence ought to be produced instead—was a non sequitur. Copper pence and tuppence had never been issued before (these denominations having traditionally been reserved for silver), and it was not clear that they would find ready acceptance now, notwithstanding the general shortage of copper coin.

In early July, when John Southern took a break from working on Soho's new mint to solicit cartwheel orders from bankers around the country, he found that they would only take the new coins "on the strap"—that is, in exchange for three-month London bills. The bankers worried that they might have trouble disposing of the new coins and wished to avoid tying up their capital while waiting to unburden themselves. From Leeds, Southern wrote Boulton that "without some such

---

13. Of course, it would have to decide whether to receive old coins by tale or by weight and whether to receive apparent counterfeits at any value.

kind of security from loss . . . you will find few enter the business with the ardour that is to be wished" (MBP 343/31). In a later letter from Newcastle, he explained that although shopkeepers would rather have the new pennies than continue to deal in worn or fake Tower halfpence, "Halfpence I find would be fully preferable and 2 d pieces are not much liked" (MBP 343/33).

The reason for bankers' and shopkeepers' aversion to the new tuppence was obvious enough: at two ounces apiece, the "absurd" coins (the adjective is Sir John Craig's) posed a serious threat to pocket linings and were therefore judged a nuisance. As for the pennies, although they were only half as heavy, they were still much heavier and bulkier than their silver counterparts had been. That the equally heavy penny Druids supplied a successful precedent was true enough. But halfpenny Druids had proven more popular still and were for that reason the only sort produced after the closure of the Parys Mine mint. Most other commercial coins were likewise halfpennies, including the first Willeys, which, though intended to serve as pennies, were refused as such. The market having so clearly favored halfpennies over pennies with respect to commercial coins, shopkeepers and bankers had every reason to fear that it would render a similar verdict concerning regal ones.

Were their fears warranted? Respecting the twopenny coins, there's little doubt that they were: the giant coins were never popular except as curiosities, collectors' items, and paperweights. Although some large orders were placed, almost all of them came from industrialists friendly to Boulton, who used them to pay their hapless workers' salaries.[14] After the workers spent them, the huge coins were seldom seen again, except by brewers and other wholesalers and, eventually, copper smelters. That shopkeepers seldom dealt with the oversized coins was revealed by Boulton's own December 1799 investigation, which found that most kept only four drawers for copper coin: one for the new pence, one for old legal halfpence, one for the better counterfeits, and one for "raps or the very worst." The shopkeepers did not bother, in other words, to make room for the occasional tuppence they were obliged to receive. Rather than trouble other customers with them, they made them their own "pocket pieces" (MBP 362/11).

Respecting penny cartwheels, the record is less clear. On the one

---

14. Of roughly £3,200 worth of tuppence cartwheels delivered by Boulton to places apart from London, £460 went to Wilkinson's various works, £600 went to Manchester, and over £300 were kept by Soho for its own use (BL Add. MSS 38423, 375–78).

hand, once it became clear that new halfpence and farthings weren't in the offing, orders poured in—to Soho, which was responsible for meeting all provincial orders, and to Mrs. Matthews, who had agreed to supply the London market from her Fenchurch Street warehouse.[15] When she first opened for business on August 24, Mrs. Matthews was overwhelmed.

> The Coin arrived at 11 o'clock last night. . . . If I had advertised before the Coin was in my possession, I believe the house would have been pulled to pieces for never did I experience such a scene of confusion as the people made in my Warehouse today. The Bankers were shy in sending their orders, but when they saw the way the public mind was disposed, they poured in on me and would take no denials. I hope you will send another delivery while the rage prevails.   (MBP 326/53)

That the "rage" persisted is evident from Mrs. Matthews's subsequent missives: "I find the town is greedy beyond description for your pence" (October 10); "I have now orders for 157 Casks[16] of Coin: send me some or I shall be torn to pieces" (October 13); "I have 240 [outstanding cask orders] on my Book" (November 10); "of the 388 Casks that I have received this year, not one is left and I await anxiously for those coming by barge" (February 3, 1798); "I am entirely destitute of Coin" (June 29). Ultimately, the demand for cartwheels remained robust enough to allow Boulton to undertake two further commissions after the original order had been filled. In all, by July 26, 1799, when the cartwheel dies were destroyed, the market had absorbed close to forty-four million pennies as compared to a mere 722,180 tuppence.

On the other hand, even though penny cartwheels were ordered faster than Boulton could deliver them, the public's reaction to them was far from being universally favorable. John Ewer, an Aberdeen hardware retailer, was one of hundreds of provincial merchants who conveyed their disappointment directly to Boulton.[17] "I am constrained to inform you," he wrote, "of the effect of the importation we made of Penny pieces which I am sorry to say does not correspond with my sanguine expectations and certainly not with the laudable intentions of government"

---

15. Another London agent—a Mr. Chippendalls—supplied coins in Salisbury Square, Fleet Street.

16. A cask contained 250 rouleaux of twenty-four pennies each, or twenty-five pounds' worth. Six casks therefore constituted one ton of coins.

17. See PRO BT6/126, "Abstract of letters received by Mr. Boulton" etc., 142ff.

(MBP 138/134, May 19, 1798). Although many of Ewer's customers accepted the pennies, they did so reluctantly, while others refused them altogether, preferring even suspect halfpence.

It seems, furthermore, that the pennies, like their big brothers, never quite managed to become a regular component of Great Britain's circulating medium. In a 1798 report to Liverpool (BL Add. MSS 38423, 349–50), Boulton acknowledged that instead of being actively circulated, they seemed to vanish into hoards. Although he blamed this on shopkeepers' practice of continuing to pay out "illegal Coin," Boulton chose to overlook the more fundamental cause—namely, the public's willingness to go on using the old copper coin, presumably because it found the smaller coins to be relatively convenient, notwithstanding their shoddiness. That at least some of these shoddy coins were still legal tender in payments up to six pence didn't help matters.[18] In short, even putting the question of denominational convenience aside, Gresham's law tended to work against the "good" pennies and for "bad" halfpennies. The traditional solution, once again, would have been for the government to recall its old coins, depriving them of their legal tender status while offering to receive them (and perhaps some counterfeits as well) in exchange for new copper. But this traditional solution could only be resorted to once the new coinage was fully capable of rendering the old redundant. Such was obviously not the case in 1797 or 1798, and it would not be the case until a substantial quantity of new halfpennies and farthings had been coined.

In the meantime, Boulton urged the government to promote the use of cartwheels by other means. In particular, he asked it to "recommend" them to the dockyards and to the army and navy paymasters, which it eventually did. The government also arranged to have cartwheels sent to Newfoundland, Cape Town, and New South Wales. Cartwheels that private retailers were unwilling or unable to hand over to their customers were thus used by the British government itself, to be fobbed off on hapless colonials, soldiers, and sailors as well as on suppliers of naval stores.[19]

On the whole, then, the cartwheels were far less popular than numerous accounts of British numismatic history have suggested. They might have been less popular still had Boulton not wisely insisted on in-

18. Cartwheels were legal tender for payments up to one shilling.
19. Boulton pennies, halfpennies, and farthings having a total face value of twelve hundred pounds were sent to New South Wales, where they were made to do double duty by means of a proclamation rating them at twice their English value (Greig 1967).

cluding in his contract a distribution allowance of four pounds per ton, so that he could make the coins available "at every mans Door in the two Kingdoms paper'd up in Rouleaus & pack'd in new casks" (Dyer and Gaspar 1992, 448). One of the more serious shortcomings of the Royal Mint's policies—making coins available only at the Tower—was thus avoided.

But neither Boulton nor anyone else took steps to correct the mint's opposite error of failing to provide for the return of unwanted coins. Like old Tower halfpence and unlike most commercial coins, the cartwheels were irredeemable: no one pledged to convert them for their face value into Bank of England notes, much less gold guineas. Consequently, once in circulation, they tended to go on a one-way trip from manufacturers' pay tables and booths to public houses (either directly or following an extra circuit through retail stores) and thence to brewing companies, which were once again left to their own devices when it came to disposing of them. Before long, complaints concerning excess supplies of copper coin, reminiscent of those heard back in the 1770s and before, were once again being heard.

Liquid Assets

Luckily, the problem of unwanted cartwheels lasted only a few years. But even this seemingly fortunate fact pointed to a final and ultimately fatal flaw in the cartwheel coinage. A further, sharp increase in the price of copper cake, from an average of £112 in June 1797 to as much as £165 in April 1805, kept brewers from being permanently saddled with useless coins. Owing to the war, raw copper fetched even more in European ports, such as at Cadiz, where it was already bringing as much as £175 a ton by early 1799 (Wager 1977, 46: see also Peck 1970, 218; app. 10(c), p. 614). Because the nominal value of a ton of cartwheels was only about £150, melting them or otherwise selling them as junk copper became worthwhile (despite penalties) once the price of copper rose substantially above that level.

Considering how brewers and others had been complaining about unwanted cartwheels piling up in their vaults, it shouldn't surprise anybody to find that rumors of cartwheels being exported to Holland and elsewhere began to be heard as early as July 1798 (MBP 326/105; Wager 1977, 45). As the price of copper continued to rise, British coppersmiths began bidding against their foreign counterparts for cartwheels. By the time the domestic price of copper cake reached its peak of £165 a ton in

April 1805, a brisk trade in cartwheel smelting had been going on for some time. On April 13, the *Times* reported on what may have been a typical (though foiled) instance of this trade.

> It having been for some time known that the late copper coin was collecting for the purpose of melting down, orders were issued for the Police to keep a strict look-out: and on Thursday an Officer . . . followed a cart with eight casks of penny and twopenny pieces, containing 18 cwt. 21 lb. from Saffron Hill, to a coppersmith's in Upper Thames Street, and secured the property for future investigation. The penalty is 100l. and forfeiture of the goods.   (PECK 1970, 614)

Harsh penalties and eagle-eyed constables notwithstanding, it appears that substantial quantities of cartwheels ended up being turned back into raw copper within eight years of having been made from it. That many also survived was testimony not so much to the success of injunctions against the melting of coin but to their bulkiness (which caused them to be placed into service as paperweights and ashtrays or consigned to piggy banks and curio cabinets before the copper smelters could lay their hands on them) and to the appearance, during the first decades of the nineteenth century, of substantial numbers of light cartwheel counterfeits.[20]

That genuine cartwheels were made so heavy to begin with, despite the bulkiness this weight entailed and the threat posed by the unstable price of copper, seems foolish in retrospect. But there was a principle at stake: namely, that coins ought not to be rated substantially above their "intrinsic value." This principle, long applied to Britain's silver and gold coins (with adverse consequences already noted), was extended to official copper coins when these were first authorized by the proclamation of 1672. According to that proclamation, the Royal Mint was to coin halfpennies and farthings containing "as much copper in weight, as shall

---

20. Although the high price of copper supplied a means for brewers and others profitably to dispose of their unwanted cartwheels, the decline in copper's price after 1805, plus the reduced standard of later Boulton copper, revived the problem of redundant copper coin once again. In October 1813, the "Wholesale and Retail Traders, Manufacturers, Brewers, Distillers, and Licensed Victuallers in *London* and its Vicinity" complained to the Privy Council Committee on Coin that they continued "to experience heavy Losses and Inconveniences, in consequence of the excessive quantity of Copper Coinage circulation in and about the Metropolis," which they could dispose of only by offering copper coins to "Mfrs, Pawnbrokers, and others, in return for Bills drawn at three months," despite being, in many cases, in no position to extend credit (BPP 1813, 237).

be the true intrinsick value and worth of a halfpenny or farthing respectively, the charges of coyning and uttering being onely deducted." In contrast, the proclamation giving currency to Soho's cartwheels called for them to have an "intrinsic value . . . Workmanship included, corresponding as nearly as possible with the nominal Value of the same." In short, the government had gained nothing from 125 years of copper coinage experience, including the largely successful and therefore especially instructive commercial coinage episode, save a slight improvement in spelling.

Well, perhaps it gained a little more than that, for it at least realized the need to make its small change harder to counterfeit. That goal was, after all, one of its reasons (the other being a simple desire to save time and money) for assigning the new copper coinage to Boulton, who had insisted that his machinery, besides coining money faster and less expensively than ever before, would make coins that could not be profitably imitated.

Alas, it did no such thing.

Sincerely Flattered

Although a parliamentary act of July 19, 1797 made counterfeiting cartwheels a felony, cartwheel counterfeits—"reasonably plausible" ones, according to Richard Doty (1998, 317)—were being detected in London and elsewhere within about two months of the originals' debut. While Doty assures his readers that "there were not enough of them to represent more than a nuisance," Boulton himself wasn't so sanguine. By October, he'd become concerned enough to put the following notice in *Piersons' Paper:*

COPPER COIN

WHEREAS an Act of Parliament was passed the nineteenth of July, 1797, for the more effectually preventing the COUNTERFEITING of the current COPPER COIN of this Kingdom, and the uttering or paying of the same: And whereas certain PENNY PIECES (described in his majesty's Royal Proclamation) have been put into Circulation but in Defiance of all Law, they have been counterfeited, by crafting others of base Metal, from Impressions made from them in Sand or Loom, and Issued in Payment, and taken by such inattentive Persons;

It is necessary therefore to inform such Persons,

THE BOULTON COPPER 175

1st. That whatever Pieces are cast in Sand, have a Manifest Roughness upon their Surface, very much un-like the smooth Polish given by Steel Dies in a Coining Press.

2dly. That they are not cast of pure red Copper, but of a Mixture of base Metals, and are of a paler Colour than the legal Coin.

3dly. That from the Contraction or Shrinking of the cast BASE METAL in casting, the Pieces are a little less in Diameter than the legal Coin, and much lighter.

4thly. That the Edges of the Counterfeits are rough and imperfect.

N. B. It may be also proper to observe, that the legal Pence weigh one Ounce, and are of equal Diameter, and seventeen of them laid in a Line, measure two Feet. Any Information on the Subject will be thankfully received, and the Parties giving it handsomely rewarded, by

M. BOULTON.

Soho, Oct. 6, 1797

Although the notice doesn't tell just how "handsomely" snitchers were to be paid, Doty (ibid.) gives the amount as one hundred guineas, which was no small sum. Boulton had more than patriotic reasons for being so generous: besides violating the royal prerogative of coinage, counterfeiters were making a mockery of his claim that his coins could not be imitated.

A year and several months passed during which Boulton's offer elicited no response. Then, in January 1799, he received the following letter.

Mr. Bolton Sir,

this is to inform you that I think I can find out A person that is A making your Penny pieces in this town & they make 3 or 4 hundred Pr week wich should be glad to have a letter from your hand in form me What Premium you Will Give mee to have them Appren'd & your letter this Afternoon to the Post Office til Caled for, for W.P. & you may Depend on me caling for it & then i will give my self the Pleasure to Call up on you in A day or 2 Sir should take it to a favour not to let Any person now about this & you will much oblige

your Most obedient Humble
Searvant
W.P. Friday Morning 11 clock.

(MBP 149/275)

Boulton paid the semiliterate "W.P." (who turned out to be a man named William Phillips), and in return heard about not one but three cartwheel counterfeiting operations, all running right under Boulton's nose, in Birmingham. With the Birmingham magistrate's permission, Boulton and fourteen of his workers joined the Birmingham constables in staging simultaneous raids on all three premises. One group headed to Navigation Street, where they caught Richard Barber red-handed. Another nabbed a fellow named Pitt, whom Boulton called an "old offender." The third group, which forced its way into the home of one Thomas Nichols, wasn't so lucky. Boulton's account of how Nichols managed to save his bacon reads like something out of a penny dreadful. According to Boulton his men

> were informed that he [Nichols] was in the upper most Shop. They mounted & enterd, but it was empty. Upon observing a secret door, they attempted to pass, but found some resistance on ye other side, & a struggle ensued at length ye Constable thrust his shaft through, & upon the sight of it Nicholls [*sic*], like Harlequin, jumped through a door upon a ladder, which he instantly kicked down and then descended into a lower room in which there was no door, & he escaped through a Window contrived for that purpose.   (DICKINSON 1936, 153)

Later, Boulton found out, to his chagrin, that Phillips had himself been faking cartwheels, having turned on his fellow forgers either to settle a score with them or simply to take the heat off himself. Though Phillips was never convicted for imitating Boulton's coins, a William Phillips, who may well have been the same man, was charged in 1807 in Warwick with counterfeiting Prussian groats (Powell 1979, 218).

As for the other culprits, one hears nothing more of Pitt, who presumably went scot-free. Barber also managed to get off the hook, thanks to the ill will that Royal Mint officials harbored toward the man who was, by their lights, usurping their authority. Having convened a grand jury, the Lent assizes at Warwick were prepared to charge Barber with counterfeiting soon after his arrest. But Barber could be indicted only with the help of John Vernon, the mint's solicitor, who was supposed to affirm the propriety of Boulton's complaint. Boulton duly wrote to Vernon, requesting his cooperation, only to have a month go by before receiving a reply wherein Vernon promised to send Mr. Powell, his assistant, to Warwick at once. But Vernon's delay had been such that, by the sheerest of coincidences, "at once" meant that Powell would arrive at Warwick on

March 26—the very day after which the Warwick judge had been forced to discharge the grand jury and acquit Barber for want of evidence (Powell 1979, 218).

While the judge himself found "the dilatory proceedings of the Mint . . . very shameful, but by no means unusual," Boulton's colleague William Cheshire saw them as part of a concerted effort on the mint's part to harass Boulton.

> The Mint wish to set at nought the authenticity of your money and so far are they from admitting propriety or power of your prosecutions . . . that they wish to have it considered that you are liable to be persecuted yourself. . . .
>
> I hope, Sir, you will excuse me for expressing the belief I entertain that the men of the Mint are endeavoring by this means to give a death blow to your coinage.   (IBID.)

Cheshire wasn't being paranoid. A few days before he let Barber get away, Vernon accused Boulton of having himself counterfeited regal copper coins by striking one hundred tons more than he'd been authorized to strike; Vernon then offered Boulton some "friendly" advice, which Boulton ignored, to the effect that Boulton ought not to press the matter of Barber's prosecution, as doing so might provide grounds for Boulton's own arrest and conviction. As we shall see, this wasn't the first time the Royal Mint tried to intimidate a rival with accusations of counterfeiting.

Barber's contribution to the counterfeit cartwheel trade was noteworthy not only because of the way he managed to get away with it but also because his forgeries, which were struck on a screw press using hand-engraved dies, were extremely accurate (Wager 1977, 51). They were not, in other words, lower-end sand-cast imitations of the sort referred to in Boulton's newspaper notice. That someone had managed profitably to imitate the cartwheel dies and design features, presumably without having to build a steam-powered mint, was especially disturbing, for this ability appeared to undermine Boulton's claims concerning the anticounterfeiting advantages of steam-struck coinage.

In truth, Boulton appears to have fallen victim to his own exaggerated claims for steam power. He managed to convince himself not only that a change in motive power, from grunting men to a puffing steam engine, could somehow make coins harder to imitate but that this change could serve instead of traditional anticounterfeiting measures, including edge markings and high-relief engravings not so readily adapted to Soho's steam-powered equipment. In short, Boulton, who had a knack for making a virtue out of necessity, was led to promote steam power as a cure-all for Great Britain's coining ills. What's surprising is that so many people believed him.

Cornered

Despite the cartwheels' shortcomings, or to some extent *because of* those very shortcomings (which caused cartwheels to disappear into hoards and, eventually, melting pots), Boulton, who had begun lobbying to have his original contract extended ever since August 1797 (Doty 1998, 318), received the Privy Council's permission to undertake a second order of five hundred tons of cartwheels. This was followed by a third contract, in November 1798, for 250 tons of pence.[21] By the latter date, Boulton was also lobbying for an equally large (if not larger) commission for regal halfpennies and farthings.

Boulton had every reason to seek these additional orders. He had a long way to go to recoup the expense of his first mint, let alone the considerably greater expense of its replacement. Any long lag between orders might force him either to lay off skilled employees who could not easily be replaced or to go on paying their salaries despite having nothing for them to do.

If Boulton was to keep his mint busy, he had to meet three challenges. He had to realize his plan for rebuilding the Soho Mint, for the original was too feeble to survive another round of cartwheel strikings and too slow to yield the twenty tons per week of halfpence that Boulton was proposing to supply. He also had to come up with enough copper to complete his new commissions. Finally, he had to secure a royal warrant for coining halfpennies and farthings, in place of the vague promises he'd been banking on so far.

Of these challenges, the first might appear to have been the most difficult. Yet the others proved equally so, in no small part because, in confronting them, Boulton found himself face-to-face with an old nemesis. The formidable Thomas Williams, MP, appeared to be doing everything he could to foil Boulton's plans, starting with buying every ounce of fine copper in the country.

---

21. Although these are the figures in the Privy Council's own records, Boulton, in correspondence, puts the total tonnage of these cartwheels at 760.

It was in the course of getting hold of copper for some of his commercial coin commissions that Boulton first realized how close Williams was to cornering the market. Williams had long been the main supplier of copper ships' sheathing, bolts, and nails for the British navy. For that reason, he needed all the fine copper he could get his hands on. To that end he had, since 1793, been using forward contracts to get first dibs on all or part of the copper-smelting companies' output, at prices reflecting the annual average price of copper at the time when the contracts were signed (Harris 1964, 110). Firms that participated in Williams's scheme had to give him three months notice to terminate their agreements. Otherwise, they were bound to sell their copper to him, no matter how much others offered for it (ibid., 111). In 1794, Williams also began to purchase Cornish ore to smelt at his own Welsh works. Those Cornish ore purchases alone allowed him to make between two and three hundred tons of sheet copper each year through 1799.

Until 1797, Boulton didn't mind Williams's copper-purchasing scheme, for good reason: between 1792 and 1796, he was among the scheme's beneficiaries, who sold substantial quantities of copper to Williams and made handsome profits by doing so. But once he had an inkling that the regal coinage contract was coming his way, Boulton's attitude toward the Copper King changed sharply (Harris 1964, 111–12). In the fall of 1796, when the East India Company placed an order with Boulton for 150 tons of coin, he found that Williams again had claims to most of Great Britain's fine copper. Boulton was only able to carry out the promised coinage by having John Company supply its own copper. The prospect of a regal contract for five hundred tons of coinage posed a far greater challenge. On March 4 and again on March 7, Boulton wrote his Cornwall agent Thomas Wilson, who was connected with Fenton & Company, the copper smelters, asking for his help, only to have Wilson remind him that both Fenton & Company and Foxes, their principal rivals, were "under positive engagements to sell all they make to Mr Williams" and that they could only sell to others with Williams's consent. "I am very much of the opinion," Wilson added, "that you will not get Copper except through Williams: why not treat him as a friend? I know the bone is Rolling: cannot you divide it?" (MBP 369/191–92, Wilson to Boulton, March 7 and 10).

Although Wilson had no way of knowing it, to "divide the bone" was, in fact, precisely what Boulton had promised to do, in an agreement he and Williams sealed with a handshake in John Wilkinson's presence almost ten years earlier. Williams was to supply Boulton with hot-rolled copper sheets for any regal copper coining Boulton undertook, while Boulton was to handle everything else, including the cold rolling. Boulton was also supposed to keep Williams fully informed of any progress he made in securing a regal contract. Williams agreed, in return, to give up his own aspirations to coin for the government.

Under the circumstances, it should have been natural for Boulton to go directly to Williams for his copper. Only Boulton had no intention of honoring his gentleman's agreement with Williams. Instead, he hoped to add the profit from rolling copper into sheets to whatever else he might earn from the regal coinage, and he decided for that reason to round up five hundred tons of fine copper on the sly, while keeping Williams in the dark as long as possible concerning the good news from Whitehall.

So instead of taking Wilson's advice, Boulton had him scrounge around for copper cake wherever he could find it, trying at first to pay as little as £100 a ton for it. Boulton quickly learned, however, that he could get nothing at all for less than £106 and little even for £108, which turned out to be the maximum price allowed for in his contract. Still he clung to his plan, displaying a friendly front all the while to the man he was trying his best to deceive. Thus, on March 6, just two days after Williams had been kind enough to write Boulton to advise him of the Treasury's plan to countermark dollars (which Williams feared might be intended as a substitute for a renewed copper coinage), Boulton, who knew the truth but kept mum about it, was asking Wilson "for all the copper he could lay his hands on" and telling him to keep the order "entirely secret from Williams" (Harris 1964, 112).

That same evening, Boulton and Williams dined together, with Boulton later informing Wilson of just how "very civil to me & friendly" Williams had been, as if to congratulate himself for pulling the wool over Williams's eyes. Boulton kept up the friendly front so that he might get some copper through Williams in a pinch; yet behind the scenes, he attacked him without mercy. The day before their "friendly" dinner, for instance, he complained bitterly to Watt that "Williams seems to have monopolized the whole" of the market for fine copper and that he was thus causing the government to think twice about ordering a new copper coinage (MBP, Boulton to Watt, March 10, 1797, quoted in Harris 1964, 112).

It was, of course, impossible for Boulton to keep his plans for regal copper coinage a secret for very long. In early March, he'd managed to get hold of twenty tons of copper from the Cheadle Smelting Company by telling Williams, who had a lien on the copper, that he needed it to complete his latest East India Company coinage. Williams sold Boulton the copper, only to discover what he really wanted it for around mid-March. The discovery infuriated Williams, both because he'd been lied to and because Boulton had violated the terms of their old agreement. On March 20, Boulton drafted a letter to Williams in which he tried to justify what he'd done by arguing, among other things, that Williams would have done the same under similar circumstances. "Now my good Sir," Boulton wrote, "permit me to ask whether you or any other prudent man in trade would not have taken time by the forlock [*sic*] and acted as I have done" (Harris 1964, 113). Whether or not the letter was sent is unclear; in any event, Williams did not forgive Boulton. According to Williams's biographer J. R. Harris, "the decisive break between the two men dates from this time" (ibid.).

Still desperate for fine copper and having burned his bridge to Williams, Boulton had only one option left, which was to smelt his own. To this end, he arranged, toward the end of March, to have the Rose Copper Company, of which he was "a leading member," buy out Fenton & Company (Harris 1964, 114). Boulton could then compete directly with Williams for Cornish ore, bypassing him altogether when it came to executing the new coinage.

Ironically enough, Boulton might have had a lot less trouble getting around Williams's copper corner if he and the government had taken advice Williams himself gave them. On March 16, 1797, the Committee on Coin interviewed Williams concerning the state of the market for manufactured copper, which was then fetching £112 a ton. Asked what he thought would happen to the price over the course of the next ten years, Williams replied,

> If the Consumption of Copper increases, as I think it will, in the same proportion for the next ten years, as it has done in the last ten years, I would not venture to engage for any considerable time, for any considerable Quantity, delivered either in London or Birmingham, for so low as £112 per Ton.   (PRO BT6/126)

Williams went on to attribute the rising price of copper to the increased consumption of it in manufacturing, especially in ships' sheathing (which consumed between four hundred and five hundred tons of copper annually in Liverpool alone); to the even higher price of copper in Europe (which precluded importation); and to reduced mine yields both abroad and at home. His own Anglesey Mines, Williams observed, "have not, for these Two last Years, produced Copper in such Quantity as they did before, and their future produce depends on Contingencies, upon which it is impossible to calculate" (ibid.).

Nobody knew the copper situation better than Williams did, which is presumably why the Committee on Coin interviewed him on the subject. Yet despite his forthright answers to their questions, the committee, in its final report, did precisely what he told it not to do; that is, it estimated the cost of manufactured copper for the proposed coinage at only £112 per ton. What's worse, the Treasury, in its subsequent revision of the committee's proposal, lowered the copper allowance to just £108 per ton, which, far from allowing for copper's likely appreciation, was considerably below its average price over the course of the preceding year. Boulton, who should have known better but did not wish to risk losing his long-sought contract, imprudently went along with the modified terms, thereby committing himself, in essence, to getting hold of five hundred tons of copper despite being reimbursed for it only at a rate at least four pounds per ton below what Williams and others were paying.[22] Then, when he realized his mistake, instead of blaming himself, or the government, he blamed Thomas Williams.

Boulton was hardly alone in making Williams a scapegoat. As the price of copper cake kept going up, from £96.12 a ton in 1797 to over £123 in February 1799, increasingly loud and bitter complaints were voiced by the Birmingham hardware men, who watched their already meager profit margins being whittled away and were convinced that Williams was to blame (Harris 1964, 115). Although the fundamental reasons for copper's rising price had little to do with Williams, who had merely been astute enough to anticipate and protect his own interests against the price increase, this did not stop Pitt and Hawkesbury from denouncing Williams (then representing the borough of Marlow) in Parliament, provoking him to demand a committee of inquiry to clear himself. According to Harris (1964, 116–18, 121–23, 135–36), Boulton played a major part in "prodding" Pitt's government into vilifying Williams, partly out of sheer animosity toward the man, but also because he hoped that doing so might lead to measures to limit copper exports and otherwise hold down copper prices.

What made the accusations leveled against Williams particularly la-

---

22. Recall how Boulton employed the same flawed strategy to secure a token contract with the Monneron Frères back in 1791 (see chap. 3).

mentable was that Williams's critics had done far more to drive up the price of copper than Williams himself could possibly have done. What's more, these critics were perfectly aware of the truth. Thanks to declining yields in Cornwall and Anglesey, Great Britain's annual production of copper ore had fallen to a level sufficient to produce only about seventy-eight hundred tons of fine copper, if that. Of that total, the East India Company alone claimed about fifteen hundred tons a year, while the Admiralty took another thousand or so tons. Finally, the copper coinage itself, having already absorbed twelve hundred tons of metal at the time of the inquiry, was expected to absorb another thirty-five hundred tons over the course of the subsequent two and a half years. In short, while the government was trying in earnest to blame the high and rising price of copper on Williams's "artificial dealings," it was gobbling up almost half of Great Britain's dwindling copper output. Boulton was well aware of these facts, having set them down himself in a paper he sent to the Committee on Coin less than a year before the inquiry (PRO BT6/117, n.d.). But his testimony to the committee of inquiry concerning the central issue of Williams's culpability was craftily neutral.

Rankled by Boulton's treachery, Williams tried to turn the tables on him. During the third week of the inquiry, which began on April 8 and lasted a month, he, like Vernon, accused Boulton of coining cartwheels illegally. Unlike the accusations raised against Williams, this one had merit, for Boulton finished his second 500-ton batch of cartwheels and was starting on a final 250-ton batch without having secured a warrant for either. In fact, Boulton had nothing at all in writing to offer the committee of inquiry in his own defense, having undertaken the new commissions solely on the basis of "verbal" (i.e., spoken) orders from the Committee on Coin (MBP 362/63, Boulton to Ambrose Weston, July 21, 1799). Although the Committee was to blame for the oversight, and one can only sympathize with Boulton's desire to continue coining so as to avoid having to lay off his mint staff, there is no getting around the fact that Boulton had broken the law, which equated making regal coins without a royal warrant with counterfeiting.[23]

Boulton managed to wriggle out of the "paltry trap" Williams set for him, Parliament having voted to retroactively legalize his illegal coining. Moreover, what came to be called the "Copper Enquiry" ended up work-

---

23. There is, however, no evidence supporting John Powell's (1979, 219) conjecture that Boulton engaged in illicit coining to compensate himself for diminished profits owing to the unexpected rise in copper's price.

ing as Boulton hoped it would, by preparing the way for a reduction in the duty on copper imports and restrictions on copper exports. Thanks to these measures, to a series of reductions in the copper coinage standard (from sixteen pence per pound weight of copper in 1797 to eighteen pence in 1799 and to twenty-four pence afterward), and to substantial increases in the price allowed for fine copper (from £108 per ton in 1797 to £121 in 1799, £169 in 1805–6, and £143 in 1807), Boulton was able to get hold of or to make all the fine copper he needed to complete his regal commissions.

As for Williams, while he certainly didn't profit from the Copper Enquiry, he at least managed to get through it relatively unscathed, if somewhat unnerved (Harris 1964, 135–36; see also Levy 1927, 142–56). When it finally came out, the report of the committee of inquiry (BPP 1799) was inconclusive; but this hardly mattered to Williams any more, for by then both his business empire and his health were rapidly deteriorating. Long beset by asthma, the Copper King was now afflicted by gout as well, which made it increasingly difficult for him to write or walk. In November 1802, he lapsed into unconsciousness, never to wake again. As if their own stamina were inextricably linked to that of their owner, the Anglesey Mines petered out around the same time.

Long-smoldering resentments harbored against this man who outmaneuvered them so often kept Williams's business peers from supplying epitaphs (or favorable ones, at any rate). Boulton, for his part, remained convinced that Williams was plotting against him to the bitter end. But Williams's former workers still thought of him as "Tom Fair Play," and his closest associate, Pascoe Grenfell, was being truthful, if unoriginal, when, echoing Hamlet, he wrote, "Take him all in all it is hardly to be expected that we shall meet his like again" (Harris 1964, 138).

Halfpennies at Last

Although Boulton's enemies didn't manage to make their counterfeiting charges stick, they couldn't have raised them at a worse time for Boulton, who was then desperately trying to get a warrant for coining halfpennies and farthings. Boulton was counting on receiving such a warrant before running through his cartwheel orders. Just as the Copper Enquiry was getting under way, on April 9, he'd written to Soho's clerk, asking him to tell Southern to adjust the "balls" on two of the mint's presses so that they'd run at the faster rates halfpence and farthings would allow and to have Küchler send plaster impressions of the proposed halfpenny dies to London.

Küchler's halfpenny and farthing designs represented a major change from the cartwheels. The cartwheels' raised rims were abandoned in favor of "concave," saucerlike fields. While Boulton, true to form, claimed that the concave designs would serve to deter counterfeiting, their main purpose, like that of the rims they replaced, was to preserve the coins' shallow engravings from wear and tear.[24] Another modification did, however, represent a genuine deterrent to counterfeiters, though one that was hardly original: the blanks for the smaller coins were to have their edges grained, or "milled," before striking.[25]

The new coins were also to be struck at the lowered standard of eighteen pence (or thirty-six halfpennies) per pound weight of copper. Boulton first proposed the lower standard in 1798, when copper reached £113 per ton—a price that made coining at the former standard of sixteen pence per pound a losing proposition (PRO BT6/380). Although Boulton's advice was followed in the government's first, 1799 commission for halfpennies and farthings, further increases in copper's price would eventually cause the standard to be lowered still further, to twenty-four pence per pound, which was slightly below the old Tower standard. The Boulton halfpennies and farthings were thus steered clear of the melting pots that consumed so many cartwheels.

On the whole, the coins Boulton was now looking forward to making appeared to have less in common with his cartwheels than they had with earlier commercial coins, including most of Boulton's own commercial products. In other words, the government was finally getting around to

---

24. The concave designs also served to accommodate a lowered standard (discussed shortly in text) while maintaining standard coin diameters and edges.

25. The edge-marking process also served to "upset" blanks—thickening their outer edges. Thus prepared, the blanks would retain their grained edges after being struck in plain, one-piece collars (Doty, personal communication, February 17, 2004). The need for a segmented collar of the sort Droz had employed was thus avoided.

Despite the lower standard to which it was made, later Boulton copper does not appear to have been counterfeited as the cartwheels had been. London memorialists, writing mainly to complain of surplus coins in October 1813, also complained about continued presence of much old counterfeit coin, which they hesitated to refuse for "fear of offending their customers," but which they hoped would eventually be done away with by recalling all the old, though legitimate, Tower halfpence (BPP 1813, 238). However, they also observed that they "have rarely seen any attempts to imitate or counterfeit the new Coin," which by then would have consisted mainly of Boulton's halfpennies and farthings.

supplying manufacturers and shopkeepers with coins resembling those they commissioned when they could have their money custom made.

Designing better coins was one thing; getting permission to make them was quite another. The new Soho Mint was ready to start coining Küchler's halfpence and farthings by the summer of 1799, and merchants had been pleading for them ever since the first cartwheels became available. But Boulton would not receive official permission to do so until November, and he would not be allowed to sell a single halfpenny or farthing until early December. For the better part of six months, one bureaucratic delay gave way to another: first, Boulton's proposal was found to be in the wrong format; then, he needed to supply separate proposals for coining and for copper. These were "accepted" by Liverpool and His Majesty in April, but the attorney general was in the country, and a royal warrant could not be prepared in his absence. By the time the attorney general returned, the secretary of the Treasury, whose involvement was also necessary, had left. So matters went for month after excruciating month.

By mid-August, with another month to go before the attorney general bagged his last partridge, Boulton was in despair. "I cannot think of any other subject at present than the Coinage," he wrote to Ambrose Weston, his solicitor, who had agreed to serve as his London agent in securing the halfpence commission.

> The delay of the coinage will be fatal to my peace, to my Credit, & to that regular system of circulation wch. I have established throughout the whole Kingdom. I receive a doz letters every day with orders for Casks of Coins and as I have many regular periodical customers they also will be disappointed & will be obliged to adopt other measures & other base Coin again. . . .
>
> If Lord Liverpool would be so obliging to call a Comm.tee I am persuaded the business might be put into some train of going on without an entire stop being put to ye Coinage for 3 months, & if the regular forms of Office cannot be obtain'd, I should be satisfy'd with the same authority w.ch I receiv'd for the 760 Ton of pence I last Coin'd viz. a letter from the Comm.tee or from Lord Liverpool: for as the King has approv'd the Specimen & the proposal for coining 550 Ton the remainder is only form & Ceremony which may be conform'd to as soon as the law officers return to Town or sooner by sending the Warrant or other papers by Express, and unless something of this kind is done the whole Kingdom will grow ill humour'd from disap-

pointment Insomuch that they will throw obstructions in the way of circulating the Coin when it does come out & set their faces against it but independent of all publick considerations it is cruel to me who am losing the interest of Seventy thousand pounds besides paying a considerable weekly expense to a set of people whom I cannot replace if I turn them off.   (MBP 362/77)

In truth, Boulton was already striking halfpennies, despite the risks of doing so, which he knew all too well. "I have ventured to coin 20 tons last week," he informed Weston in a letter of August 24 (MBP 362/82), "but it is unpleasant to do that which is not lawful." By mid-October, he'd coined another eighty tons, yet he still had no warrant and would not have one until November 4. Even then, he could not breathe a sigh of relief, for the Treasury would not allow him to sell the new coins until they were declared current by royal proclamation. Just days before the proclamation finally appeared, in early December, Boulton claimed that the coins he'd made were costing him no less than one hundred pounds a week in interest. This and other circumstances (including the Tower Mint's tendering of a rival bid) were, Boulton opined, "not encouraging rewards for the thought and money I have expended in carrying the Art of Coining to its *ne plus ultra*" (MBP 362/104–2, Boulton to Weston, December 2).

Although Lord Liverpool tried to assure him that the delays he'd suffered through were nothing more than bureaucratic bungling, Boulton had no doubt that Williams and his friends at the Treasury were behind it. They had, he told Weston, formed "a Cabal to rob me of the Coinage, my inventions, my character, and tire me out" (ibid.). But tired though he may have been, Boulton would not be defeated. By Christmas week, he was close to meeting his goal of manufacturing twenty tons of halfpennies and farthings per week, though still far from meeting his orders, which were ten times greater. To Mrs. Matthews, who had been besieged with inquiries for months, he promised two hundred casks a week "til you say stop" (MBP 326/190). So far as the records indicate, she never did.

A New Leviathan

While Boulton and Williams were locking horns in London, John Southern and James Harley were struggling to put Soho's new mint together. In January 1798, Southern, who'd been working for Soho since 1782 and was one of Watt's most capable assistants, came up with a new idea for working the coining presses in series using a vacuum drive instead of Boulton's clanking carousel. Encouraged by a five-hundred-pound bonus Boulton promised to pay him if the idea actually worked, Southern saw it through its first successful trials in mid-April. Around the same time, Southern viewed sketches for the new mint building—a curved and double-roofed shed measuring about fifty by twenty feet—into which Boulton hoped to squeeze a row of eight new vacuum-driven presses. A new engine house, with a sixteen-horsepower engine, and a new lapping-up room, were also planned. The engine house was to be placed at the southern end of the old coining shed, with the new lapping-up room immediately to its right, where it would butt up against the south end of the new coining shed. By late summer, piles of brick and oak timbers had accumulated around the construction site, and in September, Samuel Wyatt came back to Soho to supervise the new mint's construction.

By New Year's Day 1799, the new steam engine was up and ready to be set working. A month later, Boulton, who was detained in London throughout the mint's construction, was pleased to inform Sir Joseph Banks that he had "finished and set to work my Leviathan" (MBP 272, quoted in Doty 1998, 56). But Harley didn't finish the first pair of new presses until the first of February, and even those weren't moved to the new coining shed until a week later. Two more months went by before a second pair joined them.

In the meantime, Boulton, having agreed some time before to refurbish Russia's Imperial Mint, was rash enough to invite the Russian ambassador to see his new mint at work during the first week of May. With just three weeks to go and only four of eight presses ready, he promised Harley a three-guinea bonus if he finished by May 1. The extra inducement did the trick, though just barely. "I have the pleasure to write," Southern scribbled in a note dashed off to Boulton on May Day, "what I hoped you could have seen *with your own eyes to day,* that all the eight presses have been at work *together* for a considerable time this morning" (MBP 343/48).

So Boulton was not disappointed; and neither, it seems, was the Russian ambassador. Strolling from the grounds through the new mint's elegant main entrance, next to Boulton's tea room, His Imperial Majesty's London representative passed through a sumptuously furnished entry hall and into an antechamber, where a large Boulton & Watt patented "Polygraphic" portrait of Catherine the Great was surrounded by smaller portraits of Boulton and Watt and by still other Polygraphic pictures, including a fine rendering of Isaac blessing Jacob.

Beyond the antechamber was the mint room itself, as noisy as Bedlam and still reeking of the fresh paint on its dark green walls, stone-colored trim, and sky blue ceiling. Supporting the ceiling were two rows of rose-bearing cast-iron columns, which straddled a straight series of eight presses, each of which was jammed into a space scarcely exceeding a six-foot square. Attached to the upper end of the screw of each press was a large suction head, from which a spindle extended into the attic above. (Although the ambassador couldn't see it, and would not have been told of it even if he'd ventured to ask, the spindles were the first of a sequence of links leading from the presses to eight vacuum cylinders—one for each press—to which steam was delivered from the engine house by means of several "spirit pipes" hidden below the mint's raised floor.) The presses were operated by young boys dressed in blue and red uniforms and sitting in a cubical space set three feet below floor level (Joshua Gilpin quoted in Doty 1998, 58). This arrangement allowed the boys to keep their eyes on the presses' lower dies, where wayward or missing blanks might do mischief. Besides having to stop and start the presses when necessary, the boys were responsible for filling their round blank-feeding hoppers with blanks delivered from the lapping-up room in 12 × 6 × 3 inch trays.

At the time of the Russian ambassador's visit, the presses were all running like clatters, with six of them striking penny cartwheels at a rate of sixty coins per minute, while the remaining two churned out halfpence and farthings at sixty-three and seventy-two coins per minute, respectively. (Further tuning would eventually raise the last figures to seventy and eighty.) Three of Soho's old presses, updated with Southern's vacuum drive, were also striking pennies in the original mint building, though at the slower rate of forty-two coins per minute. Blanks continued to be cut at the main manufactory, where the small version of Boulton's mechanical "carousel" was still in use. Before the week was out, Boulton had to ask Southern to stop coining halfpennies and farthings, as he had yet to receive written orders for them and feared that Williams or some of Williams's "Mint friends" might again spring a trap on him. Over the next eight years, however, the new mint would supply Great Britain and Ireland with 2,950 tons of halfpennies and farthings—close to three times the weight of copper coin produced at the Tower Mint throughout the entire eighteenth century.

Besides allowing Boulton to fulfill his regal coinage commissions, the new Soho Mint served as the prototype for a brand-new Royal Mint. Matthew Boulton's hard-won coinage contracts were more than just a triumph for Soho and its founder. They marked the beginning of the end for the "old shop."

Getting Screwed

Not only since the Garbetts issued their scathing report in 1783, but for the better part of a century, the Royal Mint successfully fought off all manner of proposals for its reform. Administratively, it retained the same medieval character it possessed in the late seventeenth century, and some of its equipment was no less out of date.

Nothing better illustrates the tenacity with which the Company of Moneyers resisted technical innovation than their successful scuttling, over the course of more than a century, of repeated attempts to mechanize coinage through the substitution of screw or roller presses for shears and hammers.

While the screw press appears to have first been employed by Italian medallists, including Bramante, around the turn of the sixteenth century (Craig 1953, 117), the technology was first used to strike coins in Augsburg in the late 1540s.[26] From there, screw presses spread to other parts of Europe, including Paris, where the Monnaie du Moulin, completed in 1553, was equipped with them. They found their way from France to Elizabethan England when Eloi (or Eloy) Mestrell, a former Paris Mint employee who also happened to be a Huguenot, sought asylum there from Catholic persecution. At the time, Elizabeth was struggling to undertake the massive recoinage made necessary by her predecessors' Great Debasement, so Mestrell was allowed to set up his machinery at the Tower Mint (ibid., 123). In October 1561, his new coins "passed all trials without incident" (K. Davis 2001, 118), and that December, the queen awarded him an annuity of twenty-five pounds so that he might continue coining.

Although the Company of Moneyers was violently opposed to Mestrell's presence and methods, they could at first do nothing about these because the government had abolished their traditional, autonomous status (along with the posts of master and warden) back in 1543, substituting in its stead direct government management of the

---

26. Richard Doty, personal communication, February 17, 2004.

coinage. So, despite Royal Mint officials' opposition, Mestrell was able to go on coining money his way, under their very noses, for the better part of a decade. To the officials' dismay, Mestrell's coins "were very well received by the public," being "not only more round and more evenly struck than their hammered counterparts" but also "much more elaborate, and finely engraved" (K. Davis 2001, 118).

In 1571, however, the Royal Mint began to turn the tables on Mestrell. In that year, the moneyers arranged new trials aimed at showing that Mestrell's methods were less cost-efficient than hand hammering. In particular, the trials established that the process of preparing blanks of proper weight took more than ten times as long using Mestrell's machines. The following April, the Royal Mint's old constitution was reinstated, with the master and warden—Richard (later Sir Richard) Martin—once again assuming full responsibility for the mint's operation. Martin at once shut down Mestrell's operation, declaring, "Neither said engine nor any workmanship to be wrought thereby will be to the Queen's Majesty's profit" (Mackay 1984, 35; Andrew 1974, 857–58).

Although most coinage historians have accepted Martin's conclusion, it's hard to overlook how the moneyers opposed Mestrell's ideas even before he'd had a chance to try them. Moreover, as Professor Challis (1989, 259–60) points out, the trials took no account of the superior design of Mestrell's coins, which made them must less subject to counterfeiting. In any case, Mestrell was sent packing. As no further legitimate avenues remained open for his unique skills, he turned, out of frustration, to counterfeiting, which earned him a hearty choke at Norwich in 1578. It was, as James Mackay (1984, 36) writes, "a very sad end for England's pioneer of mechanically produced coinage."

Meanwhile, back in Paris, coins were still being struck mechanically when, in 1585, opposition to the new technology caused a reversion to hammering, with screw presses confined to medal making (Craig 1953, 147). More than three decades passed before Nicholas Briot, then engraver general at the Paris Mint, began a long but ultimately vain struggle to revive mechanized coining there. According to François Le Blanc, "Every device that intrigue and malice could contrive was put into play to foil the plans of . . . the most capable man in his vocation in all Europe."[27]

Having been rebuffed in France, Briot, like Mestrell before him,

---

27. Author's translation of French original, quoted in Craig 1953, 147.

sought greener pastures in England, where, in 1625, Charles I made him his new provider of patterns. Because his new responsibilities included the sinking of dies and striking of medals bearing the king's portrait, Briot was allowed to build and install his own "roller" and "sway" presses for the purpose.[28] Four years later, he managed somehow to get permission to strike coins with his special equipment. Briot's trials won the approval of a royal commission in 1631, and in the following year, he found himself once again the engraver general, this time at a none-too-happy Royal Mint.

Although the mint was not about to throw away its hammers, Briot kept on striking modest quantities of coins his own way for several years, both in London and in Edinburgh, where he'd been sent in 1631 to oversee a copper coinage. The reaction there to his "engines" was the exact opposite of Sir Richard's reaction to Mestrell's: Briot's machines were, by all accounts, capable of coining much more rapidly than hammers, though not always more economically. According to one Scottish witness,

> This way of coinage by the milne press and sway is a great deal more dispatching but more expensive . . . for heir the yrons [dies] are more subject to braking and defacing than the uther way, and the milne very chargeable to maintain, but this was an extraordinary brave way for coining the stirling copper money which required great dispatch, and could not have been done the ordinary way for triple more charges.   (QUOTED IN CRAIG 1953, 148)

In Royal Mint historian Sir John Craig's modern English, "Machinery could cope economically with great and sudden expansion but . . . otherwise less complicated methods were cheaper" (ibid.) As we shall see, this conclusion bears an uncanny resemblance to some Royal Mint employees' assessments, almost exactly two centuries later, of Matthew Boulton's steam-powered coining machinery. Despite it, Briot was allowed to continue striking modest quantities of coins his way even after Parliament seized the Royal Mint in 1642, his experiments coming to an end only upon his death four years later.

---

28. Coining with a roller press involves passing sheet metal through a pair of cylindrical "roller" dies with coin designs cut into the roller face. The coins are then cut from the sheets. A sway, or "rocker," press rocks a blank back and forth between a pair of dies with curved oval faces, using a lever and gear arrangement.

Although he may not have been aware of it, Briot lived just long enough to have witnessed the ultimate success of his ideas back in his native country. A contest between old and new ways of coining was held in Paris in connection with the silver recoinage of 1641, and was perceived as such a decisive victory for the screw press that the employment of coining hammers in French mints was banned once and for all in 1645. In England, however, Briot's approach to coining, though favored by the government, still had to contend with formidable opposition from the Royal Mint. When the Commonwealth invited Paris Mint engineer Peter Blondeau to further the modernization process Briot had begun, Royal Mint officials greeted him with their guns blazing. Sir John reports:

> The wrath of the moneyers exceeded all bounds; in a public battle of pamphlets vitriolic on their part, restrained on Blondeau's, the mint men boasted the defects of former Frenchmen and their pretended improvements; and prayed that an end might be made of this new runagate from France by requiring him to run the gauntlet only once round the Mint. The moneyers declared that they could in any case coin better than the interloper with some old discarded machines[29] that lay on the premises.

A contest between old and new methods was in fact arranged. Though it did not prove as decisive as the French contest before it, its outcome was such that Blondeau was allowed to set up his presses and begin coining. But to strike coins one must first have metal, and the Royal Mint saw to it that Blondeau got hardly any: when, for instance, Spanish loot worth more than one hundred thousand pounds was acquired in 1656, the mint let him coin only two thousand pounds, keeping the rest for itself. Not long afterward the Protectorate, and with it most of Blondeau's own protectors, came to grief, and Blondeau hightailed it back to France. Three months later, the Royal Mint shipped his machines to Edinburgh, which, as far as the moneyers were concerned, was as good as consigning them to the devil.

So the Royal Mint managed to evade mechanization once again—but not for long. On May 17, 1661—one hundred years exactly since the year in which Mestrell first introduced the screw press to England—the restored king, having had his fill of badly struck money and of the rampant clipping and counterfeiting it inspired, ordered the Royal Mint to

---

29. Sir John presumably means Briot's presses.

switch to screw presses as quickly as possible, so that all coins might thenceforth be struck with grained or lettered edges (Craig 1953, 157). To the moneyers' tremendous dismay, Blondeau was fetched back the following February and paid one thousand pounds to build and install new presses. By March 1662, the coining of gold and silver by machine had begun.

To Little Tower Hill

Swapping hammers for screw presses at the Royal Mint took exactly one hundred years, figuring the time from the year when Mestrell first employed the new technology in England. The official switch from manual presses to steam-powered ones took less than a fifth as long. Still, mint officials didn't exactly welcome this latest change with open arms.

Indeed, there was no more reason for the mint to embrace technological change in the late eighteenth century than there had been in the late sixteenth century. The status quo rewarded both the mint establishment and the moneyers handsomely, whereas any sort of labor-saving technological change was likely to injure the last group without rewarding the first. As long as the mint retained its monopoly status, the earnings of its officers and employees weren't adversely affected by its refusal to embrace new techniques, even (or especially) if the new techniques allowed vast improvements in efficiency.

The mint had been under pressure to reform its coining methods for many years when Boulton came up with his newfangled way of making coins. The gold recoinage of the 1770s, involving 508,161 troy pounds (or about 275 long tons) of coin, kept a staff of more than seventy workers busy for an entire decade and cost the government a whopping £750,000. The actual coining expenses alone (exclusive of both overhead and the cost of gold required to make up for deficient coins) summed to just under £115,500 (Craig 1953, 245), or £419 per ton of product. This was (to put matters in some perspective) about ten times what Soho and other commercial mints (which had to recoup their capital costs) charged for their copper coins and about four times the price Boulton was to propose for coining silver crowns.[30]

Although the Garbetts' report convinced Lord Shelburne of the de-

---

30. Although copper was harder to work with, full-bodied gold and silver coins were more costly to produce, owing to the extra care that had to be taken in sizing the blanks and to the greater value of wasted metal.

sirability of a major mint reform, starting with the abolition of the master's, warden's, and comptroller's offices, the fall of Shelburne's administration caused the momentum for reform to be lost (Dyer and Gaspar 1992, 444). That momentum was restored, however, following the Bank restriction, thanks to the utter failure of the Royal Mint's Bank of England tokens and to the (relative) success of Boulton's regal copper. The Garbett report was "dusted down" (ibid., 451); and the Privy Council's Committee on Coin, first convened in 1787 to address the lack of good copper coin, was officially reconstituted on February 7, 1798, with Liverpool as its head, to undertake the task of looking into "the present Establishment and Constitution of His Majesty's Mint" (ibid.). By now, Liverpool was entirely won over to Boulton's new methods of coining, as was Boulton's friend Sir Joseph Banks, another member of the reconstituted committee. Because the committee's other members skipped most of its meetings, Boulton's friends were in a position to see to it that Britain's future coinage (not just its copper coinage, but all of its coinage) was done Boulton's way—if not at the Royal Mint, then by Boulton himself, at Soho.

Indeed, on January 30, Liverpool, anticipating his new charge, had written Boulton to ask (1) what Soho would charge to strike new regal silver coins, (2) how many crowns and half crowns it could strike in a month's time, (3) whether Boulton and some of his "ablest Mechanics" would be willing to join a subcommittee of the new Committee on Coin in making an official inspection of the Royal Mint, and (4) how long Boulton thought it would take to refit the mint with his improved coining machinery. Boulton replied on February 18, saying that he could coin 140,000 troy pounds of silver per month, provided he could have ingots of the proper standard delivered to Soho. His coining charges would be $9d$ per troy pound (or £102 per long ton) for crowns, $10\frac{1}{2}d$ for half crowns, and $1s\ 2d$ and $1s\ 6d$ for shillings and sixpences, respectively,[31] and he could start coining within a week of getting the necessary silver. As for reequipping the Royal Mint with his machines, Boulton believed it would take at least a year. Finally, Boulton was prepared to obey Liverpool's summons to inspect the Royal Mint "at a moment's notice," although he saw little point in doing so, as he was already as familiar with

---

31. The comparable fees allowed to the master of the mint for silver coinage back in 1770 were as follows: crowns and half crowns at $1s\ 5\frac{3}{4}d$ per troy pound of silver; shillings at $1s\ 10\frac{1}{2}d$; and sixpences at $2s\ 2d$. As usual, one must keep in mind that these fees did not cover salaries or most of the mint's capital costs, which were paid out of the public purse.

its equipment and procedures as he might be after seeing them "a hundred times." To visit again, he said, "before some plan had been digested by your Lordships . . . would only tend to increase envy & jealousies, which I have had some experience of within this month" (PRO BT6/27). Come early April, the Committee on Coin determined that it had digested enough and that it was time for Boulton to revisit the Royal Mint, whether or not he was welcome there.

The handwriting was plainly on the wall: the mint could either roll out a red carpet for its would-be reformers or risk losing its "ancient prerogative" altogether (Dyer and Gaspar 1992, 452). Nothing could have been more vain, in retrospect at least, than Deputy Master James Morrison's repeated attempts to evade this dilemma by deploring "the mischievous tendency of coining money without great necessity in any other place than his Majesty's Mint" while declaring that the Tower was prepared to mint copper for less than what Soho was charging and with equal dispatch (Dyer and Gaspar 1992, 448; see also Jenkinson 1805, 196). Liverpool paid no heed either to Morrison's misgivings or to his offer, which Liverpool rightly construed as so much pure bluster.

The Royal Mint inspection began on April 27. John Rennie, a former Boulton & Watt employee who helped design the Albion Mill, also took part, having been recommended by Boulton. Over the course of several days, Rennie, Boulton, and members of the Committee on Coin subcommittee, including Sir Joseph Banks, made several visits to the mint. Boulton's brief report, submitted on May 8, was largely devoted to suggestions for improving the mint's assaying procedures: for a change, he demurred from offering advice concerning how the mint's coining department might be improved, explaining that he had no desire to "plunge . . . into Disputes with Persons, whose habits & customs have established Prejudices in favor of their old trades in their old ways; but whose Occupations have not allowed them to gain that mechanical and Philosophical Experience, which more general and more extensive manufactories afford to thinking men" (quoted in Doty 1998, 150). This was an interesting twist on diplomacy, but it did not quite satisfy the Committee on Coin, which called Boulton back to Whitehall the next day to have him spell out precisely what experience had taught him. Boulton complied by recommending, in essence, that the Royal Mint be refurbished so as to more or less replicate the mint he'd built at Soho. So equipped, it might, he observed, strike as many coins in an hour using only a bushel of coal and the labor of eight young boys as it would require fifty-five men and eleven presses to strike the old-fashioned way (ibid.).

Eventually, Boulton sent Liverpool a detailed statement concerning the machinery with which he thought the Royal Mint should be equipped. Here, he recommended a single twenty-horsepower steam engine, which was to power a new rolling mill, eight coining presses, eight cutting-out presses, two shaking machines, and several lathes. Boulton & Watt's Soho Foundry would manufacture the steam engine as well as the machines to be powered by it, and Soho engineers would put everything together, save for the rolling mill, which was best left to Rennie, "the best Millwright in the Kingdom" (BL Add. MSS 38424, 383). But Boulton understood all too well that by helping to modernize the Royal Mint, he risked putting his own mint out of business. He therefore insisted on securing "a Contract for the remainder of the Copper Coinage," to "set my mind at ease" as a condition for having Boulton & Watt reequip the Royal Mint. "[I]t is my wish and Intention," he wrote, "to act right and honourable, and do my Duty to my King and Country, and at the same time I ought to do it to my own Family in that Trade and in that state which it has pleased God to place me in, and not to apply my Head to the making of Machinery to cut it off" (ibid., 384). To allow him to retain the privilege of coining copper was, after all, the least the government could do in return for the great sacrifices Boulton had made on its behalf.

> When I reflect upon the pains I have taken for ten years, the great Sum I have long been out of pocket, and that I am continuing to lay out more Money in making weighty Experiments, and the Risk I have run of never being repaid; I say when all these things are completely at work, I shall feel a consciousness that I merit a handsome Reward, and have no doubt, but that will be equally obvious to His Majesty's Ministers, in whose Honor and Liberality I have an implicit Confidence. (IBID., 385)

As of late 1799, Boulton was still waiting for his "handsome Reward," but he had at least secured permission—*written* permission, that is—to continue coining copper, and he was prepared to do his part in the proposed Royal Mint reform. But just as Boulton was getting on board, the reform plan suffered yet another setback: Lord Liverpool's knees gave out, forcing him to retire from public life.[32]

Liverpool's invalidation came close to destroying the prospects for

---

32. Liverpool's illness may have been responsible for his initial failure to complete the Committee on Coin's official report. An incomplete draft, published in 1798, is limited to

Royal Mint reform during his or Matthew Boulton's lifetime and probably would have done so had the Bank of England not decided, early in 1804, to take a second stab at issuing countermarked silver dollars. The Bank was led to this decision, despite the utter failure of its last attempt to issue silver tokens, by the worsening shortage of silver coin. Thanks to hoarding and wartime inflation, bankers found themselves paying over one hundred pounds to obtain sixty pounds of old crowns and half crowns for their customers (Kelley 1976, 49), so they began lobbying the Treasury and the Bank of England for relief.

The Treasury proved receptive, though only, according to Lord Liverpool (Jenkinson 1805, frontspiece), because the government itself was finding it impossible "to pay the seamen of the Royal Navy, and the artificers in the great docks of the kingdom, from the want of Coins of the lower denominations." Its initial response took the form of a January 2, 1804 warrant to the Royal Mint, authorizing it to resume countermarking Spanish dollars. In a futile effort to avoid the rampant counterfeiting that had doomed the 1797 tokens, the warrant called for the dollars to be countermarked using the octagon-shaped head normally reserved for Maundy pennies in place of the smaller duty stamp applied to the earlier series.[33]

But as the Royal Mint went to work on the new Bank tokens, Boulton was preparing to best it. He had been running some of his own "experiments" in restriking silver dollars and had found that his steam-powered presses could almost completely replace the original markings found on the Spanish coins with those from a new set of dies, in effect treating the Spanish originals as so many blanks. Boulton reported his findings to Sir Joseph Banks, who, being quite won over by this latest "*chef d'oeuvre* of coining," urged Boulton to write to the Bank (MBP Banks/96, Boulton to Banks, January 27, 1804, quoted in Kelley 1976, 54). Boulton took Banks's advice on February 6, reminding the directors (as if they needed

---

a historical review that is supposed to have actually been written not by Liverpool but by Rogers Ruding. Liverpool eventually published a completed version, in the guise of a letter to the king, in 1805. This was his famous *Treatise on the Coins of the Realm*. The sections of this work concerning Royal Mint reform, that is, the ones not written by Ruding, appear to have been heavily influenced both by Boulton's own arguments and by those of Samuel Garbett, with whom Liverpool kept up a voluminous correspondence. A comparison of Liverpool's arguments with those found in Garbett's letters suggests that Garbett was the sounder thinker of the two.

33. Because Maundy money was issued in such trivial amounts, the government's claim that outstanding Maundy pennies could be used as a means for checking the authenticity of stamped dollars was far from persuasive.

to be reminded) of the failure of the last Bank dollars, assuring them that his versions would be far more difficult to counterfeit, and offering to supply them at the attractive rate of one hundred pounds per one hundred thousand pounds (ibid., 55).

When they discovered what was brewing, the Company of Moneyers threw a fit. To let Boulton get away with coining copper was one thing, for the moneyers and their masters had long acknowledged that the copper coinage did not "belong to the Mint." But to suffer his coining silver was another thing altogether, for that, as they insisted in a February 24 memorandum to the Treasury, would be to allow him to encroach upon their ancient and exclusive rights. But their protest fell on deaf ears: the proposed dollars were, they were informed, not current coin of the realm but mere tokens "issued by the Bank of England for the convenience of the Public" (ibid.).

So, with the stroke of a pen, the Royal Mint was deprived of its monopoly of silver coining, and Matthew Boulton won the privilege of being the first private coiner to compete with it legally. The Bank of England accepted his offer on March 3. Less than eight weeks later, it shipped the first of three consignments of Spanish dollars, including some bearing the Royal Mint's octagonal countermark, to Soho, in wagons escorted by Bow Street runners. Between May 15 and July 12, over one million of Boulton's five-shilling Bank dollars made the return journey to Threadneedle Street, where, from May 20 to June 2, the Bank of England offered to exchange them for those inferior Royal Mint tokens that were already outstanding (ibid., 58–59).[34]

The moneyers' February 24 memorandum played a crucial role in reviving the movement for Royal Mint reform, not only because the reply it elicited shattered the moneyers' last hopes of forestalling reform, but also because it signaled an about-face in the moneyers' official stance toward Boulton's coining system. Anticipating the failure of their legal complaint against Boulton, they added the fallback complaint that their obsolete equipment prevented them from matching his coining prowess. In other words, instead of continuing to resist or delay technical change, the moneyers now took to pleading for such change as their best hope for survival. Suddenly, the main obstacle to Royal Mint reform had melted away, and the Committee on Coin was left with the relatively

---

34. By the time of Boulton's takeover, the Royal Mint had stamped 412,140 dollars, of which 266,000 had been issued to the public.

easy task of accommodating the moneyers' own express wishes, which it did in short order by concluding, on March 5, that the Royal Mint ought to be reequipped with "the most improved Engines and Machines of all kinds applicable to the fabrication of Money" (Dyer and Gaspar 1992, 455–56; PRO BT6/127).

At first, the government intended to refurbish and enlarge the Royal Mint's old quarters—a horseshoe-shaped congeries of dark, cramped, and decaying workshops and living quarters that had accumulated along a half-mile interior stretch of the Tower's damp wall like so many barnacles on a ship's hull. Some of the rooms had long since been shored up by huge timbers, which, being themselves in danger of collapsing, were held together by iron clamps. Hopelessly outmoded and in need of constant, expensive repairs, the Tower left much to be desired even as a place for storing His Majesty's enemies and jewelry. As the site for a modern coin factory, it was a hopeless anachronism.

Moreover, as John Rennie (in his new capacity as surveyor general to the Board of Works) reported in November, the old relic of a building simply wasn't big enough to house both the king's ordnance and the sort of mint Boulton and the Committee on Coin had proposed for it. A new building would have to be built, and the government had just the place for it, on Little Tower Hill, just a few hundred yards away from the Tower, where the old royal tobacco warehouses had recently been vacated. Plans for the new facility were drawn up during the spring of 1805, and construction began in August. In the meantime, negotiations were begun with the firm of Boulton & Watt, which eventually agreed to supply two steam engines, eight coining presses, twelve cutting-out presses, six "milling" machines, four shaking machines, four lathes, a die multiplication press, and sundry other hardware, for a grand total of £16,990, while leaving the hardware for the rolling mill to Birmingham's Eagle Foundry.

Although the new mint equipment was ready by July 1807, the building was not. Pitt's death in January 1806 put progress on hold for a few months while a new government was pieced together, and the Dundee stone foundations required for the coining and cutting-out rooms had sorely tested the skills of London's best masons. By the spring of 1808, when it was at last ready to be equipped, the building had already cost almost twice the ninety-six thousand pounds budgeted for it (excluding the cost of machinery). It would take four more years and a total construction expenditure in excess of three hundred thousand pounds before the old Tower Mint could at last be vacated, signaling the ultimate triumph of Boulton's steam-powered coining process.[35]

Sadly, Matthew Boulton did not live quite long enough to witness this triumph. Having suffered from a kidney stone for many years, he was permanently bedridden some months before the Little Tower Hill project got started, and he passed away on August 17, 1809. His death would at least spare him from having to witness his own mint's sad decline, for despite the precautions he'd taken (and Matthew Robinson's remonstrations), Soho ended up playing the role of Laius to a refurbished Royal Mint's Oedipus, unwittingly fathering the instrument of its own doom. The difference, of course, was that the Royal Mint was bent on patricide from the start.

The Little Tower Hill "maiden" coinage of April 1810 proved a portent of things to come. The coinage consisted of twenty-five tons of copper struck for the East India Company's Prince Edward Island settlement near Penang. Just as the Royal Mint had learned, to its great dismay, that it couldn't take its monopoly of silver coinage for granted, the Soho Mint now discovered that the right to strike regal copper coins, rather than being guaranteed to it, was up for grabs. Moreover, the government would generally favor the Royal Mint over Soho for official projects. Again and again, Matthew Robinson Boulton offered to place his mint at the public's disposal, only to be sent away breech in hand.

Consequently, from June 1813 to June 1821, Soho did not produce any British coins; indeed, it produced no coins at all (Doty 1998, 64). By mid-1816, Boulton had been forced to lay off most of its skilled personnel, retaining only a skeleton crew of boys and women and a handful of adult men—from motives of charity mainly, at a considerable loss to Soho (ibid.). In early January 1819, after the government once again favored the Royal Mint over Soho (this time for an Ionian Islands copper coinage), George Rennie reported to his former boss, straight from the

35. The overall cost of the new Royal Mint, including its equipment, was almost five times the seventy thousand pounds Boulton had invested in his second Soho Mint. The difference was partly due to the extra cost of new metal-rolling, die-making, and assaying facilities; but it also reflected the newer project's unnecessarily mammoth scale. Sixty years after the new Royal Mint's completion (when Britain's monetary needs had grown considerably), the deputy master opined that the mint's work "could be equally well, if not better, performed in a much smaller building, and undoubtedly with a considerable saving of expense" (BPP 1870 (7), vol. XLI, p. 7.) As for the rest, one thing it did not buy was outstanding architecture: critics were divided over whether the new mint's odd blend of Renaissance and classical Greek motifs was an unforgivable muddle or just boring.

beast's belly: "you have furnished them with the Arms to fight against you & they will not rust for want of use" (ibid., 162). The final and most bitter blow came in 1821, when the Royal Mint resumed the coining of copper for the British Isles. By then, however, the handwriting had been on the wall so long that Boulton "did not even bother to complain" (ibid.).

The year 1821 did, nevertheless, witness a new round of coin making at Soho. The coins in question were halfpennies destined for the island of St. Helena, where Napoleon had recently died. They would be the last coins produced at Matthew Boulton's famous mint, for their production happened to be witnessed by an East India Company engineer named John Hawkins, who was in charge of equipping a new mint the company planned to build in Bombay. Hawkins liked what he saw, and Matthew Robinson Boulton was pleased to let him have it, lock, stock, and barrel, for the right price. A deal was eventually struck, and by September 1824, the mint that ushered in the modern era of coinage had been unceremoniously dismantled, crated up, and crammed into a ship's hold, to be unloaded again at Ballard Pier, halfway 'round the world (Doty 1998, 65).

One might suppose that Soho's decline and fall marked the end of commercial coin making in Great Britain. After all, by 1812, eighteen hundred tons of post-1805 Boulton copper (not to mention 4.5 million Soho Bank dollars) had been placed into circulation, and Britain had at its disposal a brand-new steam-powered mint with a capacity even greater than Soho's. Surely, then, the public could have no further use for commercial coins, except as collectors' items.

One might suppose, in other words, that in embracing Boulton's high-tech coining methods, the British government was on the brink of officially solving its big problem of small change.

One might suppose so. But one would be mistaken.

CHAPTER VI

Their Last Bow

HAPPY the man who, void of cares and strife,

In silken or in leathern purse retains

A Splendid Shilling; he nor hears with pain

New oysters cried, nor sighs for cheerful ale.[1]

That Sucking Sound

In early July 1809, angry clouds gathered over central England's grain-growing Champion Region. Then the rain came, in buckets.

The rain kept falling for the rest of the month and throughout August and September. Finally, in mid-October, it stopped. But by then it was too late: the grain harvest was reduced by a third, and much of what was harvested either sprouted or mildewed before it could be milled, making it unfit for bread. Grain prices shot up accordingly. Even mediocre wheat was fetching over one hundred shillings per eight-bushel quarter (Tooke 1838, 294).

On the Continent, though, the weather was kind to the crops, and prices were relatively low. So the British people had a choice: they could go begging for bread, as they'd done after the dismal harvest of 1799, or they could have truck with the enemy. Understandably, they chose the latter course. And so, notwithstanding Napoleon's Continental blockade and Britain's own orders in council, between the harvest season of 1809

---

1. Philips 1701.

and that of 1810 1.5 million quarters of wheat and flour and another six hundred thousand quarters of other grains and meals—Great Britain's largest grain imports ever for so short a period—were spirited across the English Channel (ibid., 295–301).

Thanks to Continental grain, the people of Great Britain avoided another famine—another bread famine, that is. They did so, however, only by subjecting themselves to a famine of a different, but no less familiar, sort. For the grain had to be purchased, yet it could not be purchased with British goods. French authorities might wink at grain shipments to Great Britain, but they were deadly serious when it came to keeping British goods from landing on the Continent, and they were willing to prove it by confiscating ships laden with contraband goods and by shooting their captains for good measure. So grain and other Continental goods passing through Napoleon's porous blockade could only be bought with specie—that is, with gold or silver.

Nor did the bills stop coming after 1809. A second thin harvest in 1810—this time a result of dry spring winds—sent wheat to 120 shillings a quarter, eliciting more heavy imports. Imports of other Continental commodities, including wool, silk, tallow, hemp, flax, and linseed, also rose sharply. All told, British expenditures on Continental goods leapt from just shy of thirty million pounds to over forty-one million between 1808 and 1810 (ibid., 301, 354). As if all this weren't enough, cartloads of bullion were also being sent to fill Wellington's military chests in Portugal. By the close of 1810, the Peninsular Campaign had absorbed thirty-two million pounds, over three times concurrent expenditures on grain (ibid., 352). In 1811, the same campaign would cost another fifty-eight million pounds (Kelley 1976, 74).

Little wonder that the market price of specie shot upward. Gold's price, fixed at £3 17s 6d per troy ounce before the Bank restriction, reached £4 10s by February 1809 and peaked at £5 8s five years later. Spanish silver, in turn, went from 5s 3½d per ounce just before the restriction to six shillings in late August 1811 and to over seven shillings by the autumn of 1813 (Tooke 1838, 384–85). At these rates, both guineas and Bank dollars, not to mention intact regal silver, were worth far more as bullion than as tender. In vain did the government attempt, by means of Lord Stanhope's Act (51 Geo. III c 127), to stop the traffic in guineas by imposing stiff penalties on persons caught buying or selling them for a premium. As one might expect, the act merely drove the bullion trade further underground, making it that much harder for merchants and manufacturers to get hold of guineas or dollars for legitimate uses.

Was there no other way to check the outflow of specie? In principle, the Bank of England might have held down the price of bullion, at the cost of some extra commercial distress, by aggressively stiffening the terms on which it stood ready to grant credit. But instead of "leaning against the wind," the Bank did just the opposite, expanding its deposits and notes from just over thirty million pounds at the close of August 1808 to over thirty-eight million two years later. Given this whopping increase, who can blame the Bullion Committee for placing responsibility for the high price of bullion squarely on the Bank directors' shoulders?

> Propagation in reason—a small child or two—
> Even *Malthus* himself is a friend to;
> The issue of some folks is moderate and few—
> But *ours,* my dear corporate Bank, there's no end to![2]

But rather than allow ourselves to be drawn into the bullion debates,[3] let us simply recognize how, by February 1811, the high price of bullion saw to the melting of many of Great Britain's already scarce gold and silver coins, and that it was only by means of all this melting of coin that Britons managed to feed themselves while keeping Napoleon on the run.

A London trader named Benjamin Smart (1811, 7) summed up the situation neatly in a letter of March 17, 1811. "Every country person coming into London brings guineas for sale; agents are employed all over the kingdom to collect them, and they are now sold at a premium of half-a-crown." As for silver, Smart wrote:

> A few weeks and there will not be a bank dollar left. [Standard] Silver is this day six shillings and threepence per ounce; the unstamped dollar costs [i.e., is worth] full five shillings and threepence; will any manufacturer of silver go to the market and pay that price, if he can receive them in currency for five shillings?

Correct answer: No.

---

2. Thomas Moore, "Amatory Colloquy Between Bank and Government," in Moore 1828.

3. Instead, see Henry Adams's (1871) classic treatment of the subject.

Trickle-Up Economics

It happens that just as Smart was dashing off his letter, the Bank of England announced that it was calling up its dollar tokens to save them from the silversmiths.

> Whereas the Price of Silver has risen so much since the first Issue of Bank Dollar Tokens at 5s. each, as to now make them worth more to be sold as Bullion than the Price at which they are current; and whereas it has been deemed expedient, at the Recommendation of the Right Honourable the Lords of the Privy Council for Coin, in order to prevent their being withdrawn from Circulation, that an additional value . . . be now assigned to them, the Government and Company of the Bank of England do hereby give Notice that they have given Orders to their Cashiers and other Officers . . . to receive all Bank Dollar Tokens tendered in Payment at the Bank, at the Rate of 5s. 6d. each, instead of 5s. as heretofore; and to pay and to issue all such Bank Dollar tokens as shall be paid or issued hereafter . . . at the same Rate.

But while calling up Bank dollars may have yanked Great Britain from the brink of a still greater crisis, it still left it facing a coin shortage bad enough to be referred to in Parliament as "an evil of the greatest magnitude." "Every Member of this House," Lord Folkestone observed on April 8, "knows the difficulty that there is in getting change in London, and I have been informed by letters, that the difficulty is still greater in the country." Folkestone went on:

> I have been informed, that at a fair there was no possibility of getting change for a pound note; and that in order to make small payments, it was necessary for three or four people to join to purchase what would altogether make up a pound note. It is impossible that trade can go on in the country unless this calamity is remedied.
>
> (*Bell's Weekly Messenger,* APRIL 14, 1811)[4]

Responding to the "calamity," the government took the further step, on June 26, of announcing new three-shilling and 1s 6d Bank tokens.

---

4. Here as elsewhere, when reproducing speeches in Parliament, I have restored the first-person, present voice where sources have replaced it with the third-person conditional.

The Committee on Coin, employing the same specious reasoning that informed its decision to limit the first Boulton coinage to onepence and twopence pieces, settled on these odd denominations because it feared that shilling and sixpence tokens would only drive away the last of their regal counterparts. The new Bank tokens were to be the first commission undertaken by the reconstructed Royal Mint, which was still getting the hang of its new equipment.[5] A chapter of accidents hampered production for several weeks: dies made by Lewis Pingo, the mint's septuagenarian (and senile) chief engraver, were no match for Boulton's presses; and the rolls in the new mill seemed almost as fragile, breaking down in late July and again in August (Dyer and Gaspar 1992, 470).

Despite every mishap, the mint managed, by year's end, to deliver one million pounds' worth of tokens to the Bank of England. By then, dealers were paying six shillings per ounce of Spanish dollar silver, and Bank silver was again in danger of becoming underrated. Also, the Bank of England had neither branch offices nor dealings with country bankers. Consequently, its tokens were generally available through London discount houses only, from which they were expected to trickle to the provinces. This arrangement resembled and was no better than the Royal Mint's age-old policy of delivering coins at the Tower only, with no allowance for transportation. In July, the government decided to ship Bank tokens to sixty-five major cities and towns, with quotas set according to each town's population. That helped, of course. But the quotas proved ill-matched to the various towns' needs, being filled rapidly in most places but slowly in others; and every British community of fewer than seven thousand souls still had to wait for its trickle (Kelley 1976, 84).

Continuing shortages of silver coin and especially of shillings and sixpences led to the drafting of official appeals for more silver in Birmingham, Bristol, Worcester, and other industrial cities. The appeals were directed to Spencer Perceval, the prime minister and chancellor of the exchequer, to the lords of the Privy Council Committee on Coin, to the Bank of England, to local bankers—in short, to anyone who might conceivably direct some Bank tokens the applicants' way. Provincial papers did their part by publishing editorials like the following, from the *Taunton Chronicle*.

---

5. The Bank of England had asked Soho to design new 5*s* 6*d* tokens to take the place of revalued Bank dollars, only to abandon this plan in favor of continued production of Bank dollars of the old pattern (Kelley 1976, 76–79).

SCARCITY OF CHANGE—The total disappearance of Good Coin and the extreme difficulty of procuring Silver Change, continue to perplex if not to alarm, every description of persons. The Bank Tokens have been so sparingly issued that they have hitherto served rather to gratify curiosity than to administer to public convenience. In fact, unless some means are immediately adopted to remedy this daily [increasing] evil, it will be impossible to execute the ordinary transactions of trade. The want of change is no longer merely an inconvenience, but a source of actual distress to thousands of traders and poor people; the former of whom are reduced to the alternative of giving credit, which they wish to avoid, or keeping their commodities in hand; and the latter are compelled to submit to purchases in which the liberty of choice is sacrificed to the necessity of the occasion. It is a serious fact, that several butchers and market people, on the last Taunten Market day, declared their intention of withholding all supplies which were not indispensably required by their regular customers, while others avowed their determination to abstain from attending the market altogether.   (QUOTED IN MAYS 1982, 86)

The Irish situation was no less serious: Sir John Newport, MP for Waterford and former chancellor of the (Irish) exchequer, assured Parliament: "[T]he distress occasioned, and especially among the poor peasantry, by the scarcity of silver, is most severe. Indeed, the peasant who brings his bacon or other articles to Waterford, is obliged to return home with a check as payment . . . which he is but too likely to lose, or obliged perhaps to go to market again to get his check changed" (*Hansard*, February 12, 1813, c. 509).

Cartloads of Cartwheels

With silver coin scarcer than ever, might copper take its place? Back in the 1790s, six hundred tons of commercial copper tokens had come close to doing just that, not only addressing the shortage of regal farthings and halfpennies, but also making up for the lack of shillings and sixpenny pieces. By 1811, over thirty-six hundred tons of Boulton copper—more than £680,000 worth—had been issued throughout Great Britain, not to mention six hundred more tons for Ireland. So why couldn't that serve in place of lost silver?

Part of the answer is that the price of copper also peaked during the first decade of the new century, though somewhat earlier than the prices of gold and silver and for different reasons: copper grew dear not because it was exported but because so much of it was being consumed at home—by the Royal Navy and also by the Soho Mint. The Copper King's passing did not end copper's streak, as his detractors suggested it would. Instead, the price of manufactured copper kept rising, from seventeen pence per pound in 1802 (the year of Williams's death) to twenty-three pence in 1805. At the latter price, even the 1799 Boulton copper coinage was underrated, while the original cartwheels (and all the old Parys Mine Druids) were worth almost a third more as copper than as coins (W. Davis 1904, xix). That was good news to London's brewers, who had lots of unwanted copper on their hands. But it was bad news for British industrialists, who now found themselves competing with smelters for pennies, halfpennies, and farthings.

Here again, legal penalties against melting did little to protect the coinage, although they did result in an occasional arrest, such as that reported in an April 13, 1805 notice in the *Times* (quoted in Peck 1970, 614, app. 10(c)):

> It having been for some time known that the late copper coin was collecting for the purpose of melting down, orders were issued for the Police to keep a strict look-out: and on Thursday an Officer belonging to Hatton Garden Office, followed a cart with eight casks of penny and twopenny pieces, containing 18 cwt. 21 lb. from Saffron Hill, to a coppersmith's in Upper Thames Street, and secured the property for future investigation. The penalty is 100*l.* and forfeiture of the goods.

So it happened that within a few short years of running through his original 1797 and 1799 contracts, Matthew Boulton began receiving letters from all over the country pleading for more coin, which he was of course quite unable to deliver. Replying to one such correspondent in October 1804, Boulton could offer nothing save his commiseration: for some time, he observed, Soho itself had had to meet its own payroll needs by buying Boulton copper coins in the open market, at a premium (Wager 1977, 46).

It was to make up for the loss of the old Boulton copper that the Privy Council decided to order three further batches—in 1805, 1806, and 1807—comprising another eighteen hundred tons of pennies, halfpennies, and farthings for Great Britain and a further six hundred tons for Ireland. This new Boulton copper was struck at twenty-four pennies per pound—that is, at a standard slightly below the old Tower standard. The public's eager acceptance of the "lightweight" coins marked another important step toward official abandonment of the "intrinsic value," fetish.

But the later Boulton copper, like all regal copper coin and unlike commercial copper tokens, either didn't tend to go where it was needed or tended to go there once only, never to return. Soho had improved on the standard Royal Mint practice of delivering coins at the Tower, by securing four pounds per ton from the government to cover shipping expenses. But because they were not redeemable, Soho's copper coins tended—no less than old Tower products—to pile up in London. Getting them back to the provinces would cost another four pounds per ton or something of that order; and that expense the government would *not* pay.

So Soho's latest coins, having provided temporary relief to the provinces, ended up becoming a burden to wholesalers in the capital. "By May 1808," Peter Mathias (1979, 203) relates, "petitions had started coming in from London tradesmen (particularly the brewers) that stocks of Boulton's coins, unwanted and unusable, were piling up in their vaults." "Boulton," Mathias adds, "was told not to send any more into the capital until the brewers had 'disburthened themselves.'" Between May 1808 and February 1809, Soho arranged to collect close to ten thousand pounds in its unwanted coins from the leading London brewers, to use in filling unmet demands elsewhere. Nevertheless, the situation in London worsened, while complaints also began coming in from Canterbury and Liverpool (ibid.).

In March 1813 and again in October, the London traders renewed their pleas to the Committee on Coin, complaining that they were experiencing "heavy Losses and Inconveniences, in consequence of the excessive quantity of Copper Coinage circulating in and around the Metropolis." The tradesmen, while not wishing to refuse even base copper in payments out of "fear of offending their customers," were forced to dispose of unwanted copper by selling it to "Manufacturers, Pawnbrokers, and others, in return for Bills drawn at three months, exposing themselves to losses when parties to whom they advanced change failed, and this despite being in need of ready money themselves" (BPP 1813, 237–38). As ever, the problem was rooted in the lack of arrangements for redeeming unwanted regal copper.[6]

In short, it was the 1780s all over again, but with at least one big dif-

---

6. Wager (1977, 48) instead interprets the problem as one of alternating, rather than simultaneous, shortages and surfeits.

ference—in scale. The British economy and the demand for small change that went with it had grown tremendously. Great Britain's population, which probably did not exceed 7 million in 1781, reached 8.9 million in 1801, the year of the first (decennial) census. By 1811, it was 18.1 million. During the same thirty-year interval, Britons' average nominal earnings almost doubled.[7] These raw figures alone point to something just beyond a fivefold increase in Great Britain's small-change requirements, and that's leaving aside the disproportionate rise in wages, and in manufacturing wages especially, relative to other kinds of income.

Splendid Shillings

Under the circumstances, it is hardly surprising that commercial coinage got going again. "Such was the contempt in which the Government was held on the question of coinage," William Davis (1904, xxiii) writes, "that history repeated itself," with private firms resolving once more "to supply a token coinage . . . to facilitate the trading propensities of the Nation." Because the original wave of tokens receded on its own at the start of the new century, the government had never bothered to suppress private coinage. The way was thus legally open for another round of such coinage once the need for it became urgent. That such a point had clearly been reached by June 1811 is evident from an editorial in the *Bristol Gazette and Public Advertiser*. Although the *Gazette* had been happy to say good riddance to commercial tokens only a dozen years before, it now hoped for their revival.

> [I]f large capitalists were to issue copper and silver tokens, as was done a few years since, . . . hoarders would soon find the folly of heaping useless wealth. For our own parts, we agree with the eccentric Jack Fuller,[8] that oyster shells, pieces of leather, wax candles if they would not melt, or any other substance might, by agreement, be substituted as a circulating medium: none of them are so fragile as paper. There is but one trifling objection to this, which is the impossibility of how [*sic*] can you get the butcher, the baker, the farmer, &c to consent to such agreement.   (JUNE 24, QUOTED IN WITHERS AND WITHERS 1999, 13)

---

7. British average earnings estimates, based on work by Lawrence Officer, are available at http://www.eh.net/hmit/ukearncpi.

8. John "Mad Jack" Fuller (1757–1834), an MP for Sussex from 1801 to 1812, was a well-known philanthropist and patron of the arts and sciences, best remembered today as a builder of follies.

That butchers and others could be persuaded to accept little metal discs, including privately minted ones, was, of course, an established fact. Moreover, there was no shortage of "capitalists," including some large ones, willing to give the *Gazette*'s suggestion a try, for such capitalists were themselves hard up for small change. A handful had already issued tokens, and July would see a rush of new entrants. By autumn, a commercial coinage revival was in full swing: all of Great Britain's manufacturing cities and many of its provincial capitals were once again being supplied with custom-made and locally issued small money.

Despite the far greater coinage needs of the time, the overall scale of nineteenth-century commercial coin production is supposed to have fallen short of that of the earlier commercial coinage (Wager 1977, 48).[9] There's nothing puzzling about this, since the first episode went on without the least hindrance for over a decade, while the second was less than a year old when the government began a crackdown. The really substantial differences between the new private coinage and the previous one had to do not with the overall quantity of tokens issued but with their quality and also their issuers' locations and character.

For starters, the tokens of the 1790s were mainly halfpennies, with some pennies; and almost all of them were made of copper. The nineteenth-century series, in contrast, favored larger denominations: pennies now accounted for 73 percent of all copper tokens, with the rest consisting not merely of halfpennies but also of substantial numbers of twopenny and threepenny pieces. Far more significantly, the new issues included large numbers of silver tokens, especially silver shillings. Such tokens had been almost unheard of in the earlier token episode, appearing as it petered out and then only in Scotland: J. Wright Jr. managed to issue a few Dundee silver shillings in 1797; and in 1799, Colonel William Fullarton was about to issue his own (bearing the Prince of Wales's portrait) when the Committee on Coin talked him out of it (Dykes 2002; Mays 1982, 125–26). Such exceptional cases aside, no one dared to strike silver tokens, for to do so was to encroach directly on what the Royal Mint regarded as its exclusive and ancient prerogative.

What had happened to account for the change? Bank dollars hap-

---

9. The nineteenth-century episode lacked counterparts to Charles Pye and Thomas Welch, who took the trouble to gather production statistics from eighteenth-century token makers while most were still alive and kicking.

pened. In allowing the Bank of England to issue its own silver coins beginning in 1797 and especially in allowing it to have them struck elsewhere than at the Royal Mint, the government unwittingly set a precedent. It was only a matter of time before others began thinking, "If the Bank of England doesn't have to apply to the Tower for its silver, why should we?" The legal floodgates were left open when, in reply to a memorandum of February 24, 1804, in which the mint complained about the breach of its coining privileges, the Treasury replied coolly that no breach had occurred, because Bank dollars were not coins but tokens (Kelley 1976, 55). Dublin quickly took advantage of the ruling, issuing its own silver tokens that same year. Five years later, Guernsey's Bishop de Jersey & Company issued its own five-shilling pieces. But Guernsey, though a Crown dependency, was technically no more part of Great Britain than Dublin, so this issue also did not infringe on the prerogative that so far had not been extended beyond the Bank of England.

Finally, on March 11, 1811, a Neath draper named Hopkins got together with ironmonger John Morgan to test the waters in Great Britain by issuing silver shilling and sixpence "medals" bearing their town's arms. When no action was taken against them, English bankers began to follow their example, often at their communities' urging. In Bristol, for instance, the *Gazette* put the heat on local bankers in its June 11 editorial: "As a temporary relief, the Shaftesbury and other banks, have issued local silver tokens, why cannot the banks of Bristol do the same? If they should get less profit by so doing, they owe it, in common with other tradesmen, to their customers" (Withers and Withers 1999, 15). The Bristol bankers came through, as did dozens of others in towns all over England.

Banks were not the only silver issuers. As one contemporary source (quoted in Phillips 1900, 26) put it, "Since Ministers have transferred to the Bank of England one of the prerogatives of the Crown . . . every other Bank, Banker, Agent, Merchant and Shopkeeper has taken it for granted that an equal right . . . is the privilege of all." By the end of 1811, no fewer than eighty communities had their own silver money. By mid-1812, the number had risen to one hundred (Mays 1982, 88).

Scotland, it bears noting, took no part in the silver token episode. One reason for this was Parliament's decision, immediately following the Bank restriction, to temporarily restore to Scottish banks the right they had lost in 1765 to issue fractional notes. So great was the confidence Scottish people had in their banks that they generally preferred even small-value paper to coin: in the words of one Scottish witness and pamphleteer—a certain "Malachi Malagrowther"[10]—"the [Scottish banking] system has so completely expelled gold from the country of Scotland, that you never by any chance espy a guinea there, unless in the purse of an accidental stranger" (Malagrowther 1826). Although the ban against small notes was restored in 1800, many small notes issued while the ban was lifted remained in circulation years afterward. Also, instead of commissioning their own silver tokens, Scottish industrial concerns, most notably the Ballindalloch Cotton Works and Catrine and Deanston cotton mills of James Finley & Company, turned to overstriking foreign silver coins with their own company countermarks. The promissory stamps sufficed to render the coins current where they would not have circulated otherwise (Mitchiner 1998, 2111; Symes 1997).

Besides involving a much-increased role for silver tokens, the nineteenth-century token episode also revealed a substantial northern shift in the overall distribution of token issuers. Now more than 70 percent of all issuers (and over 50 percent of English issuers) were to be found above a straight line connecting the mouth of the Severn to the Wash, as compared to 50 percent of all issuers (and only 20 percent of English issuers) operating above the same line back in the 1790s (Wager 1977, 61). The shift was a perfectly predictable consequence of the pattern of British industrial growth during the intervening decades. Statistics concerning the overall distribution of token issuers can be misleading, however, since there was a marked difference between the use and sources of copper tokens, on the one hand, and the use and sources of silver tokens, on the other. Whereas silver tokens were, as we've seen, issued in almost every important English and Welsh community and mainly in response to local pleas for more small change, the vast majority of copper tokens were now commissioned not primarily by small retail firms (as had been true in the 1790s) but mostly by large industrial firms, which used them to meet their own payrolls. These copper token issuers were concentrated "in the counties of Stafford, Warwick, and York" (Sharp 1834, ii) in England and in the Swansea copper-smelting district in Wales (Dykes 1954).

Fully two-thirds of all the copper tokens came from metal-manufacturing firms and from copper companies especially, the latter having been encouraged to take part by the post-1808 copper slump, which found them sitting on tons of cheap raw material. Six copper companies

----

10. This was a pen name of poet and novelist Walter Scott.

in all—including the Rose Copper Company (of which Matthew Boulton had been a founding shareholder), the Crown Copper Company, and the Union Copper Company—issued penny and some halfpenny tokens. Because all save one of these companies had their headquarters in Birmingham, Sheffield, or Bristol and had smelting works in Wales, their tokens circulated widely (Dykes 1954, 349).

The largest copper token issuer of all was a Midlands ironmaster named Samuel Fereday. Fereday, who had been John Wilkinson's bailiff, took over Wilkinson's Bradley works after the great ironmaster's death in 1808 (Chaloner 1946, 24), having by then become a partner in several South Staffordshire works as well (Birch 1967, 151). By 1811, Fereday had become one of Great Britain's largest employers, with close to five thousand workers on his various payrolls. To meet his huge small-change bill, Fereday placed an order for two million copper tokens (mostly pennies, with some halfpennies) with Birmingham's leading medalist, former Boulton apprentice and button maker Edward Thomason, who filled the order by sending a carriage-load of coins to Fereday's Bilston works every other Friday for the better part of two years (Thomason 1845, 45).

The newer tokens also differed from earlier ones in design. The first round of commercial coins appeared when the Industrial Revolution was just getting under way, the second when it was in full swing. Accordingly, the newer tokens tended to sport a more businesslike and "industrial" look than their predecessors (cf. Withers and Withers 1999, 11). The lettered edges that distinguished the earlier tokens were gone, vertical or diagonal graining having taken their place. And many of the newer tokens bore either mere legends or legends supplemented by local or county borough arms or wreaths, in place of the busts and industrial scenes found on their predecessors.

On the whole, then, less artistry seems to have gone into the nineteenth-century tokens, causing collectors to treat them as second-rate. But there were plenty of exceptions. Consider the shilling or half-crown tokens of John Robertson, a Newcastle-on-Tyne silversmith, with their neatly milled edges and obverses bearing the arms of Newcastle surrounded by the legend "PAYABLE BY JOHN ROBERTSON * NEWCASTLE ON TYNE." Flip one over and behold a takeoff on the Boulton-copper reverses, worthy of Külcher himself (but engraved by Peter Wyon, who was at least his equal), with Commerce sitting on a bale instead of Britannia sitting on a rock and with the legend "NORTHUMBERLAND & DURHAM 12D TOKEN—1811" instead of "BRITANNIA—1797."

Elaborate engravings were more often employed on copper tokens, in part because these tended to be manufactured in larger quantities: fancy dies were more economical for large-scale commissions, where the high cost of original hand-engraved "matrices" could be spread thin. The 1811 pennies issued by Norwich draper Samuel Barker, designed by Peter Wyon and showing Norwich Castle on their obverses and two sheep grazing on their reverses, are comparable to some of the most artistic eighteenth-century tokens (Waters 1957, vii). Just as impressive were Fereday's 1811 tokens, which bore intricate obverses depicting the smoke-churning furnaces at his Priestfield works, near Bilston. The dies for them were sunk by Thomas Halliday, another outstanding Birmingham engraver, who apprenticed with Matthew Boulton and whose Newhall Street workshop in turn served as the training grounds for almost all of Great Britain's best Victorian-era die sinkers (Timmins 1866, 565). In 1812, Fereday, yielding to critics who insisted that his copper tokens were too light, switched to heavier ones. But when he did so, he also abandoned the lovely engravings that graced the originals, neatly demonstrating a basic principle of coinage, to wit: that high "intrinsic worth" and hard-to-replicate engravings are substitutes when it comes to discouraging false coiners. As it happens, Robertson's fancy silver tokens also confirm that theory, having weighed considerably less than their more utilitarian counterparts, many of which were not rated much above their intrinsic worth.

While nineteenth-century tokens often lacked pretty pictures and, to that extent, were more vulnerable to counterfeiting than their eighteenth-century counterparts, in other respects they were better coins. The use of restraining collars, previously limited to Boulton's tokens, the Parys Mine pennies, and a few of Peter Kempson's Scottish commissions, was now relatively common (Sharp 1834, passim; Bell 1964). Also, improvements in the art of die "hubbing"—the process by which a single original matrix could serve as the basis for a large number of identical "working" dies—limited die variations among legitimate coins, making it easier to spot counterfeits. The more talented die makers, Halliday among them, could make it "very difficult to distinguish between individual [working] dies" (Withers and Withers 1999, 27) and correspondingly easy to tell the difference between coins based on authentic hand-engraved matrices and ones made from hand-engraved (as opposed to hubbed) copies. On the whole, then, despite being more homely, the new tokens were, in the words of numismatist John Taylor, "well made pieces . . . admirably suited for their particular purpose" (Bell 1964, ix).

Medalist of Merit

Although Halliday was once credited with manufacturing not only the dies for many nineteenth-century tokens but the tokens themselves, experts (see, e.g., Withers and Withers 1999, 20) are nowadays inclined to treat him as a specialist who prepared dies for others, rather than a major token manufacturer in his own right. By far the most important of Halliday's clients was Edward Thomason, who, besides making all of Fereday's tokens, also made tokens for several copper companies. Like most Birmingham coiners and like his father before him, Thomason started out making buttons and buckles. But Thomason's father articled him to Matthew Boulton in 1786, and Edward ended up sharing his master's taste for bold ventures along with his interest in numismatic products. Although his first few inventions were flops, Thomason hit pay dirt with the corkscrew he patented in 1801—a favorite to this day among wine connoisseurs. After that, he piled up one success after another, becoming Birmingham's most celebrated entrepreneur.

Some years before he got involved in commercial coinage, Thomason had established himself as one of Great Britain's leading medalists, second only to Boulton himself. The deaths of Boulton and Külcher (Soho's best medal engraver) in 1809 and 1810, respectively, not only eliminated Thomason's chief rivals but provided the inspiration for one of his most impressive undertakings: a four-inch medal commemorating the death of his former master, engraved by Peter Wyon. It was supposed to be the largest medal in all of Europe. It wasn't,[11] but it was an outstanding achievement nonetheless. Thomason would follow it with several undisputed numismatic firsts. The last and greatest of these—a series of sixty three-inch medals depicting scriptural scenes, completed in 1830—sufficed, in light of his other accomplishments, to earn Thomason a tap on the shoulder from the "Sailor King," William IV; nine foreign knighthoods; three foreign medals of merit, a medal of divinity, and nine vice-consulships. Not bad for a button-maker's son!

As Sir Edward was not one to resist crowing over his accomplishments,[12] we may leave it to him to explain his involvement in commercial coinage, provided we bear in mind his poor memory for dates.

---

11. Russia's ambassador quickly refuted Thomason's claims by producing a wider, though considerably thinner, Russian medal. Some years later, the Danish ambassador came up with a much older medal (Danish, of course) that trumped everything (Mays 1982, 21).

12. According to a contributor to the *Victoria County History of Warwickshire* (Everseley 1964, 107), Thomason's memoirs are "without doubt one of the most egotistical and snobbish productions ever published."

In 1807 there was the greatest difficulty with commercial men to obtain change in silver, but particularly in copper, to pay the workpeople their wages. During the year I put up machinery for the manufacturing of tokens or coins, because the distress and annoyance were so great with the manufacturers, that many principal establishments were determined to pass their own tokens of copper, and some of silver, and made payable at their own works, sooner than that their workmen should attend in dozens of public houses to obtain change.

(THOMASON 1845, 27)

Presumably, Thomason should have written 1811 or, perhaps, 1810: the tokens he struck to pay his own workers, which he says were the first ones he made, are actually dated 1811 and 1812 (Withers and Withers 1999, 67), and no earlier tokens from him are known. Such inconsistencies recur throughout Thomason's memoirs, which he wrote while in his seventies and published just three years before his death.

Although Thomason's Church Street facility took on some very large token commissions, Thomason cannot be said to have monopolized the token business. In two December 1811 letters to Matthew Robinson Boulton, Zach Walker Sr. identified five "principal Token manufacturers" operating in Birmingham, including Thomason, as well as three smaller ones. Separate contemporary sources reveal another eight, including Sheffield button makers Younge and Deakin, who were responsible for some of the more important silver tokens. That makes no fewer than sixteen nineteenth-century token manufacturers in all (Withers and Withers 1999, 21–24). Although most of them were striking tokens for the first (and last) time, a few, including Peter Kempson and Bonham Hammond, had been among the manufacturers of eighteenth-century tokens, while both Thomason and Halliday cut their teeth at Soho.

Conspicuously absent from the nineteenth-century commercial coinage scene was the Soho Mint itself. Soho struck its last British commercial coins—Charleville thirteen-pence truck "tickets"—in 1802, afterward limiting itself to offshore commercial coining ventures. Matthew Robinson Boulton wouldn't touch British commercial coin commissions with a bargepole, for good reason: now that Soho had become Britain's only official source of both copper coin and Bank of England dollars, he'd have been foolish to risk its privileged status by contributing to a controversial commercial coinage that was bound eventually to give way to more official coining. Still, the decision not to take part was costly: at the close of 1813, Soho's coinage account showed a loss of £1,266 18s and 3 farthings, "Arising principally from Wages paid & little work done" (MBP 60/372).

Morgan the Not-So-Magnificent

If Edward Thomason was the most notable of the nineteenth-century token makers, a man calling himself "Henry Morgan" was the most notorious. Morgan announced his entry into the business through advertisements such as the following, placed in the London *Star* on July 26.

> SILVER TOKENS AND SMALL CHANGE supplied to regimental Paymasters, Manufacturers, Farmers, Shop and Inn Keepers, Clerks of Public Works, and all other People who require Change for their Business, or to pay Workmen.
>
> COUNTRY RESIDENTS may be accommodated, per COACH, with from Five Pounds worth to a large amount, weekly, by directing, with real Name, Occupation, and abode, to M & Co. care of Mr. Heaton, No. 27, Clement's Lane, Strand, London, enclosing a remittance in Notes, or Good Bills. No letters admitted unless post paid.

Morgan's offer sounds perfectly legitimate. Yet numismatist and token cataloger William Davis (1904, xxix) denounced his activities as "an insidious malady, which was eventually sure to kill private enterprise." Arthur Waters (1957, 116) likewise condemns Morgan's "evil work," while calling the man himself a "villain."

What had Morgan done to incur such odium (le mot juste)? First, he had the effrontery to stamp his products with such inscriptions as "Issued by Royal License" and "Licensed Silver Token." As *Bell's Weekly Messenger* pointed out to its readers on November 11, 1811, the inscriptions were a sham: there was no such thing as a royal license to issue silver tokens. Morgan's "License," assuming he had one, could only have consisted of the license required of every manufacturer of silver products.

Second, Morgan was heavily involved in the production and sale of anonymous and irredeemable tokens for general circulation, as opposed to legitimate commercial coins. Of the 108 tokens (excluding proof pieces) for which he's credited, only twenty-three carry explicit promises of redemption (Clayton 1967, 41), and some of these bear fake issuers' names (ibid., 42). This record alone made Morgan a renegade: of all the different silver tokens listed by Dalton, including Morgan's issues, 84 percent are "Genuine Trade Tokens" bearing names of bona fide issuers who scrupulously honored their redemption pledges (Edmunds 1966, 179).

There was, to be fair, nothing inherently underhanded about anonymous tokens: not every businessman needing change could afford his own bespoke coins, and there weren't always enough genuine trade tokens from other sources to go around. But Morgan's silver tokens were exceptionally light, weighing perhaps two-thirds as much as most others. Their presence therefore helped blacken the reputation of all private coins, supplying crucial ammunition to those who wished to put a stop to private coinage on the grounds that its products tended to be "underweight."

Third and most seriously, Morgan was guilty of forging at least two legitimate trade tokens—the shilling and sixpence tokens of a group of Bristol traders headed by Francis Garratt. Here, *forging* is, strictly speaking, too strong a word, for Morgan's Bristol tokens were actually private token "evasives": although they closely resembled the originals, which bore their issuers' names on their reverses, Morgan (perhaps to protect himself from a charge of common-law fraud) made a point of misspelling all the names: "Fras. Garratt" became "Frans. Garrett"; "Wm. Terrell" became "Wr. Terrell"; "Grigg" became "Gregg," and so on. He also changed the obverse-side date from August 12 to August 22 or July 12. The frauds were thus quickly detected, allowing Garratt & Co. to alert the public to Morgan's "infamous deception" in an ad placed in the *Bath Chronicle* on February 12, 1812 (Clayton 1967, 43).

Why the swindle? Morgan's motive appears to have been not profit (for the "forged" tokens were too few in number to have yielded any) but revenge. Morgan, it seems, had supplied an initial, smallish batch of Garratt and Co. tokens. But when the same group undertook a much larger token issue under the guise of the Bristol Commercial Token Bank Company, they turned not to Morgan but to a rival supplier. A scorned Morgan struck back by retrieving some of the dies he'd used for the original commission, modifying them to evade the charge of fraud, and striking and issuing his own versions (Mays 1991, 78). While Morgan's "spite" issues proved more a nuisance than a calamity for Garratt and his friends, Morgan's dubious undertakings did lots of harm to the entire commercial coinage system. Numismatist Peter Clayton (1967, 38) even goes so far as to claim that Morgan was "responsible to quite a large degree for the undermining of the token economy" that began in 1813 and culminated in the blanket outlawing of private coins.

Morgan managed, ironically enough, to make advertising hay out of

the token suppression movement that his own activities helped to in-
spire. An ad he placed in the *Star* for June 24, 1813, reads:

> Local Tokens of Gold and Silver, invented and first made for Public
> Convenience in March 1811, by Messrs Morgan and Co. Die Makers
> and Medallists, at their Licenced Token Manufactory, No. 12, Rath-
> bone Place, Oxford Street, London, having been honoured with Leg-
> islation sanction and patronage by Three successive Acts of Parlia-
> ment, continue to make to any design for Companies and Individuals,
> at a short notice, in that superior style of execution which has ob-
> tained for M. and Co. during the last two years numerous and exten-
> sive orders from Bankers, manufacturers and Shopkeepers, in almost
> every city and town throughout the United Kingdom. N.B.-Unpaid
> letters will not be admitted. Dies of numerous patterns ready en-
> graved.

In fact, as we shall see, the "Three successive Acts of Parliament" to which
Morgan refers "sanctioned" tokens only to the extent of announcing the
government's repeated decisions to delay suppressing them.

This last ad also points to the mystery surrounding Morgan's identity
and the whereabouts of his mint. 12 Rathbone Place turns out to have
been home not to a mint but to a tailor's shop—a letter drop, in other
words;[13] and Morgan's name doesn't show up in any London directories
for the period when he is supposed to have been in business there. Evidently, Morgan was intent on keeping to himself both the details of his
coining operation and his real identity.

But that hasn't kept numismatists from speculating.

Most believe that Morgan, despite his advertising, was merely a token
salesman and not a manufacturer. Because a large number of the dies for
Morgan's token commissions came from Thomas Halliday's Birmingham workshop, William Davis (1904, xxix) concludes that Morgan was
serving as an agent either for Halliday himself or for Edward Thomason.
Thomason, after all, struck the vast majority of tokens made using Halliday's dies. That the shady Henry Morgan may have been "shilling" (so to
speak) for the esteemed Edward Thomason is a tantalizing hypothesis.
Thomason alone could (and almost certainly did) boast truthfully of
having taken "numerous and extensive orders from Bankers, manufac-

---

13. It happens that William Hazlitt's brother John lived at 12 Rathbone Place from
1799 to 1804.

turers and Shopkeepers, in almost every city and town throughout the United Kingdom"; and Thomason is the only token maker known to have manufactured not just copper and silver tokens but gold ones as well. But then Morgan's claims concerning all the tokens he made may have been so much humbug, like the rest of his ads' contents. Moreover, if the hypothesis that Morgan was fronting for Thomason is at all plausible, it is certainly no more plausible than the alternative suggestion that he was fronting for Halliday or for some other token maker who used Halliday's dies. In short, though Thomason never shied when it came to having Orders of Merit stuck on his breast, to pin the blame on him for Morgan's misdeeds isn't so easy.[14]

Out-of-Pocket

There was, as we've seen, a charitable intent behind many nineteenth-century tokens, including most silver ones (Morgan's were notorious exceptions). Charity was the sole raison d'être of the tokens issued by several British workhouses—or, more precisely, by the overseers of the poor in several British towns. Such tokens accounted for 8 percent of all token types issued and were issued in substantial quantities in three instances—those of the Birmingham, Sheffield, and Worcester workhouses (Wager 1977, 61).

Poor relief in England had long been the responsibility of individual parishes. Each parish elected two or more "overseers of the poor," who (along with local justices of the peace) determined who was eligible for relief, set "poor rates" and collected taxes based on them, and built and maintained workhouses. These last, which were first provided for by the Poor Law of 1601, allowed parishes the option of putting able-bodied paupers to work while housing and feeding them ("indoor relief"), instead of making payments to them at their own homes ("out-relief"). The Workhouse Act of 1722–23 went further, sanctioning a "workhouse test" by means of which relief could be denied to applicants who refused to enter workhouses. Indoor relief was thus encouraged because it was supposed to lighten the relief burden using proceeds from sales of workhouse products.

In reality, workhouses, like other public enterprises, usually lost money. They also earned the reputation, not altogether undeserved, of

---

14. Morgan's identity is the subject of a forthcoming book by Andrew Wager, who, understandably, is keeping his as-yet-unpublished findings to himself.

being crowded, filthy, disease-ridden places with horrible food, whose inmates were abused by their masters and scorned by their benefactors:

> Their's is yon house that holds the parish poor,
> Whose walls of mud scarce bear the broken door;
> There, where the putrid vapours, flagging, play,
> And the dull wheel hums doleful through the day,
> There children dwell who know no parents' care,
> Parents, who know no children's love, dwell there!
> Heartbroken matrons on their joyless bed,
> Forsaken wives, and mothers never wed,
> Dejected widows with unheeded tears,
> And crippled aged with more than childhood fears;
> The lame, the blind, and far the happiest they!
> The moping idiot and the madman gay.[15]

In fairness, the workhouses with mud walls—that is, the small ones found
in the more impoverished villages—tended to be the worst, whereas the
more impressive, brick versions in larger towns and cities weren't quite
so bad (Longmate 1974, 32). Nevertheless, their overall reputation as
unwholesome places led, in 1796, to a relaxation of restrictions on out-
relief. "Within a generation," Norman Longmate writes (ibid., 35), out-
relief went "from being the rare exception [to being] the almost universal rule," especially for able-bodied men. The workhouses began to limit
themselves to elderly persons, unmarried mothers and their children,
orphans, the disabled, and, once the French wars began, the destitute
wives of fallen soldiers and sailors. By 1803, workhouse inmates made up
only about 10 percent of British relief cases (Lees 1998, 64–68).

What no one could have anticipated at the start of the century was the
huge increase in "pauperism" (to use the contemporary term) over the
course of the subsequent two decades. Between 1801 and 1813, England's bill for poor relief rose from £4.1 million to £6,656,106. By
1818, the figure was £7,870,801. The unprecedented number of applicants for relief, especially for out-relief, confronted overseers with a
tremendous challenge: besides having to raise more money, the meager
sums they doled out to their charges, which seldom exceeded two or
three shillings per week, meant that they had to have it all in the form of
small change.

---

15. Crabbe 1783, quoted in Longmate 1974, 30.

The challenge was greatest in manufacturing towns, which saw their export-oriented industries decay as the war continued. None suffered more in this regard than Birmingham, whose toy trade was ravaged both by the closing off of European markets and by the rising price of copper. "Mr. Pitt's 'War of Humanity,'" Samuel Garbett wrote acidly, "has almost entirely annihilated our trade" (Gill 1952, 116). By 1809, according to William Hutton, no fewer than five hundred Birmingham tradesmen had failed (Hopkins 1998, 108). Gun makers alone prospered, though not nearly enough to make up for the depression of most other trades. The upshot was that many people were thrown out of work. Those men who could do so joined the army or navy. For the rest, including their wives and children, the choice was between "the workhouse or the grave" (Yates quoted in Gill 1952, 116).

Birmingham's workhouse was located at the lower end of Lichfield Street, at the site of the present Victoria Law Courts on what is now Corporation Street. The building, first erected in 1733, was given a new wing in 1779 so that it might hold as many as six hundred inmates. During the first two decades of the nineteenth century, however, more than a thousand people were sometimes jammed into it, to be set to work, if they were able, weaving, spinning, combing wool, and drawing flax. Besides providing for these workhouse inmates, Birmingham's 108 Guardians of the Poor (a board elected by ratepayers, of which Birmingham's overseers were ex officio members) were responsible for no fewer than two thousand out-relief "cases" each week, with a typical case involving two or three persons. In Easter 1817, for instance, over twenty-two thousand persons were dependent on weekly charity of some kind, but only a thousand of these were workhouse inmates (Stephens 1964, 322–23; Hutton 1819, 306).

Whereas workhouse inmates received in-kind relief in the form of food, clothing, and shelter (such as it was), out-relief consisted entirely of money payments ranging from one shilling to 2s 6d per pensioner or child (Elrington 1964, 321–24). With total relief disbursements falling just shy of twenty-one thousand in 1811 and trending upward from there to almost sixty-two thousand pounds by 1818 (Hutton 1819, 306), the Guardians had somehow to come up with very large amounts of decent copper and silver coin. Yet they couldn't expect already hard-pressed ratepayers to come up with it.

At first, Birmingham's Guardians tried to get help from the government. In early July, 1811, a deputation of them set off for London. Their mission: to meet with Perceval, explain how the change shortage was keeping them from ministering to the poor, hold out their own beggar's bowls, as it were, and say (in effect), "Please, sir, we want some more." The mission succeeded in that the men came back with three thousand pounds in Bank dollars, as well as Perceval's promise to deliver another six thousand pounds in the new three-shilling and 1 s 6 d pieces once they were ready (Perkins 1905, 57).[16] But such sums couldn't go far. Come August, finding themselves again strapped for change, town officials appealed to the government again, this time by memorializing the Committee on Coin and stressing the plight of manufacturers and their workers rather than that of the poor. The memorial, signed by Joseph Ledsam, Birmingham's high bailiff, and published in *Aris's Birmingham Gazette* on August 30, declared:

1. [T]hat the Trade of the Town and Neighbourhood suffereth great and serious Evils from the Want of small Change, wherewith to pay the Manufacturers in the different Branches of Trade.

2. That there are in this Town and Neighbourhood, many Thousands of Persons, whose weekly Labour does not produce more than from three to ten shillings, and that the Employers being compelled to pay several of them together in Pound Notes, they are under the necessity of going to Public Houses to get Change, where of course some of the Money must be spent to induce the Publican to supply them therewith, or they must buy some of the articles which they do not want, or in many cases, must take the Articles of Food on credit at an extravagant Price, paying for the same when what they have had amounts to a pound.

3. That the issue of Bank Tokens, although of great and essential Service, is by no means adequate to remedy the Evil. And your Memorialists, therefore, must earnestly request that your Lordships will speedily order a Coinage of Copper Penny and Halfpenny Pieces, which would effectively remove the Evil they labour under. (Withers and Withers 1999, 15)

---

16. Peter Kempson, Thomas Halliday, and Edward Thomason all served as members of the Guardians of the Poor at one point or another, and it would be nice to be able to say that at least one of these private coin makers was among the deputies who called on Perceval. Unfortunately, apart from knowing that Thomason's tenure was quite brief, I haven't been able to determine the dates on which each served, let alone whether they were among the deputies who went to visit Perceval.

But the Committee on Coin was not about to order any more copper coin, having not long ago placed three orders for a total of eighteen hundred tons of Boulton copper. If the Guardians wanted more money, they would just have to make it themselves.

In fact, they'd been doing just that, albeit to a very limited extent, since 1810, when they started issuing one-pound, crown, and half-crown card and leather tokens. During the autumn of 1811, having been disappointed by the government, they began making small-denomination metal tokens as well. Indeed, the Birmingham workhouse ended up being responsible for one of the largest issues—if not the largest—of silver shillings and sixpences, as well as for a very large issue of copper tokens.[17] The last consisted mainly of pennies but also of substantial numbers of threepenny tokens, all struck by local button makers. Samuel and Thomas Aston, of St. Paul's Square, struck all the threepenny tokens and some of the pennies, while the remaining penny commissions were divided between Henry Laugher of Great Charles Street (who struck the 1814 series) and Peter Kempson (Withers and Withers 1999, 76).[18] It appears that Peter Wyon had a hand in making the dies for the silver tokens, as well as those for the copper threepenny tokens. (An otherwise unknown engraver named Willets deserves credit for the rest of the copper token dies.)

In theory, Birmingham's copper workhouse tokens, which could be redeemed in Bank of England notes at the workhouse, were supposed to work much like today's food stamps, being received only at certain shops, for bread and other essentials, but never for, say, alcohol. In practice (also like food stamps, only to a far greater extent), they were treated like coin of the realm, if not like something better than available coin of the realm, not only in Birmingham, but also in nearby villages and towns. That the theory failed was good news for the Guardians of the Poor, in-

---

17. Although both Waters and Davis list a 2/6 "Birmingham workhouse" token, this extremely rare token was actually a forgery—perhaps another of Morgan's "spite" issues—to which the Birmingham overseers alerted the public in an advertisement on August 17, 1812 (Mays 1978, 241). That the forged tokens were, according to the ad, "circulated in distant counties" points to the widespread acceptance of genuine Birmingham workhouse tokens.

18. Had these tokens been struck after 1815 rather than during the preceding three years, Kempson, who (together with his partner and son, Peter Jr.) was a member of the Guardians of the Poor, would not have been allowed to supply any: section 6 of 55 Geo. III *c* 137 prohibits overseers from supplying "any goods, materials, or provisions for the use of any workhouse, or for the support and maintenance of the poor in any parish for which he shall be appointed."

sofar as its failure enhanced the demand for their tokens, allowing them to offer them to the general public in exchange for banknotes. An amount corresponding to the float from such exchanges could then be invested, with the interest taking at least some pressure off the poor rates.

Given all the gains to be had, it isn't surprising that workhouses in other communities also made and issued their own coins. Sheffield's three-story Union Workhouse, whose already huge relief payments of £18,327 in 1812 soared to just over £27,000 in 1813 (W. White 1833, 113), also began issuing pennies in 1811, as did Worcester's House of Industry—a huge complex taking up much of Tallow Hill, at Worcester's eastern end. The House of Industry tokens, which consisted of both pennies and halfpennies, were first made available on November 8, 1811. Their immense popularity can be gauged from the following notice, printed in the *Worcester Herald* on November 16.

> THE DIRECTORS of the HOUSE OF INDUSTRY finding the demand for their TOKENS greater than they at first calculated upon, and that many disappointments have occurred in consequence thereof, have now provided a sufficient quantity to supply the Public with any amount. They likewise beg to state, that as the Advantage arising from issuing these Tokens, independent of the Convenience of the trading Interest, will be applied in aid of the Poor Rates, they trust they will meet due encouragement from every Class.
>
> N.B. —These Tokens will be regularly exchanged at any time for Bank Notes at their Office in Friar's-street, and they presume to add, that their Responsibility must have a preference to the issue of any Individual.

As that last clause suggests, the House of Industry wasn't Worcester's only source of tokens. On the contrary, it found itself competing head-on with other local token issuers for what was, after all, a limited local market for very small change. The directors therefore thought it wise to prick the public's conscience so as to favor their own tokens over rival issues. They succeeded to the point where, at a meeting of local tradesmen, it was unanimously resolved to receive nothing save House of Industry and government coin. Manufacturers struck back, though, by holding their own meeting at a boozer named the Stars and Garter, where they resolved that Worcester's business couldn't manage without more change and that they therefore intended to continue issuing their own pennies and halfpennies, which were just as heavy as the best regal copper and for which they always stood ready to pay twenty shillings on the pound (Tuberville 1852, 236).

Two other large workhouses, those of Halesowen (or Hales Owen), also in Worcestershire, and of Smallburgh, in Norwich, issued their own custom-made pennies and halfpennies (Berry 1982, 43; Brunel 1974b). Most other workhouses presumably made do with what regal coin they could get hold of or with local tokens issued by others. However, the workhouse of Bradford, in West Yorkshire, settled for a clever and inexpensive compromise: rather than choosing to commission its own tokens or to employ other tokens indiscriminately, it took to countermarking tokens issued by various copper companies, especially Birmingham's Union Copper Company, with its own marks consisting of an opposed pair of sausage-shaped indentions in which the words "BRADFORD" and "UNION" appeared, in raised letters.

Thanks to such makeshifts, to making their own tokens, or to the token issues of others, Great Britain's hard-struck workhouses managed to struggle through one of the most challenging stretches in their long history—or most of it, at any rate. For the hardest times of all would be the years just following the Treaty of Paris, when a second wrenching adjustment of Great Britain's economy would swell the relief rolls more than ever. It was precisely at that time that the government, having by then cracked down on silver tokens, chose to crack down on copper ones as well, without the slightest intention of supplying anything to take their place.

Reading's Great Grecian

The most venerated nineteenth-century token source was not a workhouse or copper company or banker's consortium but a private individual, who issued tokens partly to aid his fellow citizens but also to draw attention to the British government's mismanagement of the nation's currency. John Berkeley Monck (1768–1834) attended Eton and studied at the Middle Temple. After practicing law in London for several years, he moved to Reading, where a large property that came to him upon his father's death in 1809 allowed him to devote himself to extensive charitable activities. It also made him free to pursue his passion for political economy, which had been aroused by the Bank restriction.

An unrelenting critic of Britain's paper standard, Monck endorsed David Ricardo's strict bullionist stand, laying all blame for the depreciation of the paper pound relative to specie squarely on the shoulders of the Bank of England and favoring a return to the former metallic standard. Though his views allowed for little compromise, the frank and eloquent way in which he expressed them, both in speech and in writing, combined with his indisputable concern for his fellow citizens, won him tremendous public support. After a narrow loss in 1812, he was elected to Parliament in 1820 and again in 1826. Concerning him, Miss Mittford,[19] who happened to be a constituent, wrote:

> He is a Great Grecian, and a great Political Economist—a sort of Andrew Marvell in parliament[20]. . . . He votes sometimes with one party and sometimes with another as he likes their measures; respected by all, notwithstanding his independence, and idolized here in the country for his liberality, his cheerfulness, his good-humour, and his unfailing kindness.   (QUOTED IN COOPER 1923, 122)

So well liked was Monck that when he died at Coley Park on December 13, 1834, his loss was, according to *The Gentleman's Magazine* (March 1835, 433), "deeply felt by the town at large." Hundreds of gentlemen, scholars, and tradesmen took part in his funeral, accompanying his remains four abreast from Coley Park to St. Mary's Church. Along the way, the sidewalks were jammed with other mourners, the town's businesses having closed so that they might pay their respects (Cooper 1923, 122).

The post-1811 currency famine offered Monck a perfect opportunity to take up cudgels against Spencer Perceval's government, which, far from doing what it might to end the hated restriction, was threatening to make Bank of England notes legal tender. Monck struck back in both word and deed, the former consisting of an open letter to Perceval, the second of his own substitutes for the government's "debased" currency. Reading, like many other communities, was desperately short of silver at the close of 1811. It was then that Monck began issuing his own half-crown and 1s 6d silver tokens, which he'd ordered from Thomason both for his own use—to make himself "independent of the Bank of En-

---

19. The reference is to Mary Russell Mitford (1787–1865), the English dramatist and novelist.

20. Andrew Marvell (1621–78) was a Metaphysical poet and friend of John Milton. Mitford's choice of words is rather odd, as Marvell was himself an MP, who represented Hull in the House of Commons. The "Great Grecian" epithet was originally given to Francis Dillingham, one of the translators of the King James Version of the Bible, in recognition of both his command of the Greek language and his extraordinary debating skills.

gland," as he put it—and for the use of local firms and officials, for whom he acted as a coin wholesaler. Monck's tokens, whose redemption, in banknotes, he personally attended to at Reading's Bear Inn (Childs 1910, 25), eventually made up about a quarter of the total value of silver money circulating in the borough and were practically the only silver money available in nearby villages. Bank of England tokens, in contrast, made up only about one-sixth of Reading's silver, which was a relatively high proportion, reflecting Reading's proximity to London. The rest of Reading's small change consisted of regal sixpences and shillings so badly worn that it took over one hundred of the latter to make up a troy pound.

According to an appreciative editorial in the *Reading Mercury*, Monck's tokens alone kept Reading from getting mired in a trade depression. Until their appearance, the paper noted, "almost every individual, but in particular the retail tradesmen, had cause to complain of the most disturbing scarcity of small silver money, for the purpose of change." The editorial continued:

> So great was the deficiency, that many tradesmen were compelled for want of it either to turn away their customers or give credit for very small sums, a circumstance attended with very great additional trouble, and frequently terminating in the loss of both their customers and their debt. . . . But the large and liberal coinage of your tokens has made silver this year abundant, compared with the year preceding, and has given a proportional facility to trade.
>
> (SEPTEMBER 21, 1812, QUOTED IN CHILDS 1910, 25)

Important as Monck's silver tokens were to Reading's citizens, to Monck himself they were only one small ploy in a scheme aimed at breathing new life into Great Britain's *gold* coinage. That scheme formally began with the publication, on February 12, 1812, of Monck's letter "to the Right Hon. Spencer Percival," then serving as his own ministry's chancellor of the exchequer. Assessing the state of Great Britain's coinage, Monck wrote:

> [T]here is now no longer in circulation any money but a debased specie, consisting wholly of light shillings and sixpences, or of [Bank] tokens inferior to the standard of the double [bimetallic] ratio both of quality and quantity. Even this base money and humble silver has been dealt out by the Bank of England very sparingly . . . and the

country was suffered last summer to experience the greatest difficulty from the scarcity of this sort of specie. Poor persons were obliged to receive their wages in one pound notes, and to allow a discount for change. (MONCK 1812, 4–5)[21]

Monck added that although "the speculations of individuals, who have issued local tokens, has removed in great measure the pressure of this particular inconvenience . . . the general inconveniences arising from a debased currency remain in full force" (ibid.); indeed, Monck hoped that token coins might be dispensed with altogether once the "old standard" was restored.[22] As for the government's plan to make Bank of England notes legal tender, Monck argued that it was "a measure fraught with guilt and folly" that "would be in effect an insolvent act . . . releasing from their engagements a set of wealthy debtors, very competent to pay, and imposing on their creditors a loss perfectly unnecessary, and therefore perfectly unjustifiable" (ibid., 6).

Monck wanted instead to bring the nation "back by degrees to its old standard" and to do so "with safety and honour" (ibid., 7). But just how does one revive a metallic standard "by degrees"? Monck believed it could be done by issuing gold tokens—what he called "representative guineas"—into which Bank paper might be freely converted. Although the "representative" guineas, at four pennyweight and one grain each, would be well below the "old standard," they would at least have some metallic worth and would therefore be a step in the right direction. After two years—the same delay the Bullion Committee had advised—the tokens could be freely exchanged for genuine guineas (ibid., 11).

Monck understood perfectly well—better perhaps than the Royal Mint staff—the difference between fiduciary or token gold coins and full-bodied ones. Moreover, he realized that "the high numerary value given to the guinea tokens will be a great temptation to forgery." The

---

21. Given all his blustering about the "debased" status of Bank of England tokens and given his endorsement elsewhere of John Locke's assertion that "[i]t is only the quantity of silver in any coin, that is, and eternally will be, the measure of its value" (Edmunds 1966, 177), it is only fair to note that Monck's own silver tokens weighed about two-thirds as much as their Bank of England counterparts. The difference proved crucial in keeping Monck's tokens in circulation despite the further appreciation of silver.

22. In a later letter also addressed to Perceval, Monck wrote that "the whole system of tokens, although comparatively useful, is radically bad, and a miserable corollary to the depreciation of our compulsory paper currency" (Edmunds 1966, 178). Monck here overlooks the fact that Great Britain's small-change problem, which could not be addressed save by tokens, antedated the Bank restriction.

temptation might be obviated, he wrote, "by bestowing great pains upon the dies, so as to put their imitation out of the reach of any but first rate artists, who, it may be hoped, need in this country never earn their bread by a base prostitution of their talents." After all, "I do not know that gold tokens would be much more liable to be forged than bank notes are at present, and in both cases it must be left to the vigilance of the Bank and Government to counteract these frauds" (ibid., 13).

Such, in brief, were Monck's suggestions to the government. But he doubted that the government would take them up—not, at least, without some further prodding on his part. So he chose to prod it by issuing his own "representative guineas" in the shape of "40-shilling" gold tokens bearing a portrait of Alfred the Great on their obverse, together with the inscription (from Ovid's *Metamorphoses*) "PIGNORA CERTA PETIS: DO PIGNORA CERTA"—literally, "Credible pledges thou seekest: credible pledges I thee give."[23] Using bullion supplied by Monck, Edward Thomason struck two hundred such pieces, putting six pennyweights and eighteen grains (or about thirty-four shillings' worth) of gold in each.

The government was prodded, all right: for Monck's gold tokens, unlike his silver ones, were unprecedented. Even the Bank of England, which did more business in gold than anyone both before and during the restriction, never dared to encroach on the Royal Mint's monopoly of gold coinage. Necessity had compelled the government to allow it—a private corporation—to issue silver dollars and then smaller silver tokens, in part so that the government itself might avoid the charge of tampering with the ancient standard. That step opened the way to other private silver issues, which the government tolerated both because they helped satisfy a dire need and because it knew no legal way of stopping them without discrediting the Bank's issues. But Monck's gold tokens were another matter altogether. Too valuable by far to ease the shortage of small change, they could, from the government's perspective, serve no purpose at all apart from promoting Monck's preferred scheme for ending the Bank restriction.[24] They would further undermine the Royal Mint's coinage prerogative. Moreover, their presence was embarrassing, offering, as it did, mute testimony in support of the bullionist proposition that Bank paper had depreciated and against Nicholas Vansittart's

---

23. Ovid *Metamorphosis* 2.91. George Sandys (1632) translates the phrase, "A signe thou crav'st, that might confirme thee mine: I, by dehorting, give a certayne signe." Other contemporary translations depart still further from the Latin original.

24. In fact, Monck's gold tokens never circulated, having been eagerly scooped up by collectors, for as much as five quid each, as soon as they made their appearance.

ludicrous counterclaim that a paper pound and a shilling were together worth just as much as a guinea.

Monck, for his part, was perfectly happy to see the government red-faced—the better to shame it into ending the restriction. With that goal in mind, he planned to issue a second batch of gold tokens. Taking advantage of the expiration on March 25 of Lord Stanhope's Act, Monck advertised in the *Reading Mercury* of April 10 his willingness to pay £115 in bank notes for every one hundred guineas offered to him, or a pound tuppence halfpenny per guinea—which was actually about tuppence halfpenny below the going market price.

Whether Monck managed to get hold of much gold despite his cheap offer is academic, for, guineas or no guineas, he would be kept from going through with his plan by none other than Spencer Perceval himself. Perceval, it seems, had wind of Monck's intentions, whereupon he personally called on Edward Thomason, securing Thomason's promise not to proceed with Monck's gold tokens until Perceval could interview him. Whether the interview took place—and what was said during it if it did—hasn't come to light. The upshot, though, was that Great Britain had seen its last private gold coins (Edmunds 1966, 174).[25]

By making his own gold tokens, Monck hoped to goad Perceval into doing something about Great Britain's coinage. Goad him he did. But far from getting Perceval to take steps to end the Bank restriction or to otherwise reform the government's own coinage, the Great Grecian provoked him to do something else altogether. Having staved off the private sector's latest assault upon the regal prerogative of coinage, Perceval decided to launch a counteroffensive, in the shape of a campaign to stamp out every last one of Great Britain's unofficial coins.

---

25. According to Richard Doty (personal communication, October 19, 2004), the Sheffield firm of Younge, Wilsons & Younge issued some gold half guineas struck for them by Halliday in 1812. Very few specimens are known, though Doty himself purchased one on behalf of the American Numismatic Society. Arthur Waters (1957, 16) and Christopher Brunel (1974a, 24) apparently have these tokens in mind in referring, mistakenly, to gold 1 s 6 d tokens issued by the same firm. Although Waters speculates that Younge, Wilsons & Younge's gold tokens "probably met a quick fate in the crucible" when their would-be issuers learned of the government's opposition to gold tokens, the wear on Doty's specimen suggested to him that it had "circulated widely."

CHAPTER VII

Prerogative Regained

Go, Children of my care!

To practice now from theory repair.

All my commands are easy, short, and full:

My sons! be proud, be selfish, and be dull.

Guard my prerogative, assert my throne:

This nod confirms each privilege your own.[1]

Half a Loaf

When Spencer Perceval decided to put a stop to commercial coining, he had plenty of support to draw on. For while many viewed commercial tokens as the only thing keeping Britain's internal trade flowing, others saw them as a menace, if not a disgrace.

Some opposed commercial tokens on principle, saying they infringed upon the royal prerogative of coinage. On such grounds, 120 of John Robertson's fellow Newcastle tradesmen declared that they would refuse not only Robertson's tokens but also those issued "by any other Individual whatever" (Phillips 1900, 26). (The tradesmen later relented.) Even some token issuers had qualms about stepping on the government's turf. One regretted "running away with one of the inalienable prerogatives of the crown," fearing that, if the people were allowed to "purloin" one

---

1. The Queen of the Kingdom of the Dull, to her followers, in Pope 1743, book 4.

such prerogative, they might "begin to grasp at others and that this in-road will lead to hideous consequences" (Lauderdale quoted in Mays 1991, 80).

Others pointed to commercial tokens' practical shortcomings, one of which was that they, unlike Bank tokens and regal coin, had only a lim-ited, or "local," circulation. Although most token issuers were perfectly reputable, their reputations seldom extended beyond their domiciles, and accepting tokens from other communities was risky. Thus the *Cam-brian* of November 2, 1811, after applauding local (Welsh) token issuers for helping to remedy "the considerable inconvenience resulting from the unprecedented scarcity of small change," went on to warn its readers against tokens offered "at any considerable distance from the place where they are issued" (Mays 1991, 151). Such warnings didn't fall on deaf ears. Consequently, as Zach Walker reported to Matthew Robinson Boulton on December 4, 1811, parties issuing tokens found it "difficult to pass them beyond the immediate vicinity of the Town or place whence they are dated" (quoted in Withers and Withers 1999, 16).

Opposition to commercial money was thus spurred less by familiar to-kens than by unfamiliar ones that had wandered far from home. Blanket opposition was, in turn, most likely to come from places lacking their own token sources. While shopkeepers in Bilston had nothing but good things to say about tokens issued there by Rushbury and Woolley and by Sam Fereday, their counterparts in nearby Wolverhampton, where no to-kens were issued, declared the very same tokens unfit and vowed to refuse them (Withers and Withers 1999, 16). Perhaps this refusal boiled down to sour grapes: why should Bilston profit from Wolverhampton's change shortage? But Wolverhampton's retailers also had legitimate wor-ries. Token issuers' solidity couldn't be taken for granted, after all; and if an issuer got in hot water (as Fereday, for one, eventually did), the is-suer's neighbors would get wind of it first and, by quickly cashing in their chips, would leave outsiders holding the bag.

Commercial tokens were also faulted for being irredeemable. Strictly speaking, the complaint applied not to genuine commercial tokens but to anonymous tokens for general circulation. As we've seen in connec-tion with the 1787–97 token episode, tokens for general circulation tended to gain ground whenever the future of genuine commercial coins was threatened. Rumors of an impending suppression would cause genuine tokens to be withdrawn despite a continuing shortage of small change. Anonymous tokens would then fill the void.

Until the last days of 1811, irredeemable tokens didn't pose much of a problem. But in early December, a rumor started to spread, the gist of which was, in Zach Walker's words, "that a new Govt: coinage of Silver & *Copper* is on the Tapis, & that the token System will be put an end to early next session of Parlt" (quoted in Withers and Withers 1999, 22). Anticipating a crackdown, many legitimate token issuers took steps to retire their coins. Although anxious merchants got some of them to change their minds (Mays 1991, 75–77), a permanent niche remained for anonymous tokens to fill, and that niche grew ever larger as opposition to commercial tokens made headway (Mitchiner 1998, 2093). The complaint that tokens were sometimes irredeemable was in this way self-validating.

The most frequently heard complaint against commercial tokens was that they were "lightweight," "debased," or lacking in "intrinsic value." This complaint, most often made against silver tokens, proved most influential in the chambers of Parliament, where it struck a chord with politicians still nostalgic for the old silver standard. Owing to it, the government first decided to prohibit silver (and gold) tokens, turning against copper ones only as an afterthought.

To denounce a token as "lightweight" was to claim that its constituent metal was worth less than its declared value. In Newcastle, for instance, some of Robertson's critics, having failed to discredit his tokens merely by threatening to refuse them, struck out at him again on April 28, 1812, with the following ad in the *Tyne Mercury*.

Assays have been taken at the Assay Hall, of different tokens issued in this town and neighborhood, as also of several in the south: and in general they have been found of very inferior quality, the intrinsic value of the twelve penny tokens on average does not exceed *eightpence halfpenny*, and some not more than eightpence.

(PHILLIPS 1900, 30)

That silver tokens, considered as mere bits of metal, were worth less than their declared values was true enough. But while tokens for general circulation, including most of Morgan's products, contained relatively little metal, most genuine commercial tokens were relatively heavy: the difference between their face value and their "intrinsic value" was usually between one and three pennies in a shilling, depending on the market price of silver.[2] Part of this difference—perhaps one penny's worth—

---

2. See the appendix.

covered issuers' minting, carriage, and insurance costs. Because the tokens could be redeemed at any moment and were bound to be returned
when more official silver coins became available, their issuers could
hardly expect to profit from them. On the contrary, if the price of silver
fell, token issuers would end up taking a licking.

Such considerations counted little to critics who saw any departure
from the (long-defunct) silver standard as a threat to the currency's in-
tegrity. When Bath's Francis Ellis, an especially fervent opponent of local
tokens, was offered proof that Witchurch and Dore profited little, if at
all, from their four-shilling tokens, he dismissed it as beside the point. All
that mattered, he insisted, was "that the proportion of Silver in the Bath
Tokens is much inferior to that in the current [*sic*] Coin of the Kingdom"
and that this inferiority was likely to result in "an inundation of counterfeit Bath Tokens."

> The perplexity and loss that may ultimately flow from the Tokens, it is
> easy to foresee, though not to calculate the extent of! and while it is
> yet time, may perhaps be no less worthy the consideration of the
> avowed issuers, than of the receivers of the Bath Tokens.
>
> (*Bath Chronicle*, DECEMBER 5, 1811)

Some months later, when legislation against the silver tokens was in the
works, *Bell's Weekly Messenger* denounced them all on similar grounds.

> In Coin, properly so called, . . . there are two most useful commercial
> qualities. In the first place that each coin contains a certain number
> of grains, and secondly, that these grains are of a certain purity. This
> composition . . . constitutes a certain fixed value. . . .
>
> Now the Local Tokens want both these qualities. There is no con-
> trol upon these coiners, either in respect to the quantity of the silver
> or to the assay of it. . . . The simple mischief of all these tokens is this:
> they are bad money, an adulterated coin. They are made as a matter
> of merchandise and profit, and of course the makers must have some-
> thing beyond their intrinsic value.   (JULY 11, 1812)

A final criticism of commercial tokens was related to the claim that
they were underweight. However, it had to do not with the quantity of
metal in them but with the source of that metal: local tokens were said to
have been made from melted Bank of England tokens. The allegation
implied that instead of helping to address the shortage of decent coin,

local token issuers aggravated the shortage by treating Bank dollars and tokens as raw material for their own metallic IOUs.

Such were the charges against "local" tokens. Were the charges valid, and, if they were, did they justify outlawing commercial coins? Concerning the coins' "local" character, at least some managed to secure wide, if not nationwide, acceptance. "We know for a fact," writes numismatist D. R. D. Edmunds (1966, 181), "that [some] local tokens did circulate quite acceptably outside their town of origin." In a follow-up to his letter of December 4, 1811, to Boulton, Zach Walker himself reported finding, on the basis of coin samples collected by London's principal coach companies, that tokens' circulation was "not confined to the mere neighborhood of the Manufacturers" (quoted in Withers and Withers 1999, 21).[3] Token issuers in different towns sometimes agreed to receive each other's tokens, just as banks might agree to receive each other's notes (Mays 1991, 79). Tokens issued by manufacturing firms with establishments in various districts tended to circulate in all of those districts. For example, tokens issued by Birmingham's copper companies circulated not only around Birmingham but also in far-off Swansea, where the companies had their smelting works (Dykes 1954, 349). Such exceptions made it inaccurate to stigmatize all commercial money as "local."

More fundamentally, while coins that circulated nationally were, other things equal, better than local ones, this hardly justified suppressing local issues while national coins were scarce. Local coins were, presumably, better than no coins at all. The same might be said for anonymous tokens, although they might have been scarce themselves had legitimate tokens not been threatened.

As for tokens' lack of "intrinsic value," there was, first of all, no flood of counterfeit Bath tokens, as Francis Ellis had predicted. Nor did Whitchurch and Dore fail to honor their redemption pledges. Other silver token issuers also kept their promises, despite being forced by the government to retire their tokens en masse. Moreover, the gap between tokens' nominal value and their intrinsic worth, far from being an unpardonable defect, was the only thing that kept them from succumbing to Gresham's law. The Committee on Coin had acknowledged the need for such a gap in approving the calling down of Bank dollars and in authorizing still more "debased" Bank tokens. Parliament would eventually do the same by increasing silver's mint price from sixty-two to sixty-six shillings per troy pound.

---

3. Walker ought to have written "issuers."

Even the *Weekly Messenger*, for all its grumbling about how local tokens were "adulterated," knew it wasn't possible to keep silver in circulation while cleaving to the old standard. When the Bank dollars were cried down, it defended the move on solid economic grounds.

> When Money becomes more valuable as Bullion, than as Coin, that is to say, when more can be gotten by melting it, than by passing it; when the Mint rates at five shillings what the Money-brokers will purchase of you for five and threepence, under these circumstances is it any reasonable subject of wonder that Coin should disappear? The value of Silver at the Mint is rated as if it were always the same. Silver, however, has a price in the Market which varies as much as that of any other commodity whatever. For many years past it has been rising. The consequence is, that our Coinage has entirely lost its former relation. Nothing is so much wanted as some new regulations of the Mint. Until something of the kind has been attempted, there will always be the same dearth of Money, of Coined Money, amongst us.
>
> . . . The act of the Bank is founded upon the above principles; and was the only means of preventing the total disappearance of Dollars from the hourly rise of Silver.   (MARCH 24, 1811, 90)

When, several months later, new Bank tokens were issued bearing a still smaller value of silver relative to their intrinsic worth, the *Weekly Messenger* observed that they "must not be considered as cash, but as merely what they are called, as Metal Notes." The editors explained:

> The nature of a note . . . does not require any value, except in the terms of the contract. It is a mere promise to pay and to receive, and whether that promise be given on paper or leather, or on metal, is totally immaterial: the substratum of the promise need be worth nothing. . . . Where it is not required, therefore, that such Tokens should be worth any thing, it is no reasonable objection to them that they are not worth the whole of the sum to which they express the contract.
>
> (JULY 14, 1811)

"We may cursorily observe," the editors went on to say, "that it is a matter of very great doubt to us whether the mint price [of silver] must not be altered, and put under an entire new regulation, before the King's Mint can again be set to work" (ibid.).

Much as the *Weekly Messenger* might deny it, its arguments amounted to an implicit defense of local tokens against the charge of being "adulterated" or "debased." If anything, local tokens more closely resembled "Metal Notes" than Bank tokens did, for the Bank of England steadfastly refused to treat its tokens as direct claims even to its own notes, receiving them only in exchange for silver bullion.

As for the claim that local token makers had been melting down bank silver, although William Chaloner (1946, 24) refers to "a considerable body of evidence" supporting it, one searches for that "body" in vain. As we shall see, the British government itself eventually denied that substantial quantities of Bank tokens had been melted by local token makers or otherwise. What is certain is that intact Bank silver began to vanish well before the first silver tokens appeared. Being legally undervalued, it was bound to do so, and if it reappeared at all, it would do so in the shape of jewelry, candlesticks, and salt cellars. Private token makers thus returned at least some previously undervalued silver to circulation. Because their demand for silver far outstripped what could be had by acquiring and melting Bank tokens, they also ended up importing large quantities of Spanish and Portuguese coins from the British West Indies, New South Wales, and other British colonies (Phillips 1900, 27–28).

There were, in short, holes enough in the arguments for suppressing local tokens to accommodate a fleet of coaches and their horses. If commercial coins weren't perfect substitutes for regal ones, they were at least imperfect substitutes. In resorting to them, the public helped itself to half a loaf, while waiting for the government to come up with more.

But the government wasn't about to come up with anything. On the contrary: it was preparing to wrest that half loaf away.

"A Most Dangerous and Mischievous Measure"

The flimsiness of the charges brought against local tokens didn't stop the tide of sentiment—at least, official sentiment—from turning against them. The adverse sentiment, in turn, gave rise to rumors of impending suppression, which (as we have seen) led to the proliferation of anonymous tokens, further eroding support for local issues.

So it happened that on April 27, 1812, William Huskisson pointedly asked the chancellor of the exchequer whether he planned "to bring forward any measure for the purpose of checking the circulation of local tokens." It was then that Perceval, having just stopped Monck from issuing more gold tokens, answered (to cries of "Hear! Hear!") that he intended, the very next day, to introduce "a Bill to regulate, with a view to REPRESS, the circulation of small tokens" (Phillips 1900, 30).

In fact, Perceval did not introduce his bill "to prevent the issuing and circulating of Pieces of Gold and Silver, or other Metal, usually called Tokens, except such as are issued by the Banks of England and Ireland" until May 4. Parliament would not hear it until May 7. By then, word of the bill's existence had reached the provinces, where it set off an alarm among tradesmen and token issuers, including John Berkeley Monck. Monck responded with a second letter to Spencer Perceval, alerting him to the damage his measure would do.

> I am not a defender of the system of private tokens, but heartily deplore the train of circumstances that have gradually supplanted the coin of the realm, and led to the universal introduction of baser substitutes. I am persuaded, however, that in the present condition of our currency they are absolutely necessary, and that without them there never will be silver in circulation enough to answer the numerous and pressing occasions for small payments among the lower and laborious classes of society. . . . If it is your intention to suppress these altogether, you will take away a portion of our currency, which is not only the most solid, but which is the most useful, and even necessary to the comfort of the lower orders of society.
>
> (QUOTED IN EDMUNDS 1966, 177–78)

Alas, Perceval would never hear Monck's plea. On the evening of May 12, 1812, as Monck committed his thoughts to paper, an unhinged London broker named John Bellingham shot the prime minister dead in the lobby of the House of Commons.[4]

Perceval's death caused a second reading of the Local Tokens Bill to be deferred repeatedly while a new government was cobbled together, with Charles Jenkinson's son Robert, the second Lord Liverpool, at its helm and Vansittart serving as chancellor of the exchequer. The second reading took place at last on June 25, whereupon the bill was committed to a committee of the whole House, which reported an amended version

---

4. Bellingham was tried at the Old Bailey on May 15. The plea of insanity made for him was not admitted, and he was hanged on May 18 (Phillips 1900, 30n). Justice was indeed swift in those days. On June 1, Monck's letter was published in the *Reading Mercury* under the somewhat macabre title "A Second Letter to the Late Chancellor of the Exchequer, on the Present State of our Currency, and on Bank of England and Local Tokens."

on July 1. On July 8, further amendments were agreed to. On July 9, the bill, calling for a withdrawal of local tokens by March 25, 1813, was read for a third and last time, passed, and delivered to the House of Lords for its concurrence.

Although the Local Tokens Bill encountered no serious opposition in the Commons, its reception at the upper house was to be another matter. There, local tokens had an eloquent champion in the person of James Maitland, eighth Earl of Lauderdale (1759–1839). Besides leading the Whig Party in Scotland, Lauderdale was one of his era's most accomplished—if doctrinaire—political economists, whose published writings included "Inquiry into the Nature and Origin of Public Wealth, and into the Means and Causes of Its Increase" (1804); "Thoughts on the Alarming State of the Circulation" (1805); and "The Depreciation of the Paper-currency of Great Britain Proved" (1812).[5] He was also, according to the *Dictionary of National Biography* (Leslie and Lee 1885–1900, 12:801), "a violent-tempered, shrewd, eccentric man with a fluent tongue," who relished confrontations and whose heavy-handed attempts at humor ("a joke in his mouth was no laughing matter," Sheridan once said [Hammond and Hammond 1917, 166]) often misfired. One of his characteristic effusions provoked Benedict Arnold to challenge him to a duel, from which both men emerged unscathed, if not unsullied. No fewer than eighty-six of Lauderdale's protests appear in the pages of the *Journal of the House of Lords*.

Concerning the currency, Lauderdale was essentially a conservative. An uncompromising bullionist, he favored a quick end to the Bank restriction. He also looked forward to a time when the Royal Mint would again take charge of the nation's silver and copper coinages. Yet the government's plan to outlaw local tokens appalled him. That plan, he told Lord Grenville (after learning of the measure's passage through the lower house), "was just beginning at the wrong end of the necessary reforms & doing a thing, which even I, with all my notions of the present state of the circulation could not have ventured upon" (BL Add. MSS 58943, Lauderdale to Grenville, July 10, 1812).

---

5. Besides being at odds with Lauderdale's opposition to the Local Tokens Bill, the Hammonds' (1911, 166) claim that he was "an inveterate opponent of all measures to protect the weak by State interference" is contradicted by George Hilton (1960, 60), who points out that Lauderdale was "the principal Parliamentary supporter of the truck legislation of 1817." In fact, Lauderdale was an uncompromising democrat who opposed (violently, of course) the war with France and took delight in being nicknamed "Citizen Maitland."

When the Local Tokens Bill reached the House of Lords on July 21, Lauderdale let his "fluent tongue" loose on it, calling it, in his broad Scottish accent, "a most dangerous and mischievous measure." The suppression of local tokens would, he said,

> create confusion and distress in the country, by destroying the means of carrying on the retail trade, it being only through the medium of the small change afforded by these local metallic tokens that the retail trade in the country can at present be carried on.

The price of silver, Lauderdale observed, was again on the rise; if it rose much further "even the present Bank tokens will soon be driven out of circulation." In that case, he wondered aloud, "how is the retail trade at all to be carried on?" (*Hansard,* July 21, 1812, c. 1110; see also *Times* (London), July 22, 1812, 2).

The wily Scot also had a ready reply to the charge that local tokens were "debased." Having collected "a considerable number" of specimens, he found their metallic worth to be about three-fourths their nominal value—"a fair proportion," he opined, that supplied no ground whatsoever for the government's assault. (Lauderdale's own comprehensive statistics, reproduced in the present work's appendix, actually suggest a higher proportion.) The "absolute want of small change" meant on the other hand that "the Bill, if passed, will operate as a proclamation for the manufacture of base coin, which will get into circulation, instead of tokens issued by persons of credit and for which they are responsible" (ibid.).

In fact, word of the bill's progress had already given a boost to "base" (that is, anonymous and lightweight) tokens. Yet the government was unmoved by Lauderdale's warnings. "The noble Lord and his [Whig] friends had so often raised the cry of dangerous measures," Liverpool answered, "that it was like the fable of the Boy and the Wolf" (*Hansard,* July 21, 1812, c. 1110–11). Considering the moral of the fable, Liverpool would have been wise to consider whether there was in fact a wolf lurking about. Instead, he dismissed Lauderdale's concerns, insisting that "the evil resulting from these [local] tokens loudly demands a remedy." In light of events to follow, it is worth noting that the only specific "evil" to which Liverpool referred was the canard that "those who are interested in circulating these tokens buy up the Bank tokens and withdraw them from circulation, in order that they may make a larger profit by the issue of their local tokens" (ibid., c. 1111).

So, despite Lauderdale's efforts, the government had its way. On July 28, the House of Lords passed the Local Tokens Act (52 Geo III, *c* 157) by acclamation, with only slight amendments. On July 29, it commanded the Royal Assent.

Anticipating tokens' eventual withdrawal, their holders rushed to cash them in, each fearing that others would do so if they didn't, exhausting token issuers' reserves. Token issuers, in turn, did what they could to reassure the public and forestall disorderly runs. Monck, for example, placed the following ad in the *Reading Mercury* on five occasions between August 10 and September 12.

ISSUED BY JOHN BERKELEY MONCK, 1811–1812
GOLD AND SILVER LOCAL TOKENS

WHEREAS BY an Act of Parliament passed in the last Sessions, it is declared lawful to circulate Gold and Silver Local Tokens until the 25th day of March 1813, *and no longer,* I think it my duty to call the attention of the Public to this Act, and to declare my readiness to redeem my promise, expressed on my Tokens, *at all times.*

But for the particular convenience of the holders of my Tokens in the Town and Neighbourhood; I hereby give notice, that on the first Saturday, in February next, and every succeeding Saturday, I shall attend at the Bear Inn, Reading between the hours of eleven in the forenoon and two, in order to exchange my tokens for Bank Notes, until they are *all* exchanged.

I have to thank the Public for the confidence reposed in me, and hope, that by the time Local Tokens are withdrawn, Government will be prepared to provide the country with a coinage of Standard money, the undoubted right of the subject, and will not leave the country, as it now is, a prey to a compulsory paper currency, at open discount in the Stock Market with the King's Coin and not controvertible by any legal process into pounds, shillings, pence, or Bank Tokens, or into any specie, or change whatever.

JOHN BERKELEY MONCK,
Coley Park, Reading, Aug. 8. 1812[6]

The impending withdrawal of Monck's tokens did not strike all of Reading's inhabitants as a bad thing: in a September 14 letter to the *Reading*

---

6. Monck's ad is reprinted in Edmunds 1966, 179. In the initial version of the ad, Monck wrote "proceeding" instead of "succeeding."

Mercury, an anonymous writer, signing himself "A Pioneer," wrote, "[I]t must be considered a maxim by all who understand the subject, that, THE MINT STANDARD MUST BE STRICTLY ADHERED TO," for to do otherwise was to tempt false coiners (quoted in Edmunds 1966, 186). This "pioneer" appears not to have noticed that strict adherence to the mint standard would have meant doing entirely without coin or that the person having the greatest incentive to protect Monck's tokens from counterfeiting was none other than John Berkeley Monck himself. In any case, his was a minority opinion: several days later, no fewer than 106 of the good citizens of Reading answered it with a public meeting at which they thanked "J. B. Monck, Esq., for the convenience afforded them by the issue of his silver tokens," while "expressing their surprise that an Act should have been passed prohibiting the circulation of gold and silver tokens . . . without any provision for the future supply of silver, either from the Mint or from the Bank of England" (*Morning Chronicle,* September 19, 1812, quoted in Phillips 1900, 31).

Back in Westminster, though, opinions not unlike that of the "pioneer" just quoted had gained the upper hand, leaving Lauderdale hopelessly outnumbered. Yet Lauderdale expected to have the last laugh. "As to the cry of 'wolf,'" he had told Liverpool on July 21, "I have no doubt, that long previous to the 25th of March, your lordship on this subject also will cry 'wolf!' and will be very anxious to repeal the present Bill" (*Hansard,* July 21, 1812, c. 1111).

The cocksure lord wasn't just talking through the back of his neck. "In the complete absence of the official silver coins," Sir Albert Feaveryear (1932, 192–93) observes, "the tokens served a useful purpose, and the Government had not the remotest idea how to provide a silver coinage which would work satisfactorily as a subsidiary to inconvertible paper." Under the circumstances, the government would have no choice but to call off the scheduled suppression. To do otherwise would risk provoking an all-out payments crisis.

From the Horses' Mouths

But Lauderdale would take nothing for granted. If he could spare Great Britain another crunch, however temporary it might be, he intended to do so. That meant persuading the government to change its mind about local tokens before the Local Tokens Act took effect on March 25. "You know I am sufficiently anxious," he wrote to Baron Grenville on August 12, "for a general reform of our Circulating Medium." He continued:

[Y]et I am certain that this partial reform, if such it can be called, must be productive of such mischief that it is impossible the Act should not be repealed.

There is not with all the Local Tokens at present a sufficiency of small Money for the Convenience of the Country, and the necessary quantity is not likely to be produced by giving to the bank of England an absolute monopoly of furnishing the Country with all Money of value under twenty Shillings. But that this is the Consequence of the act is evident when we reflect that there exists no standard Silver Coin and that if there did it could not circulate. . . .

I am anxious in this state of things to get every information I can on the subject & for that purpose I am about to send a Circular letter to every issuer of Local Tokens throughout the Kingdom inclosing a number of Inquiries the answers to which will put me in possession of the real State of the Country in respect to small money.

(BL ADD. MSS 58943)

So, as Parliament took its summer recess, Lauderdale went to work. Soon token issuers around the country began receiving his letter, with its accompanying questionnaire. The letter opened as follows:

In the last Session of Parliament, I opposed the Bill, entitled *An act to prevent the issuing and circulating of old pieces of gold and silver, or other metal, usually called tokens, except such as are issued by the Banks of England and Ireland respectively.*

Much as I could wish for the credit and welfare of the country, that a general revision should take place of the principles upon which our circulation is now conducted, I was then, and am now, perfectly convinced that the measure of annihilating all local tokens in the month of March next, unless it should be attended with some further arrangements, must prove highly injurious.

I am indeed of the opinion, that there is just reason to believe that, if this Act is not repealed immediately on the meeting of Parliament, the commerce of the country will sustain a most severe shock. For, in my view of the subject, it will deprive the master-manufacturer of the power of paying the wages of his workmen, and leave the poorer consumer without the means of dealing with the retail trader; whilst it would prove a source of infinite inconvenience to the community at large.

The attached questionnaire, reproduced in the appendix to the present work, listed fifteen questions concerning the recipients' tokens and the circumstances that gave rise to them.

Responses started arriving in early September and were still trickling in months later. Though they came from every corner of the kingdom, the testimony they offered was remarkably consistent: that local tokens had been resorted to reluctantly, in response to severe shortages of official small change; that Bank of England tokens met only a small fraction of retailers' small-change needs; and that in manufacturing towns at least, tokens (especially copper tokens) were often the only practical alternative to group pay.

Although the original replies have vanished—perhaps for good, perhaps into a cranny in some dusty archive—Lauderdale published a summary table of token statistics and excerpts from respondents' letters in his *Further Considerations on the State of the Currency* (Maitland 1813). The excerpts, which supply a fascinating and unprecedented bird's-eye view of monetary conditions then prevailing throughout provincial England, were making the rounds among the peers during the closing months of 1812. This work's appendix reproduces them in their entirety, so that readers might take their own measure of the act then slated to go into effect the following March.

One reply that Lauderdale didn't publish was that sent by John Berkeley Monck, who was then taking steps to redeem his tokens. Fortunately, the Great Grecian himself published his full response in the *Reading Mercury,* and Professor Edmunds (1966, 180–85) has reprinted it, along with his expert commentary. Monck concludes:

> I have done one man's part . . . to furnish this District with silver for change. I have, likewise, no doubt of the mistaken policy of prohibiting the circulation of Local Tokens, in the present circumstances of our currency; but I believe that nothing will convince Ministers of the error, but dear-bought experience. For this reason I shall henceforth follow the tide, rather than uselessly oppose it.   (IBID., 185)

Wolf!

While Lauderdale sounded out token issuers, the silver market began bearing out his predictions. As September opened, the price of Spanish silver reached 6s 4d, making the metal value of Bank tokens almost equal to their face value. Another halfpenny increase would mean a repetition of the crisis of March 1811 (Kelley 1976, 95). The crisis came in mid-November, when Spanish silver reached 6s 6d. At that price, not only were Bank tokens again undervalued, but the Bank would suffer a loss on every new token it ordered. Reluctantly, the Bank told its correspondents not to count on it for silver.

In Parliament, the tide of opinion began to turn in Lauderdale's favor. On December 8, the great Henry Thornton sounded the alarm Lauderdale anticipated months before.

> If such a measure is resorted to, what is to supply the deficiency? Small change for the common transactions of life is every where wanted, even with the aid of these local tokens; but when they are withdrawn, the governor of the Bank has admitted that that establishment has it not in its power to issue any silver to make good the loss.
>
> (*Hansard*, 1813, c. 234)

A few days later, on the eve of Parliament's holiday adjournment, Hudson Gurney rose to ask "whether it was the intention of ministers to press the provisions of the Local Tokens Act, and thereby inconvenience the country in the present scarcity of silver and the comparatively limited distribution of Bank Tokens." Put on the defensive, Vansittart drew in his horns, replying that while he "fully approved of the principle" of the Act, the government now planned to postpone "the operation of that principle . . . until about Midsummer, in order that measures might be taken in the interim to ensure a more liberal supply of Bank Tokens" (ibid., c. 346).

The matter came up again on February 3, the day on which Great Britain declared war on the United States. Vansittart began by acknowledging the "many objections . . . made against the suppression of this species of currency." He then proceeded to brush the objections aside, insisting that "even if no chance exists of the place of it being adequately supplied by any other kind, it would be wrong to continue a currency so entirely out of the control of government, so much debased, and confined, from the limited credit of the issuers, to certain districts." Finally, with the tortured logic that had by then become his hallmark, he allowed that it might be a good idea to push back the original deadline until some new Bank tokens could be struck, thus avoiding any risk of "temporary inconvenience" (ibid., c. 362). Vansittart ended by asking leave to introduce a bill that would amend the Local Tokens Act by con-

tinuing local tokens' legal status until six months after the original deadline of March 25.

But just how did the government expect to get hold of the silver that
would be needed for new Bank tokens? That was one of two good questions put to the chancellor of the exchequer on February 12. In reply,
Vansittart pointed to the recent improvement of foreign exchange rates
in Great Britain's favor: the silver, he suggested, would come from
abroad. Lord Hamilton, MP for Lanarkshire and, like his fellow Scotsman Lord Lauderdale, a hard-money Whig, found the proposition ludicrous. "If the right honorable gentleman," he said (referring to Vansittart), "has no other reason to hope for an issue of silver, than the
improvement of the exchange, the hope is a frail one" (ibid., c. 510).
But Vansittart, far from entertaining doubts, withdrew his earlier suggestion to postpone the Local Tokens Act until October 1, 1813, in favor of
having it take effect on July 5. Parliament, he said, might then "make further arrangements, should an adequate supply of Bank Tokens happen
not to be forthcoming." Samuel Whitbread, MP for Bedford, objected to
the revised plan on the grounds that the House was unlikely to be sitting
on the proposed date, but he refrained from moving to amend Vansittart's bill when the chancellor of the exchequer offered to take the matter up again before the summer recess.

The other good question posed to Vansittart concerned the government's strategy for keeping new Bank tokens in circulation once it issued
them. "Is the right honorable gentleman aware," Hamilton asked, "how
many of the £1,700,000 in tokens already issued by the Bank remain in
circulation?" "I understand," he added, "that a considerable quantity has
been melted." He then concluded:

> If such has been the fate of the Bank tokens already issued, what se-
> curity can the right honorable gentleman present that the new issues
> would not meet the same fate if they are equal in intrinsic value? If the
> Bank tokens are likely to be thus withdrawn from circulation, the lo-
> cal tokens will still be necessary. (IBID.)

Vansittart's remarkable reply was that "[c]are will of course be taken that
the value of any token issued by the Bank, should keep pace with the
market value of silver, and for such equality the public has no guarantee
upon the mass of local tokens" (ibid.). It was, of course, true that local token issuers did not "guarantee" a fixed relationship between the metallic
and nominal values of their tokens. No local token issuer could, for ex-

ample, simply cry up the nominal value of outstanding coins to keep them from being melted or otherwise withdrawn from circulation, as the government had felt compelled to do in attempting to keep Bank tokens from disappearing. But local token issuers did something much better: they promised a fixed value for their tokens relative to the nation's standard money, which they guaranteed by pledging to redeem their tokens on demand. If the government had evidence of such pledges being broken, it kept such evidence to itself. If the government thought that subsidiary coins ought to bear a value rigidly tied to the value of the metal they happened to be made of, rather than to that of the nation's standard money, then it knew less than local token issuers did about the requirements for a practical small-change system.

Having skated onto thin ice, Vansittart proceeded to plunge through it. In addition to suggesting that the government could keep new Bank tokens from being melted by routinely adjusting their face values, he denied that substantial quantities of Bank tokens had been melted down in the past. They had, he said, merely gone into hoards, from which they would emerge "when the new issue of Bank tokens takes place, and the competition of Local Tokens is withdrawn" (ibid.). Thus, in making its case for a new issue of Bank tokens, the government tacitly absolved local tokens of the very "evil" that, according to Liverpool, was supposed to warrant their suppression.

If any MP noticed that the government had abandoned its own favorite argument for suppressing local tokens, he did not reveal his thoughts to Hansard. The issue was, in any case, moot, for the question before Parliament in February 1813 was not whether to suppress local tokens but whether to put off suppressing them. Concerning this question, the government and the opposition were now in perfect accord: there could be no question of sticking to the March 25 deadline. Vansittart's new Local Tokens Act (53 Geo. III *c* 19), which amended the original by extending tokens' legal lifespan until July 5, passed in the House of Commons on February 16, was agreed to by the House of Lords on March 4, and received the Royal Assent with only two days to spare, on March 23.

Thus local tokens were granted a reprieve, which was to prove the first of several. The Bank renewed its token issues on September 18, 1812,[7] but on May 26, 1813, with the July 5 deadline approaching,

---

7. All told, between 1811 and 1816, the Royal Mint produced 18,089,064 three-shilling Bank tokens and another 10,088,190 1 *s* 6 *d* tokens, consuming just over 911,671 troy pounds of silver in the process (Kelley 1976, 120).

William Manning, the Bank's governor, "was forced to tell Liverpool and Vansittart that . . . with the state of the Market and the need for silver for foreign expenditure he could not produce a sufficient stock [of Bank tokens] for the whole country" (Kelley 1976, 100). By now, Spanish silver was fetching 6s 8½d per ounce, making each three-shilling Bank token worth 3s 2d as metal. Consequently, Manning observed, "an increase in the circulation of tokens would only result in hoarding or melting down."

When, on June 11, local tokens came up for further discussion, the government had once again to admit that Lauderdale's wolf was real: "Although there has been a considerable improvement in the rate of exchange between this and foreign countries," Vansittart explained, "the state of the currency is yet such as to render it necessary to continue the [Local Tokens] Bill for some time longer" (*Hansard,* 1813, c. 571). Yet another Local Tokens Act (53 Geo. III *c* 114) was thus offered for Parliament's consideration, this time extending the life of local tokens until six weeks after the commencement of the next session, that is, until December 1813. A vindicated Hamilton could not resist allowing himself a bit of sarcasm at "Van's" expense, by expressing his "astonishment" that the chancellor of the exchequer should propose a second continuation in light of his rosy forecast of the previous session (ibid., c. 745).

Forced to eat humble pie, Vansittart helped himself to some anodyne by proposing two further amendments to the former act. One required token issuers to redeem their issues in Bank of England notes; the other outlawed banknotes worth less than twenty shillings. Huskisson thought the amendments otiose, given existing laws. Still, he had no doubt that "the renewal of the Local Token Bill is extremely necessary, and is likely to continue necessary . . . for a very long time."

> So far am I from believing that the period will soon arrive which will enable the government to call in the local tokens altogether, that I firmly believe it will be necessary to increase the nominal value of the coin now issued by the Bank of England. The price of silver is already higher than the value placed upon the local tokens, and where bullion is wanted, there is no doubt that Bank tokens at three shillings are deemed much cheaper than other silver.   (IBID., c. 572–73)

Huskisson might as well have had a crystal ball. Although the latest Local Tokens Act earned Royal Assent on July 10, come November it was obvious that the British economy still could not manage without locally issued coin. So yet another act (54 Geo. II *c* 4) had to be passed, extending the tokens' lifetime another full year.

There were to be no more "continuances," however. Lest the public should entertain any doubts, newspapers were asked to publish notices such as the following, from the December 14, 1814, *Reading Mercury*.

> *Suppression of Local Tokens*—The Act of Parliament passed on the 26th Nov., 1813, enacts, "That from and after six weeks from the commencement of the next (now the present) session of Parliament, no gold or silver token shall pass or circulate for money; and every person who shall, after six weeks from the commencement of the next (now the present) session of Parliament, circulate or pass any such token, shall forfeit any sum not less than 5 nor more than 10, at the discretion of such justice or justices as shall hear or determine such offence;[8] but nothing in this act shall extend to prevent any person from presenting any such token for payment to the original issuer thereof, or to discharge or excuse any such original issuer from his liability to pay the same." The public will, therefore, be on their guard to observe that the provisions of the Act above alluded to expire on Monday next, after which no local tokens can be received.

Not wanting the government's opinion of local tokens to be confused with its own, the *Mercury* added:

> In common, with every person in trade, we have experienced the good effects which resulted from those weighty and respectable tokens issued in this town, and we cannot but lament the stagnation which will be felt by their being immediately called out of circulation.

The stagnation was not long in coming. In Reading itself, the bank of Marsh, Deane & Company hadn't even finished redeeming Monck's tokens, as required by law, when coin shortages struck again (Ditchfield 1887, 33). Elsewhere throughout England, trade was similarly embarrassed. The withdrawal of private silver also served to advance premiums on official issues. By April 1815, shillings commanded a premium of 4¼*d*, and even three-shilling Bank tokens were underrated. "[U]nless

---

8. The original Local Tokens Act had further specified how the penalties should be applied: "One moiety of the forfeiture to the informer and the other moiety to the poor of the parish or place where the offense shall be committed."

something be done for the nation in respect of its currency," a grammatically challenged correspondent to *The Tradesman or Commercial Magazine* (May 15, 370) wrote, "it will soon be an almost impossibility to obtain change of any kind," for "[t]he expiration and non-renewal of the act for permitting the coinage of local tokens have injured the manufacturers of Birmingham and Sheffield, &c. to an irreparability."

Former token issuers, in the meantime, were taking a drubbing. Tokens poured into shopkeepers' sorting boxes, each bearing the name of some local issuer. From there, they made their way to issuers for redemption or, if there were too few for that, to brokers who took and amassed them for a fee (Phillips 1900, 41). So far as records indicate, no legitimate claims were refused, though issuers had to be compelled by the courts to redeem amounts below one pound—a decision that, apart from being inconsistent with issuers' original pledges, took no account of the shortage of official small change that led to tokens being issued in the first place. Many token issuers suffered or expected to suffer losses. Garratt & Co. of Bristol, for example, published a balance sheet showing a net loss of £5,588 on a total issue of 640,000 (or thirty-two thousand pounds' worth) of shilling tokens (W. Davis 1904, 102).

So private silver tokens were no more—at least not genuine ones. "Baser" forms of private-sector money quietly occupied the gap left by the redemption of legitimate commercial tokens, just as Lauderdale predicted they would. Anonymous tokens evaded the ban, as did counterfeit regal coins and Bank tokens. French money also entered the scene, with old French twelve and twenty-four sous standing for sixpences and shillings. According to a French merchant who knew what he was talking about, no less than two hundred thousand pounds' worth of the defunct French coins were imported into Great Britain in the space of twelve months starting in April 1815 (*Hansard,* April 10, 1816, c. 1148). Such were the alternatives to commercial money for which Parliament, in its blind impetuosity, had cleared the way.

The MP for Copper

Interpreted literally, the Local Tokens Act ought to have put an end to copper tokens as well as silver and gold ones. Some, indeed, wanted it to be so interpreted: thus William Huskisson asked the chancellor of the exchequer on June 18, 1813, whether the version of the measure then being contemplated was meant to outlaw copper tokens. It ought to be, Huskisson argued, considering the large quantity of tokens made from that "spurious metal" and their tendency "to enhance the price of first necessities." Shopkeepers charged more when paid in tokens because tokens could be redeemed only in twelve-month bills. Or so Huskisson claimed, prompting Privy Councilor and MP for Southampton George Rose to observe that he was "not aware of the existence of the practices which have been adverted by my right honorable friend" (*Hansard*, 1813, c. 744–45).

In fact, copper tokens, like their silver counterparts, were generally redeemed not in bills but in Bank of England notes (Sharp 1834, iin). Huskisson seems to have been misled by some token manufacturers' practice of accepting payment in bills on London. As for the charge that copper tokens raised prices, though it couldn't be dismissed out of hand (workers were, after all, bound to pay more for "first necessities" when they had something to pay with than when they didn't), Huskisson offered no evidence of tokens trading at a discount, and no such evidence has come down to us from other sources.[9]

Whatever the merits of Huskisson's arguments, Vansittart disappointed him by insisting that the Local Tokens Act was not intended to suppress copper tokens. The chancellor of the exchequer did, however, welcome any "proposition" aimed at dealing with such tokens. Such a proposition was put forward at the third reading of the amended Local Tokens Act on June 29, 1813. Its author, who would be copper tokens' most vocal opponent from that time forward, was ironically enough a close associate of the man who got the copper token craze going to begin with: Pascoe Grenfell made his fortune first as Thomas Williams's "outstanding subordinate" and then as heir to his copper kingdom (Harris 1964, 49: see also Dodd 1971, 163; Watts-Russell 2003). Grenfell had been Williams' continental agent for ships' sheathing, a partner in his Holywell works, and manager of his London copper office. Upon Williams's death, he inherited Williams's Great Marlow seat (one of two for the borough, the other of which was held by Williams's son Owen), thus acquiring the vantage point from which to direct an assault on the coins his predecessor inaugurated.

Paradoxically, Grenfell wanted to see private copper tokens stamped

---

9. Huskisson was no slouch when it came to political economy, having been one of the three authors of the Bullion Report (the others were Francis Horner and Henry Thornton). He is today more likely to be remembered as the victim of the world's first fatal railway accident: he was among dignitaries invited to celebrate the opening of the Liverpool–Manchester line when, having stepped out of his own train's carriage while it took water, he was run over by Stephenson's Rocket.

out for the same reason that caused Williams to introduce them in the first place—namely, to prod the government into minting new copper coins. Grenfell had already pleaded for a new copper coinage on June 13, observing that "[w]hatever scarcity there might be of silver and gold, there surely was no scarcity of copper" that would prevent such a coinage from being undertaken (*Hansard*, 1813, c. 745). He now supplemented that proposal with one for suppressing both copper tokens and (real and fake) Tower halfpence, observing how it took seventy-three halfpenny tokens, compared to only sixteen good regal pennies, to make a pound of copper and that the public were thereby losers by "the difference between 16 and 73" (ibid.). A reasonable comparison would at least have recognized the difference between pennies and halfpennies. Furthermore, the latest Boulton copper, which was practically all that remained in circulation, was coined at forty-eight rather than thirty-two halfpennies per pound, which meant that the "loss" borne by token holders was no greater than the difference between those figures. Finally, halfpenny tokens typically weighed between nine and ten grams, or about 150 grains, each, while pennies weighed twice that amount. They were, in other words, made to the same standard, if not a slightly better standard, than the latest Boulton copper. The standard of seventy-three per pound applied not to them but to counterfeit Tower halfpennies—another thing altogether.

So Grenfell was playing fast and loose with the facts. What for? In part because, being in the copper trade, he wanted the government to coin copper yet could not get it to do so by pleading a shortage of copper coin: Vansittart's official position was that there was still plenty of regal copper coin to go around. But Vansittart was also receptive to the claim—however loosely founded it might be—that token issuers were defrauding the public. This "evil," he said, "has already attracted the attention of the Government, and is now under consideration," although "it has not yet been determined how to proceed." Were the government to decry both tokens and old Tower copper, as Grenfell proposed, it would have little choice but to order a new and massive regal copper coinage.

Loose Lips

Grenfell renewed his attack on copper tokens on December 10, recalling his earlier observations concerning the debased state of the nation's copper coin. Although he now admitted that his earlier figures applied only to counterfeit halfpence, copper tokens being "not so debased," he also introduced a new argument against the latter—one that at least had the virtue of candor. Private copper tokens, he said, are "intolerable in this country, where there are copper mines producing four times as much copper as all the rest of Europe and twice as much as all the rest of the world" (*Hansard,* 1813, c. 276). What more "effectual remedy" was there for the depressed state of the copper market, Grenfell asked rhetorically, than for "the government to meet the expence of calling in the old Tower halfpence, and at the same time to put down the counterfeit halfpence and copper tokens by act of Parliament" (ibid., c. 276–77).

In reply to this latest overture, Vansittart, instead of offering vague promises, let drop what turned out to be a bombshell: "I am happy to confirm," he said, that "considerations of expence will no longer deter us from calling in the old Tower halfpence" and that "the issue of a new coinage will soon make the counterfeit halfpence and tokens disappear" (ibid., c. 277). Vansittart added that he wished to make the government's intentions "as public as possible" so as to "prevent persons from incurring considerable loss by the manufacture of copper tokens" (ibid.).

Vansittart got his wish and then some, for word of his announcement spread rapidly, triggering a general refusal of old Tower copper. That refusal proceeded to do more harm to Great Britain's poor in the space of a few weeks than counterfeit coppers, let alone copper tokens, had ever done. A stunned and mortified chancellor of the exchequer tried to undo the damage by declaring publicly that Tower halfpence were still legal tender and that they were still being taken at full value by the government and the Royal Mint. He followed up with official proclamations to the same effect. But all was in vain: come April 4, 1814, Samuel Whitbread, MP for Bedford, reported that the refusal of old halfpence was still causing "great distress . . . in the manufacturing districts," in part by hindering the collection of poor rates (*Hansard,* 1814, c. 410). The poor, having little apart from old copper on hand, were placed in a double bind, being forced by the general refusal of copper to apply for assistance to the parish, only to have the overseers tell them that the same refusal had deprived the parish itself of funds (ibid., c. 411). According to Rogers Ruding (cited in Withers and Withers 1999, 110), the general refusal of old Tower halfpennies and farthings endured right up to the date of their official retirement in December 1818 (Withers and Withers 1999, 110; Mitchiner 1998, 2111).

Nor was the harm done by Vansittart's ill-considered announcement limited to Tower copper. As the chancellor of the exchequer had predicted, the announcement put an immediate halt to further production of all but a handful of genuine trade tokens, encouraging some issuers to withdraw their tokens altogether (Dykes 1954, 348): According to William Davis (1904, xxxiii–xxxiv), the only copper tokens "indicating their locality by legend or device" issued after 1813 were "the twopenny piece of Rugely, a few farthings, and the Sheffield Workhouse token of 1815."

Vansittart failed to consider the boost his statement would give to anonymous copper money, increasing quantities of which made their way into hapless workers' pay packets and, from there, to shopkeeper's tills. The vast majority of these anonymous tokens—William Davis records over one hundred varieties of them—were either mules or close copies, if not outright counterfeits, of genuine trade tokens and were easily confused with them, to shopkeepers' great dismay.[10] Their growing presence, particularly in the Midlands iron district, did much to make the once enthusiastic response to copper tokens "evaporate altogether . . . , leaving in its place a hostile public opinion" (Dykes 1954, 352). In Stourbridge, for instance, citizens gathered on October 24, 1815, "in order to adopt Measures to stop the Circulation of Copper Tokens," these having "become a great Inconvenience to the Public, being issued without the name of the Maker or Circulator, and much under the nominal Value." The assembled resolved to refuse anonymous tokens offered in payment and to consider persons who did otherwise "as Participants in an Evil which is a Disgrace to this Commercial Country" (Perkins 1905, 179–80).[11]

Having unwittingly undermined the reputation of both private tokens and old Tower copper, Vansittart might have been expected to move quickly on the recoinage he'd promised. Instead, for three full years, during which the copper currency continued to deteriorate, he and his government hardly budged. Waterloo brought peace to Europe in the meantime, but not without bringing depression to large swaths of British industry. The Midlands iron industry, most of whose wartime out-

---

10. A separate cause of the appearance of tokens displaying no promise of redemption was the fear among issuers, already widespread by early 1813, that such tokens might be liable to the stamp duty. In some instances, issuers switched to new tokens displaying no explicit offer of redemption, while nonetheless continuing to redeem them as they had redeemed their original issues (Withers and Withers 1999, 17).

11. The Stourbridge resolution explicitly exempted the legitimate trade tokens of twelve local issuers—including Fereday; the Birmingham workhouse; and the Rose, Crown, and Union copper companies—observing that these might continue to be received, without being reissued, "for a short Time" for the sake of "the Lower Classes" (Perkins 1905, 180).

put was consumed by munitions factories, was especially hard hit, with half its blast furnaces blasting no longer (Birch 1967, 51, 54–55). The depression ruined several legitimate token issuers, including the biggest of all: Samuel Fereday. Fereday celebrated the victory at Waterloo by throwing a huge feast, to which both his workers and the poor were invited. He might as well have held a wake, for the "peace undid him as the war had made him" (Court 1953, 189). The once-great ironmaster's undertakings collapsed one after the other, starting with his Bilston bank, Fereday & Company, which went belly-up in 1817. Fereday went personally bankrupt in 1821, after which he tried, unsuccessfully, to make a new fortune on the Continent.[12]

An impatient Pascoe Grenfell, spurred on by the economy's deteriorating state, put Vansittart on the spot for the third and last time on March 27, 1817, asking whether he intended "to bring forward any measure to suppress the issue of copper tokens." Vansittart, having learned to hold his tongue, remained seated; but Worcestershire MP William Lyttleton rose to say that he would call the house's attention to this subject after the holidays, observing (to cries of "Hear!"), "Of all the persons in Staffordshire who have issued copper tokens, not one of them is now solvent." The claim was untrue (it overlooked Staffordshire's token-issuing workhouses, for starters), but that didn't prevent it from serving its intended purpose, which was to chip away at the remnants of political support for private copper.

It was, however, not Lyttleton but Grenfell who called Parliament's attention to copper tokens again, by presenting, on April 25, 1817, a petition from the citizens of Dudley, a town of some eighteen thousand residents located in the very heart of Black Country, about ten miles northwest of Birmingham. The people of Dudley, having seen more than their fair share of broken token issuers and specious tokens, were anxious to say good riddance to private money. Their petition, as recorded in the *Journal of the House of Commons*,[13] declares in part:

That a vast quantity of Provincial Copper Tokens, not intrinsically worth more than half their nominal value, is in circulation through-

<hr>

12. For further details, see Withers and Withers 1999, 40–41. According to Birch (1967, 151), although it "was his issue of notes and coins which brought him down," Fereday "had been long embarrassed by being forced to buy pig-iron under long-term contracts with the Shropshire works at a higher price than he could command when he sold."

13. M. Perkins (1905, 177) reported, "The actual Petition cannot now be quoted, as owing to the fire which took place some years ago in the House of Commons nearly all the M.S. was burned."

out the District in which the Petitioners reside; these Tokens were originally issued by persons who employ many workmen, or by sordid and unprincipled individuals who have purchased and circulated them at an enormous profit; The House will judge of the extent to which these practices have been carried, and of the prodigious loss sustained by the Public, when the Petitioners state, that in the Town of DUDLEY, during the last eighteen months, more than Six Tons of this spurious Money have been bought by two Braziers, not to be re-issued, but as old Metal; the evil has indeed been lessened by the notorious insolvency of some who were foremost in issuing this base species of Money, but it is still foisted upon the Public, to a most melancholy and alarming degree; the Petitioners are fully aware that it is optional with Tradesmen and others whether to receive such spurious Money in payment or not, the case, however, is different with the labouring classes of the community, hundreds of whom having no alternative but to take it as the Wages of their industry, or to languish with their families in hunger and hopeless misery; it cannot therefore excite surprise, that these Tokens, through such and various similar channels, force their way into circulation, to the great annoyance and detriment of the Public, for the consequence is, that the poor, being chiefly thus paid, are unable to lay out their little earnings to the best advantage; and that shopkeepers and other tradesmen are encumbered with a load of base copper, by which they are subjected not only to great risk and inconvenience, but also to very serious loss.

The petition concluded with the plea that the government issue new regal copper coins "amply sufficient for every purpose of exchange; so that where copper is required, there is now no longer even the pretence of its being a public convenience to sanction the system of fraud and oppression." Similar petitions from the nearby towns of Stourbridge and Wednesbury were read immediately following the one from Dudley.

Grenfell made much of the claim that copper tokens were valued at almost twice their worth as metal, neglecting to observe that the claim was true only of the anonymous tokens issued after 1814, and not of those issued before, which had about the same "intrinsic value" as the last batches of Boulton copper. Grenfell declared as well that while better-off persons could afford to "lie out of their money" until they'd collected enough tokens to return them for redemption, "the poor could not engage in this species of traffic" (*Hansard*, 1817, c. 1314). He neglected to mention that the better-off persons to whom he referred included shopkeepers and publicans who accumulated tokens mainly by receiving them at par from other—including poorer—persons. He also failed to consider that persons holding less than a pound's worth of tokens might sell them to retailers and others acting as brokers, for their redemption value minus a commission.[14] Finally, he seemed to forget how, standing in the same chamber three years before, he had observed that "it was not generally known, but ought to be perfectly understood throughout the country, that the full nominal value was given, at the Mint, in Bank notes, for Tower halfpence" (ibid., April 4, 1817, c. 411). In other words, the Royal Mint's terms for redeeming its copper only differed from those of legitimate token issuers in being less well advertised.[15]

But a parliamentary debate is not a court proceeding, with penalties for false testimony or opportunities for cross-examining witnesses. So when Staffordshire MP Edward Littleton moved the abolition of all copper tokens, whether anonymous or not, his motion was seconded and approved without further debate, and he and Henry Wrottlesley were given leave to prepare a bill. The resulting measure "To prevent the issuing and circulating of Pieces of Copper or other Metal, usually called Tokens" (57 Geo. III c 46) was introduced on May 9 and passed by the House of Commons on June 7 and by the House of Lords, after amendment, on June 20. The bill commanded Royal Assent a week later. On New Year's Day, 1818, the passing of copper tokens became illegal "on pain of forfeiting for every piece not less than two shillings nor more than ten, at the discretion of the justice or justices of the peace." Anyone caught making copper tokens could be fined up to five pounds per token. Great Britain's commercial coinage experience had come to an end.

Or nearly so. In some regions, including Swansea, the law was ignored, and suppressed copper tokens circulated illegally for years—even decades—after the prescribed deadline (Dykes 1954, 349). According to Samuel Timmins (1866, 562), Fereday's tokens were "still common" around Birmingham in 1866. The act suppressing copper tokens also allowed the penny tokens of the Birmingham workhouse and of its Sheffield counterpart to remain legal until March 25, 1820, and March 25, 1823, respectively. A more precipitous withdrawal of Sheffield's to-

---

14. The commission would cease to be modest, of course, when a token issuer's solvency was in doubt.

15. An 1809 act of Parliament required local token issuers to redeem their tokens in Bank of England notes.

kens, the act's preamble explains, "would be attended with great Loss to the said Township of Sheffield, and to the Holders thereof, who are for the most part Labourers and Mechanics, as well as with great inconvenience to the Inhabitants." The preamble doesn't give the government's reasons for allowing Birmingham tokens a much shorter grace period or for denying any extension to other workhouse tokens. Nor does it explain how the inhabitants of places apart from Sheffield and Birmingham were supposed to avoid being "inconvenienced" by the outlawing of local copper, Tower copper having already been discredited. In truth, this final act of suppression was bound to harm "Labourers and Mechanics" and others for whom local copper tokens had become the principal means of payment, while exposing surviving token issuers to mass redemptions ending, in some instances at least, in bankruptcy.

And so, as Peter Mathias (1962, 29) has written, "[a] movement which had begun by being a genuine private response to a failure in public responsibility ended in a sordid liquidation," the principal victims of which "were usually humble people who could ill afford such depreciation of their savings, where they had any."

The Great (Token) Recoinage

As Lord Lauderdale understood perfectly well, in suppressing local tokens before reforming its own coinage, the British government had put cart before horse. For the arrival of the government's silver horse, the public would be kept waiting until February 1817. For that of its copper harness-mate, it would have to wait several more years. In the meantime, employers and workers had to make do with those Boulton coppers and Bank tokens that managed to come their way, with the last of the legal copper tokens, with illegal tokens and counterfeit official coins, with unmarked Spanish dollars, and with old French sous.

That a new and redesigned regal silver coinage was long overdue was as plain as a pikestaff to everyone save perhaps the one person whose job it was to understand such things. When, in the House of Commons on March 1, 1815, Grenfell pointed to the distress the silver shortage was causing, while claiming that a reformed silver coinage would cost the public no more than the Boulton copper had cost, Vansittart answered that although "[t]he evil referred to was one which it would be most desirable to remedy," any such "remedy" was best put off until the gold currency was "restored." Wait another six years, he might have said, had he known how much longer the Bank restriction would last. In the mean-

time, he suggested, the government might ban the circulation of foreign
coins—as if such a ban could somehow make up for the shortage of
official money (*Hansard*, 1815, c. 1118–19).

Grenfell, for one, didn't think so. On the contrary: he gave notice
that if the chancellor of the exchequer failed to bring forward a measure
for a new silver coinage, he would do it himself. But the right moment
was wanting. It came, following a further delay of more than a year, on
April 10, 1816. On that day, Grenfell reminded the House of the "dis-
graceful" state to which the silver currency had fallen: "it is well known,"
he said, "that in change for a pound note persons usually receive one
half in French coin, and the other half perhaps in counterfeit coin made
at home" (ibid., 1816, c. 1148). He then observed that silver had just returned at last to its old mint price. "There is now no reason whatever,"
Grenfell announced to the House that day, "that the silver currency
should continue in this debased state" (ibid.). Joining him in this opinion was Alexander Baring, son of the late Sir Francis Baring (the founder
of Baring Brothers) and MP for Taunton, who called on Vansittart for
"some assurance of relief . . . from the nuisance and disgrace under
which it labored . . . from the state of the silver coinage" (ibid., c. 1149).
To Grenfell's call for a new coinage, Baring added the specific proposal
that the standard of silver currency be altered "so that it might not be
carried out of the country on every slight variation of the price of that
metal." This idea, which pointed to a gold standard supplemented by an
avowedly token silver coinage, had been among the recommendations
offered just over a decade before by the senior Lord Liverpool in his
Treatise on the Coin of the Realm (Jenkinson 1805). By 1816, the proposal,
though still controversial, could no longer be held untried, having been
put into practice officially with Bank tokens and unofficially with local
ones. It had been tried; what's more it had worked.

Baring, who would serve as master of the mint in Peel's government,
couldn't resist taking advantage of the occasion to sound off against the
mint establishment.

> I hope that when the coinage takes place, the mint officers will pay
> some attention to their work, and take some pains to understand what
> coinage is. We have a building that cost 2 or 300,000*l.*, and a large es-
> tablishment, yet such was the disgraceful state of it, that when they
> had a few tokens to make, the officers knew nothing of the matter,
> and after many attempts all the dies were broken up. In coining gold
> [louis d'ors] for France, they had not improved their reputation, and

had concluded by blowing up the mint itself. I hope the master of the
mint will think it worth his while to know a little of his business.

(*Hansard,* APRIL 1816, C. 1149–50)

Though Grenfell was quick to distance himself from the "slur" his honorable friend "thought proper to cast upon [the moneyers'] skill" (ibid.,
c. 239),[16] he also endorsed the idea of a token silver coinage to play second fiddle to gold, which he recognized as having come from Liverpool's *Treatise.* So bimetallism, which commerce had declared dead a
century ago but which had lingered on like a rotting corpse, was to be
buried at last—provided Grenfell got his way. As was his wont, Grenfell
cinched his case with a petition, this time from the traders of Shoreditch,
Spital-fields, and surrounding neighborhoods. The petitioners complained that they

have for a considerable time past experienced, and do now suffer,
great inconvenience and embarrassment, from the imperfect state of
the silver currency, and particularly from the part of it consisting of
what are denominated shillings and sixpences, which constitute no
inconsiderable proportion of the coin which the petitioners are
obliged to receive in payment for the articles of their daily trade; that,
during many years past, very few of the shillings and sixpences in currency have appeared to be of the legal coin of the realm, but, on the
contrary, have borne evident marks of being counterfeits, but which,
nevertheless, from the want of any thing better, have passed current;
that of late there has been an immense influx of French silver coin
. . . passed for shillings and sixpences; . . . and that, unless an effectual
remedy to this increasing evil is speedily applied, the petitioners are
convinced that the consequences will be most injurious to mechanics
and to tradesmen residing in manufacturing districts, where change
for payment of wages causes a greater influx of small currency than in
other parts of the country; that the petitioners are informed that a
considerable fall has lately taken place in the price of silver; and for
this reason, and under the other circumstances above stated, they
humbly pray the House to take the subject into consideration, with a
view of securing to the petitioners, and to the public in general, the

---

16. Wellesley Pole, master of the mint since July 1812, could only reply "that the moneyers were not at first as expert in working the machinery as the person by whom it was invented, . . . a circumstance which was not at all surprising" (*Hansard,* 1816, c. 240).

advantages of a good currency in silver, consisting of sixpences, shillings, half-crowns, and crown pieces, or any other coin considered proper by the House.   (IBID., c. 242–43)

On May 21, the Committee on Coin threw its weight in, reporting to the Prince Regent that as the Royal Mint had been successfully rebuilt and reformed, its first priority ought to be the restoration of the silver coinage; the committee again endorsed Liverpool's ideas (Craig 1953, 284). Specifically, the committee proposed that sixty-six shillings, rather than the customary sixty-two, be cut from each troy pound of silver, the extra four shillings to be kept as seigniorage. A bill embodying this and related recommendations was duly drafted and introduced. While Grenfell saw it through the House of Commons, the prime minister defended it before the House of Lords, delivering to them a moving speech on May 30, paying tribute to the measure's true author, his late father (who died in 1808), and doing his best to explain its provisions. The proposed silver coins, Liverpool explained, were to be understood as mere "counters for change . . . subordinate to gold" (*Hansard*, May 1816, c. 913). Silver was, in other words, to stand "on the same principle as copper; for not being in its nature [*sic*] the standard or measure of value, [the government] had only to take care that there was enough of it for the purposes of change, and that it should not be liable to be melted down" (ibid., c. 914).

However, some members of both houses persisted in thinking of silver not only as a perfectly natural standard of value but as Great Britain's only true standard (Craig 1953, 284). Of these, the most fervent was none other than Lord Lauderdale, who, despite his defense of local tokens, saw a revival of the ancient silver standard, supplemented (one presumes) by free-floating guineas, as the ultimate solution to Great Britain's currency troubles. On June 17, Lauderdale attacked the proposed coinage measure as being "founded on erroneous principles," while predicting that it "would burthen the country with an enormous expense without any benefits resulting" (*Hansard*, 1816, c. 1122). It was, Lauderdale implied, one thing for private issuers to risk their own wealth by issuing tokens that might end up in melting pots and quite another for government to risk public funds in like manner. Despite Lauderdale's formal protest, the Silver Coinage Bill passed from the House of Lords to His Royal Majesty, becoming an act on June 22.

The plan was to issue £2.5 million in new half crowns, shillings, and sixpences, of which £500,000 were intended for Ireland. Even Baring could not fault the Royal Mint for the dispatch with which it produced the new coins: work on the specimens began while the coinage bill was still pending, and by mid-August, the mint's rolling rooms were working around the clock. By year's end, £1,800,000 in new coins, consisting mainly of shillings and sixpences but also of almost £500,000 in half crowns, had been struck;[17] and by the third week of January, coaches, caravans, and ordnance wagons laden with new coins and accompanied by full military escorts were on their way to 623 exchange stations throughout Great Britain, where they were to be exchanged for old regal silver. The terms of exchange were generous, the government having decided to receive at face value all coins of the old standard, not excluding likely counterfeits, "however defaced or reduced by weight and size." Indeed, of old coins having a total face value of £2,606,405 turned in between February 13, when the exchange stations opened for business, and the end of May, when the recoinage was complete, less than £7,000 worth were refused, even though the accepted coins were on average 22.5 percent short in weight (Craig 1953, 287: see also Perkins 1905, 75; Phillips 1900, 36–42).

Although the exchange offices were closed on February 27, and outstanding (genuine or fake) regal silver was demonetized on March 1st, the government and the Bank of England continued to receive old regal silver at par for another three months. Bank dollars and tokens were demonetized commencing March 26, 1818, "on penalty of paying for each such dollar etc., uttered, offered or tendered in payment, any sum not exceeding five pounds nor less than forty shillings" (Phillips 1900, 41).[18] But the Bank of England would continue to receive its dollars at par until May 10, 1817, while receiving its smaller tokens at par until exactly two years after their official demonetization.

And so the Royal Mint reclaimed its monopoly of Great Britain's silver money, having finally overcome its "obsession with striking silver coins containing their intrinsic value in metal" (Wager 1977, 50). The mint and the government were compelled, in other words, to supply new regal silver that was just as "light" as, if not lighter than, many of the local tokens so recently suppressed. Indeed, as James Mays (1991, 20) has noted, local tokens had played a "guinea-pig role," demonstrating the

---

17. These original half crowns were ultimately scrapped (their designs having been deemed unsatisfactory), and new ones were struck in their stead.

18. Although only £4,457,649 4s 6d in all had been issued between 1804 and 1815, the value redeemed exceeded this amount by £105,859 3s 6d. Yet many Bank dollars remained outstanding. These numbers give some indication of the prevalence of forgeries.

public's willingness to accept a token silver coinage, only to be sacrificed once the demonstration proved successful.

As for new copper coin, the Committee on Coin's report said nothing about it, and Vansittart, true to form, saw no urgent need for it, what with all the Boulton copper still (supposedly) at hand. Consequently, it was not until 1821 that the Royal Mint began striking regal copper coins—an order for two and three-quarter million farthings—for the first time since 1775. Pennies and halfpennies were ordered the following year (Craig 1953, 290; Dyer and Gaspar 1992, 488). Although the usually unerring Sir John Craig (1953, 290) imagines that these larger copper denominations were struck not at Little Tower Hill but at Soho (the Royal Mint having been too busy making farthings and Irish copper), the truth is that the Royal Mint did strike them, in large quantities, although it didn't start doing so until 1825 (Dyer and Gaspar 1992, 488). By then, of course, most of Matthew Robinson Boulton's Soho Mint had been dismantled and shipped to Bombay.

Great Britain's reformed coinage system worked tolerably well. For the next half century, contrary to Lord Lauderdale's direct prediction, the price of silver bullion never rose much above sixty shillings, so no one was ever tempted to melt the new silver coins (Craig 1953, 286).[19] When more silver coins were needed, the Bank of England ordered them, and the Treasury saw to it that they were made. New copper also was put out on a regular, if modest, basis following the large runs of 1825–27. Some commercial coins remained in use decades after having been declared illegal, but payrolls could be met and bills could be changed without them.[20] Great Britain's big problem of small change was at long last officially solved.

The question is, how? What allowed the reformed coinage to succeed where the old regal coinage had failed? To what extent did its success

---

19. Although the market price of silver bullion never rose enough during this time to give effect to Gresham's law, it did occasionally rise enough to make it unprofitable for the Royal Mint to go on coining silver (Craig 1953, 286). This happened, for example, in early 1819, causing silver coin to command a premium once again. In Manchester, for instance, employers had to pay as much as £1 6d for a sovereign's worth of small change (*Quarterly Review*, January 1926, 60, cited in Chaloner 1946, 111).

20. Bell (1976) documents the widespread use of "unofficial farthings" between 1820 and 1870, claiming that it contradicts the "oft-repeated statement that the Royal Mint provided adequate supplies of copper currency after 1820." See also Wager 2002. Other commercial coins also remained in use well into the Victorian era. According to a report in the *Birmingham Weekly Mercury* on August 4, 1888, a large proportion of outdoor relief payments there continued to consist of Workhouse tokens "even down to within forty or fifty years ago" (ibid., 49).

rest on lessons learned and techniques borrowed from commercial coin makers, whose unofficial solution to the small-change problem antici- pated the official one by several decades? What gave commercial coins and later regal ones an edge over their earlier counterparts?

The standard answer is that the new regal coins, like some of their commercial predecessors, were better because their makers employed steam-driven coining presses. This seems reasonable enough: the timing is just right, and we have Boulton's own testimony to the effect that steam-driven equipment was uniquely capable of making counterfeit-re- sistant coins, both because it was more efficient and more precise than manually powered equipment and because no back-alley coiner could af- ford it. Yet it is off the mark. In truth, as we shall see, the fundamental so- lution to Great Britain's small change problem had very little to do with steam.

CHAPTER VIII

Steam, Hot Air, and Small Change

At the MINT th' invention of the MILL,

Seem'd as if COIN was form'd by magic skill.[1]

Hello Steam Press; Goodbye Big Problem?

How could upstart commercial coiners supply better small change than the Royal Mint could after centuries of practice? What exactly did the private sector contribute toward the eventual improvement of Great Britain's official coins?

The standard view, as I've said, is that the private sector's main, if not its sole, contribution consisted of its pioneering use of steam-powered coining presses. Because such presses were capable of producing counterfeit-proof coins, the argument goes, the British government had only to employ them itself in order to officially renounce bimetallism and establish the world's first modern coinage system.

Although numismatists have taken this view for some time,[2] it has only recently come to play a major part in economists' understanding of the history of money. According to Angela Redish (1990; 2000, chap. 5) and Thomas Sargent and François Velde (2002, 13–14, 61–63, 261, 331–32), steam-powered coining presses made reliance on a fiduciary or token-based small-change system possible for the first time. "The gov-

---

Parts of this chapter originally appeared in Selgin (2003b) and are reproduced here by kind permission of the Economic History Society.

1. James Bisset, "Ramble of the Gods through Birmingham," in Bisset 1800, 30.
2. See, for example, Chaloner 1946; Peck 1947; Doty 1987.

ernment," Sargent and Velde observe, "was slow to use this technology, but private firms were not" and "[t]hey soon issued substantial numbers of high-quality convertible token coins" (ibid., 292). To modernize its own coinage "[t]he government had only to nationalize and administer this [private-market] system, which it began to do in 1816" (ibid., 271). Other nations followed Great Britain's lead.[3]

Steam Presses and the Commercial Coinage

The claim that steam power reformed Britain's coinage seems plausible. The start of the commercial coinage regime did roughly coincide with Boulton's invention of the steam-driven coining press, and Great Britain did in fact abandon bimetallism in favor of avowedly fiduciary small change soon after the Royal Mint was refurbished using steam-powered equipment. It's also true that, once these reforms were complete, small-change shortages—or severe shortages, at any rate—became a thing of the past.

Yet for all its superficial plausibility, the argument is inconsistent with the historical record. The point can be proven, first, by considering the timing of Boulton's initial application of steam power to coinage; second, by consulting the Matthew Boulton and Boulton & Watt papers; third, by accounting for each of Birmingham's pre-1798 steam engines; and, finally, by taking a more general look at sources of motive power in the Birmingham toy trades and especially in the making of steel buttons.

Everyone agrees that Boulton was the first person to strike coins using steam. If one rules out the (as-yet-unsuggested) possibility of commercial coins having been struck using water or animal power, any commercial coins made before Boulton's pioneering effort must have been struck manually. The dating of Boulton's first steam-struck coins is therefore of crucial importance. Although quite a few works give that date as 1786, their authors have confused Boulton's first employment of steam-powered presses with his first venture into coinage. As we've seen, in 1786,

---

3. Although Redish never says explicitly that steam technology was widely employed in making commercial tokens, she does say (2000, 153) that issuers of commercial coins suffered "minimally" from counterfeiting. This statement, taken together with her claim (ibid., 10) that the invention of the steam coining press alone made possible the production of coins "that were not counterfeitable or at least were very costly to counterfeit," seems to imply that most commercial tokens were steam struck. In correspondence, however, Redish claims to have understood that counterfeit-proof coins could be struck manually, though at a relatively high cost. This stance begs the question: If private firms, which received no state subsidies, could afford to strike counterfeit-proof tokens using hand-presses, why couldn't the subsidized Royal Mint have done the same?

Boulton struck coins for John Company's Bencoolen settlement, but he did so not at Soho but in a London warehouse equipped with several manual screw presses. Boulton's first steam-struck coins were the Cronebane halfpennies he made for the Associated Irish Mines Company in the summer of 1789, and Boulton didn't come up with a practicable means for steam striking coins in restraining collars until the autumn of 1790.[4] Thus Dickinson (1936, 137) is quite right in saying that when Boulton told the Privy Council Committee on Coin in December 1787 that he was prepared to coin counterfeit-proof halfpennies at no more than half of the Royal Mint's costs, he still didn't have a working steam press.

So all commercial coins struck before mid-1789 and all those struck in collar before the fall of 1790 were struck using handpresses. These make up more than half of all eighteenth-century commercial coins, for they include all of the Parys Mine Company's Druid tokens produced at its own mints in Holywell and on Great Charles Street and the several tons' worth of 1787–88 Willies struck at the same facilities. Of significance equal to their numbers is the fact that these early tokens were, by all accounts, among the highest-quality tokens of all.

The correct dating of Boulton's first steam-struck coins alone refutes the claim that steam power was essential to the success of Britain's commercial coinage and, by implication, to the success of an official coinage reform. The refutation becomes all the more thorough, of course, if it can be shown that other commercial mints refrained from employing steam-powered presses even after Soho pioneered their use. That this was indeed the case is suggested, first of all, by the Matthew Boulton and Boulton & Watt papers, which, according to both my own research and that of Soho Mint historian Richard Doty (2000, 22), never once directly refer to the use of steam presses at rival mints.[5] Although the lack of any

---

4. Although, at one point, Sargent and Velde (2002, 45) state that the steam coining press "became available after 1787," they suggest elsewhere (ibid., 61) that it was first employed in 1786. Redish (2000, 154) gives the 1786 date, referring specifically to the coins Boulton made for the East India Company.

5. Doty (2000, 22–23) reports two items that might be construed as referring to other mints' employment of steam presses. The first is a 1788 reference by Boulton to the five-foot-diameter "Flys" on the presses John Gregory Hancock had installed at the Parys Mine Company's Great Charles Street mint, which according to Hancock could be worked "so as to strike ½ pence with ¼ of 1 turn." The other occurs in a June 1789 letter from Watt informing Boulton that Hancock "braggs that he can coin in your way, at half the price you can," and advising him to "get Mr. P. [William Pitt] to make an act making it felony to use These new presses & methods." Although Doty claims that "the concept of a flywheel tends to go along with the idea of automatic machinery," a look at any contemporary dictionary of mechanics makes clear that the "Flys" referred to in the first item are merely the hand-

direct reference to rivals' steam presses doesn't prove beyond all doubt that such presses were used only at Soho, no firm could have purchased Boulton & Watt's own presses without the fact being recorded somewhere in the company's very complete accounts, and it seems just as unlikely that any firm could have replicated Boulton's innovation without Boulton or Watt referring to the fact even once in their voluminous correspondence.

Next let's look at what Birmingham's steam engines were up to during the first commercial coinage episode.[6] In 1840, the Royal Statistical Society published a survey of all steam engines ever erected in Birmingham up to that date. Using information from it and from a number of other sources, one can locate and identify the owners and principal uses of all of Birmingham's pre-1798 rotary steam engines. Table 4 lists the engines—there were only eight of them all told—along with their locations and some other information.

TABLE 4. Rotary-Motion Steam Engines in Birmingham through 1797

Erection date	Horse-power	Firm	Principal use	Location
1780	14	Charles Twigg & Co.	Metal rolling	Water St.
1783	25	Pickard's Corn Mill	Flour mill	Snow Hill
1787	18	Warren's (Old) Cotton Mill	Cotton spinning	Fazeley St.
1788	18	Phipson & Sons	Metal rolling	Fazeley St.
1791	12*	Eagle Foundry†	Boring cast iron	Broad St.
1792	16	New Steam Mill Co.	Metal rolling	Fazeley St.
1796	24	Deritend Mill	Drawing wire	Deritend
1797	16*	Old Union Mill†	Flour mill	Holt St.

Sources: Royal Statistical Society 1840, 440; Dent [1880] 1973, 340; Timmins 1866, 213; Chapman 1801; Aitken 1866, 242; and Pelham 1963, 85–88.
*Later enhanced.
†Original Boulton & Watt installations.

---

turned circular wheels found on many conventional manual screw presses. That the dies on Hancock's press could be closed with only a quarter rotation of the fly meant that it had what are known as "fast threads." Doty believes that Hancock's presses also had automatic devices for feeding and ejecting blanks and resembled Boulton's equipment in this respect only. Watt's desire to have Hancock's presses outlawed suggests, however, his doubts concerning whether Soho's steam-driven coining equipment was in fact technically and economically superior to available alternatives.

6. As table 2 (in chap. 4) indicates, one small-scale eighteenth-century token maker was located in Sheffield, and at least two were located in London. Although I haven't attempted any comprehensive review of London's pre-1798 steam engines, Boulton & Watt records indicate that none of that firm's pre-1798 London "rotatives" was employed in any sort of metalwork.

Two main conclusions can be drawn from the information summarized in the table. First, there is no positive evidence suggesting that steam from any of these engines was ever used to power presses or stamping equipment of any kind, their known uses having been metal rolling or boring, flour grinding, or grinding and sharpening tools. Second, none of the engines (which were all located along the town's circular canal network, so as to minimize costs of coal delivery) was located within a shaft's length of any commercial mint. Indeed, as figure 3 reveals, only two were located in Birmingham's toy district; and it so happens that these engines have well-documented histories that give no indication of their ever having taken part in the striking of tokens or other numismatic products.

Pickard's Steam Engines

The steam engine that once stood at 65 Water Street was the world's first rotary-motion steam engine. It was the brainchild of James Pickard and an inventor named Matthew Wasborough (or Wasbrough) of Bristol. Wasborough had had the idea of replacing a standard Newcomen reciprocating engine's connecting rod with a rack, which could be made to mesh with a large geared wheel fitted to a driveshaft. Having patented this device, along with a flywheel, in 1779, Wasborough joined forces with Pickard to erect a prototype engine. Pickard, in turn, convinced a button maker named Charles Twigg to grease the venture's wheels. Boulton and Watt, after hearing a Soho employee's report on the engine, dismissed it as a "noisy, disorderly bad machine" and went calmly to work developing their own rotative-motion engine. Then Pickard drew an ace from his sleeve: in August 1780, he managed to patent a rotary-drive mechanism consisting of a quiet, orderly crank—a rather obvious solution Watt himself had been toying with. The patent infuriated Watt, who is supposed to have complained (with an inconsistency so evidently driven by despair that it is almost touching) that (1) no patent should have been granted for something any fool could have thought of and (2) that Pickard had stolen the idea from a Soho employee who blabbed unwittingly to one of Pickard's spies between quarts of stingo at a Handsworth alehouse.[7]

Although the Pickard-Twigg-Wasborough engine was built to power

---

7. As the late Sir Eric Roll (1930, 109) observed, "the fact that Watt, usually over anxious to secure patents for the slightest improvement, had not done this [with respect to his rotary-motion drive mechanism], speaks certainly against him."

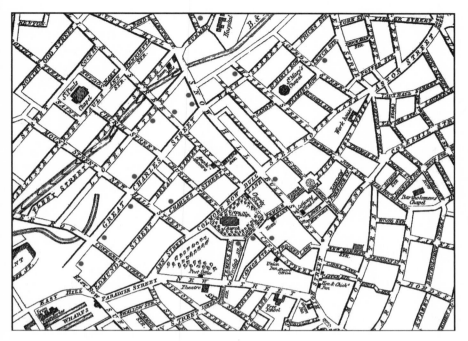

Fig. 3. The Birmingham toy district during the eighteenth-century token episode. The dots show approximate mint locations. Pickard's (later Parker's) Corn Mill and the Twigg & Company (later Muntz's) Rolling Mill appear as two small quadrangles toward the upper left of the map, just above the Birmingham and Fazeley Canal at the bottom of Snow Hill. (Courtesy of Birmingham Reference Library.)

four pairs of rolls, the fourteen horsepower it generated were applied to other purposes as well, as is made clear in a 1783 advertisement published in *Bailey's Directory*.

Boulton and Watt hagiographer Samuel Smiles (1866) has Pickard himself slip into the Wagon and Horses Inn during the summer of 1780 to suck the brains of loose-lipped Soho mechanic Dan Cartright. Having thus learned about Watt's rotative-engine plans, Pickard is supposed to have posted straight to London to secure his crank patent. This is "patent nonsense," to make a bad pun. But even if Cartright did leak the crank idea to one of Pickard's workers, as seems actually to have been the case, the fact remains that Pickard and Wasborough deserve to be credited as the original inventors of the rotary steam engine (Prosser 1881, 32–33; for further details, see Hulse 2001). The damage to Pickard and Wasborough's reputation has proven difficult to repair, with numerous writers since Smiles neglecting them entirely and crediting Boulton and Watt with what was in truth their invention. Some imagine that Watt's alternative "sun and planet" apparatus, which he came up with to circumvent Pickard's crank patent, was somehow better than a plain old crank (it was not, and it wasn't Watt's own invention either, for that matter), while others (see, e.g., Skipp 1997) actually go so far as to credit Soho with having built the Pickard-Wasborough-Twigg engine.

Charles Twigg and Co., Rollers of metal, Grinders and Borers of Gun Barrels, at the Steam Mill, Snow Hill. N.B.—This mill is erected for the above purposes, and also for the polishing of steel goods, finishing buckles, buckle chapes, and a variety of other articles usually done per foot lathes. The whole is worked by a steam engine, and saves manufacturers the trouble of sending several miles into the country, to water mills.   (QUOTED IN AITKEN 1866, 242–43)

Twigg & Company also "let" power to other users, by directing it through shafts to nearby workrooms that could be rented by the day or week. But there is no indication that he ever let power to any of Birmingham's token makers.

Twigg's fate shows how, in those crueller times, even relatively progressive businessmen could be dealt a bad hand. In 1793, he found himself heavily in debt, and over the course of the next five years, as he explained to Matthew Boulton, he'd had "to relinquish every Species of Property to satisfy those Gentlemen to whom I was indebted." At last, to avoid ending up in debtors' prison and to provide for his wife and seven children, he was compelled to announce his bankruptcy in *Aris's Gazette*, which meant selling off his last important asset: the rolling mill. On this occasion he penned a despondent note to Boulton, his old client and friend, lamenting his fate, while reminding him to credit his account for rolling he'd done for Soho just before going south (MBP 257/147). And that sad note is the last one hears of the now-forgotten sponsor of the world's first rotary-motion steam engine.

The mill that once stood at the corner of Snow Hill and Water Street was originally known as Pickard's Corn Mill. Pickard left the metal-rolling business to build it and an adjoining bakery in 1783 (Pelham 1963, 88). It was a decision Pickard would eventually come to regret, for during Pitt's "War of Humanity," the mill and bakery were thrice victimized by mob attacks triggered by grain shortages. The first of these took place in 1795, when rioters (most of them women, by the way) stormed the place, inflicting heavy damage and destroying Pickard's account books, after hearing the rumor that Pickard had buried a large stash of grain. At last the king's own dragoons arrived, read the riot act, and proceeded to arrest several mob leaders, who were being taken to the Peck Lane dungeon when the mob renewed their attack, forcing the soldiers to shoot and kill one of the rioters. In September 1800, virtually the same thing happened again, only mill employees themselves fired on the looters this time, killing four. Finally, in June 1810, when bread was once

again in short supply, yet another mob assembled at the mill. On that occasion, however, the Handsworth Volunteer Cavalry showed up on time
to disperse the crowd before it turned violent, without firing a single
shot.

Steam, Sweat, and Buttons

Although there's no reason to think that any of Birmingham's pre-1798
steam engines was used to power screw presses, that doesn't mean that
those engines played no part at all in commercial coin making. Both the
Twigg engine and that belonging to Phipson & Sons were employed in
making sheet copper, some of which may have been purchased by one or
more commercial mints. Steam power may thus have played a role in
commercial coining outside Soho. But any such role was a far cry from
the crucial one recent works have assigned it.[8]

By 1812, there were dozens of steam engines in Birmingham. That
makes locating each of them and determining its uses a Herculean task.
But other evidence suggests that whatever else these engines may have
been up to, they almost certainly played no role in striking nineteenth-
century tokens.

One small but nevertheless significant bit of evidence consists of a
pair of dies employed by Younge & Deakin in striking Scarborough's
1811–12 shilling tokens. The dies, which were preserved for a time by
Scarborough's Rotunda Museum (but have since gone missing), were
perfectly round, with a slight conelike tapering up to their faces. According to Richard Doty, such dies belong to a "straight manually operated screw press" rather than one powered by steam (personal communication, January 6, 2005). If Younge & Deakin, one of the most
important token producers of the period, struck its tokens by hand,
other, smaller-scale token makers almost certainly did the same.

The other evidence consists of information concerning the general
use of steam power by Birmingham manufacturers, especially its use in

---

8. That this indirect contribution of steam power was of limited importance is suggested by an article in the October 1886 *Birmingham Weekly Mercury* in which it is observed
that, even at that late date, "many of the Birmingham steam mills are not supposed to be
able to compete in point of excellence and precision of workmanship with some of [the]
distant country mills" run by waterpower (cited in Pelham 1963, 90). In any event, if steam
mills were capable of turning out better sheet copper, at a low price, there was nothing to
prevent counterfeiters as well as legitimate mints from acquiring copper from them. As
noted elsewhere, Soho's own rolling mill was water powered throughout the eighteenth
century and remained so until the factory was shut down.

making metal buttons and numismatic products that resembled coins. Eric Hopkins (1989, 34) explains that in Birmingham manufacturing generally, steam power "was of relatively small importance till the 1830s at the earliest." Steam power was used to make semiraw materials, including sheet metal, rather than final products, such as buttons (Allen 1966, 104–8). According to the Factory Inquiry of 1833, Ledsam & Sons, Birmingham's largest button factory (with three hundred employees), used "a small portion only" of steam power, which it let from an adjoining factory's engine. The city's second-largest button firm, Hammond, Turner & and Son (which made tokens in 1812 and 1813), relied solely on human-powered equipment.

Other sources from the same era (e.g., West 1830, 177–81; W. Smith 1836, pt. II, pp. 9–16) supply detailed descriptions of Edward Thomason's Church Street showrooms and factory at the start of the 1830s. Some years earlier, Charles Pye (1825, 88–89) had described Thomason's works as "the longest established and the most extensive in town"; and Thomason was certainly Birmingham's largest producer of numismatic products, including commercial coins, during the first decades of the nineteenth century. The descriptions don't mention any steam engine or steam-powered machines. Yet they do mention Thomason's manually operated drop hammers and screw presses. If Great Britain's largest producer of nineteenth-century commercial coins was still relying on human-powered equipment in 1836, it's hardly likely that any of the city's less important commercial mints employed steam-powered presses before then.

The general situation in Birmingham, with screw presses and other machinery being manually operated except in the heaviest trades, remained essentially unchanged until as late as the mid-nineteenth century. In February 1851, for instance, brass "coffin plates" were still being made using manual labor, although the stamping of such plates required great strength. A forty-ton press at one of the larger coffin hardware factories was powered by two strong men, each of whom earned twenty-five to thirty shillings a week (*Morning Chronicle,* February 10, 1851). Even drop hammers, which usually took three strong men to operate and were more easily adapted to steam than a screw press, were human powered, "with one or two exceptions," as late as 1866 (Timmins 1866, 307; see also Allen 1966, 106–7).

To conclude, a mass of evidence contradicts the claim that steam presses were widely employed in striking tradesman's tokens, supporting instead one found in the most exhaustive nineteenth-century work on the commercial tokens, Richard Samuel's *British Tokens* ([1881–83] 1994). "[T]he merit of applying steam power to the production of [commercial] coins," Samuel observes (March 22, 1882), "was exclusively Boulton's."

Was Steam Efficient?

If Birmingham's commercial mints were able to make high-quality, counterfeit-resistant coins without steam presses, such presses cannot have played any essential role in solving Great Britain's big problem. Might it have been the case, though, that other private mints failed to adopt Boulton's technology despite its superior efficiency? Boulton's coining apparatus was, after all, highly sophisticated for its day. Perhaps other mints wanted to employ it but couldn't do so because they couldn't buy or make the necessary machines.

It's true that Soho had more than its fair share of outstanding mechanics. But it was far from having had a monopoly on inventive genius. Although it took a great deal of ingenuity and trial and error to figure out how to deliver power to as many as eight coin presses at once from a single rotating shaft, to drive one or even two screw presses this way would have been a relatively simple matter. As for Boulton's patent, which he secured in 1790, it was granted not for the general idea of hooking up a coining press to a steam engine but for his peculiar wheel-and-escapement arrangement for delivering steam power to a battery of presses. Other mints were entirely free to experiment with steam power so long as they did not make use of this peculiar arrangement, which, in any event, was meant to handle a coinage capacity far beyond what they required.

Granted, the capital costs involved weren't trivial. Even a small (say, five-horsepower) Newcomen engine, modified for rotary motion, could cost a couple hundred pounds, which was hardly loose change for operations that were mainly small workshops. A Boulton & Watt engine might cost twice as much.[9] Coining presses specially adapted to steam power also cost more than conventional presses. Assuming that they could not finance purchases of such expensive equipment out of their retained

---

9. Newcomen engines could economically be made to operate more efficiently, though not quite as efficiently as Boulton & Watt engines, without infringing on Watt's patent, by allowing steam from them to condense in a pipe placed just beyond the main cylinder rather than in an external cylinder. In the mid-1790s, many of Great Britain's rotary steam engines were of this design (Von Tunzelman 1978, 62).

earnings, could Birmingham's commercial mints have done so otherwise?

According to experts on Birmingham's economy, many could have done so, by taking advantage of informal bonds of kinship (if their owners were among Birmingham's many Nonconformists); by applying for credit at one of Birmingham's several banks; or, most probably, by forming partnerships, as Boulton had done when he joined forces with Fothergill and as Matthew Wasborough did when he hooked up with Pickard and Twigg (Everseley 1964, 90; Duggan 1985, 45–60). Compared to the overall capitalization required to set up a button-making factory, the funds needed to pay for a small steam engine were quite modest. One button-manufacturing partnership formed in 1822 involved a capital investment of five thousand pounds, and initial business investments of this magnitude had in fact been fairly common in Birmingham for decades. Indeed, by the early nineteenth century, money could be had at competitive rates in amounts that "seemed to belie the small workshop image of the city," with investors and lenders in many instances offering "tens of thousands of pounds in a single transaction" (ibid., 59–60). It is hardly likely, therefore, that Birmingham's commercial mints refrained from employing steam power owing to a shortage of funds. Furthermore, the owners of Birmingham's eight rotary-motion steam engines might themselves have entered the coinage business without having to invest in any additional steam power. That none chose to do so suggests that possession of a steam engine did not constitute an important technical advantage in coin production.[10]

The most persuasive evidence against the hypothesis that steam-powered presses were more efficient than manually operated ones consists of the simple fact that mints employing manual screw presses managed to survive and even (it seems) to thrive, despite having to compete against Soho. Although Boulton may have hoped to gain a monopoly of the token trade after Thomas Williams's withdrawal and John Westwood Sr.'s bankruptcy, the early 1790s witnessed the entry into token making of both Peter Kempson and William Lutwyche, whose businesses would flourish until the end of the century and, in Kempson's case, well beyond. During the mid-1790s, another dozen small-scale mints entered

---

10. Although Twigg, the original owner of the Water Street steam mill, was himself a button maker and token issuer who produced some numismatic products, he did not make tokens for others. Moreover, Twigg manufactured his own buttons and numismatic products not at his Water Street facility but at a separate toy shop on Harper's Hill, near St. Paul's Square (Mitchiner 1998, 2005).

the scene, each grabbing a small share of the token market from the Soho Mint, which was never close to running at full capacity until it began coining cartwheels in 1797. Unlike Boulton, the other commercial coiners entertained no hopes of securing even a temporary monopoly. On the contrary, they all faced a positive probability that unauthorized commercial tokens would be suppressed once the government reformed its own copper coinage, as had happened in 1672 and as would happen again in 1817. It is hard to see why any of them should have been attracted to the business unless it offered reasonable profits.

Actually, one mint did stay in business despite failing to turn a profit. That mint was none other than the Soho Mint itself. "In truth," the mint's historian (Doty 1998, 50) informs us, the "Soho Mint was not a going concern and would not become one until its master secured his first regal coining contract in 1797." Boulton's net loss on his mint's output before its first regal coinage amounted to just under £2,500 on an investment of £7,780. This substantial loss suggests that the Soho Mint was, given the state of coinage technology as of 1797, a marginal operation that would in the competitive long run have been forced out of business by its more efficient rivals. Boulton was willing to endure losses because he was banking on something other than a competitive long run. That Boulton looked forward all along to landing an exclusive regal contract explains why he embraced a technology that wasn't capable of holding its own in what Sargent and Velde term a "laissez-faire" coinage regime.[11]

A comparison of Soho's charges for its 1797 regal penny and twopenny "cartwheels" with Lutwyche's charges, as supplied by him to cataloger Thomas Sharp (1834, ii) in 1793, provides qualified support for the preceding conclusion. Lutwyche charged his clients about £42 13s 4d (exclusive of the cost of copper) to manufacture one ton of halfpenny tokens. Soho, in contrast, charged the government £41 6s 8d to manufacture and deliver one of the five hundred tons of penny and twopenny coins it produced in fulfillment of its first regal coinage contract in 1797 (Doty 1998, 317). Although these figures give the lie to Boulton's claim that his equipment would cut coining costs in half, they at least appear to suggest a slight cost advantage. But even that slight advantage turns out to be illusory, for Soho was producing only sixteen pennies per pound weight of copper and half as many twopenny coins.

---

11. Sargent and Velde (2002, 266). Recall here Sir Eric Roll's (1930, 99) conclusion that Soho generally "expanded its productive capacity far beyond the limits justified by the fluctuating nature of the demand for its products."

Given the actual proportions of penny and twopenny pieces produced, which strongly favored the former, this was about a third as many coins per ton of copper as Lutwyche had offered to supply for just a bit more. Had Soho really been the more efficient mint, its costs should have been substantially lower than Lutwyche's, abstracting from differences in coin quality. That they weren't suggests that Soho was the less efficient mint, although its higher charge per coin may also have reflected Soho's higher profits or its coins' superior quality.[12]

Because coining by steam involved substantially higher fixed costs than coining by hand, steam technology was most economical for coining on a large scale. Even then, it might be inefficient, or it might be efficient only if the coining was constrained to take place under one roof. Such a constraint had been part of British coining policy since 1553, when all regal minting was assigned to the Tower mint in London (Craig 1953, xvii); and Boulton had good reason for assuming that it would be relaxed as little as possible in any reform of the copper coinage. Given his goals, his technology choice may therefore have been perfectly rational, despite not having been efficient in a competitive context.

Counterfeit-Proof Coin

If steam power wasn't the key either to making counterfeit-resistant coins or to making them efficiently, what was? A fundamental, if prosaic, answer is superior engraving. The traditional way to make counterfeit-resistant coins was to employ a die sinker whose original dies, like any superior work of art, were inimitable and therefore (to employ the terminology of Sargent and Velde) capable of being monopolized. "Superiority of execution alone," Rogers Ruding (1799, 36–37) opined,

> can protect our money from being . . . counterfeited and debased. That will immediately place it far out of the reach of many who have sufficient skill to copy the wretched workmanship of our present coins . . . whilst the expense of time required for finishing the work so

---

12. The coins to which Lutwyche's figures refer were not struck in collars. Moreover, at least some (e.g., John Fielding's 1793 Manchester halfpennies) bore indifferent engravings.

highly, will abate so much from the profit, that a greater number must be forced into circulation before the forger can be repaid.[13]

Ruding's opinion was far from novel: more than a century previously (and only three decades after England switched to "milled" coins), William Chaloner (1693), himself a notorious counterfeiter, publicly accused the Royal Mint of assisting him and his likes by making its coin easy to imitate. Chaloner suggested that his trade might most readily be discouraged by means of engravings "so curiously done that few in the Kingdom could do it so well."[14]

As we've seen, Birmingham was home to some of the world's outstanding metal engravers in the eighteenth and nineteenth centuries. Birmingham's commercial mints employed the best of them to make tokens that proved not only counterfeit resistant but tremendously popular among coin collectors. Soho went to especially great lengths to employ the best available engravers, employing no fewer than half a dozen of them on a full-time basis at one point and searching overseas as well as locally for outstanding talent.

Besides embellishing their coins with superior engravings, commercial coiners generally marked their coins' edges. In the eighteenth century, they did so mainly using incuse legends indicating where the coins could be redeemed; in the nineteenth century, they switched to graining. Such edge markings, applied to blanks before striking them, prevented what might otherwise have been an effective, though inexpensive, method of forgery—namely, casting imitation coins in sand molds made using authentic ones. Edge markings ruled out this easy and cheap alternative, forcing would-be counterfeiters to stamp their products using handmade dies, because there was no way to prevent molten copper from leaving a seam where obverse and reverse casting molds met. Al-

---

13. In a clarifying footnote (36n), Ruding adds, "[b]y superiority of workmanship is not meant anything in the least resembling the late copper coinage," meaning the regal copper coins then being made at Soho. His reasons for saying so will be considered in due course.

14. Chaloner also anticipated Boulton's favored solution to the counterfeiting problem by recommending the employment of dies of such high relief as to call for an "engine" powered by "Horses, Wind, or Water." Such an engine would, he thought, make it "morally impossible to Counterfeit Money without being discovered." Note, however, that Boulton's steam-powered presses turned out to be incapable of striking high-relief dies or of otherwise making coins that could not be struck manually. Horse-, wind-, or water-powered presses might actually have been superior in this regard.

though Royal Mint officials understood perfectly well that edge markings were a precaution against counterfeiting—the edges of the first "milled" guineas, crowns, and half crowns bore the intaglio inscription *Decus et Tutamen,* meaning "Ornament and Safeguard"—they never bothered to mark the edges of low-value coins, despite the fact that the fiduciary status of such coins made them especially tempting targets for counterfeiters. As we've seen, Boulton was to make the same mistake with his first regal copper coins.

Unlike Soho, the Royal Mint could not assign salaried posts to foreigners. Moreover, the chief engravers responsible for most of its eighteenth-century coins—John Croker (a naturalized German) and (after 1740) John S. Tanner—were no match for Birmingham's best die sinkers. Besides relying on unimpressive engravings, "the old shop," as Matthew Robinson Boulton styled the Royal Mint in 1810, "never made the least improvement for a century past" to its coins (Powell 1993, 53), the only modifications being the inevitable ones reflecting the accession of new monarchs. The mint didn't even bother to edge mark copper coins. Back-alley operators were therefore able to churn out cast imitations that, with the help of a little filing or aqua fortis, could not readily be identified as such. No wonder Ruding (1819, 4:155) characterized the workmanship of the mint's coins as "barbarous," while John Pinkerton ([1786] 1808, 186) went so far as to rank its eighteenth-century output "with that of the lowest times of the Roman empire."

Something else that may have given commercial coiners an edge, so to speak, over the Royal Mint was the invention, in Sheffield during the mid-1740s, of cast, or crucible, steel. Such steel is free of the slag and silicon particles found in blister steel. This makes it harder and more uniform and therefore far better suited for making master dies capable of withstanding multiple blows without fracturing and for making working dies that will take strikes uniformly.

For several decades, crucible steel could be obtained only in very limited quantities and for a high price from its original inventor, Benjamin Huntsman. But during the 1770s, Huntsman's trade secret—which had to do with the mixture of local clays employed to make the necessary crucibles—got out, and within a decade or so, Birmingham die sinkers could obtain crucible steel at a considerably lowered price from no fewer than seven Sheffield suppliers (Ashton 1951, 57). By that time, crucible steel was being generally employed by Birmingham's button makers, who valued dies made from it for their unique ability to take a fine polish.[15]

Boulton, for his part, began buying steel from Huntsman in the 1750s (Tweedale 1995, 39; MBP 238/231–32). Although Huntsman's earliest records were destroyed in a fire, his firm's post-1787 records and Boulton's own papers reveal a long list of deliveries of steel and die blanks to Soho (MBP 238/231–34; see also Ashton 1951, 58).[16] In April 1789, when the king's recovery led Boulton to conclude, wrongly, that he would soon begin making regal coins, Boulton wrote to Benjamin Hunstman's son William:

> I am about to undertake the striking of some millions of copper pieces which will require a hard blow in hardened steel dies. I have tried various kinds of steel but am not satisfied with any of them. I am of the opinion that the best steel you are capable of making will answer the best. . . . It must be the best you can possibly make without regard to price or expense, that being a trifling object in comparison to the quality of the steel. . . . The steel I have tried hitherto either cracks in the hardening or breaks afterwards in the striking or it is so soft as to sink in the middle and become hollow.   (CHARD 1990, 1141)

The use of steam presses made the right choice of steel especially crucial because such presses exerted more pressure than manual ones, causing dies of any given steel to fail more rapidly, especially in making heavier coins. That's why, when the first cartwheels were being struck, John Southern again insisted that Huntsman supply Soho with steel and die bosses "of the strongest and best quality without regard to prices" (MBP 343/30, July 2, 1797; see also Chard 1990, 1141–43). Thanks to good crucible steel, the number of cartwheel varieties was very small relative to the number of actual coins.

The Royal Mint seems to have remained unaware of the advantages of crucible steel until many years after it switched to steam presses: during

15. In a March 1792 "Report on Huntsman's Cast Steel" (reproduced in Hadfield 1894), Fourness & Ashworth, engineers to George III, observe: "[A]s to Dies, there is perhaps no Steel that can be made into a face of equal hardness and durability. For Buckles, Buttons, and other articles of the steel kind, to which great superficial brilliancy is requisite, there is, we believe, not another fabric of Steel so completely adequate" (ibid., 236).

16. Huntsman's pre-1800 sales records are available at the Sheffield Archives, items LD 1612–24.

the Mint Inquiry of 1837, William Busson, the mint's surveyor of money presses and coins, testified that he "took a great deal of pains some years ago to discover the best kind of steel" for making long-lasting dies. "I think now I have found it out," Busson added (BPP 1838, 73–74). What Busson finally "discovered" was Huntsman's steel, which Boulton and other Birmingham button makers had by then been using for over half a century.[17]

Crucible steel aided the detection of counterfeit coins by making legitimate ones more uniform. Working dies made from it lasted longer, as did original master dies. With the aid of a large (manual) screw press,[18] a single master die of crucible steel could be "hubbed" to make hundreds of precisely identical working dies, without cracking and without need for further resort to hand engraving to correct flaws caused by metal impurities. Millions of precisely identical coins could then be made using a single hand-engraved matrix of crucible steel. Hubbing—which Birmingham's button makers had long practiced (Dickinson 1936, 146), but which was not a normal practice at the Royal Mint until the late 1770s, when the mint had ceased to make small change (Dyer and Gaspar 1992, 430)—allowed any even slightly deviant coin to be reckoned counterfeit, thereby substantially lowering the costs of counterfeit detection. Although hubbing became standard practice at the Royal Mint after it switched to steam power, the mint's failure to "discover" crucible steel until many years later meant that its master hubs often failed after only a small number of working dies had been reproduced from them, defeating the mint's attempts to avoid unwanted variations in its coins. The Soho Mint, in contrast, is said to have "perfected the art of die hubbing to such an extent that [all its] coins of a certain denomination were virtually identical" by 1791 (Vice 1998, 53).

To conclude, much as Soho's steam-powered machines may have dazzled all who set eyes on them, those machines had little to do with the quality of its coins. As Jenny Uglow (2002, 210–11) observes, in refer-

17. According to Craig (1953, 293), the Royal Mint's "first scientific inquiry" into steel for its dies "was entrusted in 1823 to London's leading chemist, William Thomas Brande," whose "research somewhat improved the average life of dies, which had been curtailed by the steam-driven presses." Following Brande's researches, the mint was able to make up to twenty-three thousand coins of typical size with one pair of working dies. This was, however, still only half the average value of coins per working die for the mint's halfpence coinage in 1744–60 (Dyer 1993, 162).

18. Even the Soho Mint employed a manual press for die multiplication, because steam presses were not practical for conveying impression in high relief, in part because their higher striking pressures would quickly destroy even a punch made of crucible steel.

ence to both Boulton and Josiah Wedgewood: "It is easy to overstate the role of machines. It was skilled hands that made the difference in the toy trades and in pottery. But machines were new and intriguing and helped make their factories into showpieces."

Why did Birmingham's "skilled hands" take such pains to render mere pennies and halfpennies inimitable? The principle reason is that the mints' clients couldn't afford to settle for less, because they promised to redeem their tokens in standard money and might therefore be rendered bankrupt by counterfeits not demonstrably different from their own issues. Secondly, if any one mint failed to meet a client's needs, the client could take his business elsewhere. The Royal Mint, in contrast, never offered to redeem any of its token coins until 1834, when it reluctantly agreed routinely to receive excess silver coins from the Bank of England, though only in batches worth at least £250,000. It therefore suffered little, if at all, from the successful counterfeiting of its coins. The private token regime thus supplied stronger incentives for the production of counterfeit-resistant small change than did the state monopoly regimes that preceded and followed it.

Rogers Ruding, for one, was convinced that poor incentives, rather than poor machines, were at the bottom of the copper counterfeiting problem.

> Let but the skill of our first designers and engravers be stimulated by proper encouragement; and, with that, there can be no doubt of their producing a coinage, which, at one glance, may be distinguished from the work of inferior artists.   (RUDING 1799, 36n)

By electing to issue inconvertible copper coins on government account, the Royal Mint caused most of the costs related to counterfeiting to fall on outside parties. Matters changed only when commercial coiners, including Boulton, proved that it was possible to strike counterfeit-resistant token coins. The threat of a privatized copper coinage and the still greater threat of a privatized silver coinage (which loomed large once Soho began striking Bank dollars) induced the Royal Mint to embrace not only steam power but various traditional counterfeit-proofing measures employed by most commercial mints.

The convertibility of tradesman's tokens, together with their lack of even limited legal-tender status, also made it relatively easy for issuers to retrieve worn or damaged tokens and withdraw them from circulation. Thanks to this ability, token counterfeiters had no choice but to come up with convincing imitations of genuine tokens in something close to their mint condition. In contrast, the Royal Mint refused to take back its own copper (and silver) coins (no matter how worn they had become), even to exchange for fresh regal copper, so regal copper counterfeiters had merely to replicate the most dilapidated current regal coins, which, besides containing less raw material, displayed only a shadow—if that—of their original (mediocre) engravings. By failing to redeem or otherwise cry down worn small-denomination coins, the Royal Mint rendered nugatory what little anticounterfeiting effort it may have invested in them when they were first produced.

The point can be made by referring to Redish's (1990, 793) condition for profitable coinage, which is that the market price of a quantity of metal plus the mint's cost of coining that metal must be less than the metal's mint equivalent. If the Royal Mint could profit by coining copper, counterfeiters could also profit, even despite adhering to the official mint equivalent (in this case, twenty-three pence per pound of copper), as long as their costs fell short of the sum of the mint's costs and its profit.[19] The mint earned substantial profits on its copper coins, notwithstanding the royal proclamation according to which they were to be rated at no more than their "intrinsic value" plus manufacturing costs. From 1727 to 1760, the mint's average cost for prepared copper sheets was fifteen pence per pound, which, after adding four pence per pound to cover coining costs, implied an average seigniorage rate of over 14 percent (see fig. 4). This profit alone was more than enough to invite counterfeiting. But genuine regal coins were allowed to remain current despite being badly worn. The coins' worn state amounted to an ex post increase in copper's mint equivalent, owing to the reduced copper content of the worn coins. It also gave counterfeiters a cost advantage by allowing them to use dies intentionally cut shallow and without detail, if not "plain" dies bearing no engravings at all, which had the added merit of not being incriminating.[20]

---

19. Some clarification is called for here: counterfeiters, being competitive coin manufacturers, were presumably incapable of earning above-normal profits in equilibrium. They sold their products at cost (roughly half their face value) to wholesale counterfeit dealers, who in turn sold them at smaller discounts to retailers known as utterers or "smashers" (Colquhoun 1800, 16–19). Redish's profit condition must thus be understood as measuring potential gains for the counterfeiting industry taken as a whole, not specifically those of counterfeit manufacturers.

20. Some procedures for mimicking old coin, including frying counterfeits in brimstone to give them an appropriate patina, added to the costs of counterfeiting, but such costs were presumably small compared to savings on copper and die-sinking charges.

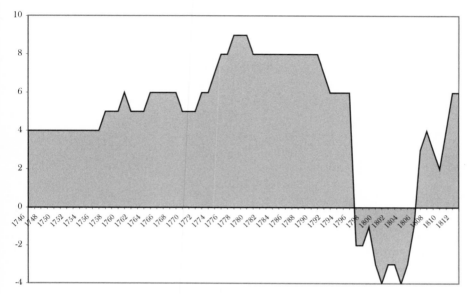

Fig. 4. Implicit seigniorage rate on regal copper coin, 1749–1816. Seigniorage is calculated by subtracting the sum of the price of sheet copper (drawn from Grenfell 1814, app.) and a constant average coin.

The situation with silver was no different. Rogers Ruding wrote at the end of the century (1799, 35–36):

> [T]he counterfeiter has only to procure a die (the sinking of which is within the ability of any workman in steel), with a faint outline of part of a bust upon it, and with a reverse totally plain: With this mean instrument he may secure a profit of nearly thirty per cent. by coining shillings, even of standard silver.

Legitimate silver sixpence were in even worse shape than shillings; and the regal copper coins were no better, many of them having been issued during the reign of George II (Oman 1967, 364).[21] "Worn" imitations of

---

21. In 1789, Royal Mint authorities claimed that there were perhaps twelve hundred tons of legitimate regal halfpennies and no less than three thousand tons of counterfeits in circulation (MBP 249/234). By taking the mint's 1785 estimate, which (after allowing for an error in the mint's calculation) placed the nominal value of authentic regal coppers at £306,000 (Craig 1953, 251–52), and rounding it down to allow for coins lost between 1785 and 1789, one arrives at a de facto mint equivalent of fifty-five halfpennies per pound of copper, as opposed to the de jure equivalent of forty-six per pound.

these coins could not be distinguished from genuine ones except perhaps by an expert medallist (Pinkerton [1786] 1808, 226).

Evidently, no new coin production technology is likely to prevent official coins from being counterfeited if older official coins, especially badly worn ones, remain current. That is one reason why the Committee on Coin was obliged, in March 1807, to admit to the Treasury that, despite Soho's having issued over 110 million new halfpennies, "counterfeit halfpence are now nearly as abundant in the circulation of London as they have been at any former time" (Wager 1977, 47; Doty 1998, 320, 330). The systematic withdrawal of old Tower copper didn't start until a few years later and didn't end until the last day of 1817 (Craig 1953, 266–67).

Why the long delay? The main hurdle to comprehensive recoinage was the cost, which had to be borne either by persons bringing worn coin to the mint or by the public at large. This hurdle grew greater with every year's delay. Already in 1755, when large numbers of William III halfpennies made from cast flans (and hence easily counterfeited) were still in circulation, Royal Mint officials estimated that a proposed recoinage would involve a loss of nine pence per pound weight of recoined copper, or £222,400 for supplying an estimated eighteen hundred tons (avoirdupois) of new copper coin. The Treasury balked, and the proposal was abandoned (Snelling 1775, 45).[22] Aggravating the problem was the fact that the mint couldn't avoid redeeming convincing counterfeits along with its own worn-out products, unless it did so by refusing many of the latter. Successful counterfeiting thus played into a vicious cycle: the greater the quantity of (convincing) counterfeit money in circulation, the higher the expected costs of recoinage and the greater the official resistance to it. Putting off recoinage only served, however, to allow the coin stock to go on deteriorating, directly adding to the costs of a recoinage, while further reducing the cost and increasing the volume of counterfeiting.

Britain's commercial coin issuers avoided a similar vicious cycle by insisting on token designs that were difficult to copy in the first place and by offering to convert their tokens into gold guineas or banknotes on demand, which made it easy for them to routinely retire and replace worn

22. When the government elected to recall and recoin light (gold) guineas starting in 1773, the recoinage ended up costing close to two hundred thousand pounds, much of which went to line the pockets of the Royal Mint's officers. The huge expense of that recoinage prompted Edmund Burke to introduce a bill that would have abolished the mint and transferred responsibility for coinage to the Bank of England.

tokens. The Royal Mint, in contrast, would not get around to routinely renewing its copper coinage until the twentieth century. Until then, its policies continued to encourage counterfeiting by allowing old and worn copper coins to remain in circulation.[23]

One aspect of Royal Mint procedures made life easier for the average eighteenth-century counterfeiter no matter whose coins he chose to imitate. This was the mint's system—or, rather, its lack of any system—for getting coins to places where they were needed (Mathias 1979, 192–95; Craig 1953, 252). As we've seen, the mint, despite selling its copper coins at face value, made them available only at the Tower, instead of offering to bear the costs of shipping them to distant towns and factories. Because regal coins were inconvertible, once they were spent by their initial recipients, they made their way to retailers and publicans, who, being legally obliged to receive them in small payments, had helplessly to watch them accumulate, unless some manufacturer offered to purchase them. While London coin surpluses gave the mint an excuse for not issuing any new coins, provincial shortages aided counterfeiters, by tempting manufacturers to do business with them, rather than incur the cost of obtaining change from London, and by forcing workers and retailers in affected areas to accept even the most transparent fakes, for want of anything better. "[A]n insuperable Difficulty has always occurred," a Privy Council committee reported in 1799, "in getting them [regal copper coins] into Circulation in all parts of the Kingdom." The report continued,

> Those who live at a Distance will not send for them and it is owing probably to this circumstance that the Counterfeits have been made use of in preference to those hitherto coined at the Tower.
>
> (QUOTED IN MATHIAS 1979, 193)

In light of this, to treat the counterfeiting problem as having been primarily, let alone entirely, a problem of inadequate coin-making technology makes little sense. The problem was to a large extent institutional rather than technological, and the solution lay not so much in improved equipment as in improved policies.

---

23. Thus William Gladstone, in reporting (as chancellor of the exchequer) the findings of an 1859 investigation of Great Britain's copper coin, remarked that "a great deal of it was in very bad condition," with over one-fifth of sampled coins still consisting of Boulton's 1797–1805 issues and with only 15 percent consisting of post-1852 coins, eight hundred thousand pounds of which had been issued (*Hansard*, August 4, 1859, c. 978–79).

Did Steam Striking Suffice?

If steam striking wasn't necessary for making counterfeit-resistant coins, was it at least sufficient? Could it serve as a substitute for traditional anti-counterfeiting methods? Boulton, of course, claimed that it could: "I have executed and perfected such an apparatus or Machinery," he told the Committee on Coin in December 1789, "as will make Coin not only superior in Beauty & Workmanship to that of any Nation in Europe but also so manufactured . . . that Counterfeiting will be prevented" (MBP 249/235). But taking Boulton's claims at face value is risky. "Like a show-man," Dyer and Gaspar (1992, 446) write, Matthew Boulton "made extravagant claims" concerning what his equipment could do, in part because he believed he could make good on the claims, but also because he was determined to obtain a lucrative regal coinage contract. He also hoped to sell his machinery to various national mints, including the Royal Mint.

One of Boulton's extravagant claims consisted of his assertion, during his 1787 testimony to the Committee on Coin, that coins made using his method would be "perfectly uniform," whereas those made by "Men will vary as their strength respectively does . . . the effect of which will appear in the difference of Diameter and Thickness of the pieces of Coin" (quoted in Redish 2000, 145). In fact, steam striking could make only a trivial contribution to the uniform thickness and diameter of coins, which depend mainly on the uniformity of the sheet metal used to make coin blanks, on the accuracy of blank-cutting tools, and on whether blanks are run through an edge-marking, or "milling," device before they're struck.[24]

Although it's true that Boulton's coins had especially round and smooth edges, this was so not because they were struck using steam presses but because they were struck using a restraining "collar."[25] Coins

---

24. The early 1780s saw many improvements in metal rolling, including a method for hardening copper by graduated cold rolling, patented by John Westwood Sr., one of Birmingham's commercial coiners (Dykes 1999, 181). The Royal Mint's own horse-powered rolling mill, though adequate for rolling gold and silver, couldn't handle copper ingots (Craig 1953, 175).

25. Unless it is put through an edging machine, a coin struck without a collar will generally be of slightly greater diameter than the blank from which it is struck. It might also not be perfectly round, depending on the coin's design and, significantly, the operating pressure of the press. Late George III halfpennies, for example, were slightly "out-of-round." In this respect, at least, most counterfeits were faithful to the originals (C. Smith 1995, 37).

could also be collar-struck by hand: in Paris, the practice dated back to 1555; and the Royal Mint itself had been doing it, albeit on a very limited basis, since the reign of Charles II (Sargent and Velde 2002, 54; Oman 1967, 330). Among commercial coiners, the Parys Mine Company, Peter Kemspon, John Westwood Sr., and William Lutwyche all employed collars in striking some of their commercial coins, while most private mints employed them in trial strikings and in making "private" (display) tokens.[26] Indeed, at the time of Boulton's testimony, he was still more than three years away from perfecting a collar and coin-ejection mechanism compatible with his presses' high operating speeds. The Parys Mine Company would, in the meantime, issue about nine million collar-struck pennies.

Concerning steam-struck versus "milled" (i.e., manually struck) coins, no one could say what all numismatists acknowledge concerning milled versus hammered coins—namely, that the difference is such as to be "obvious, upon a bare comparison of the products" (Pinkerton [1786] 1808, 74). The collar-struck Parys Mine pennies were, according to Richard Doty (personal communication, August 6, 2002), "every bit as good as [Boulton's] products, even though they were struck on hand presses" and on a scale comparable to that of Boulton's 1797 regal coinage. Of course, Soho could strike coins on a still vaster scale. But that didn't stop small-scale counterfeiters from profitably imitating its coins.

One thing Boulton didn't tell the Privy Council was that the rapid thrust of Soho's presses, when they were run at excessively rapid rates, tended to shatter dies, especially high-relief ones, even when they were made from the best crucible steel. Sixty coins per minute was about as fast as Boulton's original presses could safely be run, even for farthings and other small coins. Larger coins, like the tuppence cartwheels, had to be struck at a much slower rate to avoid damage to dies and presses (Doty 1998, 46–47, 55–56). The vacuum-type presses, though less fragile (and therefore more suitable for larger coins) were generally no

---

As for variations in thickness, although it is true that counterfeits of Soho's steam-struck coins could often be identified using a steel thickness gauge, this reflected not the inferior accuracy of screw presses but that many counterfeiters were inclined deliberately to make their coins slightly thinner and lighter than the originals, so as to enhance their profits. Had mere inaccuracy been to blame, there should have been some "heavy" counterfeits. So far as records indicate, there weren't.

26. The principal collar-struck commercial coins, apart from Soho's, were the Parys Mine pennies, at least nine tons of Hancock's Willeys, and just under five tons' worth of Kempson and Lutwyche issues, including most of Kempson's Scottish commissions. For details, see Pye 1801.

faster than their predecessors. As Sargent and Velde (2002, 55) note, manual screw presses modified to provide for automatic feeding of blanks and ejection of finished coins, like those designed by Droz for the Paris Mint, were almost as fast.[27]

Furthermore, because steam-powered presses, unlike manually powered ones, did not lend themselves to "multiple" strikings—the traditional means for avoiding die breakage when making high-relief coins and medals—Boulton had to stick to shallower dies, which (according to some numismatists at least) were easier to engrave and to copy (Pinkerton [1786] 1808, 186–87).[28] Because shallow engravings also tend to wear out more rapidly, Boulton tried surrounding his with the thick raised rims that earned the cartwheels their nickname. The thick rims had to be given up, however, because they "broke dies right and left" (Doty, personal communication, August 7, 2002) and because they caused the designs they surrounded to become caked with grime (Samuel [1881–83] 1994, 307, c. 2 [March 12, 1882]).

In short, although Boulton's presses allowed him to strike coins in collar faster than was possible by manual means, they didn't allow him to produce coins that could not also be produced manually. The cartwheels' unusual design contributed to the myth that they could be made only using Boulton's presses. However, as Ruding (1819, 4:378n) indicates, "All the [cartwheels'] boasted improvements are to be found on the patterns of Queen Anne's Money: except, perhaps, their complete circularity" (ibid., 81n); and it was actually much easier, as Richard Doty observes (personal communication, August 7, 2002), "to create the 'Boulton look' (i.e., the raised ribbon/incuse lettering) . . . with a normal screw press, with or without a collar," because such a press was easier on dies. In fact, the look was imitated by Kempson and several other commercial coiners during the 1812–17 commercial coinage episode.

---

27. In 1818, Pistrucci discovered to his dismay that the Royal Mint's steam-powered presses were too weak to fully strike in a single blow both sides of the high-relief crowns he had designed toward the end of George III's reign. Consequently, the crowns had to be run through the presses twice, slowing their output to a snail's pace of fifty per hour (Doty 1998, 164n19). Even a clumsy team on a manual screw press could do better than that.

28. Pinkerton ([1786] 1808, 2:186–87), writing in December 1797, faulted the Royal Mint both for the artistic shortcomings of its coins ("the pattern shilling of 1778 . . . is perfection itself—in the *bathos* of art; if the shilling and six-pence do not exceed it," etc.) and for their low-relief designs, which, requiring less talent to make, were also easier to copy. He recommended, per contra, the use of high-relief dies "so as to rival the ancient in this grand criterion of good coin," while criticizing the alternative proposal of "a noble lord" (Boulton) who proposed to reform Britain's coin by making it "in still less relief than now—with a circle to protect that relief."

Indeed, steam presses were generally less versatile than manual ones. Thus, when he was asked, during the Mint Inquiry of 1837 (BPP 1838, 74–75), to state the advantages of the Royal Mint's coining "plan" to that of the Paris Mint (which, having experimented with steam technology, rejected it in favor of continuing to strike all of its coins "by hand"), William Busson replied simply, but evasively, that the Royal Mint plan allowed it "to coin more rapidly." Busson's Privy Council interrogator was far from satisfied.

> *PC:* My question went not to the quickness of execution, but as to making the coin as perfect as possible; do you think, according to the French mode . . . that they can coin better?
>
> *Busson:* I think the French mode of coining is very much like the mode adopted here in casting medals, or in coining proof-pieces, which we coin by hand, and we can then coax the press according to circumstances.
>
> *PC:* Is not that a much superior mode?
>
> *Busson:* Much superior.

That the Royal Mint was still striking its proof pieces manually in 1837 is especially revealing, as these pieces were supposed to be more precise but otherwise faithful renderings of coins being proposed for mass production.

One might suppose that the Royal Mint was at least coining more economically than the Paris Mint and other mints equipped with manual presses only. Boulton had, after all, claimed as far back as December 1789 that "although my Machinery is more expensive at the outset it can manufacture Coin cheaper than the cheapest Method now used" (MBP 249/225). Later on, when Soho had all eight of its coining presses in running order, Boulton supplemented this claim with the more specific one that using his equipment, steam from one bushel of coal could do the work of fifty-five men working eleven old-style presses (Doty 1998, 150). If Boulton was being truthful, steam power might indirectly have helped to make British coins more counterfeit resistant, by freeing up resources that could then be invested in better (albeit shallow) engravings.

But Busson's further testimony during the Mint Inquiry of 1837 suggests that steam power did not supply even this more indirect advantage.

> *PC:* Is it not the case, from the scale upon which the machinery of the English Mint is constituted, it is a very expensive process to put into operation?

Busson: Very.

PC: It is not worth while to do so for anything but a considerable coinage?

Busson: No.

The trouble, according to senior moneyer Jaspar Atkinson, was that it cost the same amount to run the Royal Mint's steam engine when only one of its coining presses was operating as it cost when all eight were at work. The same observation applied to the mint's cutting-out presses, twelve in all, which were powered by a separate engine. For anything except a major recoinage, Atkinson testified (BPP 1838, 128, 132), manual striking was more economical.

Owing to the limited market for new coin, the Paris Mint decided to strike coins by hand even after it had acquired a steam engine for the purpose.

Atkinson: I asked the [Paris Mint] contractor why [the steam engine] was not set to work; he said it was so expensive he could not afford it; and six years ago, when I was there, it had been some time in a quiet state, and has so been ever since.

PC: Do your observations apply to the increased expense incurred by you in smaller coinages?

Atkinson: Yes; and the Committee will observe in looking at the accounts, our expenses now, as compared to what they were in the period of 1770 to 1781, are more than doubled; whether it was a small coinage or a large one, they are more than doubled.[29]

Atkinson's last statement suggests, intriguingly, that steam-powered coining presses may not have been efficient even for large coinages: the decision to install them in the new Little Tower Hill mint, which was made not by mint officials themselves but by the Privy Council Committee on Coin, appears to have been due more to Boulton's relentless and ultimately successful lobbying of the committee and Lord Liverpool than to any well-established advantages, economic or otherwise, possessed by his equipment.

Finally, as we've seen, Soho's official coins, starting with the cart-

---

29. The Paris Mint did eventually switch to steam-powered presses, in 1845. Elsewhere also, coins continued to be struck manually decades after Boulton's first employment of steam power.

wheels, were counterfeited despite the extralegal protection such coins enjoyed compared to commercial tokens. According to Ruding (1799, 36n; see also 1819, 4:377n), Boulton's "boasting was found to be vain almost as soon as the coins were issued; for, the workmanship of the dies being not beyond the skill of many other Birmingham artists, their ingenuity readily suggested expedients to supply the want of the so much vaunted power of the machine." In deciding to dispense with edge markings on his first regal coins, Boulton neglected the advice he'd given in his original proposals to the Committee on Coin, reverting instead to the Royal Mint's bad practice and thereby encouraging the making of plausible cast cartwheels. Soho's Bank dollars were even more vulnerable to counterfeiting, with copies good enough to fool even the bank's clerks appearing within days of the first originals. This was a classic instance of counterfeiters successfully undermining part of what Sargent and Velde (2002, 5–6) term the "standard formula" for a successful token coinage. I remind readers of these occurrences not to deny that Boulton's coins were harder to counterfeit than earlier regal coins had been but simply to show that steam striking alone was, Boulton's claims notwithstanding, no guarantee against counterfeiting.

Britain's Yellow Brick Road

In truth, the counterfeiting of regal coin continued to be a problem well into the Victorian era.[30] Britain nonetheless managed to contain the problem enough to abandon official bimetallism in 1816 in favor of a gold standard supplemented by token coins. If the steam presses at Little Tower Hill didn't make this move possible, what did?

A strengthening of legal penalties against counterfeiting, undertaken in response to recommendations made by London police magistrate Patrick Colquhoun (1800), may have helped somewhat. Perhaps the most important reform along these lines was an 1803 statute making simple possession (without lawful excuse) of as few as six pieces of counterfeit copper a crime punishable by a fine of from ten to forty shillings for each fraudulent coin (Ruding 1819, 4:85). But it seems unlikely that this reform alone could have had any great effect unless the quality of legitimate coins was also improved.

Other reforms (which, like the switch to steam power, had been

---

30. Indeed, according to Henry Mayhew ([1851] 1967, 4:377), by the middle of the nineteenth century, the forging of silver coins in London was "as prevalent as ever."

urged by Lord Liverpool) effected such an improvement and thus made counterfeiting more difficult, by eliminating local coin shortages and by replacing old Tower halfpence with fresh coins. Starting with Boulton's 1797 cartwheel coinage, the Treasury at last began to allow four pounds per ton to cover the costs of shipping regal copper coins where they were needed. This reform, coupled with Soho's large copper coin issues and, especially, the much larger silver coin issues of 1817, radically changed the nature of the counterfeiting trade. Because they were no longer "exploiting a need," John Powell (1993, 55) writes,

> counterfeiters had to change their methods. They could no longer deal in bulk but needed to slip their coins into circulation. Before 1810 a counterfeiter did not need to make an exact copy since shortages would have made his money acceptable, but after 1816 the counterfeiter had to possess the best of disguising skills.

Steam power did, of course, increase the Royal Mint's ability to produce large quantities of new coin within a relatively short period and under one roof. But this indirect contribution was hardly essential: given enough space and manual screw presses, the mint might have produced coins just as rapidly without steam, though perhaps at a higher unit cost. It was, moreover, the mint's prior mismanagement of the coinage—not its prior reliance on human-powered presses—that made such enormous issues of new coin necessary in the first place: in a well-designed coinage system, only a small part of the coin stock becomes excessively worn and in need of replacement each year.

Eventually, the government arranged, at long last, to recall and recoin all of its old and decrepit small change. In February 1817, the Royal Mint's old silver was recalled and recoined; in December, all pre-1797 regal coppers were retired. Also, in January 1818, most unauthorized coins (including evasives and commercial tokens) were legally suppressed. Thus, by early 1818, counterfeiters were forced to replicate relatively recent Soho and Royal Mint products. Although these measures followed Britain's official abandonment of bimetallism, all were understood to be necessary complements of that measure. Some years later, in 1846, a new policy was inaugurated of continuous withdrawal at the Royal Mint's expense of worn sixpences and shillings. Continuous withdrawal of half crowns began in 1871 (Craig 1953, 311). These policies mimicked the private market's solution of making small change redeemable on demand, though for silver coins only: copper coin remained subject to discrete renewals only.

The remaining and crucial challenge was to make Britain's new coins as difficult to counterfeit as the earlier commercial coinage had been. As we have seen, this challenge could not be met simply by switching to steam-powered presses. It could be met only by designing better coins. In fact, the new regal subsidiary coins were, by all accounts, far better than earlier ones. They were better not because they were struck using steam but because Soho continued to employ several of the world's best engravers (including Küchler, who designed Soho's regal copper coins) and because the Royal Mint, having put old Pingo out to pasture, drew on Birmingham talent to restaff its own die shop and engraving department, hiring (among others) Soho's George Rennie and James Lawson and a battery of Wyons.[31] Recall that it was young Thomas Wyon Jr. who, in his capacity as the Royal Mint's chief engraver, executed the dies for its new silver half crowns, shillings, and sixpences, which, according to one respected Victorian authority, were "the finest that had ever been issued in Europe" (Humphreys 1848, 111).[32]

In addition, starting with Soho's cartwheels, regal coins were struck in collar so that they would be perfectly round and uniform. They were also given smaller diameters and reliefs as high as (and, at least in the case of Pistrucci's crowns, higher than) their steam presses could readily handle. Besides making official coins more difficult to copy, these steps also reduced the rate at which they deteriorated, that rate being proportional to a coin's surface area. Finally, by the mid-1830s, the Royal Mint perfected its die-making procedures by at last switching to crucible steel and by drawing on the expertise of several former Boulton employees whom it had lured away.

Despite all of these improvements to its small change, Britain never did implement a fully convertible token coinage during the nineteenth century. It settled instead for limited convertibility only, starting in 1834

---

31. As part of his comprehensive 1815 Royal Mint reorganization, Master William Wellesley Pole also announced that the mint, instead of relying on its own staff only as it had done in the past, would select its new coin designs from entries submitted by all the best artists of the realm.

32. The same writer recalls having witnessed "the agreeable impression" Wyon's coins produced when they were first issued, especially "the extraordinary beauty the coins appeared to possess, after the flat, bent, and battered bits of silver . . . that had been so long made to pass current as coin of the realm."

with the Treasury's (reluctant) offer to receive unwanted silver from the Bank of England (Redish 2000, 152–53) and concluding with the extension of the continuous withdrawal policy to silver half crowns in 1871. In this respect, at least, contrary to what Sargent and Velde (2002, 268) suggest, the commercial mints' solution to Britain's small-change problem, though certainly "tentative," was also more—rather than less— "complete" than the official solution that supplanted it (cf. Cannan 1935, 41–42).

. . . and its Ruby Slippers

There was no shortage of skilled die engravers before the nineteenth century. Nor was there any lack of means for edge marking coins, distributing them effectively, and arranging for their regular redemption and replacement. Even crucible steel and advanced hubbing techniques had been around for several decades before the British government finally got around to modernizing its coinage system.

Why, then, did reform not come sooner? If the absence of steam technology didn't stand in the way, what did? According to Sargent and Velde (2002, xviii), if the problem wasn't inadequate technology, it must have been poor theory. Yet Sargent and Velde themselves (ibid., 268) point out that the necessary theory, or key elements of it at least, had been set forth by at least one Englishman—Sir Henry Slingsby—as early as 1661. By the 1780s, many persons—Matthew Boulton and Samuel Garbett among them—had outlined the basic requirements for a sound small-change system explicitly and thoroughly, while others, including practically everyone involved in making or issuing commercial coins, can at least be said to have understood them implicitly.

The underlying problem with Sargent and Velde's account of the small-change problem is its starting point. By beginning by asking if it was "poor economic theory or inadequate technology" that stood in the way of a solution to the small-change problem (ibid., xviii), Sargent and Velde set aside the possibility that national mint authorities simply weren't inclined to do their jobs properly. Mint authorities (or "policy experts"), as portrayed by Sargent and Velde, "struggled" and "groped" their way toward a solution to the small-change problem but had to "strain against constraints" posed by flawed theories and equipment (ibid., xviii, 23). It is as if the ethos of a medieval mint (and the Royal Mint remained an essentially medieval institution at least until Wellesley

Pole's time) were no different from that of a modern research lab or think tank—and a disinterested one at that.[33] Not a word is said about mint officials living off generous sinecures without ever having to set foot in a mint,[34] about their stubborn refusal to endow most regal coins with even the most basic anticounterfeiting devices, about senior engravers retaining their posts after going senile, or about moneyers who would rather persecute inventors than embrace their inventions.

Yet history is chock-full of instances of resistance—including violent resistance—to progressive inventions and ideas.[35] Medieval craft guilds were particularly notorious in this respect. Instead of embracing new and superior methods, guilds "defended the interests of their members against outsiders [including] inventors who, with their new equipment and techniques, threatened to disturb their members' economic status" (Kellenbenz 1974, 243). In an "aristocratic" (guild-based) system, de Toqueville explains in *Democracy in America* ([1840] 2000, 439–41), "each artisan has not only his fortune to make but his status to guard," so that "[i]t is not only his interest that makes the rule for him, nor even that of the buyer, but that of the corporation." Where, in contrast, a profession is open to all, de Toqueville continues, "each worker . . . seeks only to gain the most money possible at the least cost"; consequently,

---

33. In the most recent official history of the Royal Mint, Dyer and Gaspar (1992, 411) refer to "the antiquated medieval system by which the Mint was governed" throughout the eighteenth century.

Despite Wellesley Pole's reorganization (which phased-out sinecures, among other things), the mint was to retain many aspects of its medieval constitution for several more decades. According to a mid-nineteenth-century Parliamentary report (BPP 1849), the mint was then distinguished "from all other departments of the public service" by virtue of the status of the melters and moneyers, who "are not appointed by any public authority, but from a body controlled by self-election, assuming to possess legal corporate rights, and claiming, in this character, the exclusive privilege of executing that part of the coinage-work customarily confided to them; which, they insist, cannot, without a violation of their prescriptive rights, be intrusted to other hands." The report went on to note that the mint's coining and melting charges were, of all its expenses, "the most in excess" and that it was "evident that the parties profiting by them must have an interest in resisting any *economical* change." For further details, see Selgin 2007.

34. Until the nineteenth century, it was standard practice for Royal Mint officials to deputize others to do their jobs for them—usually for a small fraction of their own salaries—thus sparing themselves from having to actually visit the Tower. For example, George Selwyn, who served as surveyor of the melting house for most of the last half of the eighteenth century, is said to have visited the mint only for the sake of having an occasional free meal there. Such abuse was not limited to higher officials: even the mint's office sweeper hired a substitute for one-twentieth of his own salary (Marsh 1971, 184).

35. On resistance to desirable innovations in economic history, see Mokyr 1994.

each "strives to invent processes that permit him to work not only better, but more quickly and with less cost."

English guilds could resist desirable changes only so long as they enjoyed monopoly rights granted to them and enforced by the government.[36] The monopoly rights enjoyed by the Royal Mint's Company of Moneyers differed from those of other English guilds in three important respects only: they extended throughout Great Britain, were enforced with especially great zeal, and lasted a lot longer. These differences made it especially easy for the mint to resist change. That economists, who led the fight against monopoly in most commercial arenas, refrained (and still refrain) from questioning national mints' monopoly privileges also helped thwart progress.

So, having a sound theory of small change, as well as the equipment needed to put the theory into practice, wasn't enough to guarantee a solution to the big problem of small change. Institutions also mattered. If economists are right in treating monopoly privileges as the ultimate source of resistance to desirable innovations, the successful reform of Great Britain's official coinage system and the official move to monometallism did not depend so much on any particular technical breakthrough as on a change in the Royal Mint's monopoly status.[37]

How does this conclusion alter our assessment of Matthew Boulton as coiner? Paradoxically, it alters it very little. Although Boulton was far from being uniquely capable either of making counterfeit-resistant coins or of making them cheaply, he, more than any other commercial coin maker, played a crucial role in the modernization of Great Britain's

---

36. On the role of monopoly rights in thwarting improvements, see Parente and Prescott 2000.

37. Elsewhere (Selgin 2007), I discuss in some detail the ways in which monopoly privileges contributed to Great Britain's short-change problem and the extent to which eventual improvements in British coinage arrangements depended on a reduction of those privileges. This perspective on the role of monopoly contrasts sharply with that of an anonymous reader who, in response to an earlier version of this chapter, wrote: "[T]he key element for the gold standard is the government's ability to enforce its monopoly. Efficiency has nothing to do with it, except to the extent that a terribly inefficient technology might make the government reluctant to bear the costs of employing it even if it provides an enforceable monopoly." This view rests on the tacit assumption that monopolies, especially government monopolies, are necessarily "reluctant" to embrace inefficient technologies. The assumption is quite unfounded: although the technologies monopolists embrace may be "efficient" in the trivial sense of catering efficiently to the monopolists' well-being, they need not be efficient in the commonly understood sense of the term.

The suggestion that a gold standard requires a coinage monopoly is no less unfounded. For U.S. evidence contradicting it, see Summers 1976; Wooldridge 1971, 54–74.

official coinage. He did this not by coming up with a new way of making counterfeit-resistant coins but by successfully defying the "old shop's" monopoly.

To be sure, steam presses helped Boulton to achieve this result. Yet they did so not by actually making better or cheaper coins but by appearing to be capable of doing so. Besides having captivated and misled all those who beheld them, Boulton's machines allowed him to coin money on a vast scale, making his boast—that he alone could meet not only Great Britain's but all of Europe's coin requirements—fully credible. To parry Boulton's assault on its privileged status, the Royal Mint adopted both desirable and dubious aspects of his coining technique. By doing so, by recalling its old coin, and by beginning to shed its outmoded, medieval constitution, it was able at last to meet the monetary needs of an industrial economy.

And yet if desert should be paid in due COIN;
    Modern works, which the ancients surpass,
The Gods, in full synod, should lib'rally join,
    To applaud, though on COPPER or BRASS.
And when, LIKE Celestials, with justice they aim,
    To discharge debts of honor below;—
To give merit, but CURRENT and STERLING, its claim,
    "Twine a wreath for the Man of SOHO."[38]

---

38. John Collins, "Extemporary Stanzas, on Seeing the Inimitable Copper Coin of Mr. Boulton's Mint, at Soho," in Dent [1878] 1972, 188.

CHAPTER IX

Conclusion

In every cry of every Man,

In every Infant's cry of fear,

In every voice: in every ban,

The mind-forg'd manacles I hear.[1]

Matthew Boulton, together with a score of other private coiners and hundreds of private coin issuers, showed the British government how to meet an industrial economy's need for small change. What lessons might one draw from this?

The commercial coinage story shows, most patently, that private coinage need not be a recipe for disaster. Despite what William Stanley Jevons claimed, the effects of competition in coining weren't all that different from its effects in other realms. Makers of inferior coin didn't "drive the best trade" (recall, for instance, how Williams's heavy pennies were eagerly accepted, while Wilkinson's light versions were refused). Nor did competition unleash a "natural tendency to the depreciation of the metallic currency" (Jevons 1882, 82). On the contrary, most commercial copper coins were heavier than their government-supplied counterparts; and although they tended to get lighter over time, the lightening only served to compensate for a rising price of copper and so allowed the private coins to steer clear of the fate that awaits any legally undervalued money. In short, Gresham's law, understood simply as the

---

1. William Blake, "London" in idem. (1794, 46).

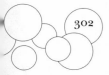

proposition that "bad money drives out good," was far less in evidence under the commercial coinage regimes of 1787–99 and 1811–17 than it had been under the older regime of state monopoly.

Commercial coins proved to be relatively "good" money for several basic reasons. Unlike regal coins, they could be refused, even in small quantities, by retailers and publicans who disliked or distrusted them. Consequently, their issuers, unlike the British Crown, could only hope to keep them current by promising to redeem them in gold or Bank of England notes. Token issuers therefore saw to it that their tokens were hard to imitate. Commercial mints, in turn, had to vie for the services of the world's best metal engravers or risk seeing prospective clients go elsewhere. Such concerns were utterly foreign to the denizens of that cluttered cloister that was the old Tower Mint.

Does any of this matter now? It matters, first of all, for a correct understanding of the theoretical requirements for a sound system of small change. In *The Big Problem of Small Change,* Thomas Sargent and François Velde (2002, 5) endorse Carlo Cipolla's (1956, 27) "standard formula" for such a system. That formula holds that small change should consist of token coins issued in limited quantities on government account and convertible into standard money. Sargent and Velde (2002, 303) add, with specific reference to the British episode, that "complete" implementation of the formula requires that "the government . . . nationalize the business of supplying small change," as the British government did when it suppressed commercial issues.

But while British experience clearly illustrates both the desirability of token coins and the importance of providing for their convertibility, that experience also casts doubt on the claim that governments can and must be relied on to supply such coins. The British government was manifestly unfit to do so until sometime after 1810. Indeed, while commercial tokens were fully convertible, Royal Mint tokens remained completely inconvertible before 1834, and are today convertible only if decrepit. In this respect at least, private coinage adhered to the standard formula more (rather than less) perfectly than the reformed regal coinage did.

The commercial coinage regime was too short-lived to serve as a definitive test of Herbert Spencer's argument for laissez-faire in coining: no one can say precisely to what extent its blemishes—and there were many—were mere symptoms of adolescence, rather than congenital. Still, the regime lasted long enough to suggest that the private sector might usefully play a far greater role in coinage than it has throughout most of history. The episode compels one to ask, first of all, whether modern governments should be in the coin-making business at all. Burke was right to observe that a mint "is a *manufacture,* and . . . nothing else." In this day and age, a government-run factory of any sort seems an anomaly; and the state's prerogative of coinage, if it is justified at all, doesn't call for a government-run mint any more than its prerogative of defense calls for government-run munitions plants.

Great Britain's experience also suggests some advantages from privatizing the issuance of coins. We've seen how private issuers were better at safeguarding their coins from counterfeiters. They might also try harder to gear their coin orders to the state of coin demand, lest they should disappoint their customers or end up saddled with batches of useless metal. To let any Tom, Dick, or Harry issue coins might (as Jevons said of Spencer's proposal) be "pushing a general principle" too far. But why not let the Bank of England commission its own small change, as it did in the early nineteenth century? Why not let the Federal Reserve issue its own quarters, dimes, and nickels? Might it not do so in a manner better calculated to avoid the wastefulness that has characterized the U.S. Treasury's handling of the coinage?[2] To imagine extending the right to issue custom-made token coins to some major commercial banks and perhaps to some other private financial firms entails no great flight of fancy. Such firms are, after all, already responsible for supplying most of the world's exchange media, in the shape of transferable deposit credits and traveler's checks, and are busy developing new types, including smart cards, that could eventually replace old-fashioned cash.[3]

Paradoxically, the very success of the private sector in coming up with popular substitutes for government-supplied cash also supplies the best argument for not taking suggestions for privatizing coinage too seriously. Controversial as it might be, even a wholesale privatization of coin production and issuance would be of little practical importance today, for coins are now "small change" in more than just the literal sense of the term: they constitute but a trivial part of most national money stocks. The vast majority of wage payments are made by check, if not through di-

---

2. I purposefully omit pennies, for I imagine that the Federal Reserve would abandon this unwanted denomination, whereas the Treasury preserves it to placate the zinc lobby. It is hard, however, to imagine the Federal Reserve badly botching a dollar coin reform, as the Treasury has done on two occasions.

3. It's true that commercial banks in most places were long ago stripped of their right to issue paper notes. But governments started granting currency monopolies to central banks because the central banks could be relied on to repay them with credit granted on generous terms, not because competitively supplied banknotes were inherently unreliable. See V. Smith 1990. Concerning Great Britain in particular, see L. White 1984.

rect bank deposits, with most of the remainder being paid in paper currency. Retail payments, in turn, are increasingly made using credit or debit cards. If British experience suggested nothing more than that coinage might advantageously be left to the private sector, it wouldn't be of much earthly use.

But the payoff of the commercial coinage story consists not in any particular reform it might suggest but in the broader lesson it teaches concerning the need to ponder governments' role in money through the same wary eyes economists tend to cast upon other government ventures. Despite being perfectly aware of the general drawbacks of monopoly and nationalization and also despite their recognition of how narrow fiscal motives led governments to usurp control of money in the first place,[4] even otherwise incredulous economists tend to take governments' monetary prerogative for granted. The outcome has been a body of monetary thought well suited toward tinkering with existing government-controlled monetary systems but not at all cut out for revealing the advantages, as well as the true shortcomings, of less top-heavy alternatives.

That monetary thought should have developed this way is perfectly understandable. Theories are shaped by experience, which they then serve, more often than not, to rationalize. "So much more does a realized fact influence us than an imagined one," Spencer wrote (1851, 402), "that had the baking and sale of bread been hitherto carried on by government-agents, probably the supply of bread by private enterprise would scarcely be conceived possible, much less advantageous." Spencer's remark is a salutary rejoinder to conservative remonstrations against hyperrationalism. It reminds us that, much as people may exaggerate the power of reason while underestimating the wisdom embodied in what Burke termed "ancient principles," they can also err the other way, treating a principle (or practice) that's sufficiently timeworn as necessarily sound. Back in Boulton's day, any well-used roadway eventually became a set of ruts from which carriages could hardly veer. Well-established government policies, it seems, can similarly confine economic thought. Perhaps awareness of Great Britain's commercial coinage experience will help nudge that thought onto less well-traveled paths.

---

4. Concerning fiscal motives, see Glasner 1998; Selgin and White 1999.

Epilogue

April 1, 1850. According to a notice in *Aris's Birmingham Gazette*, the famed Soho Mint is to go under the hammer. The notice isn't an April Fools' Day joke. The auction will commence on Monday, April 29, at 11:00 a.m.

On Thursday, April 25, would-be bidders start showing up at Soho to inspect what Fuller & Horsey's forty-six-page auction catalog calls the "Valuable Machinery and Plant . . . long celebrated and in high repute with the Government of Great Britain, as also with Foreign powers in Europe, Asia and America, the East India Company, and the mercantile and other firms of eminence in all parts of the world." The grounds, once bustling and trim, are eerily quiet and weed-infested. At the manufactory, the rolling mill's once-gleaming rolls are rust-speckled, the smithy hearths are cold, and the foot-powered spindles have been still for so long that they might shriek in pain were any attempt made to turn them. Inside the Principal Building, water trickles down the walls, plaster from the ceilings lies in sodden heaps, and every other window is broken or patched over. In the Latchet Works, to the east of the Principal Building, the six cutting-out presses, with their circular armature, bear a thick coating of dust, and surrounding workbenches are jammed with trays of punches and other tools—all of which are up for grabs. Beyond the Latchet Works, in the mint building, worm-eaten wooden patterns for the presses and frames lie scattered about. The four massive presses are complete with vacuum pumps, layers-on, and steel collars. Only the din is missing: the presses haven't clattered, and the pumps haven't hissed, for several seasons.

The "celebrated" mint whose contents are on display is, of course,

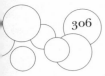

neither the mint that coined Great Britain's first cartwheels in 1797 nor the one Matt Boulton had shipped to Bombay in 1824. It is the mint Matt built when he decided to get back into coining soon after waving goodbye to Soho II. The financial crisis of 1825 had brought construction of the new mint to a halt, but by the early 1830s, business had picked up enough to justify its completion. Ten years later, the MB Mint Company was solidly in the black—an accomplishment never matched by its larger-scale forerunners (Doty 1998, 67).

Matthew Robinson Boulton died in the summer of 1842. James Watt Jr. survived him, but only by six years. The fate of both the manufactory and the mint thus came to rest with Matthew Piers Watt Boulton, who had only recently come of age. The youngest Boulton, though of a mechanical bent,[1] wasn't the least bit interested in running a factory or in making coins. So the gavel fell, marking the final curtain closing of the Soho mint's storied career.

Well, almost. For a new mint was to rise phoenixlike from the ashes of Soho, and that mint survived until just recently. Among those present at Fuller & Horsey's auction was Ralph Heaton II, a Birmingham die sinker. Heaton was high bidder for most of the mint's equipment, including all of its Boulton & Watt screw presses, which he subsequently installed at his Bath Street shop. His timing couldn't have been better, for the British Empire was expanding, and the Royal Mint alone could no longer meet all its coinage needs. Coin orders were soon pouring into Bath Street—from Australia, from Chile, and finally from the Royal Mint itself, which started by ordering blanks and then, in 1852, offered Ralph Heaton & Sons a chance to supply finished regal copper coins. "I am convinced," Ralph Heaton III wrote his father upon hearing of the offer, "[that] this is only the commencement of another Soho" (Sweeny 1981, 11). And so it turned out to be.

On March 30, 1853—not quite fifty-six years after Soho's first regal coinage contract—Heaton & Sons agreed to supply the Royal Mint with five hundred tons of regal copper coin. Other large orders quickly followed, from the Royal Mint and from governments around the globe. By 1860, according to the *Illustrated Times of Birmingham,* Heaton & Sons had coined five thousand tons of metal—enough to form a line of coins 14,800 miles long, or almost three times the distance from Birmingham to Beijing.

Having by this time outgrown its Bath Street quarters, the company

---

1. In 1868, he patented the first aileron, which showed considerable foresight since there were as yet no practical airplanes.

built a much larger plant on Icknield Street, equipping it with eleven steam-powered screw presses. By 1866, the new plant boasted three hundred employees. It had also supplemented its screw presses with a dozen Uhlhorn lever presses, which Heaton & Sons had been licensed to manufacture and sell in Great Britain. The Royal Mint, in contrast, didn't get around to installing its first lever presses—four of them only—until 1875 (BPP 1881, 588). In the meantime, it made do with the more cumbersome, less efficient, and irritatingly noisy screw presses Matthew Boulton supplied it with at the onset of the century.

When Ralph Heaton III retired in 1881, the family-owned company went public, changing its name to the Birmingham Mint, Ltd. Over the course of the next century, the company's fortunes waxed and waned. An especially bitter blow was dealt it in 1923, when the Royal Mint ended its long-standing policy of coining only for Great Britain and its possessions, by offering to coin money for Egypt, one of the Birmingham Mint's best customers. The private mint now faced the prospect of having to compete with its government-subsidized counterpart for all overseas orders. Despite the depression and wartime bomb damage, it was able to survive the next several decades, largely thanks to revenues from products unrelated to coinage, including brass sheets and copper tubes. Finally, in 1965, a surge in foreign coin orders impelled the Royal Mint to set up a consortium with the Birmingham Mint and another British private mint (the IMI Mint, which later merged with the Birmingham Mint) for export coinage, reviving Birmingham's private coining business.

Yet it wasn't until just a few years ago, in the year 2000, that the Birmingham Mint achieved its greatest triumph, in two orders: one from Germany for forty-five million pounds' worth of blanks for one- and two-euro coins and a second from another European government for fifty million finished two-euro coins. Little did the mint suspect at the time that its euro commissions would turn out to be its swan song. Soon after those commissions were completed, the Royal Mint abruptly ended its 1965 agreement awarding the Birmingham Mint a fixed share of all its foreign coining contracts. The Birmingham Mint sued for breach of contract, claiming £5.4 million in damages, while suggesting, in a memorandum to Parliament, that the Royal Mint had been "able to price down its overseas contracts by virtue of the fact that much of its fixed costs are covered by its Treasury contract."[2]

In fact, despite its subsidies and monopoly of coining for the United

2. Memorandum from the Birmingham Mint, Ltd., in BPP 2003. The hearings conducted by the Public Accounts Committee, especially its examination of Royal Mint chief

Kingdom, the Royal Mint was deep in the hole. Starting in 1997, it spent twenty-five million pounds in public funds to increase its capacity by 50 percent (from eighteen thousand to twenty-seven thousand tons of coin annually), so that it might supply 20 percent of all euro coin commissions—a share that was to prove utterly unobtainable. When, thanks partly to the substandard quality of its first euro coins, the mint ended up with a scant 5 percent of euro coin orders, it found itself severely overcapitalized and in no position to go on sharing foreign commissions. Despite breaking its agreement with the Birmingham Mint, its losses continued to mount, from less than half a million pounds in 2000–2001 to almost £6.5 million in 2001–2. These losses were, of course, borne by the British people. In 2002, British taxpayers were asked to fork over another twelve million pounds for the sake of a Royal Mint "restructuring program," the main effect of which was to undo part of the mint's 1997–98 expansion, in part by depriving 220 mint workers of their jobs. After that, the Royal Mint had to make do with "just" eight hundred full-time employees, in addition to a large part-time staff.

The Birmingham Mint, in contrast, recorded an operating profit of over £5.2 million in 2001, without consuming a penny of public money. There is every reason to think that it could have gone on making profits had the Royal Mint not deprived it of many of its foreign coin contracts. Given the circumstances, one can't help wondering why the Royal Mint should go on coining money for foreign nations. Indeed, one can't help wondering why it should coin money at all, unless it can do so efficiently. Should Great Britain join the rest of Europe in embracing the Euro, the last question will become all the more pertinent.

Nevertheless, it was the Birmingham Mint, not its Royal rival, whose future teetered in the balance. In 2003, the company went into receivership, laying off more than half of its hundred-odd employees. Since then, it has been sold. The new owners had hoped, with the city council's help, to keep the factory's old medal and commemorative coin division running as a sort of working museum. But nothing came of the plan. Instead, the mint's presses, like those of Boulton's second Soho Mint over three-score years ago, were sold and shipped to a mint in India. Then, in April 2007, most of the old plant was demolished. The 1862 façade alone still survives—the sole survivng remnant of Birmingham's great and glorious contribution to the history of modern money. For want of any other monument, long may this one last.

---

executive Gerald Sheehan, make for fascinating and often pungent reading and are available online at http://www.publications.parliament.uk/pa/cm200203/cmselect/cmpub acc/588/2102301.htm.

Appendix

Lord Lauderdale's Table of Silver Token Values (Amended)[a]

	Weight/ 1s (grains)	Metallic value/s @ 6s 11d/oz	Percent @ 6s 11d/oz	Metallic value/s @ 6s 2d/oz	Percent @ 6s 2d/oz	Reported[a] metallic value/s	Reported[a] percent of nominal value
Leeds, 1811	67.7	11.71	97.55	10.44	86.98	8.7	72.50
Manchester	64.3	11.12	92.65	9.91	82.61	8.3	69.17
Leeds	66	11.41	95.10	10.18	84.79	8.5	70.83
Nantwich	63.1	10.91	90.93	9.73	81.07	6.8	56.67
Blandford	66.7	11.53	96.11	10.28	85.69	7.3	60.83
Bath 4s	54	9.34	77.81	8.33	69.38	6.9	57.50
No place, 6s	55.4	9.58	79.83	8.54	71.17	7.1	59.17
Sheffield, 1812 2s 6d	66.9	11.57	96.40	10.31	85.95	8.6	71.67
Wiltshire, Devonshire, and Bristol	59.4	10.27	85.59	9.16	76.31	7.6	63.33
York, 1811 6s	57.6	9.96	83.00	8.88	74.00	7.4	61.67
Gloucester, 1811, county and city	54.6	9.44	78.68	8.42	70.15	7.05	58.75
Doncaster, 1812	64.1	11.08	92.37	9.88	82.35	8.2	68.33
Newark, 1811	55.2	9.55	79.54	8.51	70.92	7.1	59.17
Scarbro', 1812	63.7	11.01	91.79	9.82	81.84	8.2	68.33
Frome Selwood, 1811	63.4	10.96	91.36	9.77	81.45	8.1	67.50
Bristol	46.8	8.09	67.44	7.22	60.13	6	50.00
York, 1811	54.7	9.46	78.82	8.43	70.27	7	58.33
Northumberland and Durham, 1811	63.5	10.98	91.50	9.79	81.58	8	66.67

This appendix reproduces material from Lord Lauderdale's *Further Considerations on the State of the Currency* (Maitland 1813).

311

Appendix—*Continued*

	Weight/ 1s (grains)	Metallic value/s @ 6s 11d/oz	Percent @ 6s 11d/oz	Metallic value/s @ 6s 2d/oz	Percent @ 6s 2d/oz	Reported[a] metallic value/s	Reported[a] percent of nominal value
Newport, Isle of Wight, 1811	66.9	11.57	96.40	10.31	85.95	8.6	71.67
Devonshire, issued at Barnstaple	55.3	9.56	79.69	8.53	71.05	7.1	59.17
No place, 1812	59.4	10.27	85.59	9.16	76.31	7.6	63.33
Bristol, 1811	54.9	9.49	79.11	8.46	70.53	7	58.33
Shaftesbury Bank, March 14, 1811	54.2	9.37	78.10	8.36	69.63	7	58.33
Southampton	54.9	9.49	79.11	8.46	70.53	7	58.33
High Wycombe and Buckingham- shire	53.9	9.32	77.67	8.31	69.25	6.9	57.50
Mansfield	62.4	10.79	89.92	9.62	80.17	8	66.67
Gloucester	55.6	9.61	80.12	8.57	71.43	7.1	59.17
Gloucester, county and city	54	9.34	77.81	8.33	69.38	6.9	57.50
Bath 2s	54.1	9.35	77.96	8.34	69.50	7	58.33
Andover	57.2	9.89	82.42	8.82	73.49	7.3	60.83
Charing Cross	56.5	9.77	81.41	8.71	72.59	6.2	51.67
Bilston	58	10.03	83.58	8.94	74.51	7.4	61.67
Derby, Leicester, Northampton, and Rutland	50.1	8.66	72.19	7.72	64.36	6.4	53.33
Fazely	50.4	8.72	72.63	7.77	64.75	6.5	54.17
Sheffield	61.6	10.65	88.76	9.50	79.14	7.9	65.83
Cheltenham, 1811	56.4	9.75	81.27	8.70	72.46	7.02	58.50
North Cornwall, 1811	45.5	7.87	65.56	7.01	58.45	5.8	48.33
Bristol, August 12, 1811	57.7	9.98	83.14	8.90	74.13	7.4	61.67
Birmingham	63.3	10.95	91.21	9.76	81.32	8.1	67.50
Stockport, Cheshire	63.3	10.95	91.21	9.76	81.32	8.1	67.50
Hampshire	70	12.10	100.87	10.79	89.93	9	75.00
No place or date, Britannia 6s	55.6	9.61	80.12	8.57	71.43	7.1	59.17
Bristol 6d	61.9	10.70	89.20	9.54	79.52	8	66.67
Derby	40.4	6.99	58.22	6.23	51.90	5.2	43.33
Neath 6d	52	8.99	74.93	8.02	66.81	6.7	55.83
Fazely 6d	51.3	8.87	73.92	7.91	65.91	6.7	55.83
Stockport 6d	57.7	9.98	83.14	8.90	74.13	7.4	61.67
Wiltshire, Gloucestershire, South Wales, and Bristol 6d	54	9.34	77.81	8.33	69.38	6.9	57.50
Scarborough 6d	54.1	9.35	77.96	8.34	69.50	7	58.33

Appendix—*Continued*

	Weight/ 1s (grains)	Metallic value/s @ 6s11d/oz	Percent @ 6s11d/oz	Metallic value/s @ 6s2d/oz	Percent @ 6s2d/oz	Reported[a] metallic value/s	Reported[a] percent of nominal value
Gainsborough 6d	51.4	8.89	74.07	7.92	66.03	6.6	55.00
Leeds, 1812 6d	60.1	10.39	86.60	9.27	77.21	7.7	64.17
Bristol, 1811 6d	58.6	10.13	84.44	9.03	75.28	7.5	62.50
Bristol, 1811 6d	58	10.03	83.58	8.94	74.51	7.4	61.67
Birmingham 6d	68	11.76	97.99	10.48	87.36	8.7	72.50
York, 1811 6d	53.1	9.18	76.52	8.19	68.22	6.8	56.67
Bristol, R. Fripp & Co. 6d	52.2	9.03	75.22	8.05	67.06	6.7	55.83
Hull 6d	57.5	9.94	82.86	8.86	73.87	7.4	61.67
Poole, 1812 6d	65.6	11.34	94.53	10.11	84.28	8.4	70.00
Doncaster, 1812 6d	54.9	9.49	79.11	8.46	70.53	7	58.33
Chichester, 1811 6d	55.8	9.65	80.41	8.60	71.69	7.2	60.00
Sheffield, 1811 6d	67.7	11.71	97.55	10.44	86.98	8.7	72.50
Barnstaple, Devonshire, 1811 6d	58.7	10.15	84.59	9.05	75.41	7.5	62.50
Bristol and Wiltshire, 1811	55.7	9.63	80.26	8.59	71.56	7.1	59.17
Nantwich, 1811	53.7	9.29	77.38	8.28	68.99	6.9	57.50
Carmarthen Bank, 1811	59.3	10.25	85.45	9.14	76.18	7.6	63.33
Worcester, 1811	59.7	10.32	86.03	9.20	76.70	7.7	64.17
Lincoln, 1811	60	10.38	86.46	9.25	77.08	7.7	64.17
Chichester	54.8	9.48	78.97	8.45	70.40	7	58.33
Manchester, 1812	59.2	10.24	85.31	9.13	76.06	7.6	63.33
Bath	58.9	10.18	84.87	9.08	75.67	7.6	63.33
Blandford, 1811	56.3	9.74	81.13	8.68	72.33	7.2	60.00
Gainsbro', 1811	62.3	10.77	89.77	9.60	80.04	8	66.67
Poole	66.7	11.53	96.11	10.28	85.69	8.6	71.67
Hereford, county and city	58.8	10.17	84.73	9.07	75.54	7.6	63.33
Poole, town and city	53.4	9.23	76.95	8.23	68.60	6.7	55.83
Swansea, 1812	54.9	9.49	79.11	8.46	70.53	7	58.33
Stockport, 1812	58.6	10.13	84.44	9.03	75.28	7.5	62.50
Swansea	59.7	10.32	86.03	9.20	76.70	7.7	64.17
Epworth Isle	66.5	11.50	95.82	10.25	85.43	8.6	71.67
Leeds, 1811	63.4	10.96	91.36	9.77	81.45	8.1	67.50
Portsmouth	53.8	9.30	77.52	8.29	69.12	7	58.33
Doncaster	59	10.20	85.02	9.10	75.80	7.8	65.00
Bradford	66.8	11.55	96.26	10.30	85.82	8.6	71.67
Haverford West	55.2	9.55	79.54	8.51	70.92	7.1	59.17
Merthyr, 1811	49.5	8.56	71.33	7.63	63.59	6.3	52.50
Whitby	61.2	10.58	88.19	9.44	78.63	7.9	65.83

Appendix—*Continued*

	Weight/ 1s (grains)	Metallic value/s @ 6s 11d/oz	Percent @ 6s 11d/oz	Metallic value/s @ 6s 2d/oz	Percent @ 6s 2d/oz	Reported[a] metallic value/s	Reported[a] percent of nominal value
Rowfant House, Sussex	59	10.20	85.02	9.10	75.80	7.8	65.00
Bedworth Mill	55.7	9.63	80.26	8.59	71.56	7.1	59.17
Romsey	55.7	9.63	80.26	8.59	71.56	7.1	59.17
West Riding, Yorkshire	58.5	10.12	84.30	9.02	75.16	7.5	62.50
Gainsbro'	59.7	10.32	86.03	9.20	76.70	7.7	64.17
Newark, 1811	55.4	9.58	79.83	8.54	71.17	7.1	59.17
Launceston	55.1	9.53	79.40	8.49	70.79	7.1	59.17
Scarbro', 1812	61	10.55	87.90	9.40	78.37	7.8	65.00
Marlbro', 1811	50.4	8.72	72.63	7.77	64.75	6.5	54.17
Sheffield, 1811	60.5	10.46	87.18	9.33	77.73	7.8	65.00
Bridlington Quay	57.1	9.87	82.28	8.80	73.36	7.3	60.83
Lincolnshire	54.7	9.46	78.82	8.43	70.27	7	58.33
Bristol, No. 37 Quay, R. Fripp & Co.	58.7	10.15	84.59	9.05	75.41	7.5	62.50
Weybridge Iron Works	54.8	9.48	78.97	8.45	70.40	7	58.33
Attleboro', 1811	55.2	9.55	79.54	8.51	70.92	7.1	59.17
Doncaster	55.6	9.61	80.12	8.57	71.43	7.1	59.17
Merthyr, 1811	57	9.86	82.14	8.79	73.23	7.3	60.83
Bewick Main Colliery	58.6	10.13	84.44	9.03	75.28	7.5	62.50
London 1s 6d	41	7.09	59.08	6.32	52.67	5.3	44.17
Peterboro' 18d	57.2	9.89	82.42	8.82	73.49	7.3	60.83
Ships, Colonies, and Commerce, 1811 1s 6d	53.5	9.25	77.09	8.25	68.73	6.7	55.83
Hull, 1811 1s 6d	55.4	9.58	79.83	8.54	71.17	7.1	59.17
Attleborough 2s	58.2	10.06	83.86	8.97	74.77	7.5	62.50
Stamford, 18d	56.9	9.84	81.99	8.77	73.10	7.3	60.83
Frome Selwood, 2s	59.5	10.29	85.74	9.17	76.44	7.6	63.33
Northumberland and Durham 30d	63.4	10.96	91.36	9.77	81.45	8.1	67.50
Sheffield 2s 6d	66.5	11.50	95.82	10.25	85.43	8.6	71.67
Bath, 1811 4s	53.6	9.27	77.24	8.26	68.86	6.9	57.50
Peel Castle, Isle of Man 5s	44.9	7.76	64.70	6.92	57.68	5.8	48.33
Bath 4s	52.8	9.13	76.08	8.14	67.83	6.8	56.67
Average	57.62	9.96	83.03	8.88	74.03	7.36	61.35

[a]"Reported" values are those given by Lauderdale himself. These generally understate tokens' metallic values relative to figures based on silver prices during the second token episode.

Lauderdale's Questionnaire

1. What is the denomination of tokens you have issued?

2. What is the average weight of each species?

3. By how many dwts. in every twelve ounces is the metal of which they are composed inferior to standard silver?

4. What is the average intrinsic value of each species?

5. Are there any local tokens circulated in your immediate vicinity, besides those you have issued, and by whom?

6. What do you compute to be the total value of local tokens circulating within the district in which you reside?

7. What do you compute to be the total value of local tokens bear to the halfcrowns, shillings, and sixpences, that are in circulation near you?

8. What do you conceive to be the average intrinsic value of these halfcrowns, shillings, and sixpences?

9. Are there many tokens of the Bank of England circulated in your vicinity?

10. Has it been common to refuse change for a banknote, unless a large proportion of copper is taken?

11. Have you known a premium given to get silver for a twenty shillings banknote?

12. Has there been any attempt to issue paper notes or tickets under the value of twelve shillings?

13. Have you not known master manufacturers pay their workmen's wages with paper tickets, under the circumstance of a shop being established in the neighbourhood, where the workmen are furnished with goods in exchange for those tickets?

14. Where this has occurred, has it not been customary for the retail trader to settle his accounts monthly or quarterly with the manufacturer by whom the tickets were issued?

15. Is there a disposition to petition the two Houses of Parliament, at their next meeting, for the repeal of the Act which has recently passed, prohibiting the circulation of local tokens?

Replies to Lauderdale's Questionnaire

Bristol, June 16, 1812.[1]

The quantity of silver sanctioned by Government, now in circulation here, is not more than in the proportion of two to twenty of local tokens.

Before these were brought out, the difficulty of procuring change was so great, that eighteen shillings were readily taken for a one-pound note. The workmen employed in the various branches of business in this city, absolutely refused to take their weekly wages, and many were about to leave their employers, because they could not be paid in anything but paper. Even the local poor could not receive their pay, which in this city amounts to a considerable sum weekly, the rates for their support being from £12,000 to £14,000 per annum.

Bristol, September 1812.

It is a fact, that, at this present moment, this city is in almost as bad a state for want of coinage as it was when we first resorted to the issue of our tokens. It has been asserted by some, that what we did with the most laudable intentions was done with sinister views; but this, on a fair and impartial investigation, must to a man even of common capacity, appear to be untrue and without the slightest foundation. On the contrary, we most certainly shall (unless the present scarcity of silver causes a great advance in the price) be inevitable losers to a very serious amount. But be that as it may, the public are heartily welcome to our efforts to alleviate in some measure the general distress they, in common with ourselves, have laboured under for want of a circulating medium; and we are proud to state, that it did put in their power the means of procuring themselves, the necessaries and comforts of life, without paying an extravagant price for converting paper into specie. It is also a great satisfaction and pleasure that we can with confidence state, that the public in this city and neighbourhood, have many times both collectively and individually returned us their sincere thanks for the very great accommodation they have received through our means.

Bristol, September 3, 1812.

I have had the honour to receive your letter, and, in reply, I beg to say, I cannot avoid differing from you in your opinion on the principle you

---

1. Given its date, this first excerpt must have come from correspondence received by Lord Lauderdale before he mailed his questionnaire.

have stated. The great evil appears to me to be, that Government should omit to issue coin to the amount necessary to keep all in place. If individuals can issue tokens, and thus serve the public, does not the fact present itself, that there is no want of bullion? And if there is no want of this sort, is it not better that the Government should reap the advantage of the issue, than private individuals? Besides are not the people in this instance running away with one of the unalienable prerogatives of the crown? And if they purloin one, is it not likely they will begin to grasp at others; and that this inroad upon the constitution will lead to hideous consequences? Considerations such as these have induced me to withhold issuing tokens, and I shall be most happy to take up every one I have issued when the time comes. It will certainly behoove the Government to issue a proper supply. If they do, all will be well, but if they do not, the dreadful state of confusion, if not open rebellion, into which their misconduct will fling the country, will lay at their door. I calculate that we have not less than eighty thousand pounds of nominal value in tokens in circulation, in, and in the neighbourhood of Bristol.

Hull, September 7, 1812.

Being at the head of two considerable wholesale and retail concerns, I was one who very early felt the crippled means of carrying on my trade, for want of silver to give in change to my customers; I not only lost the benefit of my friends' custom, but in many and daily instances, I was obliged to give credit for small sums, which I have not to this day received, nor ever shall. In this situation, I and my partner were reduced to issue tokens. The relief this gave was incalculable, not only to ourselves but to our neighbours, and I can safely say that had it not been for their introduction, I do not know what this populous town and neighbourhood would have done.

Carmarthen, September 8, 1812.

During the greater part of the year 1811, we observed that the gold and silver coin were rapidly withdrawing from circulation, and these tradesmen who generally supplied us with small change, were reduced to the extremity of applying to us to issue tokens, as the dernier resort to enable them to carry on their trade with any degree of facility. Until we had acceded to their views, the distress for change was great beyond measure; the tradesmen were unable to supply their customers; and the poorer classes of the community considered themselves fortunate in procuring one moiety in silver, and the other copper of a pound note. The Bank of England in a small degree supplied us with their tokens, but in quantities very inadequate to the demand.

Frome, September 8, 1812.

Previous to the issue of local tokens, many persons were obliged to give a premium of 5 per cent for change, whilst others could not procure it even at that rate.

Tradesmen's books were filled with small debts, the greater part of which will never be discharged; in many instances the wives and children of labourers have had to suffer hunger, and the most dreadful privations, through the husband's being drove to an ale house in order to obtain change for a one pound note, part of which frequently belonged to a fellow workman. The collectors of taxes had their task increased by the impossibility of giving change for the paper currency. The overseers of the poor found the collecting rates, and the procuring of change for the payment of the paupers to be a work of unprecedented labour. Therefore, being thus plunged into intolerable difficulties, we were naturally led to seek some means of extricating ourselves, and no mode appeared so likely to do it, as that of issuing tokens. But now again the want of change is so great, that the most intimate friends will not part with it, but on condition of receiving a similar favour when required.

Gloucester, September 12, 1812.

In the months of July, August, and September 1811, change became so exceedingly scarce as to be very alarming to me, who have an extensive retail trade, producing a suspension of all settlement of accounts, whilst comparatively speaking I received no ready money. Much as this business has occupied your attention, I conceive it nearly impossible that any imaginary idea of its effects, say the embarrassment and loss to retail traders in particular, at the period stated, could equal the reality. This produced the issuing of local tokens from which I have never entertained a shadow of expectation of deriving any emolument. They were issued for my own convenience and that of others, and the only hope or wish I have ever entertained, is, that when the legislature may think proper to prohibit them, an adequate substitute may be introduced, which at present does not exist; for even with all the tokens in circulation, there is now nearly as great difficulty as ever in obtaining change for a bank note.

Chichester, September 15, 1812.

There were not many tokens of the Bank of England circulated in this vicinity; change would yet be very scarce if not assisted by the local tokens. Bank tokens begin to disappear. Previously to the circulation of local tokens, it was difficult to get change for bank notes. Frequently the whole in copper could not be obtained, to the great inconvenience of the military as well as trade, and in many cases the former (we mean soldiers) have passed through the city, when halting, without obtaining necessary food, for want of change.

Bridlington, September 18, 1812.

Local tokens compose four parts out of five of the circulating silver money. Bank of England tokens have invariably disappeared after their first circulation, even before local tokens were issued. Before this resource I used to give a premium in London to get silver, but that premium increasing, I was compelled to discontinue it, my trade not allowing me to pay so dear for the accommodation; and until the issuing of local tokens, I was daily under the necessity of refusing goods to my customers, from being unable to furnish them with change, whilst I sustained great loss by giving credit to people who came to my shop for goods, knowing I could not give them change for a note. If the local tokens are done away, and government do not issue a very large sum in specie as a substitute, trade must inevitably be at a stand, and the result of this I dare not contemplate.

Bath, September 21, 1812.

The local tokens circulated here may amount to about five and twenty thousand pounds, forming about two-thirds of the circulating silver change, the remaining third consisting of shillings and sixpences, and of bank tokens, nearly in equal quantities. It was very difficult to get a pound note changed, even by taking 15*s.* worth of copper before tokens were issued. The people here are in general crying out, "What shall we do for change, when the tokens are called in?"

Bath, October 2, 1812.

Previous to the issuing of local tokens, (gold being withdrawn) no change could be obtained. Trade was at an alarming stand; nine-tenths of our customers went away without their goods, or had them on credit. The banks could not give the least change; our drafts were returned and our credit endangered. The letter carrier carried a book in his hand, and gave credit to those he knew, whilst others went days without their letters for want of change. The issue of local tokens has removed our difficulties, and the issuers have received public thanks in the papers. From our knowledge of trade we are convinced that there is not one thousand pounds worth of Bank of England tokens, and of old silver, in circulation in this place.

Swansey, October 6, 1812.

Change is so scarce here, that during the last week I saw an instance of ten shillings of copper and ten of tokens being given for a one pound note. The tokens form five parts out of six of the silver circulation. Before they were issued all classes felt the want of silver money in an extreme degree.

At a meeting of the inhabitants convened by public advertisement, thanks were voted to the issuers of tokens. Shop notes are common in this and in the adjoining counties.

York, November 4, 1812.

Prior to the issuing of tokens, it was usual to give a premium of one shilling to procure change for a twenty shilling bank note, and customers were sent away who wished for change unless they intended a purchase to almost the amount of the note. If the act prohibiting local tokens takes effect, the greatest part of our district will be thrown into the utmost confusion, as it will be totally impossible for the lower orders, whose gains amount but to a few tokens, to procure either bank tokens or old silver in lieu of them.

Sheffield, November 21, 1812.

Four-fifths of the silver money here in circulation is in local tokens, the quantity of bank tokens very small, and there is difficulty in obtaining change even with the aid of copper; I believe it to be more scarce now than even before the local tokens were issued.

We are paying nearly £400 a week to the poor of this township; perhaps four-fifths of the cases do not average more than 8s, a head, and we are not enabled to collect more than from £100 to £150 a week in copper, (including local copper tokens). I need not point out the inconvenience this occasions to the overseers, nor the hardship it imposes on the paupers, who are of necessity obliged to be linked together, and parade the streets in numbers to get copper for an odd guinea note, and which is most generally obtained by the poor creatures spending a part of their weekly pittance.

Prior to their issuing silver tokens, the Sheffield overseers joined with the banks in getting down Bank of England tokens, which was done to some extent, and as I remember, the expence of carriage and insurance was about £12 to the £2000, but these were found to answer only a temporary purpose; they did not circulate at all—once paid away, you saw no more of them.

Barnstaple, November 20, 1812.

I enclose you specimens of leather shillings and sixpences issued in this vicinity. About three weeks ago the tradesmen who issued tokens announced by public advertisement that they would pay them off, on or before a certain day; in consequence of this about two-thirds of what had been issued was brought in for payment. The result was, that the retail trade immediately came to a stand, and several of our most respectful inhabitants called on the issuers to request of them to reissue them for two or three months. After some consideration they consented, and we now go on as formerly.

Newark, December 2, 1812.

Before the local tokens were issued, it was impossible to obtain change in silver, and the utmost efforts of the manufacturers did not enable them to pay their workmen even in copper. They were therefore forced to the highly objectionable expedient of paying them in classes, which was only a transfer of the difficulty to the lower orders amongst whom great discontent was created, as the shop-keepers could not give change when they supplied them with provisions; consequently much retail business diverted from its course, and much was disadvantageously transacted upon credit, because payments could not be taken from a pound note. Upon a Saturday evening, both individually, and in groups, the labouring classes were seen vainly soliciting change and a supply of their wants, to a distressing, if not an alarming extent and the most respectable inhabitants were fortunate in being able, in a market-day, to effect their market purchases with copper. The inconvenience arising out of the absence of silver coins is really beyond our description.

Scarborough, [n.d.].

Inconvenienced as the country was for want of silver currency, and to prevent a total stoppage of trade between the mechanic and the retail dealer, it was absolutely necessary to substitute something in its stead. To remedy this inconvenience, was one grand object in first issuing tokens, and our most sanguine expectations have been more than realized,— notwithstanding which, none more than ourselves lament the actual necessity there is for having recourse to such expedients.

It is needless to tell you, that tokens differ much in [metallic] value— yes, almost as much as the [official] coin in circulation. This is no doubt a calamity; but to put a total stop to this substitute before a sufficient quantity of legal change is issued, must occasion a suspension of business betwixt the retailer and the poorer classes of the community. Even at present it is too familiar a sight to see the shopkeeper's servant going from door to door, for a whole street together, with a guinea note in his hand in want of change, and unable to accomplish his purpose, whilst his master is at last under the necessity of either keeping his goods, or giving his customers credit, either of which is ruinous to industrious tradesmen.

Sources

Archives

Additional Manuscripts, British Library
Birmingham City Archives, Birmingham Central Library
Boulton & Watt Collection (Thomas Wilson correspondence), Cornwall Record
    Office
Matthew Boulton Papers, Birmingham Central Library
Public Record Office, National Archives (Kew)
Sheffield Archives

British Parliamentary Papers

1799. x. *Report from the Committee Appointed to Enquire into the State of the Copper
    Mines and Copper Trade of the Kingdom.*
1813 (237). xii. "'Copper Coin': Memorial of the Wholesale and Retail Traders."
1838 (465). xvi. *Report of Committee on the Establishment of the Royal Mint.*
1849 (1026). xxviii. *Report of the Royal Commissioners Appointed to Inquire into the
    Constitution, Management, and Expenses of the Royal Mint.*
1870 (7). xli. *Reports and Memoranda on the Mint.*
1881 (304). ix. *Report from the Select Committee on London City Lands.*
2003. [House of Commons. Public Accounts Committee.] *Report by the Comptrol-
    ler and Auditor General: Royal Mint Trading Fund, 2001–02 Accounts.*

Other British Government Documents

Great Britain. Parliament. *The Parliamentary Debates (Hansard). Official Report,*
    1812–16 and 1859.
Great Britain. Privy Council. Committee on Coin. 1798. "Draft of a Report on
    the Coin of this Realm."

Newspapers and Magazines

Aris's Birmingham Gazette
The Bath Chronicle
Bell's Weekly Messenger
Birmingham Weekly Mercury
The Bristol Gazette and Public Advertiser
The Daily Universal Register
The Gentleman's Magazine
London Magazine
The (London) Star
The (London) Times
The Morning Chronicle
The Reading Mercury
The Tradesman or Commercial Magazine
The Worcester Herald

Other Sources

Adams, Henry. 1871. "The Bank of England Restriction." In *Chapters of Erie, and Other Essays,* by Charles Francis Adams, Henry Adams, and Francis Amasa Walker, 224–68. Boston: J. R. Osgood.

Aitken, W. C. 1866. "Brass and Brass Manufacturers." In *The Resources, Products, and Industrial History of Birmingham and the Midland Hardware District,* ed. Samuel Timmins, 225–380. London: Robert Hardwicke.

Allen, G. C. 1966. *The Industrial Development of Birmingham and the Black Country, 1860–1927.* New York: A. M. Kelley.

Andrew, Pearson. 1974. "Labor Decries Royal Mint Machinery." *World Coins,* May, 856–64.

Andrews, C. Bruyn. 1970. Introduction to *The Torrington Diaries,* by John Byng. New York: Barnes and Noble.

Anonymous. 1739. "On the Scarcity of Copper Coin: A Satyr (in Verse)." Edinburgh.

Anonymous. 1771. "A Letter to the Members of Parliament on the Present State of the Coinage." London.

Anonymous. 1772. *The Birmingham Counterfeit, or Invisible Spectator.* 2 vols. London: S. Bladon.

Anonymous. 1801. "Matthew Boulton." In *Public Characters of 1800.* London: R. Phillips.

Anonymous. 1852. "The Button Manufacture of Birmingham." *The Illustrated Exhibitor and Magazine of Art* 1:346–49.

Ashton, Thomas Southcliffe. 1939. *An Eighteenth-Century Industrialist: Peter Stubs of Warrington, 1756–1806.* Manchester: Manchester University Press.

Ashton, Thomas Southcliffe. 1951. *Iron and Steel in the Industrial Revolution.* Manchester: Manchester University Press.

Ashton, Thomas Southcliffe. 1955. *An Economic History of England in the 18th Century.* London: Methuen.

Ashton, Thomas Southcliffe. 1962. *The Industrial Revolution, 1760–1830.* London: Oxford University Press.

Barnes, Donald Green. 1939. *George III and William Pitt, 1783–1806.* Stanford, CA: Stanford University Press.

Bell, R. C. 1963. *Commercial Coins, 1787–1804.* Newcastle upon Tyne: Corbitt and Hunter.

Bell, R. C. 1964. *Copper Commercial Coins, 1811–1819.* Newcastle upon Tyne: Corbitt and Hunter.

Bell, R. C. 1976. *Unofficial Farthings.* London: Seaby.

Bell, R. C. 1978. *The Building Medalets of Kempson and Skidmore, 1796–1797.* Newcastle upon Tyne: Frank Graham.

Berg, Maxine. 1994. *The Age of Manufacturers, 1700–1820.* 2nd ed. London: Routledge.

Berry, George. 1982. "Payable at the Workhouse." *Coin News* 20, no. 1 (December): 42–43.

Berry, George. 1988. *Seventeenth-Century England: Traders and Their Tokens.* London: Seaby.

Birch, Alan. 1967. *The Economic History of the British Iron and Steel Industry, 1784–1879.* London: Frank Cass.

Bisset, James. 1800. *A Poetic Survey round Birmingham.* Birmingham: Swinney and Hawkins.

Bisset, James. 1808. *Bisset's Magnificent Directory,* 2nd ed. Birmingham: James Bisset.

Blake, William. 1794. *Songs of Innocence and Experience.* London: William Blake.

Boase, C. W. 1867. *A Century of Banking in Dundee.* 2nd ed. Edinburgh: R. Grant.

Borrow, George. [1857] 1906. *The Romany Rye.* London: J. M. Dent.

Brewer, John. 1982. "Commercialization and Politics." Part 2 of *The Birth of a Consumer Society: The Commercialization of Eighteenth-Century England,* by Neil McKendrick, John Brewer, and J. H. Plumb. Bloomington: Indiana University Press.

Brunel, Christopher. 1974a. "Gold Tokens: But Hardly a Handful of Them." *Coins and Medals* 11, no. 4 (April): 24–25.

Brunel, Christopher. 1974b. "Token Tales in and around Norwich." *Coins and Medals* 11, no. 6 (June): 22–25, 34.

Byng, John. 1970. *The Torrington Diaries.* New York: Barnes and Noble.

Cannan, Edwin. 1925. Introduction to *The Paper Pound of 1797–1821: A Reprint of the Bullion Report.* 2nd ed. London: P. S. King and Son.

Cannan, Edwin. 1935. *Money: Its Connection with Rising and Falling Prices.* London: Staples.

Carlile, William Warrand. 1901. *The Evolution of Modern Money.* London: Macmillan.

Carlisle, Nicholas. 1837. *A Memoir of the Life and Works of William Wyon.* London: W. Nichol.

Challis, C. E. 1989. "The Introduction of Coinage Machinery by Eloy Mestrell." *British Numismatic Journal* 59:256–62.

Chaloner, William. 1693. *The Defects in the Present Constitution of the Mint Humbly Offered to the Consideration of the Honourable House of Commons.* London: A. Roper.

Chaloner, William H. 1946. "Some Problems of the Currency in the Reign of George III, 1760–1820." Paper presented to the Lancashire Numismatic Society, Manchester, December 14.

Chapman, Thomas. 1801. *Chapman's Birmingham Directory.* Birmingham: Thomas Chapman.

Chard, Jack. 1990. "Late 18th Century Coinage Dies: The Metallurgical Processes Involved." *Colonial Newsletter* 30, no. 1 (March): 1136–43.

Childs, W. H. 1910. *The Town of Reading during the Early Part of the Nineteenth Century.* Reading: University College.

Cipolla, Carlo M. 1956. *Money, Prices, and Civilization in the Mediterranean World, Fifth to Seventeenth Century.* New York: Gordion Press.

Clapham, Sir John. 1945. *The Bank of England: A History.* 2 vols. Cambridge: Cambridge University Press.

Clayton, P. A. 1967. "Henry Morgan: A Nineteenth Century Token Manufacturer of Rathbone Place." *Cunobelin: The Year Book of the British Association of Numismatic Studies* 13:36–45.

Colquhoun, Patrick. 1800. *A Treatise on the Police of the Metropolis etc.* 6th ed. London: H. Baldwin and Son.

Cooper, John James. 1923. *Some Worthies of Reading.* London: Swarthmore.

Coppieters, Emanuel. 1955. *English Bank Note Circulation, 1694–1954.* Louvain: Institute of Economic and Social Research.

Court, W. H. B. 1953. *The Rise of the Midland Industries, 1600–1838.* 2nd ed. London: Oxford University Press.

Crabbe, George. 1783. *The Village.* London: J. Dodsley.

Craig, Sir John. 1953. *The Mint: A History of the London Mint from A.D. 287 to 1948.* Cambridge: Cambridge University Press.

Cule, J. E. 1935. "The Financial History of Matthew Boulton, 1759–1800." Master's thesis, University of Birmingham.

Dalton, R., and S. H. Hammer. 1910–17. *The Provincial Token Coinage of the 18th Century.* Bristol and London: privately printed.

Darnis, Jean-Marie. 1982. "Le graveur-mécanicien Jean-Pierre Droz, 1er adaptateur des viroles plaines et brisées au mecanisme du balancier monétaire." *Actes du 9ème Congrès International de Numismatique, Berne, Septembre 1979,* 100–112.

Darnis, Jean-Marie. 1988. *La monnaie de Paris, sa création et son histoire.* Abbeville: Centre d'études Napoléoniennes.

Darwin, Erasmus. 1791. *The Botanic Garden; A Poem, in Two Parts. Part I. Containing the Economy of Vegetation—Part II. The Loves of the Plants. With Philosophical Notes.* London: J. Johnson.

Davies, Ron. 1999. "Thoughts on John Wilkinson and Bradley." *Broseley Local History Society Journal* 21:8–14.

Davis, Kirk. 2001. "The Development of 16th Century Machine Coining Technology and the Career of Eloye Mestrelle in England." *Journal of the Classical and Medieval Numismatic Society* 2, no. 3:111–27.

Davis, William J. 1904. *The Nineteenth Century Token Coinage of Great Britain, Ireland, the Channel Islands, and the Isle of Mann.* London: J. Davy and Sons.

Delieb, Eric. 1971. *Matthew Boulton: Master Silversmith.* New York: Clarkson N. Potter.

Dent, Robert K. [1878] 1972. *Old and New Birmingham: A History of the Town and Its People.* Vol. 1. East Ardsley, Wakefield: E. P. Publishing.

Dent, Robert K. [1880] 1973. *Old and New Birmingham: A History of the Town and Its People.* Vol. 2. East Ardsley, Wakefield: E. P. Publishing.

de Toqueville, Alexis. [1840] 2000. *Democracy in America.* Vol. 2. Trans. Harvey C. Mansfield and Delba Winthrop. Chicago: University of Chicago Press.

Dickinson, H. W. 1936. *Matthew Boulton.* Cambridge: Cambridge University Press.

Ditchfield, P. H. 1887. *Reading Seventy Years Ago: A Record of Events from 1813 to 1819.* Reading: John Read.

Dodd, Arthur Herbert. 1971. *The Industrial Revolution in North Wales.* Cardiff: University of Wales Press.

Doty, Richard. 1986. *English Merchant Tokens.* Chicago: Chicago Coin Club. Available at http://www.chicagocoinclub.org/projects/PiN/emt.html.

Doty, Richard. 1987. "Matthew Boulton and the Coinage Revolution, 1787–1797." *Numismatica Lovaniensia* 7:675–84.

Doty, Richard. 1998. *The Soho Mint and the Industrialization of Money.* British Numismatic Society Special Publication 2. London: National Museum of American History, Smithsonian Institution.

Doty, Richard. 2000. "The Parys Mine Company and the Industrialization of Money." *"Conder" Token Collector's Journal* 5, no. 2 (June 15): 12–23.

Drake, J. 1825. *The Picture of Birmingham.* Birmingham: privately printed.

Dryden, John. 1681. *Absalom and Achitophel.* London.

Duffy, Michael. 2000. *The Younger Pitt.* Edinburgh Gate: Pearson Education.

Duggan, Ed. 1985. *The Impact of Industrialization on an Urban Labor Market: Birmingham, England, 1770–1860.* New York: Garland.

Dyer, Graham P. 1993. "Punches and Dies in the 18th Century." In *Metallurgy in Numismatics,* ed. M. M. Archibald and M. R. Cowell, 3:160–66. Royal Numismatic Society Special Publication 24. London: Royal Numismatic Society.

Dyer, Graham P., and Peter P. Gaspar. 1992. "Reform, the New Technology and Tower Hill, 1700–1966." In *A New History of the Royal Mint,* ed. C. E. Challis, 398–606. Cambridge: Cambridge University Press.

Dykes, David W. 1954. "Some Local Tokens and Their Issuers in Early Nineteenth-Century Swansea." *British Numismatic Journal* 27 :345–53.

Dykes, David W. 1996. "James Wright, Junior (1768–98): The Radical Numismatist of Dundee." *Spink Numismatic Circular* 104 (July–August): 195–99.

Dykes, David W. 1997. "Who Was R.Y.: Searching for an Identity." *British Numismatic Journal* 67:115–22.

Dykes, David W. 1999. "John Gregory Hancock and the Westwood Brothers: An Eighteenth-Century Token Consortium." *British Numismatic Journal* 69:173–86.

Dykes, David W. 2000. "The Tokens of Thomas Mynd." *British Numismatic Journal* 70:90–102.

Dykes, David W. 2001. "John Stubbs Jorden, Die-Sinker and Medallist." *British Numismatic Journal* 71:119–35.

Dykes, David W. 2002. "The Token Coinage of William Fullarton." *British Numismatic Journal* 72:149–63.

Dykes, David W. 2004. "Some Reflections on Provincial Coinage, 1787–1797." *British Numismatic Journal* 74:160–74.

Edmunds, D. R. D. 1966. "The Gold and Silver Tokens issued by John Berkeley Monck, 1811–1812." *British Numismatic Journal* 35:173–88.

Elks, Ken. 2005. *Late 18th-Century British Token Coinage.* London: Ken Elks.

Elrington, C. R. 1964. "The City of Birmingham: Local Government and Public Services." In *A History of the County of Warwick,* vol. 7, *The City of Birmingham,* ed. W. B. Stephens, 318–39. Victoria History of the Counties of England. London: Oxford University Press.

Engels, Friedrich. [1844] 1968. *The Condition of the Working Class in England.* Trans. W. O. Henderson and W. H. Chaloner. Stanford, CA: Stanford University Press.

Everseley, D. E. C. 1964. "The City of Birmingham: Industry and Trade, 1500–1880." In *A History of the County of Warwick,* vol. 7, *The City of Birmingham,* ed. W. B. Stephens, 81–139. Victoria History of the Counties of England. London: Oxford University Press.

Feavearyear, Albert E. 1932. *The Pound Sterling: A History of English Money.* London: Oxford University Press.

Feavearyear, Albert E. 1963. *The Pound Sterling: A History of English Money.* 2nd ed. Oxford: Clarendon.

Ferrar, John. 1796. *A Tour from Dublin to London in 1795.* Dublin: John Ferrar.

Flandreau, Marc. 2004. *The Glitter of Gold: France, Bimetallism, and the Emergence of the International Gold Standard, 1848–1873.* New York: Oxford University Press.

Forbes, Sir William. 1860. *Memoirs of a Banking House.* 2nd ed. London: William and Robert Chambers.

Forrer, Leonard. 1970. *Biographical Dictionary of Medallists.* 8 vols. New York: Burt Franklin.

Franklin, Benjamin. 2003. *The Autobiography and Other Writings.* London: Penguin.

Freeth, John. 1790. *Political Songster, or A Touch on the Times on Various Subjects and Adapted to Common Tunes.* 6th ed. Birmingham: John Freeth.

Friedman, Milton. 1992. "Bimetallism Revisited." In *Money Mischief: Episodes in Monetary History,* 126–56. New York: Harcourt Brace Jovanovich.

Gallet, G. 1902. "Quelques notes sur la vie et l'œuvre du médallieur J.-P. Droz." *Musée Neuchâtelois,* November–December, 292–310.

Gaskell, Malcolm. 2000. *Crime and Mentalities in Early Modern England.* Cambridge: Cambridge University Press.

Gash, Norman. 1984. *Lord Liverpool.* Cambridge, MA: Harvard University Press.

George, M. Dorothy. 1925. *London Life in the Eighteenth Century.* New York: Harper and Row.

Gill, Conrad. 1952. *History of Birmingham.* Vol. 1. London: Oxford University Press.

Glasner, David. 1998. "An Evolutionary Theory of the State Monopoly over Money." In *Money and the Nation State,* ed. Kevin Dowd and Richard H. Timberlake, 21–45. New Brunswick: Transaction.

Goldsmith, Oliver. 1770. *The Deserted Village: A Poem.* London: W. Griffen.

Gould, B. M. 1969. "Matthew Boulton's East India Mint in London, 1786–88." *Seaby's Coin and Medal Bulletin* 612 (August): 270–77.

Greig, R. M. 1967. "Boulton's Copper Coinage in England and New South Wales." *Australian Numismatic Journal* 18, no. 3:165–72.

Grenfell, John. 1814. *Observations on the Expediency and Facility of a Copper Coinage of a Uniform Weight and Standard Value according with the Mint Prices of Gold and Silver Bullion.* London: Whittingham and Rowland.

Hadfield, R. A. 1894. "The Early History of Crucible Steel." *Journal of the Iron and Steel Institute* 46, no. 2: 224–34.

Hamer, Samuel. [1904] 2000. "Notes on the Private Tokens, Their Issuers and Die-Sinkers." Part 1. *"Conder" Token Collector's Journal* 5, no. 1 (March 15): 20–49. Originally published in the *British Numismatic Journal* 1, 299–332.

Hammond, J. L., and Barbara Hammond. 1911. *The Village Labourer, 1760–1832.* London: Longmans, Green.

Hammond, J. L., and Barbara Hammond. 1917. *The Town Labourer, 1760–1832.* London: Longmans, Green.

Hardy, Julius. 1973. *Diary of Julius Hardy (1788–1793): Button-Maker, of Birmingham.* Ed. A. M. Banks. Birmingham.

Harris, J. R. 1964. *The Copper King: A Biography of Thomas Williams of Llanidan.* Toronto: University of Toronto Press.

Hawker, Colin R. 1996. *Druid Tokens: Eighteenth Century Token Notes from Matthew Boulton's Letters.* Studley, Warwickshire: Brewin Books.

Hewitt, V. H., and J. M. Keyworth. 1987. *As Good as Gold: 300 Years of British Bank Note Design.* London: British Museum.

Hilton, George W. 1960. *The Truck System, including a History of the British Truck Acts, 1465–1960.* Cambridge: W. Heffer and Sons.

Holloway, John, and Joan Black, eds. 1979. *Later English Broadside Ballads.* Vol. 1. London: Routledge and Kegan Paul.

Hopkins, Eric. 1989. *Birmingham: The First Manufacturing Town in the World, 1760–1840.* London: Weidenfield and Nicolson.

Hopkins, Eric. 1998. "The Birmingham Economy during the Revolutionary and Napoleonic Wars, 1793–1815." *Midland History* 23:105–20.

Horden, John. 1993. *John Freeth (1731–1808): Political Ballad-Writer and Innkeeper.* Oxford: Leopard's Head.

Hulse, David K. 2001. *The Development of Rotary Motion by Steam Power.* Leamington Spa: TEE Publishing.

Humphreys, Henry Noel. 1848. *The Coins of England.* 5th ed. London: Longman, Brown, Green, and Longmans.

Hutton, William. 1819. *The History of Birmingham.* With the assistance of Catherine Hutton. 4th ed. London: Nichols and Son.

Jenkinson, Charles [first Earl of Liverpool]. 1805. *A Treatise on the Coins of the Realm in a Letter to the King.* Oxford: Oxford University Press.

Jevons, William Stanley. 1882. *Money and the Mechanism of Exchange.* New York: D. Appleton.

Johnson, Samuel. 1992. *The Letters of Samuel Johnson.* Vol. 3, *1777–1781.* Oxford: Clarendon.

Kellenbenz, Herman. 1974. "Technology in the Age of the Scientific Revolution, 1500–1700." In *The Fontana Economic History of Europe*, vol. 2, 177–272, ed. Carlo Cipolla, London: Fontana/Collins.

Kelley, E. M. 1976. *Spanish Dollars and Silver Tokens.* London: Spink and Son.

Klingender, F. D. 1947. *Art and the Industrial Revolution.* London: Noel Carrington.

Klingender, F. D. 1953. "Eighteenth Century Pence and Ha'pence." *Architectural Review*, February, 41–46.

Langford, John Alfred. 1868. *A Century of Birmingham Life.* Vol. 1. Birmingham: E. C. Osborne.

Leake, Stephen Martin. 1793. *An Historical Account of English Money, from the Conquest to the Present Time.* London: R. Faulder.

Lees, Lynn Hollen. 1998. *The Solidarities of Strangers: The English Poor Laws and the People, 1700–1948.* Cambridge: Cambridge University Press.

Leslie, Stephen, and Sydney Lee, eds. 1885–1900. *The Dictionary of National Biography.* 22 vols. London: Smith, Elder.

Levy, Hermann. 1927. *Monopolies, Cartels, and Trusts in British Industry.* London: Macmillan.

Lindert, Peter, and Jeffrey G. Williams. 1983. "English Workers' Living Standards during the Industrial Revolution: A New Look." *Economic History Review* 36, no. 1 (February): 1–25.

Longmate, Norman. 1974. *The Workhouse.* New York: St. Martin's.

Lord, John. 1965. *Capital and Steam-Power, 1750–1800.* 2nd ed. New York: A. M. Kelley.

Macaulay, Thomas Babington. 1856. *The History of England from the Accession of James II.* New York: Harper and Brothers.

Mackay, James. 1984. *A History of Modern English Coinage: Henry VII to Elizabeth II.* London: Longmans Group.

Mackenzie, Alexander. 1896. *History of the Frasers of Lovat.* Inverness: A. and W. Mackenzie.

Macleod, Henry Dunning. 1892–93. *The Theory and Practice of Banking.* London: Longmans, Green.

Malagrowther, Malachi [Sir Walter Scott]. 1826. *A Second Letter to the Editor of the Edinburgh Weekly Journal, from Malachi Malagrowther, Esq. on the Proposed Change of Currency, and Other Late Alterations, as they Affect, or Are Intended to Affect, the Kingdom of Scotland.* Edinburgh: printed by James Ballantyne and Company for William Blackwood.

Maitland, James [eighth Earl of Lauderdale]. 1813. *Further Considerations on the State of the Currency.* Edinburgh: printed for A. Constable.

Mantoux, Paul. 1927. *The Industrial Revolution in the Eighteenth Century.* New York: Macmillan.

Marsh, John. 1971. *Clip a Bright Guinea: The Yorkshire Coiners of the Eighteenth Century.* London: Robert Hale.

Mathias, Peter. 1962. *English Trade Tokens: The Industrial Revolution Illustrated.* London: Abelard-Schuman.

Mathias, Peter. 1979. "The People's Money in the Eighteenth Century: The Royal Mint, Trade Tokens, and the Economy." In *The Transformation of England: Essays in the Economic and Social History of England in the Eighteenth Century,* 190–208. New York: Columbia University Press.

Mathias, Peter. 2004. "Official and Unofficial Money in the Eighteenth Century: The Evolving Uses of Currency." *British Numismatic Journal* 74: 68–83.

Mayhew, Henry. [1851] 1967. *London Labour and the London Poor.* 4 vols. New York: A. M. Kelley.

Mayhew, Nicolas. 1999. *Sterling: The Rise and Fall of a Currency.* Allen Lane: Penguin.

Mays, James O'Donald. 1978. "Forgery of Birmingham Workhouse 2/6 Silver Token." *Seaby's Coin and Medal Bulletin* 720 (August): 241.

Mays, James O'Donald. 1982. *The Splendid Shilling: A Social History of an Engaging Coin.* Burley, Ringwood: New Forest Leaves.

Mays, James O'Donald. 1991. *Tokens of Those Trying Times: A Social History of Britain's 19th Century Silver Tokens.* Burley, Ringwood: New Forest Leaves.

Merrey, Walter. 1794. *Remarks on the Coinage of England.* Nottingham: S. Tufman.

Mitchell, Clarence Blair, ed. 1931. *Mitchell-Boulton Correspondence, 1787–1792.* Princeton, NJ: Princeton University Press.

Mitchiner, Michael. 1998. *Jetons, Medalets, and Tokens.* Vol. 3, *British Isles, circa 1558 to 1830.* London: Hawkins.

Mokyr, Joel. 1994. "Progress and Inertia in Technological Change." In *Capitalism in Context: Essays in Honor of R. M. Hartwell,* ed. John James and Mark Thomas, 230–54. Chicago: University of Chicago Press.

Monck, John Berkeley. 1812. *A Letter to the Right Hon. Spencer Percival on the Present State of Our Currency.* London: Snare and Man.

Monroe, Arthur Eli. 1923. *Monetary Theory before Adam Smith.* Cambridge, MA: Harvard University Press.

Moore, Thomas. 1828. *Odes upon Cash, Corn, Catholics, and Other Matters.* London: Longman, Rees, Orme, Brown, and Green.

Morris, Roger. 1983. *The Royal Dockyards during the Revolutionary and Napoleonic Wars.* Leicester: Leicester University Press.

Moser, Joseph. 1798. "Thoughts on the Provincial Token Coin." Parts 1–3. *European Magazine* 23 (March): 153–56; 23 (April): 232–38; 23 (May): 303–8.

Oman, Charles. 1967. *The Coinage of England.* London: H. Pordes.

Palmer, Alfred Neobard. 1898. "John Wilkinson and the Old Bersham Iron Works." *Transactions of the Honourable Society Cymmrodorion,* 23–64.

Parente, Stephen L., and Edward C. Prescott. 2000. *Barriers to Riches.* Cambridge, MA: MIT Press.

Peck, C. Wilson. 1947. "Eighteenth Century Tradesmen's Tokens. An Introduction to the Series." *Seaby's Coin and Medal Bulletin* 352 (September): 344–48.

Peck, C. Wilson. 1970. *English Copper, Tin, and Bronze Coins in the British Museum, 1558–1958.* 2nd ed. London: Trustees of the British Museum.

Pelham, R. A. 1963. "The Water-Power Crisis in Birmingham in the Eighteenth Century." *University of Birmingham Historical Journal* 9, no. 1:64–91.

Perkins, M. 1905. *Dudley Tradesmen's Tokens of the Seventeenth, Eighteenth, and Nineteenth Centuries.* Dudley: E. Blocksidge.

Philips, John. 1701. "The Splendid Shilling." In *A Collection of Poems,* 393–400. London: Daniel Brown and Benjamin Tooke.

Phillips, Maberly. 1900. *The Token Money of the Bank of England, 1797 to 1816.* London: Effingham Wilson.

Pinkerton, John. [1786] 1808. *An Essay on Medals.* Vol. 2. London: T. Cadell and W. Davies.

Pollard, J. G. 1968. "Matthew Boulton and J.-P. Droz." *Numismatic Chronicle* 8:241–65.

Pollard, J. G. 1971. "Matthew Boulton and the Reducing Machine in England." *Numismatic Chronicle* 11:311–17.

Pope, Alexander. 1743. *The "Dunciad" in Four Books.* London: printed for M. Cooper.

Powell, John S. 1979. "The Forgery of Cartwheel Pennies." *Seaby's Coin and Medal Bulletin* 731 (July): 217–21.

Powell, John S. 1993. "The Birmingham Coiners, 1770–1816." *History Today* 43, no. 7 (July): 49–55.

Pratt, J. 1805. *Harvest Home.* Vol. 1. London: R. Phillips.

Pressnell, L. S. 1956. *Country Banking in the Industrial Revolution.* Oxford: Clarendon.

[Prior, Thomas]. [1729] 1856. *Observations on Coin in General, with some Proposals for Regulating the Value of Coin in Ireland.* In *A Select Collection of Scarce and Valuable Tracts on Money,* ed. John R. McCulloch, 293–338. London: Political Economy Club.

Prosser, Richard B. 1881. *Birmingham Inventors and Inventions.* Birmingham: "Journal" Printing Works.

Pye, Charles. 1801. *A Correct and Complete Representation of All the Provincial Copper Coins, Tokens of Trade, and Cards of Address, on Copper etc.* 2nd ed. Birmingham: R. Jabet et al.

Pye, Charles. 1825. *The Stranger's Guide to Modern Birmingham.* Birmingham: R. Wrightson.

Quickenden, Kenneth. 1980. "Boulton and Fothergill Silver: Business Plans and Miscalculations." *Arts History* 3, no. 3 (September): 274–94.

Quickenden, Kenneth. 1995. "Boulton and Fothergill's Silversmiths." *Silver Society Journal* 7 (Autumn): 342–56.

Randall, John. 1879. *Our Coal and Iron Industries and the Men who Have Wrought in Connection with Them: The Wilkinsons.* Madeley, Salop: John Randall.

Raspe, Rudolf Erich, and James Tassie. 1791. *A Descriptive Catalogue of a General Collection of Ancient and Modern Engraved Gems (etc.).* London: James Tassie and John Murray.

Raven, Jonathan. 1977. *The Urban and Industrial Songs of the Black Country and Birmingham.* Wolverhampton: Broadside.

Redish, Angela. 1990. "The Evolution of the Gold Standard in England." *Journal of Economic History* 50, no. 4: 789–805.

Redish, Angela. 2000. *Bimetallism: An Economic and Historical Analysis.* Cambridge: Cambridge University Press.

Rees, Abraham. 1786. *Cyclopaedia, or An Universal Dictionary of Arts and Sciences.* London: J. F. and C. Rivington.

Reeves, Jim. 2001. "Matthew Boulton and His Influence on the English Coinage." *"Conder" Token Collector's Journal* 6 (fall):16–18.

Roll, Eric. 1930. *An Early Experiment in Industrial Organization, Being a History of the Firm of Boulton & Watt, 1775–1805.* London: Frank Cass.

Royal Statistical Society. 1840. "Economical Statistics of Birmingham." *Journal of the Royal Statistical Society,* January, 434–41.

Ruding, Rogers. 1799. *A Proposal for Restoring the Antient Constitution of the Mint.* London: privately printed.

Ruding, Rogers. 1819. *Annals of the Coinage of Britain and Its Dependencies.* 2nd ed. 6 vols. London: Lackington, Hughes, Harding, Mavor, and Jones.

Ruding, Rogers. 1840. *Annals of the Coinage of Great Britain and its Dependencies.* 3rd ed. 3 vols. London: J. Hearne.

Rule, Jonathan. 1992. *The Vital Century: England's Developing Economy, 1714–1815.* London: Longman.

Sainthill, Richard. 1844. "Memoir of the Late Thomas Wyon, Jun." In *An Olla Podrida, or Scraps Numismatic, Antiquarian, and Literary,* 1:22–37. London: Nichols and Son.

Sainthill, Richard. 1853. "Memoir of William Wyon, R.A. and His Works." In *An Olla Podrida, or Scraps Numismatic, Antiquarian, and Literary,* 2:391–401. London: Nichols and Son.

Samuel, Richard Thomas. [1881–83] 1994. *British Tokens: Articles from "The Bazaar, Exchange, and Mart," and "Journal of the Household."* Cold Spring: Davissons.

Sandys, George. 1632. *Ovid's "Metamorphosis" Englished etc.* Oxford: John Lichfield.

Sargent, Thomas J., and François R. Velde. 1999. "The Big Problem of Small Change." *Journal of Money, Credit, and Banking* 31, no. 2 (May) :137–61.

Sargent, Thomas J., and François R. Velde. 2002. *The Big Problem of Small Change.* Princeton, NJ: Princeton University Press.

Selgin, George. 1996. "Salvaging Gresham's Law: The Good, the Bad, and the Illegal." *Journal of Money, Credit, and Banking* 28, no. 4 (November): 637–49.

Selgin, George. 2003a. "Gresham's Law." *EH.net Encyclopedia,* ed. Robert Whaples. http://www.eh.net/encyclopedia/selgin.gresham.law.php.

Selgin, George. 2003b. "Steam, Hot Air, and Small Change: Matthew Boulton and the Reform of Britain's Coinage." *Economic History Review* 56, no. 3 (August): 478–509.

Selgin, George. 2005. "Charles Wyatt, Manager of the Parys Mine Mint: A Study in Ingratitude." *British Numismatic Journal* 75:114–21.

Selgin, George. 2007. "Monopoly, Competition, and Great Britain's 'Big Problem of Small Change.'" University of Georgia Department of Economics. Typescript.

Selgin, George, and Lawrence H. White. 1999. "A Fiscal Theory of Government's Role in Money." *Economic Inquiry* 37, no. 1 (January): 154–65.

Sharp, Thomas. 1834. *A Catalogue of Provincial Copper Coins, Tokens, Tickets, and Medalets.* London: Nichols and Son.

Shaw, Karl. 1999. *Royal Babylon: The Alarming History of European Royalty.* London: Virgin.

Shaw, W. A. 1896. *The History of Currency, 1252 to 1896.* 2nd ed. New York: G. P. Putnam's Sons.

Skipp, Victor. 1997. *A History of Greater Birmingham to 1830.* Studley, Warwickshire: Brewin Books.

Smart, Benjamin. 1811. *A Letter Addressed to the Honourable House of Commons, on the Necessity of an Immediate Attention to the State of the British Coinage.* London: J. Hatchard and J. Richardson.

Smiles, Samuel. 1866. *Lives of Boulton and Watt.* 2nd ed. London: John Murray.

Smith, Adam. [1763] 1896. *Lectures on Justice, Police, Revenue, and Arms.* Ed. Edwin Cannan. Oxford: Clarendon.

Smith, Adam. [1776] 1925. *An Inquiry into the Nature and Causes of the Wealth of Nations.* London: Methuen.

Smith, Charles W. 1995. "The English George III Contemporary Counterfeit Halfpenny Series: A Statistical Study of Production and Distribution." In *Coinage of the American Confederation Period,* ed. Philip L. Mossman, 23–53. New York: American Numismatic Society.

Smith, Mark. 2002. "Some Anglo-Irish Copper Mining Tokens of the Late Eighteenth Century." *"Conder" Token Collector's Journal* 7, no. 1 (Spring): 19–25.

Smith, Vera. 1990. *The Rationale of Central Banking and the Free Banking Alternative.* Indianapolis: Liberty Press.

Smith, William Hawkes. 1836. *Birmingham and Its Vicinity as a Manufacturing and Commercial District.* Birmingham: Radclyffes.

Snelling, Thomas. 1766. *A View of the Copper Coin and Coinage of England.* London: Thomas Snelling.

Snelling, Thomas. 1775. *Snelling on the Coins of Great Britain, France, and Ireland.* London: J. Thane.

Sobel, Dana. 1995. *Longitude: The True Story of a Lone Genius Who Solved the Greatest Scientific Problem of His Time.* New York: Walker and Company.

Soldon, Norbert C. 1998. *John Wilkinson (1728–1808), English Ironmaster and Inventor.* Lewiston: Edwin Mellen.

Spencer, Herbert. 1851. *Social Statics.* London: John Chapman.

Spilman, J. C. 1982. "An Overview of Early American Coinage Technology." Parts 1 and 2. *Colonial Newsletter* 21, no. 1 (April): 766–76; 21, no. 2 (July): 781–98.

Stephens, W. B., ed. 1964. *A History of the County of Warwick.* Vol. 7, *The City of Birmingham.* Victoria History of the Counties of England. London: Oxford University Press.

Styles, John. 1983. "Embezzlement, Industry, and the Law in England, 1500–1800." In *Manufacture in Town and Country before the Factory,* ed. Maxine Berg, Pat Hudson, and Michael Sonenschen, 173–210. Cambridge: Cambridge University Press.

Summers, Brian. 1976. "Private Coinage in America." *Freeman* 26, no. 7 (July): 436–40.

Sweeny, James O. 1981. *A Numismatic History of the Birmingham Mint.* Birmingham: Birmingham Mint.

Symes, Peter. 1997. "The Ballindoch Note Issues of 1830." *International Bank Note Society Journal* 36, no. 4: 43–47.

Thomason, Sir Edward. 1845. *Sir Edward Thomason's Memoirs during Half a Century.* London: Longman, Brown, Green, and Longmans.

Thompson, R. H. 1981. "French *Assignats* Current in Great Britain." *British Numismatic Journal* 51:200–203.

Timmins, Samuel. 1866. *The Resources, Products, and Industrial History of Birmingham and the Midland Hardware District.* London: Robert Hardwicke.

Tooke, Thomas. 1838. *A History of Prices and the State of the Circulation from 1793 to 1837.* London: Longman, Orme, Brown, Green, and Longmans.

Trinder, Barrie. 1973. *The Industrial Revolution in Shropshire.* London: Phillimore.

Tuberville, T. C. 1852. *Worcestershire in the Nineteenth Century.* London: Longman, Brown, Green, and Longmans.

Tweedale, Geoffrey. 1993. "Quiet Flows the Don." *History Today* 43, no. 8 (August): 30–36.

Tweedale, Geoffrey. 1995. *Steel City: Entrepreneurship, Strategy, and Technology in Sheffield, 1743–1993.* Oxford: Clarendon.

Uglow, Jenny. 2002. *The Lunar Men: Five Friends Whose Curiosity Changed the World.* New York: Farrar, Straus and Giroux.

Unwin, George, Arthur Hulme, and George Taylor. 1924. *Samuel Oldknow and the Arkwrights: The Industrial Revolution at Stockport and Marple.* Manchester: Manchester University Press.

Vice, David. 1990. "The Tokens of John Wilkinson." *Format* 40:2–8.

Vice, David. 1991. "The Cronebane Token of the Associated Irish Mine Company." *Format* 42:3–6.

Vice, David. 1996. Letter to Wayne Anderson. *Format* 39:50–52.

Vice, David. 1998. Letter to the editor. *"Conder" Token Collector's Journal* 10 (December 15): 52–53.

Von Tunzelman, G. N. 1978. *Steam Power and British Industrialization to 1860.* Oxford: Clarendon.

Wager, Andrew. 1977. "Birmingham and the Nation's Copper Coinage, 1750–1820: A Study in Local Initiative." Master's thesis, University of Birmingham.

Wager, Andrew. 2002. "How Were Unofficial Farthings Used?" *Token Corresponding Society Bulletin* 7, no. 3.

Wallace, Neil. 2003. "Modeling Small Change: A Review Article." *Journal of Monetary Economics* 50, no. 6 (August): 1391–1401.

Waters, Arthur W. 1957. *Notes on the Silver Tokens of the Nineteenth Century.* London: Seaby.

Watts-Russell, Penny. 2003. "A Copper-Bottomed Life." *An Baner Kernewek (The Cornish Banner)* 213 (August).

West, William. 1830. *The History, Topography, and Directory of Warwickshire.* Birmingham: R. Wrightson.

Withers, Paul, and Bente R. Withers. 1999. *British Copper Tokens, 1811–1820.* Llanfyllin, Powys: Galata Print.

[Whatley, George.] [1762]1856. "Reflections on Coin in General, on the Coins of Gold and Silver in Great Britain in Particular, &c." In *A Selection of Scarce and Valuable Tracts on Money,* ed. John R. McCulloch, 517–23. London: Political Economy Club.

White, D. P. 1977. "The Birmingham Button Industry." *Post-Medieval Archeology* 11:67–79.

White, Edmund. 2003. *Fanny: A Fiction.* New York: HarperCollins, Ecco.

White, Lawrence H. 1984. *Free Banking in Britain: Theory, Experience, and Debate, 1800–1845.* Cambridge: Cambridge University Press.

White, William. 1833. *History, Guide, and Description, of the Borough of Sheffield.* Sheffield: William White.

Whiting, J. R. S. 1971. *Trade Tokens: A Social and Economic History.* Newton Abbot: David and Charles.

Wooldridge, William C. 1971. *Uncle Sam, the Monopoly Man.* New Rochelle, NY: Arlington House.

Wright, James [Jr.]. 1797. "Observations on Coins." In *The Virtuoso's Companion and Coin Collectors' Guide,* by Thomas Pratten and Matthew Denton. London: Matthew Denton.

Wright, James [Jr.]. 1798. Preface to *An Arrangement of Provincial Coins, Tokens and Medalets etc.* by James Conder. Ipswich: George Jermyn.

Young, Arthur. 1776. *Rural Oeconomy, or Essays on the Practical Parts of Husbandry.* Philadelphia: James Humphreys.

Index

Page numbers in italics indicate figures and tables

commercial coin industry
  Birmingham's role in, 132
  Boulton's involvement in, 118–19
  and distribution of issuers, in
    1790s, *125*
  expansion of, in 1790s, 122–26,
    148–49
  Grenfell's attack on, 254–61
  impact and importance, 302–5
  manufacturers 1787–1797, *126*,
    146–48
  origins of, 36–37
  revival of, in 1810s, 211–16
  state of, in late 1790s, 140–48
commercial coins. *See also* Bank of En-
    gland, dollars; Bank of England,
    tokens; Parys Mine Druids
  alleged shortcomings of, 140–48,
    235–40
  anonymous, 219–20, 235–36, 240,
    243, 253, 257
  Bilston, 215–17, 260
  Camacs, 123, 141
  Carmarthen, 134
  Coalbrookdale Iron Company, 134
  collecting, 137–40
  counterfeiting of, 137, 141–44,
    216, 280–89
  Cronebane, 75–76, 123
  denominations, 212
  design of, 37, 43, 83, 85, 133–37,
    215–16, 281
  distribution of issuers, *125*, 214
  Dundee, 212
  Glasgow, 119
  gold, 231–33, 233n25
  Macclesfield, 77
  19th-century, 211–16
  opposition to, 234–40
  Penryn Volunteers, 139
  Plymouth, 133–34
  Roe & Company "beehives," 75–76,
    77
  Sheffield, 260–61
  silver, 132–33, 212–14, 241–53
  suppression of, 168, 241–53, 260
  Thames & Severn Canal, 134

"Willeys," 54–61, 120–22, 123n4,
    141
workhouse, 222–28, 260
Committee on Coin. *See* Privy Council
    Committee on Coin
Company of Moneyers, 20, 21, 190.
    See also under Royal Mint
company stores, 25
Conder tokens. *See* commercial coins
copper. *See also* Cornish Metal Com-
    pany; Parys Mine Company
  inquiry of 1799, 183–84
  mines, 68–70, 72, 108–9
  price of, 111, 144–46, *145*,
    172–73
  Williams's cornering of market in,
    178–84
copper coinage, regal. *See also* cart-
    wheels; coin shortages
  discounted by public, 123–24
  counterfeiting of, 4, 4n2, 20, 137
  maldistribution of, 22–23, 25, 210,
    289
  renewal of, commencing in 1817,
    266, 288, 296
  Royal Mint's attitude toward,
    20–23, 110
  seignorage on, 286, *287*
  supply of, in early 19th century,
    208–10
  supply of, in 18th century, 15–16,
    18, 20–23
Cornish Metal Company, 69–73,
    118–19
cotton textile industry, 7, 214
counterfeiting
  of Bank dollars, 159–61
  beneficial, 32–34
  as business, 29–31
  of cartwheels, 174–78, 295
  coins vs. bills, 4, 4n2
  of commercial tokens, 137, 141–44,
    216, 280–89
  penalties, 151n29, 295
  prevention of, in tokens, 280–89
  of regal copper coin, 20, 22, 29–34,
    142, 174–78, 295

GEORGE SELGIN is an author, speaker, and professor. Currently Dr. Selgin serves as Professor of Economics at the University of Georgia's Terry College of Business. His research covers a broad range of topics within the field of monetary economics, including monetary theory, monetary history, macroeconomic policy, and the history of monetary thought.

He has written on these subjects for numerous journals, including the *British Numismatic Journal*, *The Economic Journal*, the *Economic History Review*, the *Journal of Economic Literature*, and the *Journal of Money, Credit, and Banking*, as well as for *The Christian Science Monitor*, *The Financial Times*, *The Wall Street Journal*, and other popular outlets. He is also a co-editor of *Econ Journal Watch*, an electronic journal devoted to exposing "inappropriate assumptions, weak chains of argument, phony claims of relevance, and omissions of pertinent truths" in the writings of professional economists. His previous books include *The Theory of Free Banking* (Rowman & Littlefield, 1988), *Bank Deregulation and Monetary Order* (Routledge, 1996), and *Less Than Zero: The Case for a Falling Price Level in a Growing Economy* (The Institute of Economic Affairs, 1997). Professor Selgin holds a PhD in economics from New York University.

INDEPENDENT STUDIES IN POLITICAL ECONOMY

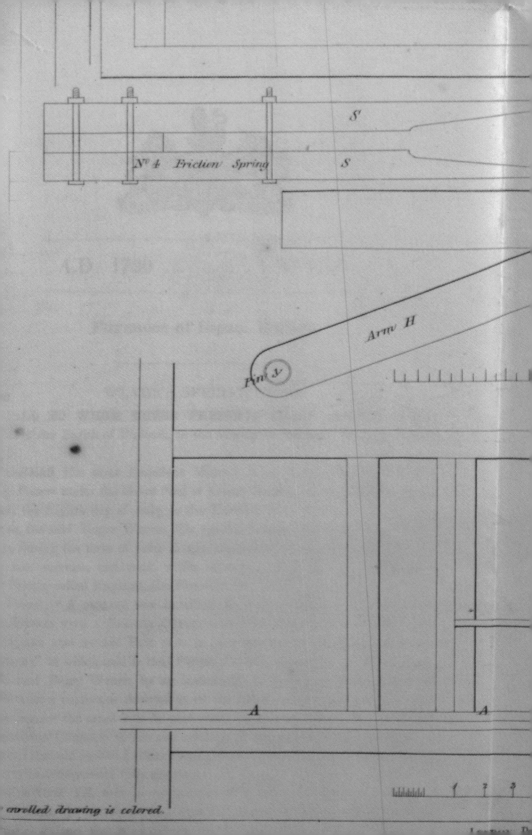

N° 4. *Friction Spring*

S'

S

Arm H

Pin y

A

A